SUSTAINABLE DEVELOPMENT

THE JOHN W. HOUCK

Notre Dame Series in Business Ethics

SUSTAINABLE DEVELOPMENT

The UN Millennium Development Goals,

the UN Global Compact, and the Common Good

edited by

OLIVER F. WILLIAMS, C.S.C.

University of Notre Dame Press
Notre Dame, Indiana

Library of Congress Cataloging-in-Publication Data

Sustainable development : the UN Millennium Development Goals, the
UN Global Compact, and the common good / edited by Oliver F. Williams,
C.S.C.

pages cm
Includes index.
ISBN-13: 978-0-268-04429-9 (pbk. : alk. paper)
ISBN-10: 0-268-04429-5 (pbk. : alk. paper)
1. Social responsibility of business—Case studies. 2. Sustainable development—Social aspects—Case studies. 3. Economic development—Developing
countries. 4. Poverty—Developing countries. 5. Public health—Developing
countries. I. Williams, Oliver F.
HD60.S8847 2014
338.9'27091724—dc23

2013044536

CONTENTS

Part III
WHERE DO WE GO FROM HERE?

FOREWORD

Bishop Kevin Dowling, C.Ss.R.

As the introduction to this volume states, "There is an astounding gap in wealth and income throughout the world. While some poor countries have become prosperous, in many nations poverty and inequalities have deepened, especially in Africa. Today there are more than one billion hungry people, up 25 percent in the last five years. Every day 17,000 children die of hunger. Too many people are jobless. Over 25 million people in sub-Saharan Africa have HIV. What is the moral response to these painful disparities?"

Yes, the statistics are numbing, mindboggling. But I only understood the statistics when I had actual experience with some of those suffering.

One day, many years ago in 1996, I sat in a miserable rusted zinc and wooden shack, one of over five thousand in an illegal so-called squatter camp in the midst of the richest platinum mines in the world, just north of Rustenburg in South Africa where I live—just one camp among several in the area housing some 350,000 destitute and despairing people. In the suffocating heat the perspiration poured down my face. In front of me on a bed were a dying baby and a woman, a single mother who had migrated from a country to the north, together with her firstborn little girl, in a desperate search for a way out of severe poverty. Her story was just one personal experience of many others, and it depicts the horror behind the need for the Millennium Development Goals.

Somehow, this woman had heard that perhaps there was a job in the mining areas in South Africa. She migrated, but she did not know that her search would end in a "poverty trap." She arrived in this shack

Based on a talk delivered at the March 2011 conference represented by this volume.

settlement located right next to a mine shaft and a hostel housing migrant workers from neighboring countries, men who had left their wives and families to find work there. She had no house, no money, nothing. So, like other women, she went to the only "salvation" there was—a tavern where men were lounging around drinking, the only pastime in such surroundings. She found a man who offered her accommodation in his own shack—but at a price. She had to provide him with sex, and the next day this became sex for money to buy food, and again and again—because, as she quickly found out, being an illegal economic migrant meant there was no job for her there and no hope of finding one. The consequences were devastating.

She inevitably contracted HIV and then fell pregnant, and her baby was born—also HIV-positive. This was before the advent of anti-retroviral treatment in South Africa, and before I was able to develop a partnership with a local company to build a hospice in-patient unit to which we could bring these "little ones" of the earth to die in peace and dignity. Because of her poverty and malnourishment, she rapidly deteriorated. That day, she and her baby were dying before my eyes. I will never forget her despairing words to me as the tears ran down her cheeks: "Father, I have no hope. There is no hope for me."

I held her in my arms as she sobbed. All I could do was entrust her to the care of my dedicated team of trained community home-care nurses in the settlement, and they cared for her in her shack until she and her baby died. Not for the first time in my life, I felt so helpless, but I also felt anger at the systemic issues and injustice which had condemned her to this shameful and degrading death. This story illustrates how poverty should not be visualized only in monetary terms; a more holistic understanding is required, which reflects all the ways a human being experiences being "deprived." In fact, a range of deprivations characterizes what it means to be a "poor" person in their actual context.

THE CHALLENGES

The eight Millennium Development Goals (MDGs) articulate several critical priorities in the quest for a more humane and just world. They also require an *ongoing analysis* of the causes of the misery experienced by millions in impoverished regions like Africa—because the tools used for analysis are being refined all the time, which can also lead to a development in conceptualizing responses. But the MDGs also demand an honest analysis by those of us who come from Africa as to why and how our political leadership, in particular, may be contributing to the problem, and what potential there is for change on the ground.

An unfortunate consequence of efforts to replace totalitarian regimes of various kinds in Africa with more democratic and participative models of government has been that several corrupt leaders have taken power only to control and exploit their country's resources for themselves and their families at the expense of their people and the nation. The efforts of regional economic groupings such as the Southern African Development Community (SADC) and indeed the continental African Union itself, with its New Partnership for Africa's Development (NEPAD), to work toward accountable governance and development by Africa's leaders has still achieved only limited success. The ideals and goals are there on paper, but ethical and values-based political governance and economic policies, not exploiting politicians, are required if we are to unlock the potential in our African communities and people. Civil society empowerment and advocacy are key to achieving accountability by governments in Africa and to gradually overcoming the poverty that diminishes and destroys the human dignity of millions. But civil society is often marginalized by those in power, and it lacks skills and resources because of its poverty. This situation calls for innovative regional and global partnerships for development, linking the private sector with impoverished people and communities.

On the other hand, there are also *structural* issues in the present globalized economic system that inhibit even the best efforts of impoverished countries and regions to come to grips with the reality of poverty and underdevelopment, with its dire consequences in terms of health care, education, child mortality, and much more.

The first constraining factor in the development of our poorest countries is the crippling national debt incurred by many of them through Structural Adjustment Programs (SAPs), which have been administered mainly by the World Bank and the International Monetary Fund. The 1997 *Human Development Report* contended that "sub-Saharan African governments transfer to Northern creditors four times what they spend on the health of their people,"[1] and that debt repayments undermine "their ability to engage in international trade on more equitable terms."[2] Poor nations, for example, changed their focus from small-scale farming to ensure food security into growing *export* crops in order to earn foreign currency to service their debts.

A more ethical analysis of the effects of such policies and global pressure over the past years from broad social movements across the world have succeeded, in part, in bringing about some form of debt cancellation or debt relief and certain modifications to the way that SAPs have been managed, for example, through the 1996 Highly In-debted Poor Countries Initiative (HIPC). But the reality for many poor nations has not yet changed significantly.

Second, consider the global trade system. Policies to govern trade are constantly being assessed and modified in the so-called Doha Round of the World Trade Organization (WTO), as well as in bilateral or regional trade negotiations. I would like to focus on just one aspect of trade policy: agriculture and agricultural support systems in relation to trade in food products. The European Union used to be a net importer of food but has now grown to become one of the biggest exporters of food in the world. Both the European Union and the United States provide substantial though different forms of support to their agricul-tural sectors, for example, significant agricultural subsidies to farmers in the European Union.

The recent rounds of WTO trade policy talks sought to make the markets in the underdeveloped South even more open to the world, but not in ways that might negatively affect the developed North. The Structural Adjustment Programs and the WTO trade rules have en-sured that the tariffs on food products in the European Union and the United States have been protected, whereas the poorer nations of the South have had to reduce their tariffs and the support needed for their local farmers, which effectively means, in the end, that they have to compete with the developed countries. It is obvious that the two cannot compete, as I think analysts who have assessed the North American Free Trade Agreement (NAFTA) in this area have shown. The net result is increasing inequality at the global level. Many small farmers in poor communities, particularly in Africa, have been forced to move off the land. There is little or no alternative employment—which leads to the kind of mass internal and international migration that I highlighted in my opening story, and to ever greater poverty.

Another factor affecting poverty reduction strategies consists of the global trends in production and consumption. The present scale of exploitation of the world's resources and the drive to achieve continual economic growth simply cannot be sustained at its present rate, and leads to ever greater inequality and environmental degradation. If we are to move toward a more equitable and just world order, then growth, reducing poverty, improving the quality of life of the vulnerable and deprived of the world, and environmental protection must be seen as *interrelated*. A high standard of life for the developed world cannot and should not be achieved at the expense of the poorer nations. The challenge here is the concept or vision of development.

Development cannot be equated simply with economic growth. *People* need to be placed at the center of development and of the way it will be implemented in different contexts. "Human development is about sustaining positive outcomes steadily over time and combating processes that impoverish people or underpin oppression and structural injustice. . . . Human development is the expansion of people's freedoms to live long, healthy and creative lives; to advance other goals they have reason to value; and to engage actively in shaping development equitably and sustainably on a shared planet. People are both the beneficiaries and the drivers of human development, as individuals and in groups."[3]

The eight Millennium Development Goals are interlinked, but for our purposes here the interrelationship between the first and the eighth goal is most important for me, especially in the light of the title of this book: "The UN Millennium Development Goals, the Global Compact, and the Common Good." These two goals are to "eradicate extreme poverty and hunger" and "develop a global partnership for development."

In view of promoting "a global partnership for development" as a means toward eradicating "extreme poverty and hunger," I believe that business companies and transnational corporations can play an important role with other actors in moving this world toward becoming more ethical and just. They can also assist in transforming the underdeveloped world into communities where objectives such as food security, providing essential services, and empowering small-scale farming and small or medium local enterprises through entrepreneurship will enable the poor to strive for a life of at least adequate dignity. The challenge is for governments and private sector companies, as well as NGOs and community organizations, to work *collaboratively* to both protect and enhance the "common good," one of the key principles of Catholic Social Thought.

Lisa Sowle Cahill clearly articulates the meaning of the common good: "That vision accentuates an objective morality, including criteria for justice and of a good society that can be known by all reasonable persons. Justice is seen as a real possibility, implemented incrementally along a spectrum of communal affiliations from the family to the nation and to the international order. Within the common good, the dignity and rights of the individual and the welfare and cohesion of the social body are balanced and seen as interdependent and mutually necessary."[4]

In my view, one important aspect of the common good is the actual *experience* of human beings in poor communities and *their* analysis of their concrete reality. The insights of these "little people" concerning how their reality can be changed for the better need to be recognized and valued. In this regard, a more participative model of development could be conceptualized and implemented, that is, a holistic development *from the bottom up*, so that individuals, communities, and entire nations can incrementally develop their innate potential, talents, and giftedness *as agents of their own transformation*. This includes enabling the poor—through different forms of partnership with government, the private sector, and NGOs—to acquire the basic skills to seize opportunities to become agents of change in their society.

Here we focus on another principle of Catholic Social Thought: subsidiarity. This principle underscores the importance of enabling and ensuring that what can be done effectively at the "lower level" should not be interfered with or blocked by the "higher level," including government. In relation to this, the role of government is to encourage, support, and monitor these local efforts, but also to ensure that local-level initiatives do not jeopardize the common good, that is, the good of the whole, or indeed the good and welfare of particular groups or minorities.

I believe that this challenge to promote and work toward the common good can be met in both ethical and constructive ways by all, including businesses and corporations. This requires a commitment to transparency and accountability especially by transnational corporations, which need to be sensitive to the reality of small-scale famers and local entrepreneurs in poor countries who lack the political or economic clout to hold these corporations accountable. In addition to working with governments, corporations can also set out to build *relational* partnerships with civil society, NGOs, and community-based organizations that commit themselves, together with such companies, to a moral framework of human rights, integral human development, and respect for the environment. Together, these parties can strive to find creative ways to respond to the concrete needs of people and societies on the ground. (I am aware that the philosophy or concept behind donor funding to NGOs in the world is changing; for instance, what is being sought are innovative responses that can then be mainstreamed and multiplied to enhance real delivery.) I have had several personal experiences of both local and international initiatives which have achieved precisely that objective, in smaller and larger ways.

For example, in the field of HIV/AIDS, consider the sixth MDG, to "combat HIV/AIDS, malaria, and other diseases." I think one foreign policy success of the Bush Administration was, and still is, PEPFAR—the President's Emergency Plan for AIDS Relief—in spite of budget cutbacks being applied at present. In addition to providing much needed funding for AIDS programs to governments in sub-Saharan Africa, the worst affected area in the world, PEPFAR also specifically targeted community-based organizations, including ones in the faith sector. Funding was allocated to them for anti-retroviral drugs and blood testing procedures. In South Africa, my own AIDS program was assessed and became one of twenty sites of Catholic community-centered AIDS programs to which PEPFAR funding was disbursed. These sites provide a high standard of care to around 70,000 patients through a network of community support mechanisms.

In my case, instead of inviting people to come to a central clinic, which would be much easier to manage than several sites, our staff takes the ARV drug regimen program to nine clinics that we have set up in some of the poorest shack settlements and villages where the two thousand patients we care for actually live—an example of innovation. We are actively engaged in discussions with the government's Health Department with a view to bringing the strengths of the community sector into partnership with local business and government, each of which have their strengths, and thus ensure and enhance the sustainability of this particular health care initiative.

The first five-year phase of these church-based programs funded by PEPFAR was scientifically analyzed by a professor from Cape Town University, who examined in detail over 45,000 patient files from the centers. His conclusion: the compliance rate and efficacy of these church-based community programs were equal to the best in the First World. What contributed to this success? I would say it was the spirituality, the ethos and sense of personal calling in the staff to the most vulnerable in society, the holistic care of the person and family in their total social context, and the organizational, financial, and program accountability by the leadership of these church-based community programs.

Another valuable initiative has been the Foundation for Hospices in sub-Saharan Africa (FHSSA), set up under the U.S. National Hospice and Palliative Care Organization in Washington, DC. What this has done is to link U.S.-based hospices with community hospice organizations in sub-Saharan Africa, not only in terms of funding partnerships but also through sending U.S. hospice personnel to the African hospices to share their skills and experience with local community workers so that more sustainable, creative, and better holistic care can be provided to patients, and indeed to the staff who care for them. So, for example, my AIDS program is partnered by Community Hospice based in Albany, New York, which this year is helping us set up an AIDS orphan center and program in a village.

At the local level, some seventeen years ago I began my journey with people and communities from my area to create what has since become the largest community-based AIDS program in the North West Province (State) of South Africa. To achieve this goal I set out to develop what I term "relational" partnerships with South African business and corporations, including the mines, based on trust and a commitment to achieve goals in which we both believed. On the one hand, this meets an important objective in the company's corporate social investment strategy by identifying a key niche area that corresponds to their organizational mission and vision in relation to society. On the other hand, from my perspective, this translates into making innovative and relevant community programs more sustainable in the short term, that is, in terms of three- to five-year funding cycles. This funding cycle requires that our administration team provides regular narrative reporting and financial accountability for the funding received, allowing the corporations to check on measurable outcomes and financial controls at any time. So, for example, we have nineteen separate annual audits for our various funding partnerships with corporations. Our experience is clear: partnerships with business *can* work, and our "little ones" truly benefit because there is *real delivery* and outcomes can be measured.

THIS PERSONAL REFLECTION underscores for me the relevance of the UN Global Compact in which you are engaged. For our purposes today, I have tried to link the first of the Millennium Development Goals, eradicating extreme poverty, with the eighth, developing a global partnership for development. And since eradicating poverty also requires dealing with the other goals—addressing the nonexistence or poor quality of education programs, the vulnerability experienced by so many women, high incidences of child mortality and inadequate maternal health care, the scourges of HIV, TB, and malaria, and environmental destruction—I have tried to link all of these to developing a global partnership.

In addition to bilateral and multilateral partnerships between governments, global financial institutions, and poor nations, the role of corporations in a global compact for the common good is of inestimable importance as we strive to implement partnerships and development programs that will incrementally change the reality of impoverished people and nations. Not only this, but it clearly demonstrates that all the companies, corporations, and NGOs involved in the UN Global Compact are striving to promote a moral and ethical vision of how everyone, including business, can indeed engage in making the world a more equitable and just global community. For this I honor you, because I have personally experienced both the validity of the concept and the efficacy of the partnership between people like you and people like myself and those in struggling communities in the world. We can make a difference! The chapters that follow outline how we can make a difference, both the conceptual foundations as well as actual experience of some of the leading companies. Congratulations to all the contributors to this volume.

NOTES

1. *Human Development Report 1997* (New York: Oxford University Press, 1997), 84.
2. Ibid., 85.
3. *Human Development Report 2010* (New York: Palgrave Macmillan, 2010), 2.
4. Lisa Sowle Cahill, "Globalization and the Common Good," in *Globalization and Catholic Social Thought*, ed. J. Coleman, W. F. Ryan, and B. Ryan (Maryknoll, NY: Orbis Books, 2005), 42.

Introduction

Oliver F. Williams, C.S.C.

Sustainability can mean all things to all persons, and many organizations are working hard to figure out what it means for them and how to implement it. The term is often used as a synonym for corporate social responsibility (CSR), corporate responsibility, and corporate citizenship. The term was first given prominence in the United Nations' 1987 *Report of the World Commission on the Environment and Development: Our Common Future* by the Brundtland Commission: "Sustainable development is development that meets the needs of the present without compromising the ability of future generations to meet their own needs." Here the focus was on the physical environment. So, for example, if a company was cutting down trees to produce paper, it should plant a new tree for each one that was cut. Destroying the physical environment was unsustainable. Today the term has been broadened so that any activity that destroys the environment necessary for business success and long-term survival is considered unsustainable. The environment necessary for business long-term survival is now thought to be not only the physical environment but also the social/ethical climate. What is clear is that in the light of globalization and world trade, many business leaders, academics, and stakeholders see that business should take a greater role in solving some of the problems of the wider society. Business is responsible not only for its private good but also, to some extent, for the common good. In the final analysis, for business to flourish, society must flourish.

To advance the vision of business and the common good, the Notre Dame Center for Ethics and Religious Values in Business at the Mendoza College of Business, in partnership with the United National Global Compact[1] and the United Nations Principles for Responsible Management Education, convened a major conference at the University of Notre Dame, March 20–22, 2011, titled "The UN Millennium Development Goals, The Global Compact, and The Common Good." The conference brought together leading businesses to outline their projects, especially those advancing the Millennium Development Goals (MDGs) designed to help alleviate dire poverty. Academics, government officials, and leaders of nongovernment organizations (NGOs) focused on some of the practical as well as the conceptual issues involved.

Globalization is a fact of life, worldwide interdependence a reality. Globalization of trade has yielded massive amounts of wealth, yet there is an astounding gap in wealth and income throughout the world. While some poor countries have become prosperous, in many nations poverty and inequalities have deepened, especially in Africa. Today there are more than one billion hungry people, up 25 percent in the last five years. Every day 17,000 children die of hunger. Too many people are jobless. Over 25 million people in sub-Saharan Africa have HIV. What is the moral response to these painful disparities?

The term "common good" conveys the idea that we ought to try to shape a world where all are able to share in the material wealth and other humane benefits that can come from economic development. Thus, for example, Pope Benedict XVI, in the 2009 encyclical *Caritas in Veritate*, acknowledges the fact that free global trade has created massive amounts of wealth but laments the fact that so many people have no possibility of sharing in that wealth and exist in dire poverty. Other major religions and the United Nations have a similar message.

While individuals and governments can do much to encourage the common good, increasingly businesses play a role, and this new role is the focus of the book. One initiative on the part of businesses to promote and enhance the common good is the United Nations Global Compact. Founded in 2000 by then Secretary-General of the United

Nations Kofi Annan, the Global Compact is intended to increase and diffuse the benefits of global economic development through voluntary corporate policies and programs. By promoting human rights and labor rights, enhancing care for the environment, and encouraging anticorruption measures, the ten principles of the Global Compact are designed to shape more peaceful and just societies. Initially comprised of several dozen companies, the Compact as of 2013 had as signatories over 7,000 businesses and 1,400 NGOs in 135 countries. One objective is to emphasize the moral purpose of business, with member companies setting a high moral tone throughout the world.

A BRIEF OVERVIEW

Whenever I reflect on the strengths and weaknesses of the UN Global Compact, I am reminded of the comment of Winston Churchill on democracy: "Many forms of Government have been tried, and will be tried in this world of sin and woe. No one pretends that democracy is perfect or all-wise. Indeed, it has been said that democracy is the worst form of government except all those other forms that have been tried from time to time."[2] While the Compact may not be the final answer, it does begin the journey. With the Compact there is a growing acceptance of universal norms for the global economy.

When the Secretary-General of the United Nations, Kofi Annan, in 2000, first promulgated the Global Compact, he had a clear vision of the problem but only a broad outline of the solution. The problem was that globalization of markets, while it created vast amounts of new wealth, did not distribute this new wealth very well. Millions of people in India and China were lifted out of poverty, but many people in the world were victims rather than beneficiaries of this new engine of wealth creation. Whether it be blue-collar workers who lost lucrative jobs on auto assembly lines in Detroit, populations of major cities in China that lost clean air to breathe, or poor peasants who were subjected to sweat shop conditions in Asia, Africa, and Latin America, increasing discontent was in the air. In former times of great economic volatility, nation-states took measures that restored social harmony and political stability. For example, the Great Depression of the twentieth century was the birthplace of the social safety net, evolving into such programs as social security, medical benefits, unemployment insurance, food stamps, and so on. The problems today are global in scope, and even where nation-states might be willing or able to regulate, they are reluctant to do so for fear of losing new investment to nations with less stringent regulations. The race to the bottom is a fact of life in developing countries.

Kofi Annan saw clearly that if globalization and its ability to create massive wealth were to continue, there must be a set of ideals that would guide business and ensure that the legitimate concerns of all, especially the least advantaged, were not neglected. This set of ideals, what has become known as the Global Compact, consists of ten principles. These focus on human rights, labor rights, concern for the environment, and corruption and are taken directly from commitments made by governments through the UN: the Universal Declaration of Human Rights (1948); the Rio Declaration on Environment and Development (1992); the International Labor Organization's Fundamental Principles and Rights at Work (1998); and the UN Convention Against Corruption (2003). The Global Compact was designed as a voluntary initiative. A company subscribing to the principles is invited to make a clear statement of support and must include some references in its annual report or other public documents on the progress it is making on internalizing the principles within its operations. This "Communication on Progress" (COP) must also be submitted to be posted on the Global Compact Website. For a good sample of the projects that companies have undertaken to advance human rights, labor rights, environmental stewardship, and the struggle against corruption, see the UN Global Compact website (http://www.globalcompact.org). Failure to submit a COP within two years of becoming a signatory to the Compact (and subsequently every year) will result in being delisted. As of July 2013, over 4,000 companies have been removed from the list of participants for failure to communicate progress.

Scholars have suggested the ethical codes are of two major types, aspirational or directional. An aspirational code offers a set of ideals, general in nature, that members of an organization are expected to hold, but it does not have any enforcement mechanism. A directional code provides detailed guidelines and sanctions for all members. The Global Compact falls in the middle of this continuum, with clear ideas and limited enforcement. The unique mission of the Compact is to foster the growth of norms and humane values in the global society, a challenge heretofore managed by nation-states for their own domestic situation. To advance the ten principles, the Global Compact has established over one hundred country and regional networks where dialogue, learning, and projects are carried forward in a local context. Kofi Annan expressed it well: "Let us choose to unite the power of markets with the authority of universal ideals. Let us choose to reconcile the creative forces of private entrepreneurship with the needs of the disadvantaged and the requirements of future generations."

Does the UN Global Compact provide an answer to critics of globalization? The answer is "yes" and "no" depending on which critics one chooses to address. Some critics see little value in the Compact unless the principles are somehow mandated by a worldwide legal framework. Since the Compact relies on transparency and the interest companies have in maintaining their good reputation as the ultimate sanction, those critics advocating a statutory approach are unimpressed.

There are, however, critics of globalization who are primarily concerned with advancing global norms for business and retrieving the moral purpose of business. These may be advocates of the Compact, considering what it has done already and may do in the future.

To be sure, there is a business case for corporate responsibility and the work of the Compact. Not only does following the Compact principles have a high likelihood of saving the company money by avoiding costly litigation, but it also enhances reputation capital, builds brands, enables a company to attract and retain valuable employees, develops trust, and so on. In addition, creating sustainable value in a company by attending to environmental, social, and governance (ESG) performance is increasingly rewarded by the investment community. The Global Compact is one of the factors advancing the trend toward a broadening of the criteria by which the market assesses the performance of companies. This broadening of criteria is reflected in two movements inspired by the Global Compact, one in the investment community and one in higher education. The Principles for Responsible Investment (PRI) is a credo subscribed to by over 1,000 investment institutions throughout the world and currently has some $30 trillion of assets under its management. The Principles for Responsible Management Education (PRME) is a code for business schools, reflecting the need to educate future business leaders with this new, broadened vision. Over five hundred business schools have already subscribed to this new initiative. Chapter 19 in this volume, by Arvid Johnson, offers a good rationale for joining PRME.

While many companies find the business case for the Global Compact compelling, it is the moral case that has the interest of some leading NGOs and critics of globalization. These critics are concerned that in developing countries where there is no enforced statutory framework to protect workers and the environment, multinational corporations are acting unethically with impunity. Many NGOs have risen to the occasion and mobilized public opinion about the need for some global standards. As for the Global Compact, there is evidence that businesses are walking the talk, and several chapters in this book discuss how businesses are meeting the challenge.

The ten principles of the Global Compact have been given added force by the UN Millennium Development Goals (MDGs), a blueprint for action agreed to in 2000 by all the countries of the world as well as leading development institutions. With the target date of 2015 for partial completion, the eight MDGs are (1) eradicate extreme poverty and hunger; (2) achieve universal primary education; (3) promote gender equality and empower women; (4) reduce child mortality; (5) improve maternal health; (6) combat HIV/AIDS, malaria, and other diseases; (7) ensure environmental sustainability; and (8) develop a global partnership for development. Facilitated by the Global Compact Office, commitment to these ideals has brought businesses into new collaborative relationships with NGOs throughout the world in order to help build a better life for the least advantaged. The MDG monitor gives an updated report on how countries are progressing in achieving the eight goals.[3] In 2015, the MDGs will be subsumed within a broader set of goals to overcome poverty called the Sustainable Development Goals (SDGs).

THE PURPOSE OF THE BOOK

The main objective of this book is to help people understand that business serves the common good on at least two levels. On one hand, just producing goods and services—doing what business does—is a great service to the common good. We have a relatively high standard of living today because of the innovation and creativity of business operating through the markets and incentives of capitalism. The second level is for business to serve the common good by helping the many who are not even in the market because they lack marketable skills and the resources to acquire them. This population is the primary target of the Millennium Development Goals, and companies have made a concerted effort in recent years to provide a "hand up" rather than a handout. In many countries, a company's deep commitment in areas such as infrastructure development, local capacity-building, education, health, job creation, disaster relief, and more can serve as far more than philanthropy. These efforts can address aspects of the societal context that are lacking or insufficient—voids which can greatly impact a company's ability to operate, compete, and thrive.

ALIGNING CORPORATE OBJECTIVES
WITH SOCIAL VALUES

In a way, the Global Compact is the fruit of a process that first took shape in the 1970s with the Sullivan Principles for South Africa.[4] The Sullivan Principles were the first instance of a shift from state-centric regulation to a new form of regulation created and implemented by the private sector and civil society. Opposing apartheid in South Africa was also the first instance where political ends were pursued by directly pressuring businesses without going through the government. NGOs, through their research and advocacy work, helped shape public opinion on the evils of apartheid. Up to this time, it was assumed that promoting and protecting civil, political, and social rights were the exclusive domains of the nation-state. What we observe here is the beginning of the demise of the strict division of labor between the private and public sectors. In large measure, this new role of business in society—advancing citizenship rights—was advocated by civil society because governments were either unable or unwilling to do it on their own.

Leon Sullivan, the charismatic leader of the Sullivan Principles, advanced a compelling argument for companies assuming this new role in society. Sullivan was fond of telling the companies, "Where there is power, there is also responsibility." Sullivan's point was not that companies had caused apartheid, or that they could buy legitimacy by dismantling it. Simply put, apartheid was wrong, and because the companies, as one of the pillars of society, had the economic power to dismantle it, they should do so. It was the right thing to do. If a company would not work to dismantle apartheid, Sullivan would publicly shame it and force it to leave South Africa. This notion that business organizations that have power and are an intrinsic part of society have to be accountable or else they lose their legitimacy is not new. In the business context, Keith Davis, in 1966, coined the phrase "the iron law of business responsibility." In contemporary business literature the term *license to operate* is often used to convey the idea that society has certain expectations of business. If business does not meet those expectations, business loses its legitimacy, and there is a price to pay as a result. In the South African apartheid struggle, there are many examples of U.S. society influencing the *license to operate* of companies perceived to be sustaining apartheid. For example, in the 1980s, 168 state, city, county, and regional authorities had some form of policy restricting their business dealings with U.S. companies thought to be irresponsible in using their corporate power in South Africa. Thus, the City of Chicago was precluded by one of these "selective purchasing ordinances" from buying buses from General Motors. GM learned the hard way about the power of the people. Similarly, companies today understand that although the Global Compact does not have an independent monitoring and verification provision, the power of the people could influence the license to operate.

Laws like the selective purchasing ordinance in the City of Chicago prepared large companies to be proactive in meeting society's expectations and to see the wisdom of collaborating with NGOs in designing and implementing ethical rules for the global community. The UN Global Compact, for example, entails self-regulation, rulemaking, and rule implementation without the assistance of governments. "Soft" transnational law complements "hard" national law, and the impetus for this law comes not from national political discussion but from transnational civil society and, to some extent, from business itself. At least in practice, there is clearly a change underway in the manner in which the responsibilities of the private and public sectors are apportioned.

More reflection on the conceptual foundations of this recalibration may be helpful, but it is clear that many in civil society find globalization more palatable with the Global Compact on the scene.

It would be inaccurate, however, to see meeting society's new expectations as the sole driver in the business quest to balance public interest with financial returns. Many of the best companies believe that they have to stand for something besides making a profit, and this belief is reflected in a company's vision, values, or mission statement. More importantly, these values are actively translated into projects that serve the common good. For example, the U.S. company Merck & Co., Inc., with 51,000 employees in 140 countries and annual sales over $ 427 billion, tells us what it stands for:

Our Vision

We make a difference in the lives of people globally through our innovative medicines, vaccines, and consumer health and animal products. We aspire to be the best healthcare company in the world and are dedicated to providing leading innovations and solutions for tomorrow.

Our Mission

To provide innovative, distinctive products and services that save and improve lives and satisfy customer needs, to be recognized as a great place to work, and to provide investors with a superior rate of return.

What We Stand For

- Excellence in science and healthcare innovation, with an emphasis on addressing unmet medical needs.
- Focus on patients and anticipating customers' needs.
- Commitment to expand access to our medicines and vaccines, and to improve global health.

Merck's purpose includes "working to help the world be well,"[5] and chapter 2 tells of one of Merck's projects that carry out this theme.

In January 2011, UN Secretary-General Ban Ki-moon announced that a small group of the Global Compact companies had agreed to assume greater leadership in tackling the sustainability challenges. Called the Global Compact LEAD, these fifty-four companies agreed to take on more of the challenges and to work with other companies not as advanced through over one hundred local networks throughout the globe. Of the seven companies profiled in this volume, four are LEAD members: Nestlé S.A.; Novartis International AG; Sumitomo Chemical Company, Limited; and The Coca-Cola Company.

THE PLAN OF THE BOOK

The book opened with a foreword by Bishop Kevin Dowling of Rustenberg, South Africa, an area ravaged by HIV/AIDS, in which Dowling outlined the challenge of meeting the needs of the poor. Following the present introduction, there are three main parts. Part I consists of seven chapters, each telling how a company is trying to advance the Millennium Development Goals. Part II contains twelve chapters by scholars who reflect on some of the conceptual issues involved with the Millennium Development Goals. The three chapters of Part III point the way for the future of the Millennium Development Goals, the Global Compact, and the common good.

Chapter 1 is written by an officer of Microsoft Corporation and outlines the philosophy of Microsoft regarding the role of business in society. Without waiting for some new, overarching theory to guide its CSR, Microsoft works from the assumption that "business is as much a part of the social fabric as educational institutions, religious institutions, and nonprofit organizations addressing a wide spectrum of issues and needs." After discussing the Microsoft philosophy, the chapter offers in an appendix an excerpt from the company's 2011 Communication on Progress (COP) report, detailing its progress in advancing the Millennium Development Goals.

Chapter 2 is authored by Dr. Themba Moeti, Managing Director of the African Comprehensive HIV/AIDS Partnership (ACHAP), with Innocent Chingombe and Godfrey Musuka. ACHAP is a unique public-private development partnership involving the government of Botswana, Merck, and the Bill and Melinda Gates Foundation. In discussing the most successful partnership project to date, the chapter provides a good overview of Merck's corporate citizenship philosophy and the company's significant contribution in advancing the MDGs, especially in the areas of health and development.

The third chapter is about Sumitomo Chemical America. Based in Japan, Sumitomo discovered a way to produce mosquito netting that keeps its insecticide quality, without requiring frequent spraying. This is a major breakthrough and holds the possibility of preventing the spread of malaria and thus reducing child mortality. Sumitomo has taken steps to ensure that these nets are available in many of the worst malaria areas in Africa.

Chapter 4 tells of Nestlé's philosophy of "creating shared value." Discovering ways to create value for the community while at the same time enhancing the company is the goal of Nestlé. The company is focused on creating shared value in the areas of nutrition, water, and rural development, and it views the Millennium Development Goals as a way of assessing the impact of company projects on a community.

Coca-Cola is the subject of chapter 5, and its focus is how Coke made partnerships a crucial element in its strategies to advance the MDGs. In its quest to create long-term value for the community, the company seeks to advance economic opportunity. Two projects are discussed in the chapter: the formation of Manual Distribution Centers, micro-distribution centers of products staffed by women; and the development of small fruit farmers in places such as Haiti, Uganda, and Kenya. There is also a discussion of the company's efforts to end child labor, advance human rights, and move toward sustainable agriculture.

Novartis is the subject of chapter 6, and in its presentation the company makes a distinction between projects to advance the MDGs accomplished through its core business and projects accomplished through its philanthropic arm, the Novartis Foundation for Sustainable Development. Perhaps one of the most active companies in advancing the MDGs, programs under the core business operation include drug donations, patient assistance or selling at cost, and not-for-profit research into neglected diseases. The Foundation's focus is in helping "the poorest of the poor," those who would probably not be reached through the core business.

Chapter 7 discusses Levi Strauss and its initiative to reach out to its own employees on the HIV/AIDS issue. With over 15,000 employees in one hundred countries, Levi Strauss had concerns about the effectiveness of its HIV/AIDS programs, and the chapter outlines a new global approach taken by the company.

The twelve chapters of Part II contain the reflections of thirteen scholars on various conceptual issues. Perhaps the most controversial issue in a discussion of the UN Global Compact and the Millennium Development Goals revolves around the notion of human rights. The 1948 Universal Declaration of Human Rights listed what is thought to be the full gamut of rights, many of which are reflected in the Millennium Development Goals, for example, the right to life, education, health care, food, and so on. The 1948 Declaration calls upon states as well as "all organs of society" to promote human rights. Some argue that business, as an "organ of society," should not only be *invited* but should be *morally obliged* to advance human rights. As it stands now, the UN Global Compact only requires that business do no harm in the area of human rights and invites companies to take on projects to advance human rights through advancing the MDGs. Chapters 8, 9, and 10 explore some of the issues involved with human rights.

Chapter 8 by Georges Enderle discusses the framework on human rights developed by John Ruggie for the UN. Known as the "Protect, Respect and Remedy" framework, it assigns the duty to protect and advance human rights to states, the duty to respect (not to harm) human rights to business, and the duty to provide remedies for alleged violations of rights to business and states. Enderle explores this framework and related issues, leaving it open whether business has a moral responsibility to *promote* human rights, that is, whether business has more of a responsibility than the Ruggie framework postulates.

Douglass Cassel in chapter 9 offers a lawyer's perspective on the United Nation Global Compact Principles 1 and 2 on human rights. While many critics of these principles call for "greater specificity and more teeth," Cassel argues that the significant contribution of the Global Compact is that it is an instrument that is raising the consciousness of business people that human rights must be taken seriously. If you want more specificity and teeth, there are other norms and regimes, but the key role of the Global Compact is to gain universal acceptance for the idea that human rights are the concern of business. In reviewing the projects of Global Compact companies that are advancing the MDGs, there is clearly truth to this point.

Daniel Malan, in chapter 10, discusses the Integrative Social Contracts Theory first put forward by Thomas Donaldson and Tom Dunfee. Malan argues that this approach steers a course between relativism and absolutism in applying human rights in the business context and provides a moral framework for responsible corporate citizenship.

Chapters 11 and 12 offer some insight on the crucial role of partnerships with business, civil society organizations, and government if progress is to be made on the MDGs. Chapter 11 is authored by the ambassador to the United Nations from the UK, Philip Parham. Parham writes from the perspective of government and suggests how the vision of the MDGs can be advanced. Chapter 12 is by a scholar of peace studies, Hal Culbertson. Culbertson outlines the role of business and NGOs in peace building and discusses how collaborative alliances can yield much fruit in advancing the MDGs.

Chapter 13 suggests that at least part of the motivation for a business's participation in advancing the MDGs is to enhance the good reputation of a company. James O'Rourke offers seven key factors that are entailed in managing the reputation of an organization and argues that this task is the key responsibility of a chief executive.

Environmental leadership is the focus of chapter 14. Deborah Rigling Gallagher discusses two major UN Global Compact initiatives, Caring for Climate and the Environmental Stewardship Strategy. The chapter provides a good understanding of the progress made as well as the challenges ahead.

Mark Kennedy in chapter 15 offers a creative response to the old debate about the purpose of business. Arguing that today business must "pursue purposeful profit," he states his point as follows: "To succeed in the long term, companies must engage and benefit society in a manner that complements and supports its overall strategy."

In chapter 16, Ante Glavas makes the point that companies practicing social and environmental responsibility benefit from enhanced employee performance. Presenting a number of research studies, Glavas argues that ideas such as the MDGs and the UN Global Compact increase employee engagement and productivity in a business.

Chapter 17 by Thomas Harvey argues that today the business economy is the most powerful force shaping all the institutions of the world. Given this power and the accompanying human and financial resources, business has a responsibility to advance the MDGs guided by the ideas of the UN Global Compact. Only if it does so, he argues, will there be a just global economy.

Chapter 18, by Gerald F. Cavanagh, S.J., and Eric Hespenheide, offers guidance for companies trying to embed the ten principles of the Global Compact into their day-to-day operations. Called the UN

Management Model, this approach has been helpful for students trying to understand company participation in the MDGs.

The final chapter of Part II, chapter 19, focuses on what business schools can do to prepare future leaders for the global economy. In 2007, at the Global Compact meeting in Geneva, a group of world-class academics announced a new initiative to prepare business students for the world envisioned by the Global Compact. Called the Principles for Responsible Management Education (PRME), these principles outline an agenda for business schools educating for a sustainable economy. The chapter presents a rationale for joining PRME by Arvid Johnson, the former dean of the Brennan School of Business at Dominican University in Chicago and currently the president of the University of St. Francis in Illinois.

Part III offers some reflections on the future of the UN Global Compact and the MDGs. While Kirk O. Hanson in chapter 20 addresses some more proximate suggestions for change, Sandra Waddock in chapter 21 argues for a major systemic change. We "need a new narrative about the role of business in society, as well as about the common good and how all can contribute to it." Arguing for a fundamental reform of capitalism, Waddock offers much food for thought.

My final chapter makes the case for an expanded version of the Ruggie "Respect, Protect and Remedy" framework. I argue that there is a moral obligation, under certain conditions, for a company to participate in advancing the MDGs. A survey of the various scholars engaging this issue is provided.

I am most grateful for our many benefactors who help support the work of the Center for Ethics and Religious Values in Business at the University of Notre Dame, and, in particular, William Lehr Jr., formerly a senior officer of Hershey Foods and the Chairman and CEO of Capital BlueCross. Also, a thank you is in order to Deb Coch, administrative assistant at the center, whose work enabled this project to move from an idea to a finished product.

The essays in this volume were first presented at a conference in March 2011 at the University of Notre Dame; the conference was organized by the center with the cooperation of the United Nations Global Compact Office and the Principles for Responsible Management Education (PRME) secretariat. To our partners, we owe a great debt of gratitude, in particular to Georg Kell, executive director of the Global Compact; Jonas Haertle, head of the Principles for Responsible Management Education Secretariat; and Lee Tavis, professor in the Mendoza College of Business at Notre Dame. To be sure, I want to thank all those who contributed to this volume and added to our understanding of the expanding role of business in society.

Finally, I want to express my gratitude to Professor Stephen Yong-Seung Park, Director of the Institute for Peace through Commerce and Dean of International Affairs at Kyung Hee University in Seoul, South Korea. I served at Kyung Hee University as an International Scholar during the 2012–13 academic year, and this time enabled me to focus on preparing the volume for publication.

NOTES

1. See http://www.globalcompactfoundation.org.

2. Winston Churchill, Speech to the House of Commons, November 11, 1947, *Hansard Parliamentary Debates*.

3. See http://www.mdgmonitor.org/index.cfm.

4. See S. Prakash Sethi and Oliver F. Williams, *Economic Imperatives and Ethical Values in Global Business: The South African Experience and International Codes Today* (Notre Dame, IN: University of Notre Dame Press, 2001). The discussion in most of this section is taken directly from Oliver F. Williams, C.S.C., "Responsible Corporate Citizenship and the Ideals of the United Nations Global Compact," in *Peace through Commerce*, ed. Oliver F. Williams, C.S.C. (Notre Dame, IN: University of Notre Dame Press, 2008), 432–34.

5. See http://www.merck.com.

Part I

BUSINESS AND THE MILLENNIUM
DEVELOPMENT GOALS

1 | The Role of Business in Society: The Microsoft Vision

Daniel T. Bross

People everywhere—from corporate board rooms to the halls of academia to the corner café—agree that corporations are obliged to fulfill certain responsibilities in the course of doing business, but that is often where the agreement ends. It is not easy to reach a consensus on exactly what corporate responsibilities encompass and to whom they apply, let alone how corporations should measure their success in meeting those responsibilities or be held accountable for their actions or inaction.

Corporations are legal entities, sanctioned and granted charters by one or more governments and the people they represent. Those charters spell out various obligations and responsibilities that corporations are required to meet, usually including an expectation that the business will in some way serve, or at least not harm, the public interest. But although corporations in a free society exist by virtue of public permission and require tacit public approval to continue operating, to what extent does that obligate a corporation to assume partial responsibility for societal problems or to help solve them?

Does a corporation's responsibility begin and end with making a profit for its shareholders, or does it have a broader responsibility to others who are affected by its business and to society in general? Should a corporation stay focused exclusively on its bottom line, or does it also have an obligation to be concerned about human rights, the environment, and other social issues?

People often speak of corporations and society as though they are unrelated, yet business is as much a part of the social fabric as educational institutions, religious institutions, and nonprofit organizations addressing a wide spectrum of issues and needs. Every business, no matter what its size, is also like the proverbial pebble dropped in a pond. It sends out ripples that change the society in which it operates.

That understanding is at the heart of corporate social responsibility, the idea that companies do have a responsibility to society and should operate in ways that lessen their negative effects and/or enhance their positive effects on the environment, on the people whose lives they touch, on the communities in which they do business—whether local or global—and on society at large.

THE EVOLUTION OF CORPORATE
SOCIAL RESPONSIBILITY

Corporate social responsibility (CSR) is a not a new idea, but the concept has changed over time and continues to evolve even now.

According to classical economic theory, a business was considered socially responsible if it maximized profits while operating within the law. This is a low bar compared to today's more progressive view that corporations, while continuing to earn healthy profits, should also exercise good governance principles and pursue responsible business practices that benefit not only their shareholders but also their employees, customers, and partners as well as the society in which they all coexist.

The roots of our modern view of corporate social responsibility stretch back to the ancient Hebrews. The Torah offers clear instructions to landowners—among the leading businessmen of their day—about their social obligations. The Book of Leviticus, for example, says: "When you reap the harvest of your land, you shall not reap all the way to the edges of your field, or gather the gleanings of your harvest. You shall not pick your vineyard bare, or gather the fallen fruit of your vineyard; you shall leave them for the poor and the stranger" (Lev 19:9–10).

Other religions, from Christianity to Islam to Hinduism, developed similar precepts, all based on the belief that their God (or gods) expected business owners to balance their pursuit of profits with an equally important duty to society. Those ideals persisted through the centuries and were practiced to a greater or lesser degree during various eras, but one of the best ways to trace the evolution of corporate social responsibility within the context of free enterprise, where the concept has attracted both strong support and aggressive opposition, is to look at how it developed in the United States.

Merchants in colonial America were thrifty, but charity was a virtue that was valued just as highly, and many business owners gave liberally to churches, orphanages, poorhouses, and other social institutions. In the early 1800s, wealthy entrepreneurs such as Steven Girard—a banker and merchant who was the richest person in the United States during his lifetime—began to establish or make large gifts to schools, colleges, hospitals, and other worthy causes. Legendary industrialists and entrepreneurs such as John D. Rockefeller and Andrew Carnegie, who made their fortunes during the economic boom of the late 1800s, became even more famous as philanthropists who used their wealth to further public health and education, support medical and scientific research, and improve the lives of ordinary Americans.

The rise of social Darwinism in the latter half of the nineteenth century, popularized by the influential English philosopher Herbert Spencer, temporarily slowed the expansion of corporate social responsibility. Social Darwinism promoted "survival of the fittest" in business as well as nature and justified ruthless competition by claiming that charity and benevolence, in which strong, successful individuals supported those who were weaker and less successful, violated the laws of evolution.

Social Darwinism lost momentum in the United States after Spencer's death in 1903, and during the early twentieth century three ideas emerged that helped to justify broader corporate responsibility. First was the notion that executives and managers were the trustees of corporate power and that their positions implied a duty to protect stakeholders. Second was the idea that managers had an obligation to balance the multiple interests of stakeholders, social as well as economic. And finally there was the service principle, which was the belief that the prosperity that individual managers, executives, and corporate officers created by building successful businesses could eliminate social problems such as poverty and hunger.

Not every U.S. business leader embraced these ideas. Some continued to maximize profits with little regard for the welfare of their workers, let alone any sense of duty to society, but many others started to apply these principles to their businesses.

In 1953, an American economist named Howard Bowen, who is sometimes called the Father of Corporate Social Responsibility, published his landmark book *Social Responsibilities of the Businessman*, which set forth the idea that large businesses were important centers of power and decision making whose actions touched the lives of citizens in many different ways.[1] One of the questions Bowen posed in his book was, "What responsibilities to society may businessmen reasonably be expected to assume?" In answer, Bowen gave perhaps the first clear definition of corporate social responsibility: "It refers to the obligations of businessmen to pursue those policies, to make those decisions, or to follow those lines of action which are desirable in terms of the objectives and values of our society." It was Bowen, perhaps more than anyone else, who firmly redefined the relationship of business to society and its problems in terms of corporate responsibility rather than individual charity.

Conservative economists, most notably Milton Friedman, soon began to argue strongly against corporate social responsibility. Friedman claimed that the only social responsibility a business had was to increase its profits; that governments, not companies, should address social problems; and that business leaders who advocated corporate social responsibility were "preaching pure and unadulterated socialism."

In an article he wrote for *The New York Times Magazine* in September 1970, Friedman asserted that corporate executives were merely the employees of shareholders—the actual owners of the company—and if they used corporate funds to address social issues, "the corporate executive would be spending someone else's money for a general social interest. Insofar as his actions in accord with his 'social responsibility' reduce returns to stockholders, he is spending their money. Insofar as his actions raise the price to customers, he is spending the customers' money. Insofar as his actions lower the wages of some employees, he is spending their money."[2]

Later in the article, Friedman reminded readers that in his book *Capitalism and Freedom*, "I have called [corporate social responsibility] a 'fundamentally subversive doctrine' in a free society, and have said that in such a society, 'there is one and only one social responsibility of business—to use its resources and engage in activities designed to increase its profits so long as it stays within the rules of the game, which is to say, engages in open and free competition without deception or fraud.'"

Despite Friedman's arguments and those of other conservative economists, acceptance of corporate social responsibility as a fundamental practice has continued to grow throughout the business community—in developed countries and emerging economies worldwide as well as the United States.

Although CSR recognizes that companies are in business to create wealth by developing and delivering products and services that people need, and acknowledges the value of those activities, it also views a corporation's profit-making activities in the context of broader social priorities. CSR covers issues that affect all companies, such as fair labor practices and greenhouse gas emissions; those that are specific to a particular industry, such as the efficient and sustainable use of water; and others that are limited to the impact of a single business on one local community or ecosystem. As a result, in recent years CSR has evolved into a coherent and comprehensive way of thinking about the role of business in society.

THE BUSINESS CASE FOR CORPORATE SOCIAL RESPONSIBILITY

It is easy to understand why many different constituencies—from governments to the general public—would prefer that every corporation be socially responsible in the way it conducts its business. And it's reasonable to expect that, on a personal level at least, many corporate executives and managers might want the same thing. But for corporate decision-makers to adopt CSR as an integral part of their long-term strategy and day-to-day operations, they have to believe that it is good for their business.

After all, corporations already do a lot of things that benefit society. They offer customers high-quality products and services, create wealth for investors, represent business opportunities for partners and suppliers, and provide jobs that enable employees to support their families and to energize the economy with their own purchases and investments. The taxes paid by corporations and their workers also help to finance essential government programs and vital infrastructure. And depending on the nature of their business, corporations may perform valuable scientific research, develop innovative technologies, or create life-saving drugs. Why should they consider doing more than that, or potentially change the way they operate to address social priorities that are not always easy to measure on a profit-and-loss statement?

First, keep in mind that multinational corporations are not engaged with just one society. Different cultures define the relationship between business and the rest of society in different ways. People, governments, and organizations in Europe, for example, have a very different view of the role that various sectors of society should play than their counterparts in Asia or the United States. So the role of business in society and the legal responsibilities that help to define it often vary greatly from country to country, depending on culture, form of government, and societal norms.

Every year, major U.S.-based corporations are seeing more of their revenue coming from outside the United States, as trade balances shift and emerging economies gain momentum. Yet despite this trend, a surprising number of those companies remain extremely U.S.-centric. These companies may have numerous customers, suppliers, partners, and facilities in dozens of nations worldwide, but they persist in viewing the world and the global marketplace through the single lens of where they are based rather than the multiple lenses of where so much of their business actually occurs. Many such companies are more likely to opt for short-term profits over strategies that could lead to long-term success in cultures that place a high value on priorities such as ending human rights abuses or conserving their natural resources.

Given today's global economy and the "flat world" in which businesses operate, such cultural differences can be either keys or barriers to success. To compete effectively, both now and twenty years in the future, U.S.-based global companies must develop a better understanding of how various governments and cultures define the role of business in society. To succeed in other countries, where so much of the global market is now concentrated, U.S. companies must be attentive, respectful, and responsive to local culture and societal norms. Without this strong connection to customers in other nations, U.S. companies cannot succeed long-term in the global economy.

UNITED NATIONS GLOBAL COMPACT

The UN Global Compact, which the United Nations describes as "a set of core values in the areas of human rights, labour standards, the environment and anti-corruption," offers corporations a way to clearly define and communicate their commitment to corporate social responsibility. The ten principles that constitute the UN Global Compact address issues such as eliminating child labor, avoiding complicity in human rights abuses, and promoting greater environmental responsibility.

The UN Global Compact is the largest voluntary corporate responsibility initiative in the world, with more than 10,000 corporate participants and other stakeholders from more than 135 countries. As such, it provides a framework that can enable companies to think in a more comprehensive way about issues that can help to define their role in society and that may improve their ability to develop a sustainable global business model. Companies that choose to adopt the Global Compact and to align their business strategy and operations with its ten principles can help to ensure that "markets, commerce, technology and finance advance in ways that benefit economies and societies everywhere."

When joining the UN Global Compact, companies agree to issue an annual Communication on Progress, a public disclosure report about the progress they have made in implementing the ten principles of the Global Compact and in supporting the UN Millennium Development Goals, which include eradicating extreme poverty and hunger, promoting gender equality, reducing child mortality, and other critical initiatives.

As an example, Microsoft, in its 2011 Communication on Progress report, noted the following work in response to "Principle 9—Encourage the development and diffusion of environmentally friendly technologies":

- Released Windows 7, its most energy efficient operating system to date, for retail sale in October 2009
- Created a free "power savings calculator" that is available to customers
- Along with the European Environment Agency (EEA), launched Air Watch in November 2009, a new application that enables EU citizens to access up-to-date, easy-to-understand information on air quality.[3]

Also included in the Communication on Progress report is Microsoft's report on its progress with the Millennium Development Goals (see the appendix to this essay).

Companies, such as Microsoft, that support the UN Global Compact and annually disclose their progress in making its principles an integral part of their business inspire greater trust among customers and other stakeholders at a time when public trust in U.S. corporations is at near-record lows. In 2011, only 46 percent of U.S. residents surveyed for the annual Edelman Trust Barometer—a key trust-measurement tool consulted by many corporations—gave a positive response to the question, "How much do you trust business to do what is right?" That figure was down from 54 percent in 2010.

A company's participation in the UN Global Compact also has become a litmus test for a growing number of investors and governments around the world. The Dow Jones Sustainability Index, for example, will not list companies unless they have signed the Global Compact. And one way in which many governments now evaluate companies that want to move into new markets is to see whether they have adopted the UN Global Compact.

The UN Global Compact can also help companies mitigate risks. In this age of instant communication, twenty-four-hour news cycles, and citizen journalism, when information and misinformation can travel around the world in seconds, active participation in the Global Compact can serve as the foundation for a company to remind customers, shareholders, governments, and the media of the responsibilities it has assumed and the good work it is doing to fulfill those commitments. That information can help the company put into context any inadvertent mistakes or temporary problems in its supply chain or other parts of its business operations.

FOR COMPANIES THAT want to become or remain global leaders in the twenty-first century, corporate social responsibility is no longer just something nice to do; it has become an essential component of their long-term business strategy. Despite the skepticism of some economists and other observers, socially responsible companies are finding that they really can do well by doing good, that is, there is no inherent conflict between making a profit and making the world a better place.

While working on another project in the 1980s, Merck developed a drug called Mectizan that would cure river blindness (onchocerciasis), a disease that was endemic in many developing countries. The disease is caused by a parasitic worm that is transmitted by the bite of black flies. As the worm grows, it causes terrible itching, muscle aches, weakness, and, eventually, permanent blindness. The people who needed Mectizan couldn't afford it, so in 1987 Merck started giving away doses of the drug and "committed to continuing the supply of Mectizan free of charge to whoever needs it, wherever they are in the world."

The program, which has cost Merck hundreds of millions of dollars, saved hundreds of thousands of people from going blind, enabled them to work and take care of their families, and helped to revitalize the economies of several countries.

Asked about the rationale for the large donation, then Merck CEO Roy Vagelos said,

> Some argue that corporations should not be in the business of making donations, contending that their first obligation is to reward stockholders with higher dividends and not squander company resources on gifts. I disagree. Our policy on Mectizan and other gifts made Merck a place where people were proud and excited to work because they wanted to make lives better around the world. It helped us recruit the best people and build company morale. It was consistent with Merck's fundamental corporate philosophy of doing well by doing good. It served the

global society Merck serves. It also served Merck's stockholders, because corporate social generosity is often followed by higher profits as the corporation becomes a better, more attractive workplace for the best talent.

The world is not perfect, it never will be, and so the work continues. There will always be more problems to solve, more injustices to overcome, and more lives to improve. That is what makes business so challenging and rewarding in today's global economy. (See chapter 2 of this volume for further discussion of Merck.)

APPENDIX. UN Millennium Development Goals Communication on Progress: Microsoft Commitment and Contribution, January 2011.

COMMITMENT TO LOCAL AND GLOBAL DEVELOPMENT

The mission of Microsoft is to help people and businesses throughout the world realize their full potential. This means mobilizing our resources across the company and around the world to create opportunities in the communities where we do business, and to fulfill our commitment to serving the public good through innovative technologies and partnerships. Our overall goal is to enable sustained social and economic opportunity for everyone, including those at the middle and bottom of the world's economic pyramid.

The Millennium Development Goals (MDGs) are an important influence on our strategy and activities because of our shared emphasis on global and local partnerships to change lives, and the clarity provided by the focus on real measures of human development within defined timeframes. Our efforts are also guided by our support for the United Nations (UN) Global Compact, which shapes both our business practices and corporate citizenship strategies.

In the past decade, Microsoft has initiated or joined partnerships with a number of United Nations agencies and other multilateral organizations that have internationally-agreed development goals, including the MDGs at the core of their mission and goals. In 2007, Microsoft joined the MDG Call to Action, in which leading companies pledged to implement concrete initiatives that apply their core business, skills, and expertise in a transformative and scalable manner that will enhance growth and wealth creation to help meet the MDGs. In 2010, the United Nations held the MDG Summit in New York to review the progress that has been made in the past five years. Leading up to the meeting, Microsoft's founder and Chairman, Bill Gates, served as a member of The MDG Advocacy Group created by UN Secretary-General Ban Ki-moon to build further political will and mobilize global action to make the MDG Summit a turning point in our collective effort to achieve the Goals by the 2015 target date.

In November 2010, the United Nations Foundation honored Microsoft with the inaugural Corporate Award for leadership in advancing UN causes, recognizing the work Microsoft is doing to help achieve the MDGs.

A MULTIFACETED APPROACH

For more than three decades, as our company has grown, so has our commitment to global and local development. Through our global community programs, Microsoft supports schools, public libraries, and local community organizations with access to technology and skills training, and we enable employee volunteering in Microsoft-sponsored initiatives and other programs in communities around the world. Since 1983, Microsoft and its employees have given US$4.6 billion in cash, services, and software to nonprofits around the world through localized, company-sponsored giving and volunteer campaigns, with US$603 million given in fiscal year 2010 alone.

In 2003, Microsoft expanded the company's Corporate Citizenship focus through two Microsoft Unlimited Potential global programs: Partners in Learning, which focuses on supporting primary and secondary school education worldwide, and the Community Technology Skills Program, which focuses on providing jobs and opportunity training and access to technology for groups that are underserved by technology.

In 2007, building on our experience with these programs and partnerships, we announced the Microsoft Unlimited Potential global commitment to extend the benefits of technology by creating new products and programs that will help bring social and economic opportunity to everyone. We have an initial goal to reach an additional one billion people by 2015.

Microsoft Unlimited Potential is based on our conviction that the key asset we can bring is not simply funding—it is our expertise in using technology to design solutions to help address the problems that are faced by underserved populations, including those who experience poverty, joblessness, and inadequate education. At the same time, we are guided by the conviction that reducing global poverty also requires developing the workforce and creating jobs alongside meeting basic education and health needs. Therefore, we are also accelerating and deepening our partnership initiatives to help underserved people—especially youth—gain access to job opportunities, become micro-entrepreneurs, and earn better livelihoods.

SETTING BOLD GOALS ON IMPACT AND RESULTS

Through Microsoft Unlimited Potential, we have set the year 2015 as the first major milestone with a goal of reaching one billion additional people who have not yet seen the benefits of technology. In doing so, our aim is to signal our commitment to contribute, through partnership, to the achievement of significant action and results that improve livelihoods and opportunities for underserved people and communities.

The day-to-day activity of our core software business also generates significant economic opportunity and creates jobs in every country where Microsoft operates. In 2009, we commissioned the International Data Corporation (IDC) research group to study the economic impact of Microsoft business in over 50 countries. IDC found that in 2009, 14.9 million jobs worldwide were attributable to Microsoft and its nearly 700,000 partners, suppliers, vendors, service providers, and distributors. This ecosystem of partners has invested almost US$180 billion in local economies. In the Middle East and Africa, for example, 46 percent of information technology (IT) industry jobs are currently related to Microsoft and its ecosystem of partners, many of which are local companies. Additionally, IDC projected that software-related employment will grow more than 7.5 percent over the next four years. This growth will create 320,000 new IT jobs in that region by 2013, with our company a major contributor to this growth. The study also found the software industry alone paid US$771 billion in government taxes globally, helping to finance vital public services, including education. You can find additional information about Microsoft business impact at http://www.microsoft.com/presspass/ presskits/economicgrowth.

MICROSOFT INITIATIVES AND PARTNERSHIPS TO SUPPORT THE MILLENNIUM DEVELOPMENT GOALS

Because technology is an important tool for the delivery of development programs and resources, Microsoft is contributing to many of the Millennium Development Goals. The remainder of this paper provides details about specific Microsoft programs, initiatives, and partnerships that aim to contribute to the MDGs. We welcome suggestions and feedback on how Microsoft could contribute further.

POVERTY

MDG 1: End extreme poverty and hunger
- *UN MDG Target 1: Reduce by half the proportion of people living on less than a dollar a day*
- *UN MDG Target 2: Achieve full and productive employment and decent work for all, including women and young people*
- *UN MDG Target 3: Reduce by half the proportion of people who suffer from hunger*

Microsoft contributes to MDG 1 in four ways:
- Response to complex global humanitarian emergencies and crises.
- Ongoing support for the world's refugees.
- Partnerships with UN agencies to foster IT capacity development in support of UN goals.
- Support for local community training centers to expand employability skills and economic opportunity, with a particular focus on women and young people.

Humanitarian Emergencies and Global Crises

Microsoft's support for people and communities in need around the world is grounded in the passion and commitment of our employees. For many years, and through numerous and complex humanitarian emergencies and crises, our employees have been among the first and most sustained contributors of their time, money, and expertise with the company's on-going support and matching programs. Microsoft is also supporting a wide range of nongovernmental organizations' (NGOs) emergency response capabilities through relationships with NetHope.org and the Interagency Working Group on Emergency Capacity Building (ECB). Since 2005, Microsoft has donated more than US$44 million in cash and software to NetHope and its member agencies to support nonprofit technological innovation and program. One such program is the NetHope Academy that was established in Haiti following the earthquake last year. The NetHope Academy provides local IT skills training to build in-country technical expertise.

The company supports its employees' commitment with donations of cash, software, technology assistance, and volunteers in close partnership with some of the world's leading nonprofit organizations. For example:

• Following the devastating earthquake in Haiti on January 12, 2010, the Inter-American Development Bank working through its public-private partnership with Microsoft along with technology partner Infusion developed the Haiti Integrated Government Platform (HIGP) solution. The HIGP was launched to aid in the coordination of reconstruction efforts and help strengthen Haiti's institutional capacity, promote good governance and facilitate a transparent approach to post-disaster recovery. The solution provides the Government of Haiti with several key communication components including integrated email for the first time since the earthquake, and the "Government of Haiti" intranet and external website. HIGP also supports the Interim Haiti Recovery Commission website—the official online tracking database for recovery projects. The platform is the central point for all new reconstruction projects and is a hub for over 3,000 NGOs, the Interim Commission for the Reconstruction of Haiti, and the 18 UN organizations.

- Following the 8.8-magnitude earthquake that struck the coast of Chile in February 2010, Microsoft activated our disaster response protocol to monitor the situation in Chile and offer support. We helped customers and partners resume operations, used Bing Maps to provide before and after imagery of the affected areas to help aid organizations focus their responses, and partnered with the Chilean government, Entel, Olidata, and Fundación Vida Rural to increase access to the Internet in the affected areas. Many Microsoft employees in Chile volunteered by conducting food, clothing, and donation drives to help their neighbors.
- In response to the devastating flooding in Pakistan in August 2010, we provided technical support to lead response organizations, promoted employee giving and volunteering and assessing where our resources can be most helpful for the impacted region and communities, and donated over $300,000 to relief organizations working in Pakistan.
- In 2008, Microsoft contributed to the aid relief efforts following the Myanmar hurricane and earthquake in China through technical resources, donations, and volunteer support. In China, the Microsoft Asia research lab team created and posted an interactive Live Search map to provide news from each village that was hit by the earthquake, and to help find missing people. Ready within 24 hours, the site enabled people to post their status and whereabouts, the government to post names of known victims and those rescued, and family and friends to list people they were seeking.

Support for the World's Refugees

For the past decade, Microsoft has invested in helping relieve the plight of the world's refugees—among the most underserved groups of people on earth—through financial contributions, software donations, and technology consulting to employee volunteer involvement, partnership development initiatives, and public awareness campaigns. Microsoft partners with a range of intergovernmental organizations, businesses, and nongovernmental organizations to improve refugees' access to education, skills training, employment, and legal protection.

In 1999, Microsoft entered into its first public-private partnership with a United Nations agency, the United Nations High Commissioner for Refugees (UNHCR), to apply our technology and skills in support of its mission to assist and protect refugees during the war in Kosovo. The partnership was renewed in 2006 and again in 2009 for three years. Together, UNHCR and Microsoft aim to embrace refugees as part of the worldwide community's technology movement and support ICT education and learning in challenging environments. In the partnership, Microsoft supports UNHCR by providing technological expertise, while UNHCR contributes its know-how in addressing challenging refugee issues.

Over the past 11 years, our partnership has expanded considerably and is now focused on three main areas:

- The development of a standardized system for refugee registration (ProGres) and status administration that is now used in more than 300 camps.
- Providing IT training opportunities for refugees through the Community Technology Access (CTA) program, which makes access to education, vocational training, and the opportunity to apply technology to improve livelihoods possible.
- Co-sponsorship of the Seattle, Washington-based Volunteer Advocates for Immigrant Justice (VAIJ) program, which offers pro bono legal counsel for detainees who are facing deportation.

Partnerships with UN Agencies and Intergovernmental Organizations

We have initiated or joined a range of partnerships with a number of UN agencies, multilateral organizations, and national development agencies—including the United Nations Educational, Scientific and Cultural Organization (UNESCO), the United Nations Development Programme (UNDP), the International Telecommunication Union (ITU), the United Nations Industrial Development Organization (UNIDO), the United Nations Environment Programme (UNEP), the Inter-American Development Bank (IDB), the World Food Program, the Food and Agriculture Organization (FAO), and the United States Agency for International Development (USAID)—to support their use of technology in delivering their missions and bringing technology to the people they assist.

As an example, the Microsoft partnership with UNDP began in 2004 and includes a range of joint initiatives to foster IT capacity development and to support UNDP goals—such as promoting democratic governance, facilitating trade, helping with disaster relief, and implementing pro-poor programs—through technology solutions.

Support for Local Community Training Centers to Expand Employability Skills and Economic Opportunity, with a Particular Focus on Women and Young People

Microsoft Unlimited Potential—Community Technology Skills Program

Since the Community Technology Skills Program (CTSP) began in 2003, Microsoft has provided more than US$350 million in cash and software grants to more than 1,000 community partners. These donations have supported over 40,000 technology centers in more than 100 countries and regions to accelerate skill development and help employers find qualified candidates. In 2010, we surpassed our goal and reached more than 170 million people since 2003 through CTSP participation. In FY2010, we reached 29 million and our goal in FY2011 is to reach an additional 23 million.

Technology for Emerging Markets Group at Microsoft Research India

The Technology for Emerging Markets group at Microsoft Research India seeks to address the needs and aspirations of people in emerging-market countries. This includes those who are increasingly using computing technologies and services, and those for whom access to computing technologies remains largely out of reach. Several of the team's research projects focus on technology innovation to enable expanded economic opportunity for the urban and rural poor in developing countries:

*   Digital Green seeks to disseminate targeted agricultural education to small and marginal farmers through digital video. The system sustains relevancy in a community by developing a framework for participatory learning. They digitally record progressive farmers and experts, train

local extension staff, and motivate other farmers to improve their practices by narrowcasting relevant content.

- Mobile Banking (m-banking) has created excitement and is seen to hold much promise as a socioeconomic development tool. The group is looking at a range of existing and proposed m-banking and m-payment solutions across countries, understanding the usability of m-banking systems by low-literate clients, as well as assessing the social and economic context and impact of the new channel on low-income households.

- Financial Service Delivery to the Poor: Microsoft Research is conducting primary research on understanding how low-income households access and use financial services from formal and informal providers, including microfinance providers. The organization is investigating ways in which using technological solutions to enable various aspects of financial service delivery can result in more cost-effective operations and cheaper, better quality finance for the poor.

EDUCATION

MDG 2: Achieve universal primary education
- *UN MDG Target: Ensure that all boys and girls complete a full course of primary schooling*

To help expand education opportunities worldwide, Microsoft is partnering with government, intergovernmental organizations, and academic and industry leaders to facilitate access to high-quality education through dynamic, learner-focused technologies and resources. Through Microsoft Unlimited Potential programs such as those listed below, we provide innovative solutions for both students and teachers to improve education around the world.

Partners in Learning

In 2003, we launched Partners in Learning (PiL) with the goal of improving teaching and learning through access to IT, localized curricula, and support for Innovative Teachers Networks. In 2008, we decided to extend our commitment and increase our investment to the program to US$500 million between 2003 and 2013. By the end of 2010, PiL had touched the lives of nearly 200 million students and teachers in 114 countries.

Education Licensing

The Microsoft Academic Volume Licensing programs provide simple, flexible, volume-based pricing. We offer several options that are customized to meet the needs of students, teachers, academic institutions, and governments, depending on their requirements.

Local Language Program

Through the Microsoft Local Language Program (LLP), we have introduced one billion people worldwide to the benefits of technology in their native languages. Through providing Language Interface Packs (LIPs) for programs such as Microsoft Office and Windows, people can now use and build software in their native languages, thus helping to prevent the loss of language diversity and preserving endangered languages. Through LLP, Microsoft supports 95 languages that are spoken in every region of the world. In 2010, Microsoft announced 59 new LIPs for both Windows 7 and Office 2010 and rolled out a new product called Caption Language Interface Packs (CLIPs), which allows for a smooth transition between languages and greater computer literacy in multiple languages. For more information, visit http://www.microsoft.com/llp.

Imagine Cup

Each year, Microsoft hosts Imagine Cup, now the world's premier student technology competition. By encouraging young people to apply their imagination, passion, and creativity, the competition aims to bring forward innovations that can make a difference in the world today. Imagine Cup 2010 was held in Warsaw, Poland. The theme of the competition was "Imagine a world where technology helps solve the toughest problems facing us today." The UNDGs served as inspiration and guidance for the final projects. More than 325,000 students from over 100 countries registered for Imagine Cup 2010. Imagine Cup has reached over one million students in the past five years alone. For more information, visit http://irnaginecup.com/.

Innovative Products and Platforms

Innovation is imperative in both how technology is made available and how content is delivered. At Microsoft, we recognize the importance of innovation as it relates to education. A few examples of products and platforms we have developed to improve education are:

- MultiPoint is a shared resource computing technology that provides policymakers, teachers, and students with access to technology at an affordable and competitive price point. To date, the MultiPoint offerings include Windows Multi-Point Server 2010, and a new Windows product that enables multiple users to simultaneously share one computer. For more information, visit http:/www.microsoft.corn/rnultipoint.
- REDU is a campaign developed by Bing from Microsoft that launched in September 2010. It is designed to expand and encourage the national conversation around education reform in the United States by providing information and resources to learn, a community platform to connect, and tools and initiatives to act. United in the belief that "every child deserves a great education," REDU is powered by Bing's commitment to empower people and aims to creatively drive positive social changes through its powerful content, unique network, and expertise in education. Visit REDU today at http://www.bing.com/redu.
- KoduTMGame Lab is a free visual programming language that enables students to design, program, and test their own games and virtual worlds, facilitating critical thinking through games. An Australian pilot showed that Kodu motivated students and improved critical thinking, creativity, and collaboration.
- Live@edu provides a familiar and reliable Microsoft Outlook web app that can be used to create a branded online community in the cloud for schools to stay connected with their students throughout their lives. As a "cloud based service," it's an example of how school communities are often pioneers with technology. Over 10,000 schools in more

than 130 countries are already using it, serving more than 11 million students, staff, and teachers.

Partnership with UNESCO

Since late 2004, Microsoft has also been engaged in a partnership with UNESCO to:

- Create teacher networks for the exchange of teaching best practices, pedagogic learning methods, and learning content materials;
- Connect Web-based communities that will advocate and foster the exchange of know-how and experiences for literacy experts globally;
- Provide capacity building to localized community initiatives such as the Community Multimedia Centers; and,
- Use technology in support of language preservation and native tongue education programs.

Launched in January 2008 after 5 years of research, Microsoft, UNESCO and their industry partners are supporting teachers to help students develop ICT skills through the multilingual ICT Competency Framework for Teachers (ICT-CFT). The ICT-CFT provides much-needed guidance for Ministries of Education and curriculum providers on how to improve teaching through ICT. The Framework provides a syllabus as the key reference for training providers, listing guidelines on what teachers should know to apply ICT to education in their own creative ways and training examples.

Microsoft also supports UNESCO's Community Multimedia Centers (CMCs) in Senegal, Mali, and Mozambique by providing the community radio facilities with software, training, and multimedia curricula. In Senegal, 24 CMCs have been established in areas of isolation and poverty. Mozambique currently has 20 CMCs in operation and Mali maintains nine centers.

As part of Microsoft Partners in Learning, UNESCO, local educational authorities and Microsoft are developing projects for the inclusion of information technologies in teachers' training, in partnership with teachers' colleges, pedagogical institutes, and schools of education through the Next Generation of Teachers (NET) initiative. The priorities of this program include creating a platform for the advancement of best practices and the adoption of innovation, providing training and access to technology resources, engaging with teachers and developing their confidence to use technology in the learning process.

WOMEN

MDG 3: Promote gender equality and empower women
- *UN MDG Target: Eliminate gender disparity in primary and secondary education*

Microsoft is strongly committed to supporting women in the IT workplace and has created and supported organizations and programs for women in the high-tech industry. In particular, we support gender equality and women's empowerment through Microsoft Unlimited Potential programs that support education and teachers, bring technology into the classroom and promote young people's interest in both science and creativity, supporting higher education and research, promote entrepreneurship in universities and in local communities, and support technology skills training.

Additionally, many of our community partners around the world in the Microsoft Community Technology Skills Program run IT training courses for immigrant and refugee women, helping them acquire skills that will increase their access to services, employment, and education. For example:

- Microsoft IT Academy—a Microsoft Unlimited Potential program—is a partnership with schools, universities, and community colleges to provide faculty and students with tools and curricula to promote business-ready technology skills. One of the features of the program is the focus on attracting women through part-time and flexible schedules, women and IT careers clinics, and female instructors.
- The Graduate Women's Scholarship Program is a one-year scholarship program for outstanding women graduate students and is designed to help increase the number of women pursuing a PhD. Each year Microsoft Research recognizes 10 outstanding graduate students who

represent a selection of the best and the brightest in their fields by awarding them each a US$15,000 scholarship.

• Through the DigiGirlz technology program, we encourage high school girls to explore careers in technology by connecting them with Microsoft employees and providing them with hands-on computer and technology workshops. Each year, girls visit Microsoft offices as part of DigiGirlz Days or attend our DigiGirlz High Tech Camps where they listen to executive speakers, participate in technology tours and demonstrations, network, and learn through hands-on experience in workshops.

• Microsoft is a proud supporter of the Global Give Back Circle, a non-profit organization that aims to mentor and educate Kenyan girls so they can lift themselves out of the cycle of poverty. As part of our Community Technology Skills Program, Microsoft set up two IT training labs that provide nine-month training courses for girls in the gap period between high school and college. The labs both equip girls with marketable skills and provide them with a place to live. Through this program, many Kenyan girls have been lifted from the cycle of poverty and gone on to pursue college degrees.

• The Institute of International Education's Women in Technology (WIT) program was launched in 2005 with support from the US State Department and Microsoft. The WIT program is now active in nine countries in the Gulf and North Africa region, and has trained more than 10,000 women in IT, entrepreneurship and professional skills; and built the capacity of more than 60 local women's organizations in the region. Along with new jobs created in WIT training centers at local women's organizations, hundreds of women have reported finding jobs, being promoted, or securing internships following the training.

HEALTH

MDG 4: Reduce child mortality
• *UN MDG Target: Reduce by two-thirds the under-five mortality rate*

MDG 5: Improve maternal health
• *UN MDG Target 1: Reduce by three-quarters the material mortality ratio*
• *UN MDG Target 2: Achieve universal access to reproductive health*

MDG 6: Combat HIV/AIDS, malaria, and other diseases
- *UN MDG Target 1: Halt and begin to reverse the spread of HIV/AIDS*
- *UN MDG Target 2: Achieve, by 2010, universal access to treatment for HIV/AIDS for all those who need it*
- *UN MDG Target 3: Halt and begin to reverse the incidence of malaria and other major diseases*

To help combat endemic infectious diseases that contribute to poverty and marginalization and contribute to improved maternal and child health, Microsoft is partnering with intergovernmental organizations and academic and industry leaders to support awareness, education, and fundraising; contribute to cutting-edge research; and provide technology support to enable dissemination of research and health care information.

Microsoft Research

Since 2003, Microsoft Research has been helping in the quest to develop a vaccine for the human immunodeficiency virus (HIV), which causes acquired immunodeficiency syndrome (AIDS). This research supports the search for an immunogen—the part of the vaccine that triggers an immune response. Researchers elsewhere are working on the other central component of vaccine design, the vector, or the part of the vaccine that delivers the immunogen. As part of this research, Microsoft Research works with many prestigious universities and research facilities throughout the world. For more information on Microsoft research, visit http://research. mcrosoft.com/en-us/.

PEPFAR—HIV-Free Generation Program

The Partnership for an HIV-Free Generation, or HFG, is a global public private partnership to promote HIV prevention in countries that are heavily affected by the disease. Launched in 2008, HFG is currently under pilot in Kenya with the goal of reducing new HIV infections among youth aged 10–24 by 50 percent over a five-year period.

Microsoft is a member of the ICT working group of HFG and has worked with Warner Bros. Entertainment to support the development of a computer game called "Pamoja Mtaani," which means "Together in the Neighborhood." The game integrates prevention messaging and entertainment to educate youth by presenting real-life situations, changing HIV risk perception, attitude, and behavior. For more information on HFG, visit http://www.pepfar.gov/ppp/hivfree.

ENVIRONMENT

MDG 7: Ensure environmental sustainability
- *UN MDG Target 1: Integrate the principles of sustainable development into country policies and programs and reverse the loss of environmental resources*
- *UN MDG Target 2: Reduce biodiversity loss, achieving, by 2010, a significant reduction in the rate of loss*
- *UN MDG Target 3: Halve the proportion of the population that is without sustainable access to safe drinking water and basic sanitation*
- *UN MDG Target 4: Improve the lives of at least 100 million slum dwellers by 2020*

Environmental sustainability is a serious, global issue that requires a comprehensive response from all sectors of society. To address this challenge, Microsoft is focusing on responsible environmental practices, software and technology innovations, and global partnerships. The goal of Microsoft is to reduce the environmental impact of its operations and products and to be a leader in environmental responsibility.

- Microsoft is committed to reducing the impact of our own operaions, through energy-efficient design of new buildings and innovation in the design and operation of Microsoft data centers, and policies to promote employee use of public transport. Microsoft voluntarily measures its carbon footprint and provides annual reports on greenhouse gas emissions to the Carbon Disclosure Project (CDP).
- Energy Efficient Computing: Microsoft is helping to reduce the impact of computing on the environment through power management at the software and enterprise level. The Windows 7 operating system is designed to provide more energy-saving features than any previous Microsoft operating system. Through a combination of platform

innovations, enterprise tools, and Microsoft engagement with hardware and software partners, Windows 7 enables individuals and businesses to significantly reduce PC power consumption. And, with Microsoft System Center software, customers can manage the energy use of their data centers, servers, and desktop computers from one central location. We have also created a "power savings calculator" within the Microsoft Assessment and Planning Toolkit, a free resource that is available to customers. The calculator provides a report of potential savings from adopting energy-efficient computing technologies and over 215,000 customers and partners downloaded the toolkit in FY2010.

- Innovative Solutions to Environmental Challenges: Microsoft Unified Communications (UC) solutions streamline communications and collaboration, reducing the need for business travel and commuting. For example, the ClearFlow feature in Live Maps enables drivers in over 70 cities to find routes based on the least traffic, which reduces travel time and pollution. With Microsoft Virtual Earth, customers can visualize data to gain insight into global trends and patterns. Both the United States Environmental Protection Agency and the European Environmental Agency rely on Bing Maps technology to share environmental information with citizens, scientists, and policymakers.

- Streamlining Our Own Operations: In 2010, Microsoft opened and operated new data centers that consume 50 percent less energy than those built just three years ago. In FY2011, we will continue to work to reduce the Power Use Effectiveness (PUE) of our new data center designs. Our goal is to construct new data centers that average 1.125 in PUE (the industry average is currently 2; optimal energy use is 1) by 2012.

Microsoft has formed partnerships with governmental, nongovernmental, academic, and industry organizations to drive global action on environmental sustainability.

- Climate Savers Computing Initiative (CSCI): Microsoft and other CSCI partners—such as World Wildlife Fund, Intel, Hewlett-Packard (HP), and other software and IT companies—offer a unified voice on the importance of sustainable computer use. CSCI offers clear guidance to individuals and businesses on how to take advantage of industry innovations and best practices that improve energy efficiency and power management. Microsoft is committed to CSCI's goal of reducing the IT industry's carbon footprint by over 50 million tons a year.

- The European Environment Agency: Microsoft has worked with the European Environment Agency (EEA) to launch revolutionary online tools to broaden awareness of the impact of climate change. In 2008, our partnership launched Eye on Earth, a pioneering project that leverages the latest Microsoft cloud technologies to gather information about European air and water quality across the 32 EEA member states. In September 2010, Microsoft and EEA launched the Eye on Earth mobile application to make it even more accessible to the EEA's nearly 600 million citizens.
- The William J. Clinton Foundation: Microsoft and the Clinton Foundation are creating tools so that cities around the globe can measure, track, and improve their greenhouse gas (GHG) emissions. With these tools, cities can collaborate and share best practices on the most effective ways to reduce GHGs.
- Equipment Refurbishers: Through the Microsoft Authorized Refurbisher programs, Microsoft provides low-cost licenses for Microsoft software to help equipment refurbishers extend the useful life of over 500,000 computers per year.

Microsoft Research is committed to delivering breakthrough innovations in research in the areas of energy efficiency and conservation, weather study and prediction, air pollution and quality, climate change, and hydrology. Microsoft Research efforts range from sensor networks to assist scientists in understanding global ecological issues by tracking animals, to Web-enabled sensors that could be used in businesses and homes to monitor energy consumption.

Microsoft Research also has several projects that aim to provide technology expertise and tools to scientists in an effort to improve how data is accessed and used. Such projects include studying how the build-up of greenhouse gases in the atmosphere leads to changes in Earth's climate, and understanding the impact of increased population and industry on rivers and balancing this with the need to conserve wildlife and protect ecosystems.

More information on these and other initiatives is available at www.microsoft.com/environment.

GLOBAL PARTNERSHIP

MDG 8: Develop a global partnership for development
- *UN MDG Target 1: Address the special needs of least developed countries, landlocked countries, and small island developing states*
- *UN MDG Target 2: Develop further an open, rule-based, predictable, non-discriminatory trading and financial system*
- *UN MDG Target 3: Deal comprehensively with developing countries' debt*
- *UN MDG Target 4: In cooperation with developing countries, develop and implement strategies for decent and productive work for youth*
- *UN MDG Target 5: In cooperation with pharmaceutical companies, provide access to affordable essential drugs in developing countries*
- *UN MDG Target 6: In cooperation with the private sector, make available benefits of new technologies, especially information and communications*

As a private sector technology partner, Microsoft can contribute toward target 4 and target 6 of the Millennium Development Goals to develop a global partnership for development; to support partnerships to enable expansion of the benefits of new technology, especially ICT; and to help expand access to jobs, training, and economic opportunity for under-served people.

Research4Life—Collaboration with WHO, UNEP, and FAO

Since early 2007, Microsoft has been working with the World Health Organization (WHO), the United Nations Environment Programme (UNEP), and the Food and Agriculture Organization (FAO) along with Cornell and Yale Universities and major academic publishers on Research4Life, an initiative to provide and empower research in 103 of the world's poorest developing countries. Research4Life is designed to overcome the digital divide in access to leading research by providing free or very low cost online access to the major journals in health, environmental science, and agriculture to local, nonprofit institutions in developing countries. It now has over 5,000 institutions registered as users.

Research4Life stems from a speech made in 2000 by former UN Secretary-General Kofi Annan who reiterated the importance of using

ICT and public-private partnerships in supporting development. It was officially launched in January 2002 with some 1,500 journals from six major publishers. Microsoft is the lead technology partner on the project and is working to enhance the platform's search and security features. Today, over 8,100 peer-reviewed journal titles from more than 150 publishers are available to institutions in 103 countries, benefiting thousands of scientists, academics, health workers, and researchers.

The Research4Life online library, one of the largest online medical libraries in the world, enables users to search and access full-text articles provided directly from the Pubmed (Medline) database. Publishers play a key role in the initiative by providing free or low cost access to their content, representing an annual value of over US$6 billion. Cornell and Yale Universities provide key bibliographic and other support.

Shape the Future

Shape the Future helps governments to imagine and attain universal technology access for all their citizens. The goal of Shape the Future is to help build the Public/Private Partnerships (PPPs) that lead to greater employability, economic recovery, and a better future. Each Shape the Future solution is customized to meet the specific needs of the government and its citizens, offering favorable financing, software, hardware, training, and support that no single provider could provide. Microsoft has established more than 50 public-private partnership projects with governments worldwide over the past four years and has helped governments and partners successfully navigate toward digital inclusion. For more information, visit http:/www.microsoft.com/industry/publicsector/pta/.

Microsoft Innovation Centers

Microsoft Innovation Centers (MICs) are state of art technology facilities for collaboration on innovative research, technology, or software solutions, involving a combination of government, academic, and industry participants. The centers provide local communities with a comprehensive set of programs and services to expand workforce skills, create jobs, strengthen innovation, and improve competitiveness. First established in 2006, a network of over 100 Innovation Centers now serves 110 communities in 60 countries and regions around the world. Through Unlimited Potential, Microsoft is expanding its resource commitment to Microsoft Innovation Centers and anticipates opening and supporting 200 centers in an additional 25 countries.

Unilateral Software License for NGOs

In 2010, Microsoft announced the immediate availability of a unilateral software license for nongovernmental organizations (NGOs) and small, independent media operating in countries: Armenia, Azerbaijan, Belarus, China, Kazakhstan, Kyrgyzstan, Malaysia, Russia, Tajikistan, Turkmenistan, Uzbekistan, and Vietnam. This unilateral software license agreement grants NGOs and small, independent media organizations a limited, non-transferable, royalty-free right to use Microsoft software products already installed on their PCs. We are making this software license available in countries where our current program is in place but the benefits are not as widely known or understood as we would like.

Partnership with the Bill and Melinda Gates Foundation

Microsoft partners with the Bill & Melinda Gates Foundation to supply and sustain free public access to computers and the Internet through public libraries. The foundation funds projects that evaluate local technology needs, purchase and upgrade equipment, train library staff, and help libraries build public support for sustained technology access and funding. Since 1997, Microsoft has donated software worth more than US$285 million to more than 23,000 libraries around the world as a part of these efforts. For example, so far we have donated $23 million worth of software to 1,466 libraries in Canada and $3.4 million to 378 libraries in Chile. By supporting public access to computing, we help ensure that those who do not have computers available to them at home, work, or school can still realize the benefits of technology. Microsoft donations are expected to reach an additional US$100 million internationally over the next two years as we continue to work in partnership with the foundation.

Partnership with the ITU

The International Telecommunications Union (ITU) and Microsoft are working together to support ITU's development agenda across the organization's three sectors (standardization, radio communication and development) to make ICT more accessible globally and trustworthy. ITU was the lead UN agency for the first two World Summits of the Information Society (WSIS), in which Microsoft broadly participated. At the second WSIS, Microsoft signed the Connect the World pledge—a multi-stakeholder initiative to "Connect the Unconnected" one billion people at the bottom of the development pyramid by 2015.

As part of the Connect the World pledge and to help accelerate the implementation of the WISS goals, ITU and Microsoft created ITU Global View, a visual online solution to map ICT statistics and trends across geographies. The solution visualizes data such as number of telephone lines, mobile and broadband subscribers, and Internet users, and presents the data under categories that are thematically shaded according to subscriber/user ratio. The platform is hosted and maintained by ITU, and is open to governments, industry, international organizations, and civil society—allowing users to check status, identify gaps, and avoid overlap in collaborative efforts to achieve the WSIS goals.

Partnership with UNIDO

In July 2006, Microsoft formed a partnership with the United Nations Industrial Development Organization (UNIDO) to pool expertise to support small and medium-sized enterprises (SMEs), and foster greater innovation and competitiveness in developing countries by harnessing the use of ICT.

Microsoft is also assisting UNIDO with its AfrIPANet initiative to help policymakers tailor their strategies to attract investment and facilitate more sound and informed investment decisions. As part of this initiative, UNIDO and Microsoft are creating an ICT tool to support the work of national agencies including investment promotion agencies (IPAs) and private sector intermediary organizations in more than 20 countries in sub-Saharan Africa. The platform will host the Africa investor database of over 15,000 enterprises and will enable national organizations to monitor trends in investment flows, formulate policies and strategies based on empirical evidence, evaluate the effectiveness of interventions on investor behavior, and target and support quality investors. The District Business Information Centers (DBICs) program in Uganda assists SMEs to access relevant market information over the Internet, supporting local growth and competitiveness which is often hampered by a lack of technical training, business advisory services, and access to relevant hardware and software. In this context, the DBICs provide integrated business information solutions to SMEs on a demand-driven basis to help their development. Eight centers have been established in various districts throughout rural Uganda.

Partnership with the Organization of American States

The partnership between Microsoft and the Organization of American States (OAS) began in March 2001 when a Memorandum of Understanding (MOU) was signed to collaborate on technological and educational development programs in OAS member states. This relationship was extended in 2003 to focus on the acceleration of e-Government technologies in Latin America and the Caribbean.

The main goal of the public-private partnership is to accelerate development in the region through strategic investments in ICT across three main areas:

- Educating political leaders on the relevance of ICT for governments and as a strategic tool for development strategies;
- Creating reference cases and best practices in the use of technology in key socioeconomic areas; and,
- Ensuring that ICT becomes part of the hemispheric policy discussion at the highest level represented at ministerial summits and in the Summit of the Americas.

Microsoft and OAS's Partnership in Opportunities for Employment through Technology in the Americas (POETA) program provides technology and job training centers for people with disabilities and other vulnerable groups throughout Latin America, helping them enter growing economic sectors including telecommunications, telemarketing, and the hospitality industry.

NOTES

The Appendix was originally published as part of *Microsoft Communication on Progress 2011* for the UN Global Compact.

    1. Howard R. Bowen, *Social Responsibilities of the Businessman* (New York: Harper, 1953).

    2. Milton Friedman, "The Social Responsibility of Business Is to Increase Its Profits," *The New York Times Sunday Magazine* (September 13, 1970).

    3. Microsoft Corporation, *UN Global Compact—Communication on Progress* (January 2011).

2 | A Public and Private Partnership: The ACHAP Experience in Botswana

Themba L Moeti, Innocent Chingombe, and Godfrey Musuka

HIV/AIDS is one of the greatest threats to development for African countries, particularly those in southern Africa, where Botswana is located. HIV/AIDS is acknowledged as Botswana's greatest health and development challenge. Thus, dealing aggressively with HIV/AIDS and its consequences has the potential to result in significant progress toward the attainment of key Millennium Development Goals (MDGs). HIV/AIDS causes mortality among the population of both adults and children, and negatively affects maternal and child health. It also makes communities more vulnerable to another major disease, tuberculosis. HIV has also increased the vulnerability of the population to poverty and hunger through reduced incomes and increased dependency ratios, as breadwinners become sick and die. This chapter seeks to illustrate Merck's corporate social responsibility in health and development and also its commitment to the UN Global Compact, by highlighting the link between its support to the Government of Botswana's HIV/AIDS response and progress toward the attainment of the Millennium Development Goals (MDGs) through a unique public-private development partnership with the Government of Botswana and the Bill & Melinda Gates Foundation.

Given that Botswana suffers from one of the most severe HIV/AIDS epidemics in the world, the high costs of setting up and maintaining its national HIV/AIDS response have negatively affected other development priorities and remain a threat to the government's capacity to deliver the health and social services essential to improving and sustaining human development.

The African Comprehensive HIV/AIDS Partnerships (ACHAP) is a country-led, public-private development partnership formed in year 2000. It has been active in the country since 2001 as a key player in assisting the Government of Botswana (GoB) to address the scourge of HIV and AIDS, thus contributing to improved human development.

As a result of an effective HIV response, Botswana has seen a substantial reduction in mother-to-child transmission and HIV-related mortality for a decade starting in 2001, and it continues to register a reduction in HIV transmission rates. However, important challenges still lie ahead, especially about how best to sustain the gains seen so far.

INTRODUCTION

In his foreword to the Millennium Development Goals 2010 report, Dr. Ban Ki-moon, the UN Secretary-General, stated: "The Millennium Declaration in 2000 was a milestone in international cooperation, inspiring development efforts that have improved the lives of hundreds of millions of people around the world. The Goals represent human needs and basic rights that every individual around the world should be able to enjoy—freedom from extreme poverty and hunger; quality education, productive and decent employment, good health and shelter; the right of women to give birth without risking their lives; and a world where environmental sustainability is a priority, and women and men live in equality." Botswana is one of 189 countries that made a commitment to the eight ambitious MDG targets, which provide a framework and roadmap for time-bound and measurable goals to be reached by 2015.

The year 2011 marks a decade of Botswana's commitment to this declaration, and coincidentally also ten years since the establishment of the African Comprehensive HIV/AIDS Partnerships.

ACHAP was established to help the GoB address the HIV/AIDS epidemic and its associated development challenges through a comprehensive approach across the spectrum of prevention, treatment, care, and support. The total grant commitment from the Bill & Melinda Gates Foundation and the Merck Foundation for the period between 2001 and the end of 2009 totaled USD 106.5 million. In addition, Merck donated two antiretroviral medicines, CRIXIVAN® (Indinavir) and STOCRIN® (Efavirenz), for use in the national antiretroviral (ARV) treatment program for the duration of the partnership. In 2008, it added two more medicines to its donation, namely, INSENTRESS (Raltegravir) and ATRIPLA (Efavirenz Tenofovir Emtricitabine). The two foundations have now made a commitment for a second phase of support totaling about US$60 million for the period 2010–2014, and the Merck medicines donation will also continue to 2014.

In this essay we describe how this unique partnership, aimed at addressing one of the most severe HIV/AIDS epidemics globally, has, in turn, made important contributions toward the attainment of several of the country's MDGs. Notable MDGs for Botswana that can be linked to the impact of HIV/AIDS and therefore are influenced by the country's HIV response, to which ACHAP has contributed significantly, include the following:

- Goal 1. Eradicate extreme poverty and hunger
    o   Reduce by half the proportion of people living on less than a dollar a day
- Goal 4. Reduce child mortality
    o   Target 4a. Reduce by two thirds the mortality rate among children under five
- Goal 5. Improve maternal health
    o   Target 5a. Maternal mortality ratio
- Goal 6. Combat HIV, AIDS, malaria, and other major diseases
    o   Target 6a. Halt and begin to reverse the spread of HIV/AIDS
    o   Target 6b. Achieve by 2010 universal access to treatment for HIV/AIDS for all those who need it
- Goal 8. Develop a global partnership for development
    o   Target 8e. In cooperation with pharmaceutical companies, provide access to affordable essential drugs on a sustainable basis.

THE BIRTH OF ACHAP

The creation of ACHAP emerged from Merck's prior experiences with other philanthropic projects on access to medicines, including the Mectizan Donation Program (for onchocerciasis or river blindness) and the Enhancing Care Initiative (ECI) (for HIV/AIDS) with the Harvard AIDS Institute. Through these experiences Merck learned that the donation of medicines alone may not be effective without support for strengthening the health care infrastructure to ensure that medicines are used effectively. Although the particular model of engagement was not initially clear to Merck officials, they always intended ACHAP to be a highly collaborative project.[1]

According to L. Distlerath and G. Macdonald,[2] Merck initiated the concept of a public-private partnership based on the following three main ideas:

- Private sector management and thinking could make a significant, effective, and efficient contribution in the design and implementation of HIV/AIDS response strategies;
- The organization formed to deliver this initiative would be based on equal partnership with a national government in a Public-Private Partnership (PPP) model. The rationale was that national commitment was essential for the effectiveness of the HIV/AIDS interventions, and hence the organization (later formed as ACHAP) had to work through the government;
- The initiative would invest large sums of money in one location, to allow a comprehensive range of interventions to be implemented, to serve as a model that would demonstrate how private sector resources could produce effective interventions.

In August 1999, Merck, realizing that it could not alone provide all the resources needed for an effective partnership, began to seek partners for additional funding as a first step toward the formation of ACHAP. Merck approached the Bill & Melinda Gates Foundation, which, after reviewing the proposal, was optimistic about the project. The Gates Foundation was also very impressed by Merck's commitment to the partnership project. After unsuccessfully approaching a number of other potential partners, who, among other factors, had preferences for the establishment of pilot projects in several locations rather than a large project in one country, Merck and the Gates Foundation proceeded with the concept.[3]

Botswana was finally selected as the location for the project in the spring of 2000, based on the following criteria among others:

- High adult HIV prevalence, which stood at 38.5% in year 2000;
- Commitment of the country's political leadership to fighting the HIV/AIDS epidemic;
- The relatively small population of the country, which according to the last census (1991) stood at 1.6 million;
- Relatively well-developed health infrastructure;
- Stable and peaceful political environment[4]

The Government of Botswana welcomed this partnership, since after attaining middle-income status in the mid 1990s,[5] Botswana had lost much of its traditional bilateral development assistance, particularly in the health sector. The resources brought by the ACHAP partnership at that time were the largest external contribution that the country had received, and which it badly needed, for tackling an epidemic on this scale.

One of the early project communications describing the initiative, its programs, and the partners' commitment eloquently captures the significance of the partnership to Botswana's HIV response.[6] In his foreword to this ACHAP document, President Festus Mogae described the urgency for a treatment program as part of Botswana's response and how the support of Merck and the Gates Foundation was critical to the establishment of this program: "An estimated 260,000 Batswana out of a population of 1.6 million are now living with HIV/AIDS. Without affordable and accessible treatment, most of them will develop AIDS and die within a decade. We need the support of the global community to ensure our future survival. To this end, cultivating public/private partnerships is a priority on Botswana's HIV/AIDS agenda. The African Comprehensive HIV/AIDS Partnerships (ACHAP) is an integral part of Botswana's comprehensive response to the HIV epidemic." He further stated, "We need to implement care and treatment programs alongside our prevention drive to look after those people already living with HIV/AIDS—and to ensure their continued contribution to family life in Botswana and the ongoing economic growth of the nation. This is the area in which the support of partners such as ACHAP is crucial."

The commitment of the partners to a comprehensive HIV/AIDS response addressing national priorities and contributing to global impact was also clearly stated in the document by then-President, Chairman, and CEO of Merck, Mr. Raymond Gilmartin: "In Botswana, we are working with the government and our partners to improve prevention, care, and treatment for HIV/AIDS including training, education, testing, counseling, and medical care. It is a country-led process: their priorities, their needs—leveraging our resources, experience and commitment to help. By working together, pooling our knowledge and resources, we can mount effective solutions to this critical challenge—and make a world of difference for people in Botswana and the millions of people around the world living with HIV/AIDS today."

The vision of the partnership as a model which, if successful, could translate its lessons to other parts of the world was also aptly described by Patty Stonesifer, CEO of the Bill & Melinda Gates Foundation: "Stopping the transmission of HIV is the Bill & Melinda Gates Foundation's number one global health priority. We believe that the experiences and successes in Botswana will not only demonstrate that we can turn the tide of this disease, but will hasten our ability to build similar initiatives across the developing world."

The formation of the partnership was therefore not merely of significance to the HIV/AIDS response in Botswana; its success also had the potential to influence the establishment of AIDS treatment initiatives in other parts of sub-Saharan Africa.

BOTSWANA'S MDG INDICATORS AROUND THE TIME OF THE ESTABLISHMENT OF ACHAP

In the period before the impact of HIV/AIDS became apparent, Botswana's investment of its mineral wealth in socioeconomic development, combined with good governance, resulted in significant improvements in several indicators of human development.

- Real per capita income increased tenfold from US$300 in 1966 to US$3,300 in 1999.
- Primary school enrollment rate rose from 50% in 1966 to 97% in 1999.
- Adult literacy rates increased from 41% in 1970 to over 79% in 1999.
- Mortality rate among children under the age of 5 fell, from 151 per 1,000 live births in 1971 to 56 per 1,000 live births in 1991.
- Infant mortality rate fell from 108 deaths per 1,000 live births in 1966 to 38 deaths per 1,000 live births in 1999.[7]
- Life expectancy at birth increased from 55.5 years in 1971 to 65.3 years in 1991.[8]

The impact of HIV/AIDS changed many of these trends. This section of the essay attempts to explain the linkage between the HIV situation at the time of ACHAP's establishment and Botswana's status with respect to the Millennium Development Goals, with a particular focus on goals 1, 4, 5, 6, and 8. There is growing evidence from the scientific literature that HIV/AIDS impacts the other MDGs in many ways, through its interaction with poverty and income inequality, education, gender inequality, maternal health, and child mortality. Therefore in countries most affected by the epidemic, failure to address HIV will be a major obstacle to attaining other MDG targets.[9] This analysis, through a focus on the MDGs, illustrates how HIV/AIDS threatened to undo four decades of progressive socioeconomic development, and the manner in which Botswana's HIV response and ACHAP's contribution to it have helped mitigate this negative impact, positively contributing to Botswana's progress toward attainment of the Millennium Development Goals.

GOAL 1. ERADICATE EXTREME POVERTY AND HUNGER

Until the mid-1990s, the leading human development challenges Botswana faced were addressing unemployment and the eradication of poverty.[10]

By the late 1990s, the profound impact of HIV/AIDS on the very fabric of society at all levels had become apparent, with the majority of deaths occurring in income earners between the ages of 25 and 50.[11]

HIV/AIDS had a direct impact on households, increasing dependency levels—and in a country where 47% of the population were estimated to be living in poverty, this would create a downward spiral pushing many families toward poverty and some to extreme poverty. Botswana had the choice to mount a robust response or surrender all her development gains to HIV/AIDS.[12]

At the household level, the frequency of funerals, dominated by those of the young, increased sharply. Extended families were called upon to provide care and support.[13] Also as a result of the high adult mortality, the cumulative number of children below the age of 17 years that were expected to have lost one or both parents due to AIDS rose to about 126,700 by the end of 2007.[14]

The link between poverty and HIV/AIDS in Botswana is illustrated by Weiser and others.[15] In a study of the linkages between food insufficiency and HIV/AIDS conducted in Botswana and Swaziland, they demonstrated that food insufficiency is an important risk factor for increased sexual risk-taking among women in these two countries. Women in both countries who reported food insufficiency were nearly twice as likely to have used condoms inconsistently with a non-regular partner or engaged in transactional sex, and were also more likely to have had intergenerational sexual relationships and to report a lack of control in sexual relationships that placed them at greater risk of HIV.

Economic and other models on the impact of HIV/AIDS in Botswana have played an important role in providing supporting information to assist policy decisions for the response, as well as providing projections to guide the continued implementation of certain interventions, such as a large public sector treatment program. For example, while there were considerable concerns about the long-term sustainability of the national treatment program at its inception, economic modeling studies of various scenarios have provided indirect evidence of HIV/AIDS impacts. A study by the Botswana Institute for Development Policy Analysis on the macroeconomic impacts of HIV/AIDS, conducted in the year 2000, projected that by 2021 the economy as measured by gross domestic product would be 24% to 38% less than it would have been without HIV and AIDS.[16] Simulations of various models have also indicated that some of the negative consequences of HIV/AIDS in Botswana due to impacts on labor supply and productivity can be offset by a successful treatment program, thus providing evidence that even from an economic perspective, a successful treatment program benefits the macroeconomy and reduces the poverty impacts of HIV/AIDS. Investment in Botswana's treatment program by the funders of ACHAP and the Government of Botswana has therefore helped mitigate levels of poverty that would otherwise have arisen.[17]

GOAL 4. REDUCE CHILD MORTALITY

The global target for Goal 4 is to reduce the under-five mortality rate by two-thirds between 1990 and 2015. Based on its achievements recorded in 1991, Botswana set itself national targets of reducing

- the infant mortality rate from 48 per 1,000 live births in 1991 to 16 per 1,000 live births in 2016;[18] and
- the under-five mortality rate from 63 per 1,000 live births in 1991 to 27 per 1,000 live births by 2016.[19]

Botswana was on track to significantly reducing child mortality, continuing a trend maintained from the 1970s, until HIV/AIDS made its impact felt in the mid-1990s. Between 1991 and 1994, the under-five mortality (U5MR) rate fell from 63 per 1,000 live births to 50 per 1,000 live births in 1997. Over the same period the infant mortality rate (IMR) fell from 48 per 1,000 in 1991 to 37 per 1,000 in 1997. Since 1997, both the U5MR and the IMR have deteriorated, respectively reaching 76 per 1,000 and 57 per 1,000 as of 2005—due mainly to HIV and its associated impact on the infant and the mother. While child survival is correlated with a number of factors, including poverty and the quality and accessibility of health care, Botswana's high HIV and AIDS burden was recognized as an immediate threat to child survival.[20] Thus both the 2004 and the 2010 Botswana MDG Reports ascribe to HIV/AIDS a significant role in this rise in child mortality, relating it in part to rising adult HIV prevalence and mother-to-child transmission of HIV. Between 1992 and 2000, HIV prevalence rates among pregnant women attending antenatal clinics doubled from 18% in 1992 to 36.2% in 2001.[21] Prior to the introduction of the national PMTCT (Prevention of Mother-to-Child Transmission) program, it was estimated that between 20% and 40% of children born to HIV-positive mothers who did not enroll in the program experienced mother-to-child transmission of HIV.

In a later section of this essay we describe the impressive reductions in mother-to-child transmission of HIV as a result of Botswana's successful PMTCT program, with more than 90% of HIV positive pregnant women enrolling and MTCT rates reduced to less than 4%, and estimated significant reductions in HIV-related mortality. Therefore, it is unclear why apparently strong child health and survival interventions, combined with a successful PMTCT program, have not been able to sustain the downward trend in child mortality. These include 90% of children fully immunized by age one, 94% of pregnant women attending antenatal clinics, and 94% of deliveries supervised by skilled attendants.[22]

This would suggest that improvements in access to HIV prevention and care, while having significantly reduced HIV transmission and likely HIV-related deaths, may not in themselves be sufficient to mitigate other factors that may be prominent, including poverty (with 30% below the poverty line), infant feeding practices which may increase the risk of non-HIV causes of death (acute respiratory infections and diarrhea), and issues of service quality with an increasing burden on stretched human resources.[23] This illustrates the complex interplay between HIV/AIDS and the other goals in achieving the MDGs.

GOAL 5. IMPROVE MATERNAL HEALTH

The *Botswana Millennium Development Goals Status Report 2010* pointed out that in the early 2000s, Botswana's maternal death rate was high, even though the overwhelming majority of expectant women in Botswana had access to preventive health services such as prenatal care and were assisted by trained health professionals during delivery. The 2004 report indicates that in 1996, a trained midwife assisted 94 out of 100 pregnant women during delivery. This ratio improved to 97 in year 2000.

The global target on improving maternal health is to reduce the maternal mortality ratio (MMR) by three-quarters between 1990 and 2015. With a base level of 326 deaths per 100,000 live births in 1991, the national target is to reduce this rate to 150 deaths per 100,000 live births in 2011,[24] while Botswana's attainment of the global target would be to reduce maternal deaths to 82 per 100,000 live births by 2015. By 2005 Botswana had reached a figure of 135 deaths per 100,000 live births and seemed on course to meet the global target. Since 2006, however, rates have begun to rise. While data from health facilities suggest that about 10% of maternal mortality is directly HIV-related, HIV/AIDS through immunosuppression is thought to increase the risk due to indirect causes such as anemia, malaria, and tuberculosis and more directly through sepsis and hemorrhage, making HIV/AIDS an important maternal health challenge.[25]

Despite strong interventions to ensure maternal health—95% of the population living within 8 kilometers of a health facility, free antenatal services, near-universal antenatal care at 94% in 2007, and 98% of deliveries attended by skilled birth attendants in 2008—analysis of the maternal mortality trends suggests that the country will not meet its maternal mortality target in 2015.[26]

GOAL 6. COMBAT AIDS, MALARIA, AND OTHER DISEASES

High HIV Prevalence

The first case of AIDS in Botswana was diagnosed in 1985. Since then the epidemic has spread rapidly with an increasing toll on morbidity and mortality, such that by the late 1990s and early 2000s, Botswana had the highest reported HIV-prevalence rates in the world.[27]

Evidence for the fast pace with which the epidemic spread within the country is provided by annual sentinel HIV sero-prevalence surveys among pregnant women from 1992—with an increase from 18% of women attending antenatal clinics (ANCs) in Botswana's health facilities between the ages of 15 and 49% HIV-positive that year, to 38.5% in the year 2000 and about 36.2% by the year 2001.[28]

Figure 2.1, extracted from the National AIDS Coordinating Agency, Botswana National Strategic Framework for HIV/AIDS 2003–2009, illustrates the changes in HIV prevalence among pregnant women visiting antenatal clinics between the period 1992 and 2002.

Figure 2.1. Trend in HIV Prevalence among Pregnant Women, Botswana, 1992–2002

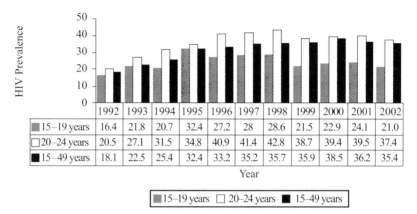

	1992	1993	1994	1995	1996	1997	1998	1999	2000	2001	2002
15–19 years	16.4	21.8	20.7	32.4	27.2	28	28.6	21.5	22.9	24.1	21.0
20–24 years	20.5	27.1	31.5	34.8	40.9	41.4	42.8	38.7	39.4	39.5	37.4
15–49 years	18.1	22.5	25.4	32.4	33.2	35.2	35.7	35.9	38.5	36.2	35.4

Year

15–19 years   □ 20–24 years   ■ 15–49 years

HIV-Related Morbidity and Mortality and the Need for Antroretroviral Therapy

The impact of HIV was devastating, and the health care system quickly became overwhelmed, with about 60% of medical hospital beds being occupied by people with an HIV-related illness.[29] Figure 2.2 illustrates that statistics of hospital mortality among people aged 15–44 rose rapidly in the early to late 1990s. As can be seen, AIDS-related mortality rose fivefold—and also resulted in a significant increase in mortality due to TB, which is closely associated with HIV/AIDS in Botswana.

With patients presenting at a very late stage of the disease and having no real prospects of recovery, there was a growing sense of futility and frustration among health care workers and patients alike. Referring to the situation at the Princes Marina Hospital in Gaborone, the country's main referral hospital, prior to the rollout of the Botswana's national ARV program "Masa" (which means "new dawn" in Setswana), one of the early Masa program physicians said: "The wards were 100% packed. People were sleeping on the floor. Not enough nurses to go round, and there was absolutely nothing you could do."[30]

In light of the severe impact of HIV/AIDS on Botswana's young and economically active adult population, it was recognized that the

Figure 2.2. Trends in Patient Mortality, Ages 15–44, Botswana, 1992–1997

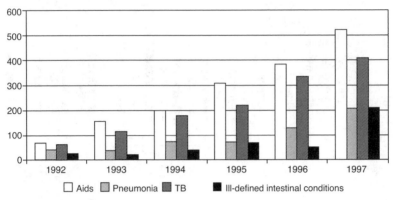

□ Aids ■ Pneumonia ■ TB ■ Ill-defined intestinal conditions

Source: UNDP, *The Botswana Human Development Report 2000*

scale of the epidemic was such that prevention interventions alone would not be sufficient to rapidly mitigate its effects. The country's high HIV infection rates among the economically active age group, with rates among pregnant women of over 30%, presented a strong argument for initiation of such a program. However, many questions about costs, human resource capacity, and infrastructure requirements remained unanswered. While a middle-income country, Botswana was still considered poor in resources for the establishment and maintenance of an ARV treatment program in terms of its health care infrastructure and providers. ACHAP provided the opportunity for assistance—determining the resource requirements for establishment of such a program, and being a partner that could provide both technical and financial support for its establishment. Treatment existed in the private sector for the few patients who could afford it, and in 2001 the Botswana-Harvard HIV/AIDS Partnership for Education and Research began a pilot HIV care and treatment program at the country's main referral hospital in Gaborone, which by the end of the year had placed about 350 patients on treatment.[31] The Government of Botswana therefore saw HIV/AIDS treatment being delivered in the context of its own facilities, albeit by a research organization that had capacities beyond those of most of its facilities, which increased the pressure to grant access to a wider patient population. The Government of Botswana approached the African Comprehensive HIV/ AIDS Partnerships for help in setting up an ARV treatment program.

ACHAP, using its access to global managerial networks, engaged the consulting firm McKinsey & Co. to conduct a feasibility study in collaboration with ACHAP and the Ministry of Health.[32] The study assessed the number of people requiring ARV therapy, how well the country was prepared to deliver such a service, the resources required to fill gaps in the health system, and the optimal implementation model and approach for Botswana.[33]

One of the findings of this feasibility assessment was that in 2001, the eligible population for ARV therapy by established criteria was estimated at 110,000 people.[34] This number was expected to grow linearly to 260,000 by the year 2005, driven by the dynamics of the HIV epidemic and assuming that all patients would be treated as soon as they became clinically eligible. The study by McKinsey had proposed establishing the capacity to treat 19,000 patients within the first year. President Mogae announced Botswana's bold step to introduce a national ARV treatment program to the UN General Assembly in 2001, and the consequences of not providing treatment on a wide scale were clearly summarized by the President in June that year: "We are threatened with extinction. . . . People are dying in chillingly high numbers. It is a crisis of the first magnitude."[35]

Modeling studies estimate that by the end of 2001 about 70,000 people had died of AIDS in Botswana's population of about 1.7 million people.[36] This high AIDS-related mortality rate also reduced life expectancy at birth by at least ten years, from 65 years in 1990–1995 to about 55 years.[37]

ACHAP's Contribution to Botswana's National HIV/AIDS Response Program

In many ways, the year 2000 was a defining moment for Botswana's HIV/AIDS response, in which the injection of new energy began and the response was taken to a new level with the realization of how large a threat the epidemic posed:

- A definitive study on the macroeconomic impact of HIV/AIDS was published, enabling the country's policy makers to appreciate the severe economic impact HIV/AIDS would wreak on the Batswana if a truly comprehensive response was not mounted.

- The health impact of HIV/AIDS on Botswana's economically active citizens had become apparent, and with about 25% of the adult population HIV infected, the loss of these persons to AIDS would have dire social and economic consequences.
- The orphan population was rising, as already poor families were being pushed further into poverty.
- The Human Development Report 2000, a detailed analysis of the human development consequences of HIV/AIDS in Botswana, was released by the United Nations Development Program in collaboration with the Government of Botswana. This report documented, in a way that many in the health and social development sectors could readily appreciate, the intricate linkages between the devastation of the epidemic at its peak and the ability of the health and social sectors to cope.
- The period 2000–2010 was the decade in which the ARV treatment program and the PMTCT program came to the fore—transforming the lives of many, and creating the kind of hope for tens of thousands of individuals and families that was unimaginable in the previous decade.

An analysis of the linkage between the impact of ACHAP's support to the HIV/AIDS response in Botswana and progress toward the achievement of the Millennium Development Goals is therefore appropriate in that the Millennium Declaration and ACHAP's establishment both occurred in the year 2000. Much of the work and progress that Botswana has made toward achievement of the MDGs, since tracking of progress began, has also been during the same period that ACHAP has been actively supporting HIV/AIDS interventions in Botswana.

ACHAP's support to the national HIV response in Botswana evolved progressively over the period 2001–2010—from a broad comprehensive response supporting many initiatives across the four pillars of prevention, treatment, care, and support in an initial proposal-driven phase in its first four years, to a more focused strategy with a few clearly defined areas of focus from 2005 onward. The first few years of ACHAP's work from 2001 to 2005 were focused on building capacity, setting up systems and developing infrastructure, supporting strategy development at sectoral and national levels, and supporting the country to generate strategic information to help inform and coordinate management of the response. In this role, ACHAP worked with a wide spectrum of partners from national ministries, research and academic institutions, and civil society organizations at national and community levels.

The Masa ARV Treatment Program

From the outset, the vision for Botswana's national treatment program was that it would be truly national in scope. Through its partnership with the Government of Botswana, ACHAP played an instrumental role in the establishment and roll out of the "Masa" treatment program, which has provided treatment free of cost to Botswana citizens since January 2002, in both urban and rural areas across the country. As with the other aspects of its HIV support to the Government of Botswana, a holistic approach was taken with respect to establishment of the treatment program, with support provided in nine major areas.[38] These included:

- Policy planning and project management
- Information, education, communication, and community mobilization
- Training of health care workers
- Staff recruitment and retention
- Drug supplies and logistics
- Laboratory and testing infrastructure and logistics
- Information technology support for patient monitoring
- Procurement and upgrading of space
- Generation of strategic information, monitoring, evaluation, and operational research.

The enrollment in this program as of April 2011 was 151,946, which represents about 87% of the total number of patients on treatment (175,000) in the country, 61.8% of whom were female and 6.4% of whom were children under the age of 13.

The program was established using a phased approach, starting in four initial sites in its first year. It had been projected that the program should enroll 19,000 patients in its first year[39] and about 20,000 annually thereafter. But by the end of the first year only 3,500 patients were enrolled,[40] and by January 2004 only 17,500 patients out of an estimated 110,000 eligible patients had been enrolled.[41] Slow enrollment in the program was thought to be due in part to low uptake of HIV testing due to fears of stigma and discrimination, as well as issues of access to counseling and testing services. The country's leadership was disappointed that, despite the huge investment and opportunity, more people were not coming forward to access this life-saving free treatment. The country's PMTCT program, which was launched in 1999 and expanded countrywide by the end of 2001, was also affected by slow uptake, with only 34% of eligible women enrolled in the PMTCT program by 2003.

In an attempt to increase the uptake of HIV testing and ART treatment, the Government of Botswana introduced the policy of "routine" or "provider initiated" HIV testing (with the possibility of "opting out") in its public health facilities in January 2004.[42] ACHAP was supportive of this key policy change during the time of its discussion, and it provided technical and financial support as well as advocacy for its implementation, providing rapid test kits and logistic support for data recording and reporting. There were many human rights concerns about Botswana's routine HIV testing policy, including concerns that it may be coercive, that counseling might no longer be practiced, and that it might increase the degree of gender-based violence toward partners.[43] However, following the introduction of routine HIV testing, there was a discernible increase in treatment uptake over the next year, and now over 90% of people offered testing in this setting are tested. In June 2004 UNAIDS and WHO, partly based on the experience in Botswana, introduced changes in testing policy recommendations and recommended the routine offer of HIV testing by health care workers in a wide range of health encounters.[44] Botswana's routine HIV testing policy in public health care settings has been an important aspect of the program's success at reaching the majority of people who need treatment. Research by Weiser and colleagues in Botswana on routine HIV testing found that among the most common facilitating factors were the knowledge that treatment was available (65%) and that results would be confidential (64%), and the fact that results would be available the same day (45%).

Laboratory and Diagnostic Capacity Development

ACHAP helped to upgrade the quality and capacity of Botswana's clinical laboratories to support the diagnosis and management of patients as well as conduct relevant research. ACHAP purchased and installed equipment for CD4 cell count, viral load testing, and other diagnostic and monitoring test services at the central HIV reference laboratory (the Botswana-Harvard AIDS Institute HIV Reference Laboratory), opened on World AIDS Day in 2001. To decentralize diagnostic and monitoring capacity, ACHAP also helped equip fourteen district and primary hospital laboratories, reducing test turnaround times and therefore improving treatment access to thousands of patients in locations remote from the major centers. In addition, ACHAP supported the recruitment and placement of laboratory technicians in clinical laboratories. Decentralizing diagnostic and laboratory capacity has been a critical element in success of the program.

Infrastructural Development Support

At the launch of the ARV program, most of Botswana's health facilities were small. Given the large additional patient burden due to HIV/AIDS, it became necessary to create additional space in the existing health facilities to deliver outpatient HIV treatment services.

ACHAP therefore supported procurement and upgrading of additional clinical space, building thirty-five Infectious Disease Care Clinics (IDCCs) in health facilities so that ARV treatment could be available in all districts in the country. ACHAP spent US$5.2 million between 2001 and 2009 on the Masa program for construction, renovation, and furnishing of the thirty-five ARV treatment facilities in the country, including the upgrading of ARV infrastructure for the Central Medical Stores (CMS). The facilities that were built or renovated with funding from ACHAP were widely distributed geographically, to cover all districts in the country. They were built to specifications determined by the Government of Botswana but using ACHAP's own procurement processes in order to expedite service provision compared to government processes.

Human Resource Capacity Development:
Training of Health Care Workers

One of the immediate challenges Botswana needed to address in delivering a national ARV treatment program was that the majority of
health care workers lacked experience in treating patients with ARV
medicines. A countrywide needs assessment had been conducted by
the Botswana Ministry of Health and the Botswana-Harvard School
of Public Health HIV/AIDS Initiative, which culminated in a five-
year plan for developing and implementing a treatment and care
training program tailored to the needs of the Botswana health sector.[45] ACHAP funded the development of this program, known as
"KITSO" (an acronym for "Knowledge, Training, and Innovation
Shall Overcome AIDS," but also the Setswana word for "knowledge")
and has continued to fund its implementation to date. This program,
comprising eight core modules and four specialty tracks, has been
central to the success of Botswana's treatment program, creating the
trained manpower across several health disciplines, including doctors,
nurses, pharmacists, laboratory technicians, and various cadres of lay
personnel, to provide ARV treatment services in 32 main IDCCs
and over 160 clinics throughout the country.[46] Over 7,500 health care
workers have been trained through this program. The didactic and
distance-learning KITSO training was complemented, until 2005, by
a clinical preceptorship program developed by ACHAP, which provided clinical mentorship by specialized HIV/AIDS physicians and
nurses from leading institutions in the developed world. Through this
program, ACHAP sponsored a total of 51 HIV clinical specialists
(36 doctors and 15 nurses). On average, each doctor preceptor trained
more than ten medical officers through hands-on training, and nurse
preceptors trained thirty-two registered nurses through hands-on
training.

Human Resource Capacity Development:
Human Resources (HR) Recruitment

One of the important aspects of ACHAP's support of the national
HIV/AIDS treatment program in Botswana has been the strengthening

of the overall health system. To address the shortage of skilled health workers, in the face of growing health care demands due to the HIV/ AIDS burden, additional staff were required to provide treatment at a growing number of health facilities as the program expanded. ACHAP has supported the recruitment of over two hundred staff in various health disciplines since the project's inception. Nearly ninety such staff were recruited to enable expansion of the treatment program to the clinic level, to improve its accessibility in rural areas. At these district level facilities, most of these staff also provide general health services, so other aspects of health care have benefited from the HIV program support.

To enable the expedited growth of the health care workforce to effectively deliver the ARV treatment program, ACHAP and the Government of Botswana adopted a unique three-pronged human resource solution, with sustainability as its underlying philosophy:

1. GoB, together with ACHAP, assesses critical and urgent HR requirements for selected parts of the national response and develops HR proposals for ACHAP's consideration.
2. Using these proposals, ACHAP procures an agreed number of positions using GoB recruiting guidelines.
3. Based on GoB conditions of service, ACHAP provides funding for these positions over an agreed period (ranging from 12 to 24 months), allowing time for the government to develop the required positions in its establishment with subsequent transfer of personnel to the government payroll.

This approach facilitated timely deployment of critically needed staff to run the ARV treatment program, enabling Botswana to rapidly roll out the program to the thirty-two project sites, providing the ART access that resulted in a significant reduction in HIV/AIDS related mortality. This also enabled Botswana to be one of only two countries to meet the global treatment access targets of the WHO "3 by 5 initiative" (launched in 2003) within the set time frame. Using GoB conditions of service for recruitment, with an initial contract period financed by ACHAP, the Government of Botswana has been able to absorb over 90% of these staff into its own establishment in a sustainable way with initial savings by the GoB. It is unlikely that growth of human resource capacity to deliver the program would have occurred to this extent, in the absence of this form of support.

Merck Medicines Donation

Merck has donated medicines to the national ARV program through ACHAP since the program's inception, initially providing two medicines in the period 2002–2008. In November 2008, Merck announced the donation of two further medicines until the end of the current phase of support in 2014. The medicines donation has been a very important contribution to the program, reducing considerably the costs to government of provision of the ARV program. The value of the Merck medicines donation by the end of December 2010 was about US$92 million, with an estimated 47% of patients on treatment including Merck-donated medicines.[47]

Information, Education, and Communication

The Masa program brand and a highly successful campaign that included social marketing, patient education, health promotion, and media relations resulted from ACHAP's engagement of private sector expertise in communications, public relations, and marketing. Through this unique approach for communications support to a public sector program, combined with other adherence support initiatives, the Botswana treatment program has reached high coverage rates (over 90%) and maintained high treatment adherence rates, with secondary resistance rates of less than 4% after eight years of ARV provision.[48]

Supporting Structures for Generation of Strategic Information for the Program

Since the inception of the Masa program, ACHAP has supported initiatives to generate information useful in program management and to monitor the program's progress, quality, and impact. ACHAP supported the development of a data recording and reporting and a monitoring and evaluation system for the Masa program, to ensure the production of good quality data. This support included the provision of human resources for managing the collection of data, support for IT infrastructure, including cabling/IT networks both at central level and Masa sites, and systems development and management.

HIV Prevention

Over the decade of its partnership with the Government of Botswana, ACHAP has supported the national HIV prevention strategy in a number of ways. First, when the enrollment of eligible women in the early years of the PMTCT program was found to be disappointingly low,[49] the shortage of midwives to provide antenatal services and counseling was identified as a constraint. To address this shortage, the government introduced a cadre of lay PMTCT counselors, and ACHAP in partnership with a local faith-based NGO, the Botswana Christian AIDS Intervention Program, supported the establishment of eleven counseling centers and implementation of a lay counselor training program which, among others, provided lay counselors to support the PMTCT program. The presence of these lay counselors, combined with introduction of the routine HIV testing program that ACHAP also supported, led to an increase in the uptake of PMTCT, from less than 34% in 2003 to about 77% by the end of 2004.[50] Botswana now has one of the most successful PMTCT programs, with over 90% of HIV-positive pregnant women receiving antiretroviral treatment for PMTCT as of 2010, and it has succeeded in reducing mother to child transmission rates from between 20% to 40% to less than 4%. Figure 2.3 shows estimates for the proportion of pregnant women living with HIV who received ART for PMTCT, with projections that coverage rates of up to 95% will be attained by 2015.

   With respect to prevention, ACHAP has also supported several other key areas. These include the procurement and distribution of condoms at the national level, complementing government supplies. In addition, ACHAP has supported blood safety efforts, contributing logistics and supplies and supporting a youth HIV prevention program linked to blood safety. ACHAP has also supported in- and out-of-school youth HIV prevention programs in collaboration with the Ministries of Education and the Ministry of Youth Sport and Culture. In 2007, ACHAP

Figure 2.3. Estimated Percentage of Pregnant Women in Botswana Living with HIV Who Receive ART for PMTCT

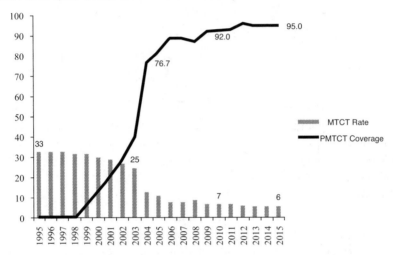

Source: NACA, "Botswana HIV Prevention Response Modes of Transmission Analysis," 2008

provided financial and technical support to the National AIDS Coordinating Agency (working in collaboration with other partners under NACA's coordination) for the development of a national plan for scaling up prevention (2008–2010). This plan identified a number of key drivers of the epidemic in Botswana, prioritizing these for prevention interventions, which have also informed prevention priorities for Botswana's 2nd National Strategic Framework (2010–2016).

THE CONTRIBUTION OF ACHAP TO BOTSWANA'S PROGRESS TOWARD THE ACHIEVEMENT OF THE MDGS

In the sections above, we have described the ways in which one of the most severe HIV/AIDS epidemics globally has affected Botswana's population, reversing earlier positive development trends with the strong potential to end the country's progress toward the Millennium Development Goals. We have also described Botswana's response to the HIV/AIDS epidemic. Botswana recognized that a robust response would be required if the country was not to surrender its development gains to this epidemic. We also described how a novel public-private partnership, namely, ACHAP, funded by the Bill & Melinda Gates Foundation and Merck/The Merck Company Foundation, has made very significant contributions to Botswana's fight against HIV/AIDS and contributed to the mitigation of the impact of HIV/AIDS. In this section we will provide an analysis of how ACHAP, as a significant partner in Botswana's HIV response, has helped mitigate the negative impact of HIV/AIDS in Botswana, and in a number of areas has enabled Botswana to remain on a positive trend toward attainment of certain MDGs. This analysis acknowledges two important points:

- The Botswana Government is the main funder of Botswana's HIV response. It is estimated that the Government of Botswana funds 70–80% of the response. This is a partnership in the true sense, with donor funds leveraging those of the national government.
- Several other development partners support Botswana's HIV response. The most notable is the U.S. Government's PEPFAR program; other partners include the European Union, the Global Fund to Fight AIDS, TB and Malaria, the Clinton Foundation, and various UN family organizations, all of which have played an important role in technical support for the response.

ARV Treatment Program

Perhaps the most effective contribution that ACHAP has made to Botswana's HIV response is its key role in the establishment and implementation of Botswana's national, publicly funded ARV program. This is also the area in which ACHAP's contributions toward MDG progress have been most direct. With ACHAP as one of its major development partners, Botswana has experienced considerable success. By 2007, coverage of people living with HIV and AIDS and eligible for antiretroviral drugs ranged from 82% in the areas with least coverage to well over 90% in areas of high coverage. This was a significant achievement, considering that only 7.3% had access in 2003.[51]

In addition to financial and technical support to establish programs, one of the most important contributions ACHAP has made
to the HIV response in Botswana has been the generation of strategic
information through various assessments, program evaluations/reviews,
conduct of studies, participation in national AIDS impact surveys to
determine national trends, and support for the conduct of modeling
and other studies to assess program trends and impacts.

Millennium Development Goal 6 includes two key global HIV-
related targets:

- 6a. Have halted by 2015 and begun to reverse the spread of HIV/AIDS
- 6b. Achieve, by 2010, universal access to treatment for HIV/AIDS for
  all those who need it.[52]

Related to these global targets, Botswana has further articulated
two national targets:

- Halt and reverse the incidence of HIV particularly among youth by
  2016.
- Reduce the number of infants born to HIV-infected mothers who are
  HIV positive by their 18th month by half by 2006, and to less than 1%
  by 2016.[53]

In 2007, discussions between ACHAP and the Government of Botswana[54] identified the need to update the country's projections for
people requiring treatment, compared to the original projections when
the program was established. Through a collaborative study with the
Government of Botswana under the coordination of the National
AIDS Coordinating Agency, ACHAP contracted the Futures Institute to support the development of projections for various indicators
of the response.[55] Using HIV sero-surveillance data among pregnant
women, national population-based AIDS impact surveys, and other
program data applying modeling techniques, new estimated trends for
HIV prevalence, annual number of new infections, number of people
in need of treatment, AIDS deaths, and the effects of the ARV therapy
and PMTCT programs were developed, with projections to 2015.[56] According to these estimates, the trend in the number of Batswana in need

of and eligible for ARV treatment is upward, compared to those who received it between the periods 1990 and 2009.

One of the most important outcomes of this work was the estimation of the impact of the ARV program in reducing AIDS-related mortality, with estimates that in the five-year period between 2002 and 2007, approximately 53,000 lives were saved as a result of the treatment program. This almost halved the rate of AIDS-related mortality in a period of five years, and it reversed the previous trend of rapidly rising mortality before the advent of treatment. It has further been estimated that if ART rates remain high, over 130,000 deaths could be averted by 2016.[57]

While achievements indicated above clearly relate to MDG 6, with reductions in HIV/AIDS mortality, they also contribute toward MDG 1 on poverty, since the majority of deaths averted due to success of the treatment program are among young, economically active people. The avoidance of these deaths has contributed to a reduction in poverty levels, by mitigating the impact on the labor force. This has also contributed to mitigating the projected increase in dependency rates and rates of orphanhood.

With respect to the national MDG 6 target of reducing the number of HIV-infected infants born to HIV-positive mothers at 18 months by half by 2006, and of reducing mother-to-child transmission to 1% by 2016, Botswana appears to be on course to achievement of this target. In 2009 the estimated rate was 3.8%.[58] The Government of Botswana is contemplating introducing universal HAART (a standard drug combination often called "highly active antiretroviral therapy") for HIV-positive pregnant women, and it is anticipated that with this change, mother-to-child transmission rates will likely fall even further.

The work that ACHAP undertook, in collaboration with the Government of Botswana and the Futures Institute, provided estimates of HIV incidence both retrospectively and as projected future trends, which suggested that the adult epidemic in Botswana peaked in the mid 1990s at about 5% incidence and by 2007 had been reduced to an estimated incidence of about 2.4%.

With respect to the global MDG 6 target of having halted and begun to reduce the spread of HIV/AIDS by 2015, although the number of new infections in Botswana is still very high, and although population-based prevalence rates appear to have stabilized at about 25% in the adult population,[59] there is evidence of a reduction in the rate of new infections, with declining prevalence rates among young people. Antenatal seroprevalence data among young people aged 15–24 (according to a 2009 antenatal seroprevalence survey) show a consistent reduction in prevalence among women aged 15–19 and 20–24 since 2001. Population-based surveys and HIV/AIDS impact evaluation studies in 2004 and 2008 have shown a reduction in HIV prevalence among women, from 18.2% in 2004 to 10.7% in 2008.

With respect to the national MDG 6 target on reduction of HIV incidence especially among young people, Botswana is moving in the right direction, although the challenge of reducing further the high incidence and prevalence rates still remains. The stabilizing prevalence rate in the face of evidence of reduction of new infections is thought to be due to the fact that a large number of people are being kept alive by an effective treatment program.

With respect to the global MDG target (6.b) that relates to universal access to treatment, defined as providing antiretroviral therapy to at least 80% of those people in need by 2010,[60] with ACHAP having played a central role, Botswana has surpassed this universal treatment access and MDG 6 target, having attained a national coverage rate of over 80% of patients in need of treatment by 2007[61] and 94% in need of treatment by the end of 2010.[62] WHO listed Botswana among eight developing countries that had achieved this target as of December 2009.[63]

Prevention of Mother-to-Child Transmission (PMTCT) and Child Mortality

Botswana's successful PMTCT program has made important contributions to reducing HIV transmission in children. By supporting the routine HIV testing initiative, and by supporting PMTCT through training of lay counselors and supply of rapid test kits, ACHAP contributed to the rapid rise in PMTCT uptake from 2004, which has resulted in mother-to-child transmission rates rapidly falling to less than 4%. Transmissions fell from a peak of about 4,000 in 1999 to less than 900 in 2007.[64] With the anticipated introduction of universal HAART for PMTCT, Botswana seems to be on target to attain its national target of reduction of mother-to-child transmission to less than 1% by 2016, as well as its goal of an HIV-free generation by 2016.

The Merck Medicines Donation

The Merck medicines donation has been a very substantial contribution to the attainment of Goal 6 on HIV/AIDS in Botswana, by increasing the government's ability to provide treatment on a wide scale through reduction in the overall medicines cost. This donation will continue to the end of the current project term in 2014. The donation also partially addresses Target 8e, relating to improving access to essential medicines. Aspects related to sustainability are beginning to be addressed, with a progressive downscaling of the medicines donation over a five-year period to the end of 2014. Modeling projections have estimated that if the national target in Botswana was met by 2015, then 60,000 HIV infections could be averted among HIV-negative men by 2021.[65]

Factors Contributing to ACHAP's Success

Key elements that have contributed to ACHAP's success in helping Botswana fight AIDS effectively—and make significant progress toward MDG goal 6 in particular—have been the following:

1. Its ability to move quickly without the burden of the bureaucracy of government. This has been used to advantage in areas such as procurement of infrastructure for service delivery and human resource recruitment, to name two examples.
2. ACHAP's unique governance structure, which has enabled a close working relationship with government with a high level of mutual trust. This has been useful in overcoming many of the early challenges of the partnership and enabling the frankness to address new ones.
3. Commitment of a significant quantum of resources over a significant period, enabling a sustained period of support in which genuine achievements can be made.
4. The ability for the response in Botswana to innovate, with the support of a partner able to respond quickly to emerging needs and issues.

CHALLENGES

Although Botswana has achieved significant successes in ARV treatment and the prevention of mother-to-child transmission of HIV, and although it has evidence that infection rates are declining, particularly among young people, still, transmission rates are high, and projected estimates suggest that the rate of decline of new infections in the adult population may be leveling off. The current prevalence by global standards is extremely high. Therefore, there is a need for Botswana to urgently strengthen its prevention efforts by scaling up the use of new, cost-effective, evidence-informed interventions to complement existing efforts. Second, Botswana's HIV response will benefit from the development of new prevention interventions to augment what is currently being implemented in the country. The development of the National Plan for Scaling Up Prevention with ACHAP support identified a number of factors considered to be important risk factors for individuals and important drivers of the epidemic at societal levels. Table 2.1 presents a summary of important risk factors and drivers.

In order to address these factors, beginning in 2008, ACHAP, in collaboration with the National AIDS Coordinating Agency and other partners in the response, supported the development and implementation of a multiple concurrent partnerships campaign to raise the level of awareness in the general population on the risks of multiple partners. In addition, ACHAP has identified scaling up access to safe male circumcision as a priority intervention in its second phase (2010–2014). Over 20% of ACHAP's second-phase budget is dedicated to safe male circumcision and, in collaboration with the government and other partners (notably the Botswana PEPFAR program), aims to assist Botswana to reach its national target of circumcising 80% of eligible men in the age group 0–49. ACHAP's focus is on the 15–29 age group, and the intention is that ACHAP's support should contribute to reaching at least 25% of the national target.

A second priority in ACHAP's second phase is supporting prevention interventions focusing on young women due to their very high vulnerability to HIV/AIDS, with the aim of reversing the trend whereby young women's HIV prevalence has risen almost sixfold in their transition from the 15–19 age group to the 20–29 age group. Development of

Table 2.1. Summary of Risk Factors and Drivers at Individual and Societal Levels

Risk Factors	Contextual and Structural Drivers
Multiple concurrent partners	Sociocultural norms and values
Low levels of male circumcision	Gender inequality and low status of women
Low levels of consistent condom use	Income inequality, poverty
Sexually transmitted infections	Human rights, stigma and discrimination
Lack of knowledge of HIV results	Distribution of health services
Cross-generational sex	
Transactional or commercial sex	
Alchohol and drug use	

Source: NACA, "Botswana HIV Prevention Response Modes of Transmission Analysis," 2008

these interventions follows a combination prevention approach, taking into account risk factors such as cross-generational sex and the impact of multiple concurrent partnerships, as well as structural factors such as sociocultural norms, gender and income inequality, and ensuring access to effective biomedical interventions such as early access to treatment. It also requires seeking future opportunities to support access to promising new interventions, such as the use of PrEP ("Pre-Exposure Prophylaxis") and microbicides as evidence of the effectiveness of these interventions increases.

THE ROAD AHEAD TO THE MDG 2015 GOALS

Merck's support for ACHAP, in partnership with the Bill & Melinda Gates Foundation and the Government of Botswana, has enabled several important achievements in the country's fight against HIV/AIDS and in progressing toward achievement of the Millennium Development Goals. By supporting the establishment and implementation of a highly successful treatment program, over 150,000 people have been put on treatment in a public sector program, enabling about 94% of people needing treatment by current criteria to access it, and leading to the attainment of the MDG target related to universal access to treatment. High treatment coverage rates along with low rates of treatment failure have enabled those on treatment to remain productive, reducing the poverty impact that AIDS would otherwise have had on Botswana's population and helping sustain socioeconomic development. By helping reduce HIV transmission from mother to child and thus HIV-related mortality among children, ACHAP has contributed toward the goal on reducing child mortality. However, trends in overall mortality among children are not yet reducing, with evidence from studies on infant feeding practices among HIV-positive mothers suggesting that avoidance of breastfeeding may lead to worse outcomes; factors such as this and others may need to be taken into account to ensure that the desired improvements in infant survival with effective PMTCT programs are achieved.[66]

Enhancing sustainable interventions has been a key priority of ACHAP's work; ACHAP is therefore providing support to the Government of Botswana to determine comprehensively the resource implications of adoption of the revised WHO/UNAIDS treatment guidelines as the country moves toward their adoption. In addition, support is being provided for a study in collaboration with the Botswana Harvard Partnerships to carry out research into the "Cost-effectiveness of Botswana National Models of HIV and AIDS Care," in order to generate local evidence on the most cost-effective approaches for delivery of HIV/AIDS treatment to inform continuing country choices. ACHAP's support in its second phase focused on taking to scale effective prevention efforts such as male circumcision and reducing the high vulnerability of young women to HIV/AIDS. These remain urgent priorities toward attainment of the Millennium Development Goals for 2015.

NOTES

We would like to acknowledge the support of ACHAP's funders, Merck/The Merck Company Foundation and The Bill & Melinda Gates Foundation, for the support that enabled ACHAP's contribution to the fight against HIV/AIDS in Botswana, in partnership with the Government of Botswana.

Information used for this essay was obtained from ACHAP archived documents, Government of Botswana public documents and reports, and international peer-reviewed journals.

1. Ramiah Ilavenil and Michael R. Reich, "Building Effective Public-Private Partnerships: Experiences and Lessons from the African Comprehensive

HIV/AIDS Partnerships (ACHAP)," *Social Science & Medicine* 63 (2006): 397–408.

2. L. Distlerath and G. Macdonald, "The African Comprehensive HIV/AIDS Partnerships—a New Role for Multinational Corporations in Global Health Policy," *Yale Journal of Health Policy, Law, and Ethics* 4, no. 1 (2004): 101–9.

3. Ramiah and Reich, "Building Effective Public-Private Partnerships."

4. Ibid.

5. World Bank, "Botswana Country Brief" (2011), available at http://web.worldbank.org/WBSITE/EXTERNAL/COUNTRIES/AFRICAEXT/BOTSWANAEXTN/0,,menuPK:322821~pagePK:141132~piPK:141107~theSitePK:322804,00.html (last accessed December 13, 2011).

6. ACHAP, "ACHAP Brochure" (2003), available at http://vih-msd.info/secure/downloads/resources/publications/ACHAP_brochuer.pdf.

7. United Nations Development Program (UNDP), *The Botswana Human Development Report 2000: Towards an AIDS-Free Generation* (2000), available at http://hdr.undp.org/en/reports/national/africa/botswana/botswana_2000_en.pdf.

8. Central Statistics Office (CSO), "Health Statistics (2009)," Government of Botswana; and National AIDS Coordinating Agency, *Botswana AIDS Impact Survey (III) Report* (2009) (Gaborone, Botswana: Government of Botswana, 2009).

9. UNAIDS, "AIDS Plus MDGs: Synergies that Serve People" (2010), available at http://www.unaidsrstesa.org/sites/default/files/aids_and_mdg.pdf.

10. UNDP, *The Botswana Human Development Report 2000.*

11. Ibid.

12. Ibid.

13. M. McFarlan and S. Sgherri, "The Macroeconomic Impact of HIV/AIDS in Botswana," IMF Working Paper WP/01/80 (June 2001).

14. National AIDS Coordinating Agency (NACA), "HIV/AIDS in Botswana: Estimated Trends and Implications Based on Surveillance and Modelling" (2008); available at http://www.unaids.org/en/dataanalysis/knowyourepidemic/countryreportsonhivestimates/20080701_botswana_national estimate 2007_en.pdf.

15. S. D. Weiser, K. Leiter, D. R. Bangsberg, L. M. Butler, F. Percy-de Korte, et al., "Food Insufficiency Is Associated with High-Risk Sexual Behavior among Women in Botswana and Swaziland," *PLoS Medicine* 4, no. 10 (2007); available at http://www.plosmedicine.org/article/info:doi/10.1371/journal.pmed.0040260.

16. UNDP, *The Botswana Human Development Report 2000.*

17. K. Jefferies, A. Kinghorn, H. Siphambe, and J. Thurlow, "Macroeconomic and Household-Level Impacts of HIV/AIDS in Botswana," *AIDS 2008* 22, supplement 1 (2008): S113–S119.

18. The date 2016 links these global development targets to Botswana's own national vision statement by its Vision 2016 Council, *Vision 2016*; available at http://www.vision2016.co.bw/.

19. Government of Botswana, Ministry of Finance and Development Planning, *Botswana Millennium Development Goals Status Report 2010*; available at http://www.undp.org/africa/documents/mdg/botswana_2010.pdf.

20. Ibid.

21. Government of Botswana Ministry of Health, *Annual Sentinel Surveillance Report* (2007).

22. Central Statistics Office, *Botswana Family Health Survey 2007* (Gaborone, Botswana: Central Statistics Office, 2009).

23. Government of Botswana, *Botswana Millennium Development Goals Status Report 2010*.

24. Ibid.

25. Ibid.

26. Ibid.

27. UNDP, *The Botswana Human Development Report 2000*.

28. Government of Botswana Ministry of Health, *Annual Sentinel Surveillance Report* (2007).

29. African Comprehensive HIV/AIDS Partnerships, *The Front Line in the War against HIV/AIDS in Botswana: Case Studies from the African Comprehensive HIV/AIDS Partnerships* (Gaborone, Botswana: ACHAP, 2004).

30. ACHAP, *The Front Line in the War against HIV/AIDS in* Botswana.

31. P. J. Kanki and R. G. Marlink, eds., *A Line Drawn in the Sand: Responses to the AIDS Treatment Crisis in Africa* (Boston: Harvard Center for Population and Development Studies, 2009).

32. Ramiah and Reich, "Building Effective Public-Private Partnerships."

33. E. Darkoh, "Testimony before the African Sub-Committee of the US Senate," April 7th, 2004; available at http://foreign.senate.gov/imo/media/doc/DarkohTestimony040407.pdf.

34. D. de Korte, P. Mazonde, and E. Darkoh, "Introducing ARV Therapy In the Public Sector in Botswana: Perspectives and Practice In Antiretroviral Treatment," case study (Geneva: World Health Organization, 2004).

35. Maggie Farley, "At AIDS Disaster's Epicenter, Botswana Is a Model of Action," *Los Angeles Times* (June 27, 2001); available at http://articles.latimes.com/2001/jun/27/news/mn-15017.

36. NACA, "HIV/AIDS in Botswana: Estimated Trends and Implications Based on Surveillance and Modelling" (2008).

37. CSO, "Health Statistics (2009)."

38. Kanki and Marlink, *A Line Drawn in the Sand*.

39. Ramiah and Reich, "Building Effective Public-Private Partnerships."

40. AIDS Online, "AIDS in Africa—Botswana"; available at http://www.aidsonline.org/africa/botswana.php#p42.

41. S. D. Weiser, M. Heilser, K. Leiter, F. Percy de Korte, S. Tlou, et al., "Routine HIV Testing in Botswana: A Population-Based Study on Attitudes, Practices, and Human Rights Concerns," *PloS Medicine* 3, no. 7 (2006); available at http://www.plosmedicine.org/article/info:doi/10.1371/journal.pmed.0030261.

42. Ibid.

43. Ibid.

44. Ibid.; also UNAIDS, "UNAIDS/WHO Policy Statement on HIV Testing," available at http://www.who.int/rpc/research_ethics/hivtestingpolicy_en_pdf.pdf.

45. Kanki and Marlink, *A Line Drawn in the Sand.*

46. Government of Botswana Ministry of Health, Annual Sentinel Surveillance Report (2007).

47. Government of Botswana, *Botswana Millennium Development Goals Status Report 2010.*

48. Ibid.

49. Ibid.

50. NACA, "Botswana HIV Prevention Response Modes of Transmission Analysis" (Government of Botswana, 2008).

51. Government of Botswana, *Botswana Millennium Development Goals Status Report 2010.*

52. UNAIDS, "AIDS Plus MDGs: Synergies that Serve People."

53. Government of Botswana, *Botswana Millennium Development Goals Status Report 2010.*

54. University of KwaZulu Natal, "ACHAP's Madikwe Forum: An Innovation in a Public/Philanthropic Partnership" (Durban: Health Economic Research Division, 2009).

55. J. Stover, B. Fidzani, B. C. Molomo, T. Moeti, and G. Musuka, "Estimated HIV Trends and Program Effects in Botswana," *PLoS ONE* 3, no. 11 (2008); available at http://www.plosone.org/article/info:doi/10.1371/journal.pone.0003729 (last accessed December 14, 2011).

56. NACA, "HIV/AIDS in Botswana: Estimated Trends and Implications Based on Surveillance and Modelling" (2008).

57. Ibid.

58. NACA, "Botswana HIV Prevention Response Modes of Transmission Analysis" (2008); and Government of Botswana, *Botswana Millennium Development Goals Status Report 2010.*

59. NACA, *Botswana AIDS Impact Survey (I)* (Gaborone, Botswana: Government of Botswana, 2001); NACA, *Botswana AIDS Impact Survey (III) Report* (2008); and NACA, "HIV/AIDS in Botswana: Estimated Trends and Implications Based on Surveillance and Modelling" (2008).

60. World Health Organization, "Treatment and Care for People Living with HIV," in *Towards Universal Access: Scaling Up Priority HIV/AIDS*

Interventions in the Health Sector (Geneva: WHO, 2010); available at http://www.who.int/hiv/pub/2010progressreport/ch4_en.pdf.

61. Government of Botswana, *Botswana Millennium Development Goals Status Report 2010*.

62. Ibid.

63. World Health Organization, "Treatment and Care for People Living with HIV."

64. Stover et al., "Estimated HIV Trends and Program Effects in Botswana."

65. L. Bollinger, J. Stover, G. Musuka, B. Fidzani, T. Moeti, and L. Busang, "The Cost and Impact of Male Circumcision on HIV/AIDS in Botswana," *Journal of the International AIDS Society* 12, no. 7 (2009); available at http://www.ncbi.nlm.nih.gov/pmc/articles/PMC2695421/.

66. T. Doherty, D. Sanders, et al., "Implications of the New WHO Guidelines on HIV and Infant Feeding for Child Survival in South Africa," *Bulletin of the World Health Organization* 89 (2011): 62–67.

3 | Sumitomo Chemical and the Millennium Development Goals

Scott Mitchell

The Sumitomo Chemical Group includes over one hundred subsidiaries and affiliates, operates businesses in five sectors (basic chemicals, petrochemicals, IT-related chemicals, health and crop sciences, and pharmaceuticals), and provides products worldwide that support a wide variety of industries and help improve people's daily lives. "Our business must benefit not only ourselves but also communities and society at large." This statement is at the heart of the Sumitomo family's business philosophy, as outlined more than 350 years ago by Masatomo Sumitomo. It forms the core of Sumitomo Chemical's corporate values today.

Sumitomo Chemical was founded in 1913 as a fertilizer manufacturing company, which produced fertilizers by converting harmful emissions from smelting operations at the Besshi Copper Mine in Niihama, Ehime Prefecture. Created to provide solutions to overcome an environmental problem and to help increase agricultural production, the company strives to exemplify the Sumitomo family's business philosophy. Its conviction that the essence of corporate social responsibility (CSR) is to contribute to the sustainable development of society through business activities is encoded in the company's DNA.

One of the central policies of the Sumitomo Chemical corporate vision is to help meet global challenges, from improving people's lives and health to increasing energy and food security, building a low-carbon society, and contributing to the sustainable development of the global community by taking full advantage of the power of chemistry.

OUR COMMITMENT TO THE FUTURE OF AFRICA

Mosquito-borne disease transmission poses one of the greatest threats to the tropical world and, with the advent of global warming, is also of increasing concern for temperate countries. Of all the mosquito-borne diseases, malaria remains one of the greatest problems in tropical countries, adversely affecting population health and economic development. Malaria kills between one and two million people every year, with 90 percent of the deaths occurring in sub-Saharan Africa. The most vulnerable sections of the population consist of pregnant women and children.

Malaria is both preventable and treatable. Given the costs and logistics of rapid diagnosis and treatment in many African countries, the old saying "Prevention is better than cure" remains true. If the infected mosquito can be prevented from biting people, the cycle of disease transmission is broken. This protection can be effected in many ways, from indoor residual spraying of insecticides (IRS) to the use of aerosols and mosquito coils.

The Olyset® Net, an insecticidal mosquito net that helps prevent the spread of malaria, symbolizes the CSR initiatives of Sumitomo Chemical. Mosquito nets are not new; they have been around for at least a century. What is relatively new is the addition of insecticide to those nets: the development of insecticide-treated bednets provided a means to protect people throughout the night and at the same time kill mosquitoes. The advent of pyretheroid insecticides made a very effective addition, offering rapid action and good kill of insects with low toxicity to people.

The first insecticide formulations marketed for treatment of nets required manual dilution and dipping of nets. These treatments are depleted after consecutive washings and therefore last from only six months to one year before losing efficacy. The logistics of regular redipping of nets, especially in remote villages, was so difficult that it was rarely totally successful. It soon became apparent that long-lasting factory treatment was required so that no retreatment of the nets would be needed during their subsequent life in the field.

Sumitomo Chemical, with over 2,000 employees dedicated to research and development, is a world leader in the discovery of innovative solutions for control of insect pests affecting the health and welfare of mankind. Sumitomo Chemical was the first company to develop a long-lasting insecticidal net (LLIN, also referred to as LN), which changed the face of malaria control programs.

Sumitomo's focused approach led to the development of Olyset Net—a high density polyethylene net with the insecticide incorporated within the fibers of the net. This innovation allowed the nets to be distributed without the need for teams to return regularly to retreat them. LLINs are designed to survive for several years in the field without further maintenance and to perform for at least twenty washes without losing insecticidal activity.

Mosquito nets may seem an obsolete technology, but a great many people worldwide are still in need of the protection they provide. Children in Africa, in particular, are especially vulnerable to malaria, an infectious disease transmitted by the *Anopheles* mosquito. It is a sad fact that, as reported by UNICEF in 2010, malaria takes the life of one child every 45 seconds. Those who do not die from malaria still suffer from a high fever and must stay in bed for several days. This in turn leads to increased poverty due to the loss of employment and educational opportunities as well as the high cost of medical treatment.

Malaria is one of the biggest barriers to economic development in Africa, and the economic losses caused by the disease are estimated at 12 billion dollars annually. Stopping the spread of malaria was therefore included in the Millennium Development Goals (MDGs), which set forth targets and action plans to be urgently implemented and achieved by 2015 based on the Millennium Declaration adopted by the United Nations in September 2000.

Malaria Control Initiatives and the Olyset Net

The World Health Organization (WHO) has been implementing the Roll Back Malaria campaign since 1998. The WHO's attention was drawn to the Olyset Net, which, as noted above, retains its insecticidal efficacy for five years or longer even with repeated washing and the passing of time. The fibers of this highly durable net are made from high density polyethylene resin, kneaded together with an insecticide, which is then gradually released to the surface of the netting fibers. Sumitomo Chemical developed the Olyset Net through Creative Hybrid Chemistry, combining its proprietary technologies in two separate fields of insecticides and resin processing.

In 2001, the WHO endorsed the use of Olyset Net, calling it the first "long-lasting insecticidal net." With results from a limited regional trial indicating impressive decline in the local rate of malarial infection, the distribution of long-lasting insecticidal nets has become one of the major means of controlling malaria.

In 2008, the WHO, promoting the policy of "universal coverage," enlarged the pool of candidates for malaria control, which had previously been limited to pregnant women and infants. Under this policy, the organization aims to distribute one long-lasting insecticidal net per two people in malaria-prone areas.

Creating Employment through Local Production

In 2003, Sumitomo Chemical provided its Olyset Net manufacturing technology, free of licensing fees, to A to Z Textile Mills Limited, a Tanzanian manufacturer, with the aim of kick-starting local production of the nets in Africa and building the framework for Public-Private Partnerships with international organizations such as the WHO and the United Nations Children's Fund (UNICEF).

Subsequently, in order to respond to a rapid increase in demand, Sumitomo Chemical and A to Z Textile Mills established the joint venture Vector Health International Limited in 2007.

As of July 2010, the local production capacity in Tanzania totaled approximately 30 million nets, and the number of people employed by the company in Africa reached 7,000, with over 80 percent of those jobs filled by women. According to the University of London School of Oriental and African Studies, the Olyset Net business is clearly contributing to local economic development.

To meet the increased demand created by the quest for "universal coverage," Sumitomo Chemical has increased the total Olyset Net production capacity of its production bases in the three countries of Tanzania, China, and Vietnam to 60 million nets per year as of mid-2010.

The Intimate Connection of Malaria and Poverty

Malaria is a disease of poverty in two senses, forming a vicious cycle: it is both a root cause and a consequence of poverty. As mentioned above, it has a devastating economic and social impact. Sick children miss school, their parents miss earning opportunities, and economic development is stifled. And for the poor, the high cost of malaria treatments often rules out the means of prevention. We believe that eradicating poverty and narrowing the gap between the rich and poor will secure the baseline of social stability and sustainable development.

Educational Support

For Africa to achieve development, it is critical to provide local people with education. African countries, however, have a shortage of schools, and many children have to study outdoors or in overcrowded classrooms.

Sumitomo Chemical has been supporting education in Africa by returning a portion of its revenues from the Olyset Net business to local communities. In cooperation with two non-profit organizations called World Vision Japan and Plan Japan, we have supported nine projects to construct primary and secondary school buildings as well as dormitories for teachers and school lunch facilities in the five countries of Ethiopia, Kenya, Uganda, Tanzania, and Zambia. Once the construction is complete, we continue to provide support for school fees and supplies, thereby helping the next generation of leaders get the education they need.

THE CYCLE OF GOOD AND THE MDGS

We believe that Sumitomo's Olyset Net business contributes to the development of African society in many ways. Not only does the business help prevent malaria, but it also provides employment opportunities through its factories in Africa, as well as other countries. Furthermore, a significant proportion of its revenues is returned to the local community through the support of education, thus benefiting society at every step. This is where we see sustainable development: a sustainable way for the private sector to be directly involved in the development of society.

Nations, regions, international organizations, nonprofit organizations and NGOs, and businesses throughout the world are working together to achieve the Millennium Development Goals for 2015, listed below:

Goal 1. Eradicate extreme poverty and hunger
Goal 2. Achieve universal primary education
Goal 3. Promote gender equality and empower women
Goal 4. Reduce child mortality
Goal 5. Improve maternal health
Goal 6. Combat HIV/AIDS, malaria, and other diseases
Goal 7. Ensure environmental sustainability
Goal 8. Develop a global partnership for development

Through its Olyset Net business, Sumitomo Chemical is working to prevent the spread of malaria and thereby reduce child mortality and improve maternal health. Moreover, we are conducting a wide range of other activities to contribute to the achievement of the MDGs.

We believe that the private sector has more contributions that it can make. Although philanthropic contributions are very important, in order to enable sustainable development businesses need to think of new ways to contribute through their business activities. The Olyset® Net business is a perfect example, which embodies the Sumitomo credo.

We will continue to make contributions to the sustainable development in Africa through our business operations that improve people's lives.

NOTE

This essay and data are drawn from Sumitomo Chemical CSR Highlights, October 11, 2010; Sumitomo Chemical Olyset® Net Technical Information 2011; and Sumitomo Chemical CSR Department PowerPoint Presentation 2011.

4 | Doing Well by Doing Good—
The Nestlé Way

John Bee

Good food, good life is what Nestlé is all about. As the world's leading nutrition, health, and wellness company, Nestlé has a long history of providing quality products supported by an expertise in nutrition, health, and wellness, and it is the largest private funder of nutrition research globally.

Nestlé's strategy is guided by several fundamental principles. Our existing products grow through innovation and renovation, while maintaining a balance in geographic activities and product lines. Long-term potential is never sacrificed for short-term performance. The company's priority is to bring the best and most relevant products to people, wherever they are, whatever their needs, throughout their lives.

WHAT IS CREATING SHARED VALUE?

Nestlé uses the term "creating shared value" to describe the relationship we have with the societies we serve and in which we operate. We often illustrate it in the form of a simple pyramid (fig. 4.1). It aims to show that, while sustainability and compliance are fundamental to our business, creating shared value goes beyond, aiming to create new and greater value for society and our shareholders within our chosen areas of focus. It is, however, important to note that we see creating shared value as built on strong foundations of *compliance* and *environmental sustainability*. For us, you cannot create shared value if you don't comprehensively address the first two layers of the pyramid first.

In Nestlé's context, *compliance* means abiding by national laws and relevant conventions, as well as our own regulations, which often go beyond our legal obligations. For example, we support the Universal Declaration of Human Rights (UDHR), which stands at the basis of the UN Global Compact's Human Rights Principles, and our CEO Paul Bulcke signed the UN Global Compact CEO Statement for the sixtieth anniversary of the UDHR. Our strong support for the UN Global Compact and our detailed commitments to the Fundamental Conventions of the International Labor Organization (ILO) or other relevant instruments are laid out in our Nestlé Corporate Business Principles (NCBP) and related policy documents, and their application is verified through our internal corporate group auditors.

Figure 4.1. Nestlé's Creating Shared Value Pyramid

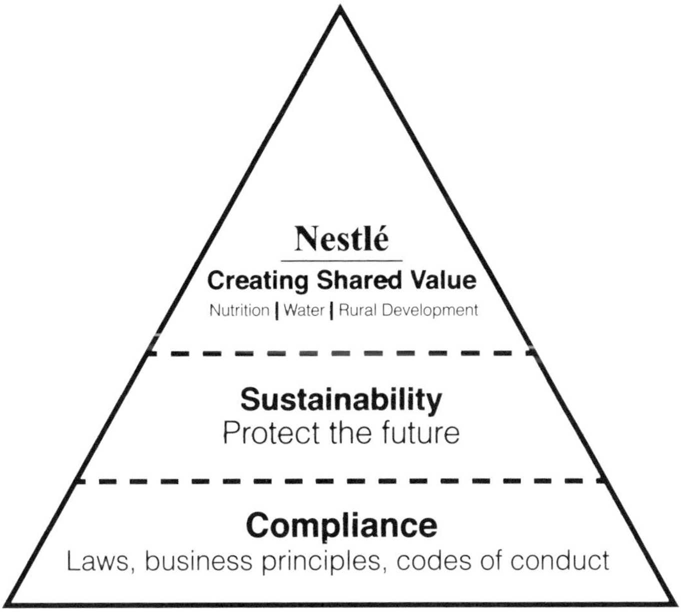

Nestlé
Creating Shared Value
Nutrition | Water | Rural Development

Sustainability
Protect the future

Compliance
Laws, business principles, codes of conduct

Beyond that, how we do business is based on *sustainability*—ensuring that our activities preserve the environment for future generations. In line with the definition of the UN's Brundtland Commission, sustainable development to Nestlé means "development that meets the needs of the present without compromising the ability of future generations to meet their own needs."

We have found the UN Global Compact and its ten principles to be most helpful to us in addressing the pyramid's two foundation layers, while the UN Millennium Development Goals (MDGs) are useful in assessing the societal impact of our value creation.

Moving beyond compliance and sustainability, creating shared value enhances the way we conduct our business by bringing shared value to both our shareholders and society overall. We believe that long-term success is assured if the benefits are jointly shared between the company and the community, where a strong partnership built on trust can be nurtured. To quote Harvard's Michael Porter and Mark Kramer, "shared value . . . involves creating economic value in a way that also creates value for society by addressing its needs and challenges. Businesses must reconnect company success with social progress. Shared value is not social responsibility, philanthropy, or even sustainability, but a new way to achieve economic success. It is not on the margin of what companies do but at the center."[1]

As a food and beverage company, we have identified nutrition, water, and rural development as the areas where Nestlé can, in particular, optimize the creation of shared value. These activities are core to our business strategy and operations and vital to the welfare of the people in the countries where we operate.

Nutrition: because food and nutrition are the basis of health and of our business—it's the reason why we exist.
Water: because the ongoing quality and availability of this resource is critical to life, to the production of food, and to our operations.
Rural development: because the overall well-being of farmers, rural communities, small entrepreneurs, and suppliers is intrinsic to the sustainability of our business.

Through these focus areas, which are very much interlinked, we aim to demonstrate and measure systematic and continuous improvement in each of these areas, and our annual "Creating Shared Value" reports are statements of record, charting our progress to our stakeholders. Creating shared value underpins everything that we do to build trust in our company. Simply put—*It is "the way we do business."*

NESTLÉ AND THE UN MDGS

Nestlé's concept of creating shared value has close parallels with the UN Millennium Development Goals (MDGs) because it focuses our business on generating value for our employees, our shareholders, and society as a whole.

In 2006, we issued our first report on those Nestlé activities that contribute to achieving the UN goals. In 2010, a decade after the creation of the MDGs, we again took stock of our actions related to the MDGs and charted 292 Nestlé business activities and programs that support these goals.

The nature of our business means that we have the most impact on MDG 1—eradicating extreme poverty and hunger. Through our creating shared value concept, we work directly with over 556,000 farmers to help them improve the quality and quantity of their produce and, as a result, increase their family income. This also brings greater access to nutritious and safe food to regions of their countries.

Through many of our business activities and related projects, we promote gender equality and education for women and girls, and, in some regions, we create new opportunities for women to participate in income-generating activities, such as dairy farming (MDG 3).

We are continually improving the nutritional quality and taste of our products, fortifying many of them to address the deficiencies of specific populations (MDGs 4 and 5).

As a company committed to continuous improvement, we are making considerable investments to stay at the forefront in reducing the environmental footprint of our operations and those of our entire value chain (MDG 7).

We wholeheartedly support the attainment of the MDGs, but we also recognize that eliminating global poverty and its consequences will take more than fifteen years. Much progress has been made, but it will require many more decades of effort to eradicate poverty and hunger.

NESTLÉ AND THE UN GLOBAL COMPACT

Since joining the UN Global Compact (UNGC) in 2001, we have embraced its ten principles, integrated them into the Nestlé Corporate Business Principles, and continuously supported them. Our annual Communication on Progress illustrates our efforts in the issue areas of human rights, labor practices, the environment, and anti-corruption. Our full Communication on Progress is available online.

Commitment and systems: The Nestlé Corporate Business Principles, endorsed by the chairman and CEO, form the basis of our culture and reflect our values of fairness, honesty, and respect for people and the environment. A revised version of the NCBP was developed during 2010 and translated into fifty languages. A comprehensive communication and training toolkit has been provided to all countries where we operate, where local plans have been launched to ensure each employee lives up to these principles. Compliance is monitored through external audits and the Nestlé group audit function. Our code of business conduct outlines minimum standards of behavior in key areas, our new employee relations policy outlines international standards and sets a tone of open dialogue on labor matters, and the Nestlé supplier code commits suppliers to comply with our core integrity standards.

Human rights and labor practices: Since November 2008, Nestlé has worked with the Danish Institute for Human Rights (DIHR) to review our human rights policy and assess our labor practices and human rights compliance. In July 2010, we signed a two-year partnership through which the DIHR assists us in integrating human rights into our corporate systems. Nestlé recognizes the "corporate responsibility to respect human rights," as outlined in the UN Framework on Human Rights and Business proposed by John Ruggie, Special Representative of the UN Secretary-General on Business and Human Rights. In cocoa-growing areas of the world, for example, child labor is a challenge, so Nestlé and others in the International Cocoa Initiative (ICI) continue to tackle child labor and improve access to education. In Colombia, Nestlé is a founding participant of "Guías Colombia" (Guidelines for Colombia), which brings together companies, governments, NGOs, and trade unions. We also have a formal dialogue with Alliance Sud, a group of Swiss NGOs examining the impact of our activities and our relationships with trade unions and local communities on national development and human rights. In 2010, all operating companies implemented action plans and are tracking progress on our gender balance initiative, a program launched in 2008 to help develop the environment, culture, and leadership that give equal opportunities for everyone. In Nestlé, a global network of so-called gender balance champions—business leaders acting as ambassadors—regularly shares best practices across the organization.

Environmental sustainability: Our aim is to continuously improve our performance and produce tastier, nutritious food and beverages that are better for the environment. We assess the environmental impact of our value chains, including procurement, logistics, manufacturing, marketing, and consumer engagement, using a life cycle approach. Nestlé is also a founding signatory of the UN Global Compact's CEO Water Mandate and has provided a Communication on Progress on water since 2009. We are committed to use palm oil only from sustainable sources by 2015, and we were the first company to commit to eliminating tropical rainforest deforestation in our supply chain. Through our collaboration with the Forest Trust, we are working with our suppliers to meet a series of principles to achieve this.

Anti-corruption: The company's code of business conduct and the NCBP condemn any form of corruption and bribery, and our supplier code of conduct requires our partners to embrace our "zero-tolerance" approach. Having performed a thorough anti-corruption risk assessment, we have developed an anti-corruption training tool to provide employees with specific guidance on avoiding inappropriate behavior, supplementing existing training efforts in this area. Our code of business conduct introduced whistle-blower procedures in 2008, and we are complementing our local hotlines with a group-wide integrity reporting system.

In 2009, Nestlé also became a member of the UN Global Compact LEAD, a leadership platform comprising a select group of UN Global Compact "champion" companies, which was scaled up in 2011. Furthermore, Nestlé was a Patron Sponsor of the UN Global Compact's Tenth Anniversary Leaders Summit in June 2010, and the company is an active member of several of the Compact's working groups and initiatives. This, and our various other UNGC engagements, give us a set of guidelines and frameworks that are especially useful in fulfilling the "compliance" layer of our creating shared value pyramid. The UNGC framework also helps us fulfill the environmental sustainability layer of the pyramid.

In fact, at this level we can see our first evidence that a long-term approach to growth, mindful of the interests of society, can be achieved without that growth bringing about negative effects on the societies in which a company operates.

In a decade in which Nestlé's production in terms of tonnage increased by nearly 73 percent, our water consumption per ton of product fell by 61 percent, waste water generation by two-thirds, energy consumption by 44 percent, and greenhouse gas generation by over 50 percent over the same period. So Nestlé is growing at the same time as it reduces its environmental impact; and because that investment takes place with a decidedly long-term perspective, it also delivers long-term benefit to shareholders, notably a reduction in operating costs and risk.

Having prepared our foundations of compliance and environmental sustainability, we can turn our attention to how Nestlé creates value for the communities where it operates, at the same time as it creates growth for shareholders.

Creating shared value is not a panacea for all social needs, nor can it penetrate every single aspect of our activities without regard to relevance. According to Porter and Kramer, "Inevitably, the most fertile opportunities for creating shared value will be closely related to a company's particular business and in areas most important to the business. Here a company can benefit the most economically and hence sustain its commitment over time. Here is also where a company brings the most resources to bear, and where its scale and market presence equip it to have a meaningful impact on a societal problem."[2]

We aim to demonstrate and measure systematic and continuous improvement in each of these areas, and our annual "Creating Shared Value" reports constitute our statements of record, charting our progress to our stakeholders.

NUTRITION AT NESTLÉ

Nestlé is the world's largest manufacturer of products fortified with essential micronutrients that would otherwise be missing from diets in most developing populations around the world.

Our locally adapted Popularly Positioned Products (PPPs) provide people on lower incomes with products of nutritional value at an affordable price and appropriate serving size. With many consumers suffering from deficiencies in key micronutrients such as iron, iodine, vitamin A, and zinc, we fortify billions of servings of Nestlé products. Many of these are PPPs, such as iodine-enriched Maggi products (bouillons, seasonings, and noodles), of which we delivered 90 billion fortified servings in 2010. Nestlé invests CHF 12 million a year into direct R&D for dehydrated and liquid milk-based products, and this know-how is applied in affordable milks for local populations in emerging countries, fortifying them with relevant micronutrients in each location. At the end of 2010, our affordable milk range was available in eighty countries.

In addition to helping combat micronutrient malnutrition, Nestlé's innovative food science technology has created new businesses and jobs, such as "Ate Vôce" door-to-door distributors in the favelas of Rio de Janeiro and Sao Paolo. To date, we have empowered more than 6,500 micro entrepreneurs, most of them women, in this respect.

In terms of over-nutrition, we are systematically innovating and renovating products, using our 60/40+ process, so as to guarantee both consumer preference and superior nutrition performance (nobody will eat a nutritionally superior product if the taste is not right, so there is no benefit). This year, over 6,500 products were renovated in this way.

While products are at the core of our commitment to deliver nutrition value, we are also aware that nutritional knowledge the world over is often lacking. This is why our Nestlé Healthy Kids Global Programme delivers often unbranded nutrition education in partnership with health ministries, universities, or NGOs in fifty-eight countries worldwide.

WATER AT NESTLÉ

Turning to the key focus area of water, here is another area where our work as a founding signatory of the UNGC CEO (United Nations Global Compact Chief Executive Officer) Water Mandate has brought useful guidance, because we measure our progress against the mandate's key elements.

This year, for example, on public policy engagement, Nestlé has formally recognized the human right to water; and we remain a committed leader in the public policy debate on restoring the balance between water withdrawals and the availability of naturally renewed water. In 2009, we led a joint project, which included the International Finance Corporation of the World Bank Group and McKinsey, producing the report *Charting Our Water Future: A New Economic Framework to Decision-Making.*

In our own direct operations, we withdrew 144 million m^3 of water in 2010. This equates to 3.29 m^3 per ton of product, 5 percent down from the 2009 level. And we operate 292 waste water treatment plants, whether legally required to do so or not.

In the agricultural supply chain, which accounts for 70 percent of fresh water use, we now have twelve water projects linked to the Sustainable Agriculture Initiative. For example, one related to coffee growing in China has saved 80 percent of water used in the production and washing process; and another in Vietnam will save 1 billion cubic meters of water annually.

Our community engagement in water projects extends across several projects, from leveraging the water filtration plant at our Kabirwala factory in Pakistan to delivering clean water to the local community, to our partnership with the International Federation of the Red Cross and Red Crescent Societies (IFRC) to bring water and sanitation to 53,000 people in the cocoa-growing villages of West Africa.

RURAL DEVELOPMENT AT NESTLÉ

We have known for some time that our biggest rural impact was through many of our 443 factories. Over half of our factories are in developing countries, and of those, over half are in rural areas. This year we completed an exhaustive survey of our factories to examine the extent of our reach, and found that 60 percent of our factories are in rural areas, providing local employment to over 148,000 people. But we also decided to analyze the nature of their development impact. What we found was quite encouraging. As a few key highlights, 32 percent of rurally located factories in developing countries provide clean drinking water to local communities, over half of them provide formal apprenticeships and contribute to local educational facilities, and more than two-thirds have waste water treatment facilities.

When one thinks of rural development, more often than not, one means agricultural extension programs. We are very active here, too. We see investment in capacity building among farming communities as key to our continued success, given that there could be 10 billion mouths to feed on the planet by 2050 but only a maximum of 20 percent more agricultural land available for farming.

We purchase substantial quantities from our farmers directly (so they keep more of the income than they would by using middle men)— 12 million tons of fresh milk alone, in over thirty milk districts worldwide, where we help them build productivity with financial assistance, feed, and breeding and vaccination advice. In the past few years, we also announced plans to invest over CHF 330 million in rejuvenating capacity in coffee and cocoa growing communities around the world between now and 2020.

These long-term investments are not only investments in the health of our own business; at the same time they are delivering what are often more immediate benefits to the societies they serve. These examples embody our creating shared value approach and are therefore more sustainable and scalable than could be achieved by philanthropy alone.

That said, we make no proprietary claim to creating shared value. In fact, every other year, the Nestlé Prize in Creating Shared Value, an award of CHF 500,000, is made to encourage and reward an outstanding innovation or project that focuses on improving access to and management of water; on delivering high nutritional value to populations suffering from nutritional deficits; or on improving the lives of farmers and rural communities.

The Nestlé Prize is open to NGOs, small enterprises, and individuals with a project that is innovative, is already implemented on a pilot or small-scale basis, is applicable on a broader scale or to other communities, and is based on a sound and sustainable business model.

No company can act alone on a journey like the one Nestlé is undertaking in creating shared value. We call on the expertise of our Creating Shared Value Advisory Board of world-renowned experts in business strategy, nutrition, water, and rural development. They guide us on what our priorities should be as we make our plans for the years and decades ahead. We also engage with stakeholders, partners, and opinion formers such as the UN Global Compact members and ask them to tell us how we are doing.

Nestlé's long-term commitment to creating shared value works in good times and, perhaps more importantly, in challenging times. This is, for us, the essence of operating a truly sustainable business, because we are asking our shareholders to invest so that their earnings will grow over time, but in such a way that the societies on whose welfare our own livelihood ultimately depends also benefit from our presence, our activities, and our long-term commitment to them.

NOTES

1. From Michael E. Porter and Mark R. Kramer, "Creating Shared Value," *Harvard Business Review* 89, no. 1 (January–February 2011): 62–77.
2. Ibid.

5 | Coca-Cola and Society

Holly Hermes

The Coca-Cola story is one that spans over a century, includes more than two hundred countries across the globe, and touches at least 1.7 billion people every day. In 2010, Coca-Cola's 139,600 employees helped generate over $35 billion dollars in revenue. As companies grow in size, their spheres of influence expand, and today there are a host of multinational companies affecting the lives of people on every continent. We live in a world that is growing more interconnected at an exponential rate. This interconnectedness is enabled by a variety of factors but is most significantly influenced by business. Companies have connected us across continents and cultures. Companies have provided the technology and platforms for us to communicate, travel, trade, and learn from one another. The Coca-Cola Company has provided the world with something many of us do not immediately recognize: a shared experience. In the company's view: "Coca-Cola is more than just a beverage: it is a moment of refreshment and connection that transcends cultural differences and helps tie our diverse world together."

Companies often expand their global reach through strategic partnerships, and this has been the case for Coca-Cola. The company has made partnerships a priority, and they continue to be a primary driver behind its success. Bottling and distribution partners have brought Coke to parts of the world that other companies still consider inaccessible, which gives us a clear competitive advantage. Understanding the importance of partnerships, Coca-Cola made these relationships a critical component of its corporate citizenship strategy. These partnerships have enabled the company to leverage its resources and influence in the most meaningful ways to address some of the most pressing social and environmental challenges of our time.

With significant influence comes significant responsibility, and this is not lost on the Coca-Cola Company, which joined the UN Global Compact in March 2006. As the company has grown in size, both financially and physically, so has its commitment to the communities in which they do business. Coca-Cola sees this commitment not just as a responsibility but, more importantly, as a strategic imperative. Muhtar Kent, the chairman and CEO of the Coca-Cola Company, affirmed in 2011 that "the economic, environmental, and social implications of business are more important than ever. In a world where populations are growing, natural resources are stressed, communities are forced to do more with less, and our consumers' expectations are expanding, we understand that sustainability is core to our business continuity and how we create long-term value."[1] The creation of long-term value has been the driver behind Coca-Cola's sustainability strategy, coined "live positively." The company has identified seven areas that are core to its business and in which it exerts significant influence. The company's vision for corporate citizenship is also in concert with the UN Global Compact and Millennium Development Goals.

The Coca-Cola Company realizes that its business success is tied to the health of the global community. Creating opportunities for communities to thrive, economically, socially, and environmentally, is a critical component of the business strategy at Coca-Cola and has become embedded in the culture of the company.

CREATING ECONOMIC OPPORTUNITY

Economic health is both a component and a by-product of business operations. Coca-Cola's Micro Distribution Center Model is the perfect illustration of this concept and a response to the following statement by Jane Nelson of Harvard's Kennedy School of Government:

"[I]t is through core business operations and value chains that companies are likely to make the greatest contributions to development. Until relatively recently, core business operations and value chains have not been a key part of the corporate social responsibility (CSR) debate, and their development impacts have not been rigorously analyzed, evaluated or reported on."[2] Coca-Cola saw both the challenge and the opportunity to address the inadequacy of philanthropy and traditional CSR in achieving the Millennium Development Goals. Coca-Cola Sabco (South African Bottling Company) developed a distribution model in the early 2000s in East Africa in response to the challenges of distribution in emerging/developing markets, called Manual Distribution Centers (MDCs). The MDCs are independently owned, low-cost manual operations created to service primarily an emerging urban retail market where classic distribution models were not effective or efficient. These centers, while commercially successful, also created new businesses, thousands of jobs, and much-needed income in local economies. Similar models are now being implemented by other bottlers in North and West Africa and in Asia.

This success prompted Coca-Cola to enhance the model through its "Business Call to Action" commitment in May 2008. The company embarked on a research project in partnership with the International Finance Corporation (IFC) and the Harvard Kennedy School to investigate the mechanics of the system of Manual Distribution Centers and its current and potential socioeconomic benefits. The project identified three key areas of development contribution: creating opportunities for entrepreneurship and employment, catalyzing human development, and promoting women's economic empowerment. MDCs create thousands of jobs and income for the broader support of dependents. In Africa there are over three thousand of these small businesses, employing over 13,500 people directly. The model enables the development of basic business skills through daily coaching and hands-on experience and facilitates the engagement of large numbers of women in the marketplace. MDC owners represent a growing number of entrepreneurs who are in business not only to survive but also to employ others, increasing the incomes of those in their community and raising productivity—which is critical to ending the cycle of poverty.

Rosemary Njeri of Nairobi, Kenya, started as a Coca-Cola stock-ist (delivering the Coke product) and is now Nairobi Bottler's most recognized distributor. Her MDC operates under the contraction of her name, "Rosinje," and her whole family has benefited as they gain first-hand experience in how to run a business. Stella Msangi, owner of Stella MDC in the Masaka District, Dar es Salaam, has a similar story. She also has a family that benefits from her ability to work while at the same time caring for her young children. The MDC concept has given Stella and her husband ownership experience after they purchased the storage facility in which the MDC operates. These women are examples of the economic opportunities that the MDC model has created for female entrepreneurs. Over a thousand of these businesses in Africa are owned by women, and more than 50 percent of new MDCs created since 2009 are owned and run by women. The use of micro-distribution centers has continued to grow. In countries such as Kenya, Tanzania, Uganda, Ethiopia, and Mozambique, these centers represent the vast majority of sales, and their use is growing rapidly in North and West Africa—particularly in Nigeria, where over 80 percent of the micro-distribution centers are owned by women.

The MDC model was initially developed to solve a business prob-lem, but at the same time it had far-reaching benefits for local com-munities, especially in developing countries. Coca-Cola has not only developed a model that will continue to expand its market into the hardest-to-reach places, but has also facilitated learning in how the pri-vate sector can accelerate the achievement of the Millennium Develop-ment Goals. The learning only grows richer as the model continues to expand, and it is a significant contribution to both business and the global community.

Coca-Cola has also looked at other areas in the value chain to cre-ate economic opportunity. In Uganda and Kenya, Coca-Cola identi-fied an opportunity to invest in local economies by inviting mango and passion fruit farmers to be suppliers to the company. Project Nurture is a four-year, $11.5 million program, in partnership with the Bill & Melinda Gates Foundation and TechnoServe, to double the income of more than 50,000 small fruit farmers by 2014. The farmers provide fruit for juices produced locally in the Coca-Cola portfolio and in turn receive training on how to improve the quality of their fruit, production methods, access to credit sources, and overall organization of their farmer groups.

The Haiti Hope Project is another undertaking by the Coca-Cola Company to invest in local economies through expanding its supplier base to include Haitian mango farmers. This is a five-year, $9.5 million partnership with the Multilateral Investment Fund of the Inter-American Development Bank, USAID, and TechnoServe which started in September 2010, with the goal of doubling the income of 25,000 farmers over five years. In January 2011, Odwalla (a beverage company purchased by Coca-Cola in 2001) launched the flavor "Haiti Hope Mango Tango" to replace "Haiti Hope Mango Lime-Aid" and committed to donating ten cents for every bottle sold, up to $500,000 per year of the initiative. The Haiti Hope project highlights Coca-Cola's commitment to disaster relief and repairing economies. These projects truly emphasize the importance of evaluating the entire value chain when looking for opportunities to build up local economies and the importance of partnering with NGOs for sustainable and successful outcomes.

STRENGTHENING THE SOCIAL FABRIC

Coca-Cola leverages this same strategy in engaging with critical social issues. The company knows it is responsible not only for the well-being of its employees but for the entire value chain from suppliers to consumers. Coca-Cola knows that communities need to be healthy in order for businesses to succeed. Suppliers, employees, consumers, and their families need communities that are safe, stable, and enable growth. The protection of basic human rights is non-negotiable for the Coca-Cola Company, and it has developed a human rights statement guided by international human rights standards. Coca-Cola seeks not only to meet these standards but also to exceed them, using its resources to address social issues in its sphere of influence. Through partnerships on a global and local level, for example, Coca-Cola is actively engaged in efforts to end child labor, especially in the harvesting of sugar cane in countries including El Salvador, Honduras, Mexico, and the Philippines. The company is also committed to the prevention of human trafficking and forced labor, and it mandates that suppliers adhere to both a workplace rights policy and supplier guiding principles. Coca-Cola performs supplier assessments to ensure responsible practices and policies, and the company provides guidance on proactive steps suppliers can take to align themselves with the guiding principles.

In 2009 Coca-Cola became a founding member of the Global Business Initiative on Human Rights, in partnership with the UN Global Compact, to focus on human rights in emerging markets. This organization provides a forum for companies to collaborate on issues and share best practices. Coke also partners with the Danish Institute for Human Rights and Aim Progress to advocate for the protection of human rights and facilitate learning in the business community on these issues. These partnerships have enabled the company not only to contribute its resources but also to benefit from knowledge-sharing and from the experience other stakeholders bring to the table. The partnerships also hold participating members accountable while providing critical tools and support.

Inclusion and diversity are important to the Coca-Cola Company, and it works to advance these principles with respect to both suppliers and employees. In 2009 the company spent over $460 million with minority and women-owned business enterprises, and over a quarter of the company's leadership is female. Coca-Cola has developed a Women's Leadership Council tasked with accelerating the development and retention of female leaders within the company. In September 2010, the company announced "Five by Twenty," a global women's initiative to empower five million women across the business system by 2020. The initiative will focus on providing training, access to financing, and networks of peers and mentors in order to overcome the obstacles that prevent women from growing their businesses.

The physical health of people throughout the value chain is another priority for the Coca-Cola Company. The prevention and treatment of HIV/AIDS continues to be a critical area of involvement. Coca-Cola has developed a comprehensive, continent-wide program in Africa that benefits over 60,000 associates and their families. The company also seeks to impact communities through sponsorship of programs conducted across Africa with strategic partners: the African Network for Children Orphaned and At Risk (ANCHOR), the African Broadcast Media Partnership Against HIV/AIDS, and Dance4Life.

Coca-Cola recognized the opportunity to make a unique contribution to the fight against disease in Tanzania by leveraging its supply chain capabilities to improve access to medicines. Coke partners with the Global Fund to Fight AIDS, Tuberculosis, and Malaria, and Tanzania is one of the largest recipients of financial support from the Global Fund. Coke embarked on a five-month project with Accenture Development Partnerships to share appropriate aspects of its supply chain to help address the challenges that hinder the distribution of these critical medications.

Safe drinking water and sanitation are also imperative to disease prevention. To date, Coca-Cola has 320 community water programs in 86 countries that aim to support access to water and sanitation as well as improve education and awareness. In 2009 Coca-Cola announced the Replenish Africa Initiative (RAIN), a six-year, $30 million commitment to provide access to safe drinking water for communities throughout Africa. By 2015, RAIN will provide at least two million Africans with clean water and sanitation.

Coca-Cola recognizes its significant opportunity to contribute to global health through the beverages it produces. The company aims to increase the number of fortified beverages it offers and has developed a variety of products with added vitamins, minerals, and other beneficial ingredients. Beverage innovation with consumer health in mind birthed a product in the Philippines called NutriJuice, which is fortified with vitamins and minerals to address iron deficiency among children. Coca-Cola also introduced the "mini can" in 2009—a 7.5-ounce, 90-calorie serving that helps consumers manage their portion sizes and caloric intake. In 2010, the company launched six hundred new products globally, which included portion-controlled options and more than 150 low- and no-calorie beverages. Coca-Cola is using its core capabilities to create products that address the global need for healthier choices.

INVESTING IN THE ENVIRONMENT

Coca-Cola recognizes that communities cannot thrive economically and socially at the expense of the environment they inhabit. The company knows that it will not be able to produce its products or find consumers to purchase them if the health of the environment in which it operates is compromised. A healthy ecosystem provides the highest quality product resources and contributes to the health and stability of local communities and the people who live and work there—which are building blocks for a successful business environment.

Coca-Cola's business depends on a healthy, sustainable agricultural supply chain because agricultural products are key ingredients in almost every one of the company's beverages. Coca-Cola began this journey at the very root of its global supply chain by incorporating sustainable agriculture criteria into its long-term ingredient sourcing plans for sugarcane, oranges, and corn. The company knew it needed to engage both suppliers and other organizations with more expertise in environmental issues. Coca-Cola developed a partnership with the World Wildlife Fund and sugarcane producers in Australia, Belize, Brazil, El Salvador, Guatemala, Honduras, and South Africa, to launch pilot projects that demonstrated innovative growing and production methods that could benefit producers, communities, and the environment. The company also became a member of the Better Sugarcane Initiative, which develops standards for sustainable sugarcane production. Project Nurture and the Haiti Hope Project, mentioned above, will enable the company to locally source more of its ingredients for certain products, which will also contribute to the reduction of environmental impacts. Coca-Cola knows that helping farmers optimize agricultural practices to increase crop yields and reduce crop costs is strategic and good for both business and the environment.

Coca-Cola recognizes the importance of staying continually engaged in these issues, not just to satisfy the environmental community but, more importantly, to ensure the long-term health and success of its business. The company knows that partnerships are critical and has joined the Sustainable Agriculture Initiative in order to continue to engage stakeholders throughout their agricultural supply chain. This allows Coca-Cola to benefit from and contribute to shared knowledge and to support the development and implementation of internationally accepted criteria for sustainable agriculture.

Water is easily the most essential ingredient in the vast majority of Coca-Cola's products and is needed to produce the other ingredients on which the company relies. Water is also critical to the economic and social health of the communities in which Coca-Cola does business. Water is quickly becoming a scarce, if not threatened, resource in almost every corner of the globe; by 2025, two-thirds of the world's population may live in areas with moderate to severe water shortages. The Coca-Cola Company became one of the first six companies to commit to the UN Global Compact CEO Water Mandate in 2007. This unique public-private initiative assists companies in the development, implementation, and disclosure of water sustainability policies and practices. For Coca-Cola, responsible water stewardship is becoming non-negotiable, and collaboration with other businesses, governments, and civil society organizations has enabled the company to develop ways to make a positive difference in addressing the world's water challenges.

Coca-Cola has decided to focus its efforts on three main areas: improving water-use efficiency, treating all wastewater from manufacturing, and replenishing water through the support of healthy watersheds and community water programs. The company has been able to improve its system-wide water efficiency for seven straight years. Eighty-nine percent of its global facilities (approximately 95 percent of reported volume) are now compliant with wastewater discharge standards, which represents a major company commitment given that 70 percent of industrial wastewater is currently released untreated in the developing world. Coca-Cola has 320 community water programs in 86 countries, including watershed protection, community water access, rain water harvesting, reforestation, and agricultural water use efficiency. In India the company is now a "net zero" user of groundwater by recharging the amount of groundwater used in operations. This is happening through support of rainwater harvesting, drip irrigation, and other initiatives, such as helping restore traditional water storage systems that local communities use. Such projects, including the RAIN commitment mentioned above, were made possible only through partnerships with organizations such as the World Wildlife Fund, USAID, CARE, the United Nations Development Program, and others.

Accountability is a critical factor in these improvements. In 2009, Coca-Cola worked with external experts to quantify the impact of community water partnership work. Based on this work, the company estimated that 22 percent (29.4 billion liters) of the water used in finished beverages was replenished in 2009.

Coca-Cola's manufacturing and distribution processes also present a significant opportunity for the company to reduce its environmental impact. In light of this, Coca-Cola has committed to use the best possible mix of energy sources and improve overall energy efficiency. The largest component of the company's climate footprint is found in the refrigeration equipment used to keep beverages cold. Coca-Cola made the decision to invest more than $60 million over the past decade to advance climate-friendly cooling technologies and has transitioned to HFC-free insulation foam for all new refrigeration equipment. It now has more than 277,000 units of HFC-free refrigerated equipment in use and has reached its goal of improving the energy efficiency of coolers by 40 percent. In 2012 Coca-Cola of Japan announced a new type of vending machine that does not require electricity during the daytime to keep drinks cold, reducing the energy footprint by as much as 95 percent. Coca-Cola leveraged its partnership with the World Wildlife Fund to set global targets through 2015 for energy efficiency and climate protection, compared with 2004 baselines. The company aims to grow business but not system-wide carbon emissions from manufacturing operations, as well as reducing absolute emissions from manufacturing operations in developed countries by 5 percent.

Coca-Cola also sees the reduction of greenhouse gas emissions through renewable energy resources as a strategic imperative. Some bottling partners are now installing solar panels on their facilities to help reduce energy use and greenhouse gas emissions, and additional investments are being made in biodiesel and wind power generation technologies.

Packaging plays an essential role for Coca-Cola's business in meeting consumer needs and preventing waste by protecting products during delivery. The company has adopted a vision of zero waste and has made significant contributions to the beverage industry in this area. Coca-Cola led the market in advancing breakthrough technologies for increasing recycled content and renewable material use in beverage packaging. Since introducing the first beverage bottle containing recycled content material in 1991, the company has invested in building state-of-the-art bottle-to-bottle recycling facilities around the world to increase the availability of food-quality recycled material. After it introduced the PlantBottle, a fully recyclable PET plastic bottle made with up to 30 percent renewable material, it didn't take long for other companies to follow Coca-Cola's lead, and the entire industry is now seeing marked improvements. With PlantBottle™ technology, Coca-Cola aims to reduce and eventually completely replace the use of non-renewable fossil fuels in plastic packaging.

Coca-Cola has not overlooked the importance of improving its current packaging, and has reduced the weight of the 8-ounce glass bottle by more than 50 percent, 12-ounce aluminum can by more than 30 percent, and 20-ounce PET bottle by more than 25 percent. Its system also contributes hundreds of millions of dollars toward collection of bottles and cans for recycling. Today, Coca-Cola recovers approximately 35 percent of the equivalent bottles and cans placed in the market and invests directly in seven plastic bottle-to-bottle recycling plants, including the world's largest in Spartanburg, South Carolina.

Coca-Cola is continually looking for small ways to improve current processes, while at the same time setting ambitious goals for the future.

Guided by the seven areas of focus laid out in the Live Positively Campaign (the driving force of sustainability at the company), Coca-Cola has developed a "2020 Vision" for economic, social, and environmental sustainability. As noted above, the company aims to empower five million women throughout its system by 2020, and it will continue to give back 1 percent of operating income to help develop and sustain communities worldwide. The company aims to achieve a 98 percent performance level for company-owned and company-managed facilities, upholding the standards set in its *Workplace Rights Policy*. It has committed itself to supporting at least one physical activity program in every country in which it operates, and it supports the Healthy Weight Commitment Foundation in reducing the total annual calories consumed in the United States by 1.5 trillion. The Coca-Cola Company will continue to develop products fortified with additional nutrients to meet global consumer needs, investing more than $50 million in research.

The company wants to improve water-use efficiency by 20 percent, and it is committed to returning to communities and nature an amount of water equivalent to what is used in all beverages and production processes by 2020. It is aiming to improve the energy efficiency of all cooling equipment by 40 percent and plans to phase out the use of HFCs in all new cold drink equipment by 2015. The company has a goal of sourcing 25 percent of PET plastic from recycled or renewable material by 2015 and improving packaging material efficiency per liter of product sold by 7 percent. It also aims to recover 50 percent of the equivalent bottles and cans used annually. Coca-Cola has committed to grow its business but not its system-wide carbon emissions from manufacturing operations through 2015, and to reduce absolute emissions from manufacturing operations in Annex 1 (developed) countries by 5 percent by 2015, compared with a 2004 baseline.

The Coca-Cola Company knows that these goals are ambitious but achievable through collaboration. Strategic partnerships have been the key to success in the past and will continue to play a central role in the future. As a leader among the UN Global Compact companies, Coca-Cola not only advances the Millennium Development Goals but also provides many best practices for other companies to follow.

NOTES

1. *2009/2010 The Coca-Cola Company Sustainability Review*, 2; available at http://www.coca-colacompany.com/stories/sustainability-reports.

2. Jane Nelson, Eriko Ishikawa, and Alexis Geaneotes, *Developing Inclusive Business Models: A Review of Coca-Cola's Manual Distribution Centers in Ethiopia and Tanzania* (Harvard Kennedy School and International Finance Corporation, 2009), 6; available at http://www.hks.harvard.edu/m-rcbg /CSRI/publications/other_10_MDC_report.pdf.

6 | Achieving the UN Millennium Development Goals

The Contribution of Novartis

York Lunau

Novartis has been contributing to the realization of the UN Millennium Development Goals since their launch in 2000. First and foremost, Novartis contributes through its core business—the discovery, development, and marketing of innovative drugs, helping to save millions of lives and improve quality of life for hundreds of millions of patients. Since not every patient has access to these drugs, Novartis carries out extensive access-to-medicine programs, such as drug donations, selling at cost, or patient assistance programs. In line with its core business, Novartis also conducts voluntary, not-for-profit research into neglected diseases such as malaria, dengue fever, and tuberculosis. The first part of this essay is dedicated to the contribution Novartis makes toward the achievement of the MDGs.

Beyond the core business, philanthropic commitments by Novartis contribute specifically to the realization of the MDGs. The Novartis Foundation for Sustainable Development (NFSD), fully funded by Novartis, is a competence center for corporate responsibility and international health, focused on the poorest of the poor. It is committed to "development with a human face," and its supported projects in developing countries are largely focused on the achievement of the Millennium Development Goals—particularly in relation to health. The second part of this essay covers the contribution of the Novartis Foundation for Sustainable Development to the achievement of the MDGs.

CONTRIBUTING TO SOCIETY THROUGH CORE BUSINESS

Both the commitment and contribution of Novartis to achieving the Millennium Development Goals are rooted in its core mission—to discover, develop, and successfully market innovative products that prevent and cure diseases, ease suffering, and enhance quality of life. This core business is, in turn, grounded in the Novartis definition of corporate citizenship, which stipulates that business success must be attained with integrity and in an environmentally sustainable manner. As a responsible corporate citizen, Novartis strives to be responsive to an array of stakeholders, reflected by four pillars that underpin the company's corporate citizenship commitment:

1. Patients
2. People and Communities
3. Environment
4. Ethical Business Conduct

Patients benefit from a diversified but focused portfolio of innovative pharmaceuticals, generic medicines, and consumer health products, as well as vaccines and diagnostic tools. The Novartis Pharmaceuticals division focuses on cardiovascular diseases, cancer, mental disorders, such as Alzheimer's, and rare diseases, such as Muckle-Wells syndrome. The Sandoz division is the second-largest producer of generic medicines in the world, with a range of products including treatments for tuberculosis (TB) and epilepsy. Among the vaccines developed by the Vaccines and Diagnostics division to prevent viral and bacterial diseases, Novartis offers a single vaccine against five deadly childhood illnesses: Haemophilus influenza type b, diphtheria, tetanus, pertussis, and hepatitis B. In this manner, the core business of Novartis contributes to achieving the MDGs by helping to combat disease and promote well-being. In 2009, an estimated 930 million people were protected and treated with Novartis products. Nevertheless, the company recognizes that many people in the world cannot easily access much-needed health care solutions. Therefore, of this 930 million, 79.5 million disadvantaged people living in developed and developing countries benefited from Novartis access-to-medicine programs valued at USD 1.5 billion. Some 94 percent of the people benefiting from these programs are malaria patients, through the at-cost provision of Coartem® for public sector use. Another example is the Patient Assistance Program (PAP) for treatment against two rare forms of cancer: chronic myeloid leukemia and gastrointestinal stromal tumors (Gleevec®/Glivec® and Tasigna®). Diverse access modalities are applied, ranging from copayment (patient/Novartis) and shared contribution (Novartis/other organizations) to full donation. In 2009, 38,000 patients were reached in this manner.

Other global access-to-medicine initiatives include treatments against malaria, TB, and liver fluke. In India, Novartis has introduced a social business model, Arogya Parivar—meaning "healthy family" in Sanskrit—which targets the health needs of rural populations living at the bottom of the pyramid. Arogya Parivar aims to improve access to health care through a network of community health educators, mainly women, who help promote disease awareness among villagers. They refer patients to rural practitioners who facilitate treatment compliance. In collaboration with city doctors, Arogya Parivar also organizes health camps, free of charge, wherever there is no rural practitioner in the village. A selected range of generic and over-the-counter drugs produced by Novartis is available through rural pharmacies. Emphasis is laid on products such as calcium or zinc formulations, which are simple to use, offered in small packs, and target maternal and child health.

In addition, the Novartis Institutes for Developing World Medical Research conduct pro bono research on malaria, TB, dengue fever, and diarrheal diseases. These initiatives complement core business activities in combating disease, reducing child mortality, and improving maternal health.

As a health care company, the prime contribution of Novartis is directed toward reaching the health-related MDGs. Yet it is also active in realizing other MDGs, such as promoting gender equality, empowering women, and eradicating poverty. Within the core business, this is visible in relation to Novartis employees, their families, and the communities in which company operations are located. The Novartis commitment to people and communities includes a group-wide initiative to promote diversity and inclusion. Diversity means recognizing and embracing the existence of individual differences such as gender, ethnic origin, and religion, but also styles of thinking and leadership. Inclusion is about creating an environment that leverages such individual differences by providing opportunities to all associates to contribute to business goals. Part of this diversity and inclusion initiative is to ensure fair and equitable working conditions for all employees. Novartis believes that a diverse organization is more likely to be a creative and innovative one—and one better prepared to serve its customers' needs.

In another pioneering endeavor, Novartis was the first multinational company to establish living wage levels for employees across its worldwide operations. The aim is to ensure a decent minimum living standard that guarantees affordability of basic necessities, including food, clothing, accommodation, schooling, and medical care in a given local context. These wage levels are updated annually, and any salaries falling below those levels are adjusted according to annual fluctuations in inflation, food costs, and exchange rates. In 2009, for the first time, no salaries below living wage levels were found, compared to 93 cases in 2005. Such initiatives not only create a conducive working environment, fostering employee engagement and resulting in improved productivity, profitability, and customer focus, but they also contribute to sustainable livelihoods in the wider community and hence to the eradication of poverty as stipulated in MDG 1. The collaboration with Indian NGOs and the nonprofit business association Business for Social Responsibility to define and measure living wages around the world is a tangible reflection of the Novartis commitment to MDG 8.

Ensuring environmental sustainability—as stipulated in MDG 7—is an integral part of company strategy. Novartis considers that careful stewardship of natural resources is not only important for the company but also critical for society and future generations. In addition to minimizing negative impacts and managing risks, Novartis is committed to providing safe workplaces for all associates and third-party personnel through its Health, Safety & Environment (HSE) management and reporting systems. This commitment extends to minimizing the impact of pharmaceuticals in the environment by managing its products over their entire life cycle. To tackle greenhouse gas emissions, Novartis has devised a climate and energy strategy comprising both internal and external measures to reduce its carbon footprint. Together, these initiatives help support targets 7a and 7b of MDG 7, namely, to "integrate the principles of sustainable development," "reverse loss of environmental resources," and "reduce biodiversity loss."

The aim of the Novartis commitment to ethical business conduct is to ensure that decisions are made responsibly, sustainably, and with an awareness of their societal impact. To achieve this, a set of core values and ethical standards has been established that gives behavioral guidance to associates with regard to all business-related activities and processes (e.g., leadership, performance management). For instance, the Novartis Integrity and Compliance program has developed training courses on the Novartis Code of Conduct and Corporate Citizenship Guidelines that deal with marketing practices, bribery, and corruption. By addressing the protection of human rights such as nondiscrimination due to gender, age, race, or disability, as well as respect for labor standards (e.g., fair working hours, holidays, or maternity leave), these courses support MDGs 1 and 3. They are compulsory for all employees.

In the same spirit, human rights compliance assessments have been piloted, using a questionnaire-based self-assessment tool developed by the Danish Institute for Human Rights and the Novartis Foundation for Sustainable Development. So far, Novartis country offices in Turkey, Taiwan, South Africa, and Indonesia have participated. Suppliers to Novartis must adhere to a specific Third-Party Code which defines minimum standards and is used internally in procurement processes. Last but not least, employees have the option of reporting to a Business Practice Officer (BPO) any incident of misconduct or human rights violation within the company's sphere of influence.

The following sections give four examples of how Novartis contributes to the achievement of different MDGs. The first example focuses on environmental sustainability, and the next three target patients and their health.

ENVIRONMENTAL SUSTAINABILITY THROUGH ENERGY EFFICIENCY AND CARBON OFFSETS

Although pharmaceutical companies operate with relatively low energy requirements compared to other industries, still, Novartis is committed to environmentally sound business conduct. To promote environmental sustainability in its business activities, Novartis focuses on reducing energy consumption, in particular CO_2 emissions. This is in line with the first target of MDG 7, namely, to "integrate the principles of sustainable development into country policies and programs and reverse the loss of environmental resources." While this MDG primarily targets nation-states, Novartis made a voluntary commitment to the Kyoto Protocol in 2005. This is driven both by a moral imperative—because climate protection is the right thing to do—and by a business case: using less energy and more renewable sources will reduce the company's energy bill in the medium to long term. Moreover, increasing carbon dioxide emissions and associated climate change will affect biodiversity and water supply, both crucial factors for pharmaceutical companies. Biodiversity loss and rainfall reduction would harm the product pipeline and production processes.

In line with the Kyoto Protocol's binding targets for greenhouse gas (GHG) emission reduction, by 2012 Novartis reduced its annual on-site GHG emissions by 5 percent, using 1990 as a baseline—an ambitious goal given the company's expanding business activities. This amounted to a reduction of about 30 percent of GHG emissions compared to 2005. To reach this goal and drastically reduce emissions—by approximately 100,000 tons of CO_2 per year—Novartis pursued a dual strategy. On the one hand, the company aimed to improve efficiency of energy use in existing business operations and adopt renewable energy sources wherever economically viable. On the other hand, in lieu of purchasing certified emission reduction credits to compensate for exceeding emissions limits, Novartis has set up two carbon-offset projects in Argentina and Mali.

Examples of renewable energy solutions include boilers fired by bagasse (sugar cane–based residue) in Mahad, India, or wood chips in Wehr, Germany, solar panels in California, and a "carbon-free campus" at Novartis headquarters in Basel, Switzerland. The bagasse and wood chips are used at production sites to power boilers for steam generation. In Vacaville, California, four thousand photovoltaic solar panels have been arrayed on 20,000 square meters to supply 20 percent of the site's electricity needs. This installation has tripled the company's solar electricity capacity and will eliminate 1,400 metric tons of CO_2 emissions per year. Last but not least, Novartis is relying exclusively on renewable energy in the transformation of its headquarters in Basel, by cooling the buildings with Rhine river water and heating them using incinerated waste. The resultant steam is free from carbon dioxide. Solar panels on some Novartis campus buildings complement this energy mix.

One major carbon-offset project, a forestry plantation in Argentina, was started in 2007. Three million trees have been planted on 34 square kilometers of former farmland between 2007 and 2009 to serve as natural forest. The plantation has already received Forest Stewardship Council certification—the most widely recognized label for sustainable wood products. This project contributes to counteracting deforestation, as stipulated in the first target of the MDG on environmental sustainability. In addition to environmental benefits, this sustainable forestry project is improving local livelihoods by creating jobs via its wood products business, thereby helping to reach the second target of MDG 1: "Achieve full and productive employment and decent work for all, including women and young people." Thanks to this project, Novartis was able to offset approximately 125,000 tons of its carbon dioxide emissions between 2007 and 2012.

In Western Mali, local small-scale farmers have voluntarily planted 1,800 hectares of jatropha on their own land. Selling the jatropha seeds brings cash income to farmers, and demand is steadily increasing. The seeds can be used to produce biofuel to generate renewable electricity (e.g., for rural electrification), and their residue can serve as a much-needed biological fertilizer. As with the forestry project in Argentina, this income-generating opportunity contributes to achieving the second target of MDG 1. In order to ensure food security, the project encourages farmers to plant jatropha in association with food crops (agriforestry). This initiative enables Novartis to obtain certified emission reductions from carbon sequestration (thanks to the plantations) and biofuel production. Estimated emission reductions from the Mali project amounted to approximately 75,000 tons by 2012.

Both projects will be certified under the Clean Development Mechanism, a scheme run by the United Nations agency overseeing the Kyoto Protocol, or under voluntary carbon-offset schemes. The Novartis Health, Safety & Environment team has forged partnerships around these two carbon-offset projects with a range of stakeholders, including carbon asset management companies, forestry contractors, local entrepreneurs, and others across Argentina and Mali. This underlines the company's commitment to MDG 8, whereby the special needs of least developed and landlocked countries like Mali are addressed and new technologies made available.

COMBATING MALARIA THROUGH
GLOBAL PARTNERSHIPS

Malaria is a major killer. An estimated 243 million people are affected annually and around 863,000 die each year of the disease, mostly children under the age of five. Although the global TB burden is slowly decreasing, two million people still die every year, and access to quality TB care is a major challenge. Overall achievement of MDG 6 therefore remains out of reach, but Novartis has contributed to target 6c, to "have halted by 2010 and begun to reverse the incidence of malaria and other major diseases," directly through the discovery, development, and delivery of safe and efficacious medicines.

The main channel for this contribution is the Novartis Malaria Initiatives. Since 2001, the company has provided its artemisinin-based combination therapy (ACT) Artemether/Lumefantrine (Coartem®) without profit for public-sector use in developing countries. Development and distribution of this product showcases global partnership at work, as called for under MDG 8: together with its Chinese partners, Novartis transformed an herbal remedy against fevers, used for centuries in traditional Chinese medicine, into an effective modern treatment that earned regulatory approval in both developing and developed countries, including the United States.

To make Coartem® widely available, Novartis opted for a dual branding and tiered pricing system. While the drug is sold at a commercial price under the brand name Riamet® in wealthy, nonendemic countries, it is sold as Coartem® in the developing world.

In malaria-endemic countries, three pricing models exist. First, in the public and not-for-profit health sector, Coartem® is sold at an average price of USD 0.76 per adult treatment and USD 0.36 per child treatment (as of 2011). Under an agreement with the World Health Organization (WHO), endemic countries can order treatments through the WHO, with funding mainly provided through grants of the Global Fund to fight HIV/AIDS, TB, and Malaria. Novartis ensures delivery of the medicines, including insurance and quality control, and the WHO is responsible for distribution and technical advice in recipient countries. Other international organizations, such as the United Nations Children's Fund (UNICEF), the United Nations Development Program (UNDP), Crown Agents, and the IDA Foundation order directly from Novartis.

Second, in the private sector, which provides treatment and care for around 60 percent of the population in many countries in sub-Saharan Africa, Coartem® is sold at a higher price in the premium sector, that is, pharmacies. Third, in the non-premium private sector, Novartis has granted low prices—similar to those in the public sector—to pilot initiatives such as the ADDO (Accredited Drug Dispensing Outlets) program in Tanzania. These initiatives have paved the way for the Affordable Medicines Facility for malaria (AMFm), which aims to make ACTs widely available through the non-premium private sector at an affordable price. Together, these varied collaborations contribute to target 8e: "in cooperation with pharmaceutical companies, provide access to affordable essential drugs in developing countries."

As of 2011, Novartis delivered more than 340 million Coartem® treatments worldwide without profit, saving an estimated 850,000 lives. In combination with preventive measures such as long-lasting, insecticide-treated bed nets and indoor residual spraying, the introduction of Coartem® as a first-line treatment has reduced child mortality by more than 60 percent in countries such as Rwanda, Ethiopia, and Zanzibar. Moreover, in collaboration with the Medicines for Malaria Venture (MMV), a pediatric formulation called Coartem® Dispersible has been developed. It is sweet-tasting and designed to disperse quickly in small amounts of water. Though children account for 90 percent of malaria-related deaths, there was no treatment formulated for infants and children: Coartem® Dispersible is the first and only ACT designed specifically for this critical patient group. Both formulations, conventional and dispersible, have cure rates above 97 percent.

In addition to substantially reducing child mortality (MDG 4), the Novartis Malaria Initiatives also contribute to improving maternal health (MDG 5). In collaboration with the WHO, the Malaria Initiatives helped evaluate the efficacy and safety of ACT in pregnant women. This research contributed to the evidence base that ACTs can be used during pregnancy, as stipulated in the revised malaria treatment guidelines issued by the WHO.

Education and information being a key factor in disease control, the Malaria Initiatives include training material for health care workers to reinforce proper treatment instructions as well as information for patients and mothers or other caregivers, with pictograms on blister packs to ensure patient adherence. In 2009, Coartem® Dispersible was acknowledged by the Healthcare Compliance Packaging Council for its unique packaging, featuring pictographic instructions especially useful among illiterate populations. Up to twice a year, Novartis brings together the managers of national malaria control programs across sub-Saharan Africa for best practice workshops. This allows an exchange of experience on community awareness, health care worker training, stock management, and distribution, as well as on health impact measurement.

Innovation and new technologies can help expand access to medicines in the most remote areas, as illustrated by the SMS for Life pilot program led by Novartis in Tanzania. This twenty-one-week pilot enhanced the visibility of antimalarial stock levels in public health facilities to help eliminate stock outs. In collaboration with the Tanzanian Ministry of Health and Social Welfare, the Roll Back Malaria Partnership, IBM, and Vodafone, the initiative used mobile phones, SMS messaging, and electronic mapping technology. At the start of the pilot, only 23 percent of the 129 health facilities had all five ACT dosage forms in stock; by the end, the rate had increased to 74 percent. Overall, the SMS for Life team found 94 percent data accuracy between the data submitted by SMS and the physical stock counts. The scale-up to cover 5,000 health facilities in all 131 districts of Tanzania was scheduled for late 2010, with the expectation of expanding SMS for Life to other African countries and include medicines for diseases other than malaria.

DONATING DRUGS AGAINST LEPROSY, TB, AND LIVER FLUKE

Through its partnership with the WHO, Novartis has been donating Multi-Drug Therapy (MDT) for the treatment of leprosy to all patients worldwide since 2000, leading to the cure of more than five million people. MDT comprises three antibiotics, two of which have been developed by Novartis. Most of the global supply of MDT is delivered through this collaboration with WHO. Before 2000, the drugs were provided free by two Japanese foundations. Since 1984, a total of 14 million patients have been cured, shrinking the global number of detected cases to 250,000. Only two countries have not yet reached the elimination target (less than one case per 10,000 inhabitants). The Novartis Foundation for Sustainable Development has been supporting this drug donation program since 1986 in many countries, including India, Sri Lanka, and Brazil. Social marketing campaigns have helped reduce the stigma of leprosy as a disease associated with deformities and have resulted in earlier detection, diagnosis, and treatment. Integration of leprosy diagnosis and treatment into all general health services has occurred, while mobile clinics have improved access.

Although hidden cases persist in former high-burden countries such as India or Brazil, the fight against leprosy can be considered one of the biggest public health success stories. Novartis is committed to providing free MDT and remains an engaged partner in striving for a world free of leprosy.

Between 2005 and 2012, Novartis undertook to donate 500,000 treatments against TB to adult patients in Tanzania. As the in-country average annual caseload amounts to 60,000, this donation covered the entire nation for about eight years. The gold standard fixed-dose combination therapy, reducing the treatment period from eight to six months, is made available through the Global Drug Facility of the Stop TB Partnership. The Novartis Foundation and the Tanzanian Ministry of Health and Social Welfare complemented the drug donation with the introduction of a Patient-Centered Treatment approach. This gives patients the choice of taking the treatment at home or at a health facility. In 2009, 73,000 patients in Tanzania were treated, thanks to this program.

Finally, in collaboration with the WHO, Novartis also donates treatments against liver fluke (fasciolasis), a disease prevalent in South America and East Asia. As of 2011, Novartis manufactures the only WHO-recommended drug against liver fluke. In 2009, 387,000 patients in Peru, Bolivia, and Yemen benefited from this program.

All three donation programs are conducted in collaboration with supranational agencies such as the WHO, embodying target 8e, namely, "in cooperation with pharmaceutical companies, [to] provide access to affordable essential drugs in developing countries."

NOVARTIS INSTITUTES FOR DEVELOPING WORLD MEDICAL RESEARCH: VACCINES AND TREATMENTS AGAINST NEGLECTED DISEASES

Novartis is at the forefront of research and early-stage development of vaccines and treatments against major killers such as malaria, TB, dengue fever, and diarrheal diseases. While TB kills an estimated two million people annually, 20,000 deaths occur every year due to dengue hemorrhagic fever, and diarrheal diseases cause more than two million fatalities each year. Research on neglected diseases is conducted by two dedicated research institutes at Novartis— the Novartis Institute for Tropical Diseases (NITD) in Singapore, and the Novartis Vaccines Institute for Global Health (NVGH) in Siena. Both form part of the Novartis Institutes for Developing World Medical Research (NIDWMR), which mobilize the most advanced biomedical knowledge and cutting-edge technologies to discover vaccines and drugs for neglected diseases of the developing world.

While NITD focuses on dengue fever, drug-resistant TB, and— since 2005—on malaria, NVGH concentrates on developing a broad range vaccine against salmonella infections, for example, the bacterium Salmonella Typhi that causes typhoid fever. Clinical testing of a conjugate vaccine for Salmonella Typhi started in 2010. The aim is to develop a cost-effective vaccine for six-week-old children, since they usually are brought to a health facility at this age for vaccination. NITD succeeded in discovering spiroindolones, a new class of compounds to fight malaria parasites, and received the 2009 Project of the Year award from Medicines for Malaria Venture. The institute also offers teaching and training for graduate students and post-doctoral fellows.

Both institutes operate through global partnerships, thus contributing to MDG 8. NITD was set up as a public-private partnership between Novartis and the Singapore Economic Development Board (EDB). Its malaria research is being supported by the EDB, Medicines for Malaria Venture, and the Wellcome Trust. NVGH works in partnership with the Global Alliance for Vaccines and Immunization (GAVI), the Bill & Melinda Gates Foundation, and the Wellcome Trust. Vaccines and medicines discovered by both institutes will be made available on a not-for-profit basis to poor patients in developing countries.

Funding neglected disease research remains a challenge. To this end, Novartis has spearheaded efforts to establish a multi-stakeholder fund for research and development for neglected diseases. The fund would allocate resources to conduct clinical trials on the most promising compounds and would be overseen by a board composed of representatives from governments, donors, and other stakeholders.

Finally, Novartis has also granted access to its compound library to the Drugs for Neglected Diseases initiative (DNDi), the Institute for OneWorld Health (iOWH), and MMV, to support their discovery-stage research on sleeping sickness and Kala-Azar, a deadly disease transmitted by infected female sand flies.

As with Novartis access-to-medicine programs on malaria, TB, leprosy, and liver fluke, these research and development initiatives address target 6c of MDG 6, to "have halted by 2010 and begun to reverse the incidence of malaria and other major diseases." In addition, they contribute to reducing child mortality (MDG 4) and improving maternal health (MDG 5).

THE NOVARTIS FOUNDATION FOR SUSTAINABLE DEVELOPMENT

Innovative Philanthropy for Better Health

For over thirty years, the Novartis Foundation for Sustainable Development (NFSD) has served as a competence center for corporate responsibility and international health, focused on disadvantaged people in developing countries. The foundation is committed to "development with a human face."

The foundation operates independently from the commercial day-to-day business of Novartis but is an integral part of the company's corporate responsibility portfolio, focusing on those who would not otherwise be reached through the core business. Forming a bridge between Novartis and the outside world, the foundation facilitates dialogue between the private sector, the state, and civil society, driving innovation and pioneering new concepts for jointly improving the health situation of disadvantaged people worldwide. The foundation operates in three overlapping modes: project and program work; dialogue and networking; and think tank activities.

Through project and program work, the foundation contributes to the achievement of the health-related Millennium Development Goals 4, 5, and 6 by strengthening health care systems in developing countries and ensuring that medicines donated by Novartis reach patients in need. In all projects, the foundation adopts a comprehensive approach embracing the other MDGs where possible, namely, gender equality and empowerment of women. To guarantee sustainability, the foundation deploys a business mindset and outcome-based thinking in all projects.

NFSD-supported projects are focused on improving access to health care, strengthening human resources in health care, and empowering vulnerable groups.

To increase its impact, the Novartis Foundation works with local, national, and international partners, in line with MDG 8 on global partnerships for development. One of the partners is the Millennium Villages Project (MVP), a large-scale initiative spearheaded by Jeffrey Sachs of the Columbia University Earth Institute in New York. Through a holistic approach addressing all eight goals, MVP aims to help impoverished communities in rural Africa achieve the MDGs. The project operates in eighty village clusters and, as of 2011, has reached nearly 400,000 people. As well as financing one of the village clusters, the Novartis Foundation donates artemisinin-based combination therapy (ACT) Coartem®, produced by Novartis, for the treatment of uncomplicated malaria to all Millennium Villages. The foundation also collaborates with MVP in implementing a telemedicine project in Ghana.

Improving Access to Health Care

Access to health care and medicines remains a challenge for many people in developing countries. Availability and affordability of safe and efficacious medicines are crucial factors impacting on access, which in turn affects the ability to combat disease, as well as child and maternal mortality, as stipulated in MDGs 4, 5, and 6. The complexity of access issues, however, can extend far beyond the health care system. To meet the health-related MDGs, many different factors and causalities must be targeted. In all supported projects, the NFSD fosters a comprehensive approach to ensure sustainable improvement of access to health care services.

The Novartis Foundation has developed an access to health care framework, defined as the degree to which a patient's resources, needs, and expectations (demand) are aligned with a health care system's services and providers (supply). Access to health care and medicines can only be sustainable if the local health care system and services meet demand.

Drawing on this framework, the ACCESS project aims to analyze and improve access to effective malaria treatment and care in three rural districts in Tanzania, in particular for pregnant women and children under five years of age.

Supported by the foundation in collaboration with the Ifakara Health Institute (IHI) and the Swiss Tropical and Public Health Institute (Swiss TPH), the ACCESS project intervenes on the supply side by facilitating training for health care personnel and performance assessments in health facilities. Not only infrastructure and equipment, but also job expectations, motivation, and clinical skills of health care staff, as well as facility management and patient satisfaction, are continuously measured. Emphasis is placed on malaria case management. Improvements in quality of services are rewarded through a performance-based incentive system. The ACCESS project also introduced the Rapid Diagnostic Test, on a pilot basis, to diagnose malaria more easily and accurately. Geographical accessibility to malaria drugs has been improved by supporting the expansion of Accredited Drug Dispensing Outlets (ADDOs) to the project districts. The proportion of patients who received the right drug and advice according to their symptoms in such private-for-profit drug shops improved to 80 percent in 2008, compared to 35 percent in preexisting outlets.

On the demand side, ACCESS informs people about the causes, symptoms, modes of transmission, and appropriate treatment of malaria through social marketing campaigns in schools and villages. Previously, many Tanzanians believed the convulsions seen in severe cases of malaria were caused by evil spirits, and therefore they initially consulted traditional healers for treatment. Thanks to various information campaigns, the proportion of convulsion and fever cases (a common indicator for malaria) treated in health facilities has increased. Quality of care work aims to ensure that patients are satisfied with the services and come back during subsequent illness episodes.

To address the affordability of health care, ACCESS supports women's groups with grants, which they can loan to their members for investment in productive income generation (e.g., piggery, beer brewing, food kiosks, and vegetable gardens) and entrepreneurial training. Around 53 percent of the women have experienced an average monthly gain of more than USD 20 from these activities. In return, they commit to sleeping under bed nets, using ante- and postnatal care, and conducting community sensitization with regard to malaria and other health issues. These activities contribute to the achievement of MDGs 1, 3, 4, 5, and 6. ACCESS also supports a community-based health insurance scheme to make health care more affordable.

Results show that from 2004 to 2008, the proportion of investigated fever cases treated with an antimalarial within 24 hours increased from 66 percent to 89 percent, indicating improved treatment-seeking behavior. The proportion of investigated fever cases treated with a recommended antimalarial within twenty-four hours in the correct dosage could not, however, be improved, mainly due to poor availability of the recommended drug in drug shops and unsatisfactory provider compliance. Nonetheless, the overall mortality for children under five years of age has dropped significantly from 28.4 to 18.9 cases per 1,000 person-years as part of a longer trend dating back to 1997. This is in part thanks to the ACCESS interventions and the national program on Insecticide Treated Nets, since malaria is a major cause of overall child mortality.

The same framework serves as a model for the Initiative Accès in Mali, supported by the foundation and the regional authorities for health and social development. On the supply side, it focuses on improving access to primary health care by increasing quality of care, strengthening the organization and management of health centers, and enhancing geographical accessibility of services for people in remote villages. On the demand side, interventions include a health insurance scheme (the largest rural scheme in the region today), viable income generation, and access to credit.

The initiative, which mainly addresses MDGs 4 and 5, covers thirteen health areas in the region of Ségou, reaching 170,000 people in 210 villages. Its main beneficiaries are pregnant women, young mothers, and children under five years of age. Annual performance assessments of quality of care in health facilities and management of health centers show that the community health associations managing these increased their average score from 119 to 131 points out of 150, through improved internal governance, management, and support to health care personnel. During the same time, average treatment costs in a health center decreased from USD 4.20 to USD 3.70.

In 2009, the health insurance scheme had over 2,000 beneficiaries, compared to 1,151 in 2004. In total, 1,300 women have gained access to loans through some thirty women's groups, with a repayment rate of nearly 100 percent. While 77 percent of interviewed women used the loan for productive activities (involving, e.g., poultry, sheep, peanut seeds), 23 percent used it to solve socioeconomic problems (health, education). The average net gain per month per woman amounted to around USD 18. The initiative thereby also contributes to the achievement of MDGs 1 and 3.

Access to TB treatment is also a major challenge, since the disease is very complex to treat, requiring a combination of drugs administered over six to eight months. Lack of patient adherence during this lengthy period has led to the emergence of multi-drug-resistant (MDR) TB. Therefore the TB treatment recommended by the World Health Organization is DOTS (Directly Observed Therapy Short-course), an approach that requires patients to take their medicines under direct daily observation by a medical professional.

Even though Novartis donates gold standard treatments to all patients in Tanzania, access and adherence to TB treatment is not guaranteed. In collaboration with the National TB and Leprosy Programme of the Ministry of Health and Social Welfare, the Novartis Foundation has therefore taken the DOTS strategy in Tanzania one step further. Patient-Centered TB Treatment (PCT) gives patients the choice to follow treatment either at a health facility, or at home supervised by a family or community member. Results showed that 88 percent of TB patients opted for home-based treatment. Previously, patients had to walk long distances every day to be treated in already overburdened health facilities.

More important, results indicate that although the majority of patients are observed by a treatment supporter at home, treatment completion rates improved from 72 percent in 2005 (the year before PCT was introduced) to 77.5 percent in 2007, while the rate of unfavorable treatment outcomes was reduced from 28 percent to 22.5 percent. PCT—together with the TB drug donation of Novartis to Tanzania—contributes extensively to the achievement of MDG 6.

Strengthening Human Resources in Health Care

Skilled human resources are the backbone of any performing health care system. But many developing countries face a human resource crisis due to health workforce shortages, migration, and lack of adequate training. Increasing health interventions aimed at reducing child and maternal mortality and tackling diseases such as HIV/AIDS, malaria, and TB require more and better-trained health personnel. In order to meet the health-related Millennium Development Goals, great emphasis therefore has to be placed on human resource development. The Novartis Foundation's commitment to human resource development in health dates back to the 1960s, when its predecessor foundation supported the creation of a health training center in rural Tanzania to strengthen the health care system of the newly independent nation. Over the decades, the foundation has continuously supported the center to train different types of health care personnel. Today, the Tanzanian Training Center for International Health (TTCIH) in Ifakara is one of the most promising of its kind in East Africa, in terms of both quality of training and financial sustainability.

Over a two-year course, former Clinical Officers go through comprehensive practical and theoretical training to become Assistant Medical Officers (AMO). The degree is similar to a university medical degree and a priority cadre for the Tanzanian Ministry of Health and

Social Welfare. Educating more AMOs helps increase the quality and range of health services, especially in rural areas where health workers are needed most. The TTCIH has established expertise in maternal and child health, both of which are crucial to the achievement of the health-related MDGs.

Since 1961, the training center has trained over two thousand health workers. In 2009, it trained three hundred students in internal and external courses, generating over USD 1 million in gross income. As a result, it will now be able to offset the financial support of the Novartis Foundation, becoming more independent financially and investing in new courses, thus further improving overall quality.

One of the major MDG challenges remains reducing child mortality. In 2009, more than nine million children died worldwide before reaching their fifth birthday. The majority of these deaths could have been prevented through a relatively small number of simple, low-cost interventions such as pre-, ante-, and postnatal care, vaccinations, and antibiotics. Again, the crucial factor is the development of skilled human resources for health. To strengthen the skills of health care personnel working with sick children, the Novartis Foundation—together with the World Health Organization (WHO)—has developed an e-learning tool for the Integrated Management of Childhood Illness (IMCI). IMCI is a WHO/UNICEF strategy that aims to significantly and rapidly reduce infant and childhood mortality in order to meet MDG 4.

Called ICATT (IMCI Computerized Adaptation and Training Tool), the program facilitates the management, with minimal personnel intervention, of the most common pediatric diseases, such as pneumonia, diarrhea, malaria, measles, and malnutrition. ICATT can be easily adapted to country-specific features such as treatment guidelines and rolled out for the training of health care personnel in IMCI. So far, ICATT has been tested and introduced in Tanzania, Peru, and Indonesia and is being further rolled out by WHO.

The tool facilitates faster and more flexible upscaling of IMCI training. Training time and costs are reduced, and consequently more people can be trained in the management of childhood illnesses. The foundation is developing a similar tool for training in maternal health, thus aiming to contribute to the achievement of MDG 5.

In an effort to strengthen human resources in rural areas, the foundation started a telemedicine project in Ghana in cooperation with the

Millennium Villages Project (MVP). The project will be implemented through the local MVP infrastructure in Bonsasso. The goal is to provide quality primary health services that are affordable, sustainable, and meet the needs of patients through appropriate mobile and information technologies.

First, the project aims to reduce unnecessary transportation and to improve the referral system. Implementation of a knowledge system for treatment referrals will ensure resource availability and supply and improve transportation access and infrastructure. Second, health care personnel will be trained in the use of mobile technologies and teleconsultation for health. Capacity-building in human resources, logistics, and institutions will be conducted, ensuring gender balance throughout.

Finally, a system will be implemented to monitor and evaluate performance and quality of services and to measure in a timely fashion the effects of telemedical consultations and mobile health. Through the collection of routine data, adaptation of indicators, and quality assurance, the ultimate goal of the monitoring and evaluation system is to inform—and improve—policy and practice.

Empowering Vulnerable Groups

As a result of the AIDS pandemic, millions of children in sub-Saharan Africa are growing up without parents, jeopardizing their health, well-being, and sometimes their very survival—not to mention the overall development prospects of their countries. In keeping with all MDG objectives, the Novartis Foundation co-founded and continues to support the Regional Psychosocial Support Initiative for Children affected by AIDS, Poverty and Conflict (REPSSI), whose main objective is to help orphans cope with their loss and regain confidence.

As of 2011, the initiative has reached over three million children and aims to reach five million by 2011. REPSSI has experienced tremendous growth and is today recognized as the leading organization worldwide in the field of psychosocial support. Its leadership position has earned the political and practical support of the Southern African Development Community (SADC), UNICEF, governments, and other high-level stakeholders. Collaborating with 140 local nongovernmental organizations, REPSSI develops and disseminates courses and tools for psychosocial support.

Through its partners and income-generating activities, REPSSI assists thousands of children and households with income-generating measures to get out of extreme poverty, thus helping achieve MDG 1. REPSSI's partner Consol Homes, for example, together with the government of Malawi, supports over ten thousand communities with a savings and loans program to improve farming yields. Although REPSSI generally does not provide school fees for orphans, the initiative helps increase school attendance, specifically for girls, through its psychosocial support, school-based interventions, and advocacy. In this way, REPSSI contributes to the attainment of the MDGs on increasing primary school enrollment and promoting gender equality.

REPSSI's main objective is to give psychosocial support to children orphaned by HIV/AIDS. All REPSSI publications in the thirteen project countries include training units on HIV/AIDS prevention and treatment. Together with UNICEF and other partners, REPSSI conducts reproductive health education through social marketing campaigns and training for caregivers, teachers, and child-focused organizations. Contributing to the achievement of MDG 4, REPSSI helps improve access to HIV counseling and testing as well as adherence to antiretroviral therapy in Tanzania and Zambia, thus reducing mother-to-child transmission of HIV/AIDS.

In 2007, the Novartis Foundation initiated and funded research in collaboration with the Swiss Academy for Development (SAD) and REPSSI to identify essential elements of a successful minimal Psychosocial Support (PSS) package. The results will be fed back into the programs studied and made available to relevant stakeholders. The ultimate aim of this research collaboration is to facilitate a paradigm shift in aid interventions by strengthening evidence-based programming for affected children and families.

In a similar vein, the Novartis Foundation has been active since 1986 in empowering disadvantaged people affected by leprosy. Spreading the message that "leprosy can be cured," the foundation has played a key role in reducing the stigma attached to the disease and helping patients reintegrate into society. A prerequisite for the campaign's major success was free provision of multidrug therapy (MDT) from 2000 onward by Novartis to all leprosy patients worldwide.

The prevalence of leprosy has been reduced dramatically, thanks to MDT. Nevertheless, many former leprosy patients suffer from disabilities, which continue to cause social stigmatization. The Novartis Comprehensive Leprosy Care Association (NCLCA), supported by NFSD, aims to prevent disabilities through early detection of leprosy. At the same time, the project helps those with deformities reintegrate into society through disability care, including surgeries, grip aids, and physiotherapy.

By passing knowledge on to local health workers and empowering patients to become autonomous, the project has greatly increased the impact of disability care in India. The project directly reaches between 800 and 1,000 patients annually, and the adoption of NCLCA's modalities—such as grip aids, self-care kits, and health education booklets—by the Indian government has increased the impact further still. As of 2011, nearly 28,000 self-care kits have been distributed to patients through the Indian National Leprosy Eradication Program. Other countries such as Myanmar, Tanzania, and Sri Lanka have also adopted the tools developed by the NCLCA. This initiative furthers the aims of MDGs 1 and 6.

THE ROAD AHEAD

The UN MDG Report 2010 revealed that there is still much to be done if the eight goals are to be reached. Sustained efforts are needed in order to further reduce hunger and child and maternal mortality, as well as to fight diseases such as HIV/AIDS, malaria, and TB. The wealth of experience amassed in the last ten years has highlighted best practices and tools that can help achieve the MDGs or at least speed up progress toward them. The MDGs can only be met if everyone contributes—governments, international organizations, civil society, and the private sector, including pharmaceutical companies such as Novartis. Moreover, focus must be directed to the areas where progress is currently insufficient.

In line with their core competencies, Novartis and its Foundation for Sustainable Development are committed to supporting such targeted efforts. Through its pro bono research on TB, dengue fever, malaria, and diarrheal diseases, Novartis aims to contribute to the development of a new generation of medicines and vaccines. As of 2012, the Novartis Institute for Tropical Diseases had tested at least two potential treatments in patient trials. Drug donation programs for the fight against leprosy and TB will be or have already been prolonged to help sustain elimination and control efforts. The Novartis Malaria Initiatives have committed to supporting the Affordable Medicine Facility for malaria (AMFm) in order to expand access to Coartem® for disadvantaged people through the non-premium private sector.

In future years, the Novartis Foundation for Sustainable Development will step up its work on improving child and maternal health services. It will continue to build human resources expertise in this area by supporting the Tanzanian Training Centre for International Health, extending the ICATT e-learning tool to maternal health, and through its new telemedicine project in Ghana. Under the access initiatives in Mali and Tanzania, poverty will be addressed through health insurance protection, access to credit, and support of viable income generation activities. By targeting women's groups, these measures not only help facilitate financial access to health services but also contribute to greater gender equality and women's empowerment.

With regard to environmental sustainability, recent data shows that Novartis has succeeded in slightly reducing its absolute emissions since 2005, despite an expansion in production and sales. But in order to meet targets beyond 2012, further internal energy-efficiency improvements, increased use of renewable energy, and additional carbon-offset projects will be required.

Finally, none of these endeavors would be as effective or sustainable without successful partnerships. Therefore Novartis and the Novartis Foundation for Sustainable Development will continue to maintain existing global partnerships for development, as well as forge new ones, thus contributing to the full realization of the Millennium Development Goals.

NOTE

This chapter in its original form was published by the Novartis Foundation for Sustainable Development, Basel, Switzerland, and is used here with permission. For further information, please see www.novartisfoundation.org and www.corporatecitizenship.novartis.com.

7 | How Global Employers Can Address HIV/AIDS

The Levi Strauss & Co. Story

Kirk O. Hanson

The global epidemic of HIV/AIDS, first identified in the early 1980s, initially provoked fear and avoidance, but later, extensive research, public health campaigns, and treatment regimens that became available to a growing proportion of the victims of this disease. Slowly, the disease was turned from one that victims "died from" to a disease "one lives with." In 2013, the disease is increasingly understood as a preventable and treatable chronic illness and not one to be irrationally feared.

At the same time that governments rushed to create preventive campaigns and established programs to identify victims of the disease and make treatments available, other institutions, including corporations, worked to do their part. It was obvious from the beginning that local governments and their public health efforts would not be enough to halt the epidemic. It would also take the effort of national governments, multinational organizations, global philanthropies, and employers.

For employers, responding to HIV/AIDS was at first very difficult. Because the disease was first discovered among gay employees, many companies hesitated to address it directly or openly. They feared that the company or its employees might be stigmatized as word spread inside and outside the company that some employees had the disease and that the company had created programs to address it.

Later, companies became more comfortable with the notion that they should respond actively to HIV/AIDS, recognizing that the disease was an important employee health issue—and even a strategic issue. For employers, effective HIV/AIDS programs were easiest to establish in developed societies and where the companies employed large numbers of people. It was much more difficult to create effective programs in developing countries and in places where those companies had small offices, often with just a few sales, retail, or technical employees. But efforts to defeat the disease and efforts to treat all employees equitably required just that.

LEVI STRAUSS & CO. AND HIV/AIDS

Since the 1980s, Levi Strauss & Co. (Levi's) has been a leader in the business response to HIV/AIDS. Acutely aware of the early growth of the disease in Levi Strauss's hometown of San Francisco and among an alarming number of its own employees, then CEO Robert D. Haas committed the company to create a workplace program for its own employees and an active community aimed at education and prevention of HIV/AIDS. Throughout the 1990s and into the 2000s, the company partnered with other companies through the Business Coalition for HIV/AIDS, the United Nations, and other governmental and nongovernmental organizations to create effective HIV/AIDS programs and to encourage other corporations to take similar strong action.

But by 2006, the company, a global employer with more than 15,000 employees scattered in over one hundred countries, came to believe that its programs, while extensive, might not be serving the needs of all its own employees, particularly those in developing countries and in its smallest offices. Did these sales, retail, and technical staff have the same access to HIV/AIDS programs that employees did in the United States and in other countries where Levi's had large numbers of employees? Company officials reluctantly concluded they did not.

In addition, Levi Strauss had long been committed to the welfare of workers in its supply chain, and it was concerned that the employees of the companies that sewed, washed, and finished Levi's apparel might not have the same protections and education regarding HIV/AIDS that Levi's own employees had. The company had long prided itself on its pioneering work promoting the welfare of employees in its supply chain, although they were not directly employed by Levi's. In 1991 the company had established its Terms of Engagement, which established standards for working conditions and environmental protection that launched the "supply chain standards" movement.

These concerns about the global effectiveness of its HIV/AIDS programs led to a reevaluation in the late 2000s of Levi's company-wide HIV/AIDS efforts and the development of a new global approach, described in this chapter.

ABOUT THE COMPANY

Levi Strauss & Co. is a casual apparel firm, which markets its broad array of clothing and accessories worldwide in both company-owned and independent retail outlets. In 2010 the company employed 16,200 persons, operated in 110 countries, and had global sales of $4.4 billion and net income of $381 million.

Levi's was founded in 1853 by Levi Strauss, a Bavarian immigrant who settled in San Francisco and established a dry goods store. In 1873, Strauss and a Reno, Nevada, tailor secured a patent for denim overalls whose pockets were secured by rivets, the first blue jeans. In 1890 the basic overalls were designated model 501, the model number they retain in 2011. Between 1890 and the late twentieth century, the company's product line expanded, encompassing various styles of men's pants, women's wear, and eventually shirts and other garments, as well as accessories. In the period after World War II, wearing blue jeans became increasingly common among workers and the young. By the late 1960s, the baby-boomer generation had adopted the casual denim style and appeared to many to be a "blue jean army." Competitors sprang up quickly to compete with Levi's and produce blue jeans and other casual clothes, which were Levi's specialty.

Descendants of Levi Strauss led the family company until the 1970s and then again in the 1980s and 1990s. For fourteen years, Levi's was a public company, but in 1985 it went private again. Descendants of Levi Strauss and their relatives continue to own most of the stock in the company. Headquartered in San Francisco, the company at first produced most of its clothing in the United States, but began to shift production abroad in the 1980s.

Levi Strauss himself was a noted philanthropist in San Francisco, and his descendants continued and developed the company's "citizenship" programs throughout the history of the firm. After the 1906 San Francisco earthquake and in the Depression of the 1930s, Levi's became known for extending credit to others and for softening the impact of these events on its employees. In the 1950s and 1960s, Levi's fought segregation in the American South and insisted that its facilities be integrated.

In the 1970s, the company pioneered "community involvement teams," which empowered groups of employees at its many locations to volunteer and make contributions to the local community. In the 1980s, these teams were developed at an increasing number of Levi's global locations. In 1991, as already mentioned above, Levi's adopted its Terms of Engagement, which required independent suppliers of Levi's apparel to adopt employee safety and work standards and environmental policies. In the 1990s Levi's was one of the first employers to expand the definition of "family" to encompass domestic partners and their children.

THE HIV/AIDS PANDEMIC

The disease that came to be known as HIV/AIDS was first detected in the United States in 1981, in California and New York, though it probably had entered Haiti around 1966 and the United States about 1970.

AIDS (Acquired ImmunoDeficiency Syndrome) is a disease that weakens the body's natural immunity system and allows various infections such as pneumonia (called "opportunistic infections") to ravage the body. Treatment of AIDS involves aggressively treating these opportunistic infections before they can progress and slowing down the decline of the body's immune system, or rebuilding it so the infections do not take hold in the first place. Many deaths occur because the infections progress rapidly and because for years no drug was available to slow down the progression of the AIDS disease or build up the immune system.

AIDS was first detected among gay men and then in injecting drug users. By 1982, when the name AIDS was adopted, clusters were also found among hemophiliacs and Haitians in the US. It was also found in Europe. By the following year, AIDS had been detected among women and children who were not injecting drug users. Approximately a thousand people had died in the United States from the disease by the end of 1983. In 1984, scientists identified HIV (human immunodeficiency virus) as the cause of AIDS and detected the spread of the disease to Africa. By two years later, in 1986, it had been found in eighty-five countries. By 1990, 8 million people were living with HIV/AIDS worldwide.

The 1990s was the height of the epidemic, which is thought to have peaked in 1999. Researchers, often supported by governments, worked feverishly to create a treatment for the disease. In 1987 a drug called AZT was approved for treating AIDS. While its effectiveness was strongly questioned, it was shown to reduce the risk of mother-to-child transmission of HIV, and infant HIV infections started to fall in developed countries. By 1996, a combination antiretroviral (ARV) treatment regimen was shown to be highly effective against HIV, and by the following year AIDS deaths began to decline in developed countries due to the use of new drugs. However, the ARV drugs were very expensive, and few in the developing world had access to them.

The data indicating that the epidemic probably peaked in 1999 also showed the impact of government, philanthropic, and international organizations, which rushed to establish preventive programs and to make the ARV regimen available across the globe, particularly in the developing world. Nonetheless, new infections in the developing world have remained high through the 2000s. Increased availability of the ARV drugs has reduced deaths in the developing world, yet in 2013, there are still areas where HIV/AIDS is spreading rapidly and where deaths are still common. Even where ARV drugs are available, many still do not have access to them due to the lack of accurate diagnosis of the disease, the high cost, or poor distribution and clinical services.

GOVERNMENT RESPONSES

The response of governments to HIV/AIDS, not surprisingly, was most intense in the developed world and often irregular in the developing world. In some countries, governments clearly failed to grasp the severity of the epidemic and dismissed it as a public health concern. In 1988 the U.S. government conducted its first national AIDS education campaign. In the same year, the world's health ministers met to discuss AIDS and established a World AIDS Day. In 1995 a Joint United Nations Programme on AIDS (UNAIDS) was established. The UN Global Fund was established in 2002 to boost the response to AIDS, TB, and malaria. And in 2004, the United States launched a major initiative championed by President George W. Bush called PEPFAR, committing the United States to contribute $15 billion to combat AIDS worldwide. In his final State of the Union address, Bush proposed that the United States commit another $30 billion over five years. Private philanthropic support for anti-AIDS programs also grew in the 2000s, including a $338 million commitment from the Gates Foundation to fight the spread of HIV/AIDS in India. By 2006, annual global spending on AIDS in low and middle-income countries reached $8.9 billion.

By 2010 governments became more confident that HIV/AIDS could be managed and had begun to remove travel bans on HIV-positive people, led by the United States, South Korea, China, and Namibia.

HIV/AIDS IN 2011

While the number infected had statistically peaked a decade earlier, approximately 2.5 million new cases worldwide of HIV/AIDS were reported in 2010, down only about 19 percent from the peak. Infection rates were down over 25 percent in Sub-Saharan Africa, the areas of greatest concern. Deaths from the disease had peaked in 2004 at 2.1 million but still totaled 1.8 million in 2009. The percentage of the adult population (ages 15–49) infected had dropped from 5.9% to 5.0 percent in Sub-Saharan Africa by 2010. However, nowhere else in the world was the rate of infection above 1 percent. It was estimated that 10 percent of adults in South Africa were infected.

As of 2009, approximately 33 million people around the world were infected with HIV, but only 25 percent knew they were infected, creating a significant potential for continued infection. It was estimated that 7,000 people were infected with HIV every day—and that even in 2009, 1.8 million people still died of HIV/AIDS annually.

Also, in the United States, HIV/AIDS had not been conquered. In 2010, a million U.S. citizens were living with HIV/AIDS. One-quarter of these did not know they were infected, and one-half were not receiving care. It was estimated that 50,000 U.S. residents were newly infected with HIV/AIDS each year. One out of four living with the disease was a woman, and it was the leading cause of death for African American women ages 25–34.

THE BUSINESS RESPONSE TO HIV/AIDS

Corporate efforts to address HIV/AIDS began in the 1980s, though they were often held back by fear of the disease and by the early perception that this was a "gay disease." Some companies feared that having an HIV/AIDS program would stigmatize those that made use of the program.

Levi's own engagement with HIV/AIDS began in 1982, when a group of employees in San Francisco asked to distribute literature concerning AIDS during the lunch hour in the large atrium of the company's headquarters building. These pioneering employees believed San Francisco was being stricken by a serious disease and that there was little information available about it.

While it was not uncommon for employees to hand out leaflets in the atrium, the company immediately recognized that this request was special and that some might assume those distributing or taking the leaflets were either gay or infected with AIDS. At the time, there was considerable fear in San Francisco over the unfamiliar disease. After discussion in the Executive Committee of the company, Executive Vice President Robert Haas, great grandnephew of Levi Strauss himself, joined the employees in handing out the leaflets, primarily to lessen the potential stigma and fear.

From that beginning, over the next few years Levi's developed a comprehensive set of policies to address HIV/AIDS. These policies and the company's attitude became a model for corporate programs to address the disease. Among the policies were the following:

- The company does not have a special AIDS policy. Instead, it addresses the needs of employees with AIDS and their co-workers within the framework of its general approach to employee relations.
- The company does not test job applicants for AIDS, and there are no AIDS screening questions on employment applications.
- Employees with AIDS are treated with compassion and understanding—as are employees with any other life threatening disease.
- Employees with AIDS can continue to work as long as they are medically cleared to do so; they are also eligible for work accommodation.
- Employees are assured of confidentiality when seeking counseling or medical referral.
- Company medical coverage, disability leave policy, and life insurance do not distinguish between AIDS and any other life-threatening disease.
- The company's medical plan supports home health and hospice care for the terminally ill.
- A case management strategy is implemented whenever an individual employee becomes critically ill.
- Managers are held accountable for creating a work environment that is supportive of an employee with AIDS.
- The company regards itself as having a responsibility to educate its employees, so that neither unwarranted fear nor prejudice affects the work environment of people with AIDS.
- Individual, family, or group counseling is available to employees and their families through the company's Employee Assistance Program (EAP) or through outside agencies.
- The EAP staff also conducts department and management counseling sessions upon request about issues such as how to handle rumors about AIDS, how to deal directly with people's feelings when a colleague becomes ill with AIDS, what colleagues can do to be helpful to a person with AIDS, and how to deal with the grief associated with the death of a colleague.

Three aspects of Levi's approach were particularly important. The first was the commitment to educate everyone in the company about the nature of HIV/AIDS, its prevention, and treatment. The company believed education could greatly influence the spread of the disease and could reduce the stigma that sufferers faced in society. The second was a commitment to "reasonably accommodate" the needs of people with AIDS, enabling them to continue to work wherever possible. Because of this policy, employees would not fear to get tested and to seek help from the company. In other organizations, those testing positive for the HIV virus found they were summarily fired. The third was a commitment of the company to alert the outside world, particularly other companies, to the need to respond to the AIDS crisis. Levi's executive and employees contributed money, time, and leadership to efforts to fight HIV/AIDS and to urge others to do so. Robert D. Haas became a San Francisco, national, and later global spokesperson urging corporate and government action on HIV/AIDS.

Other companies followed Levi's lead, and "HIV in the Workplace" efforts became the first phase of the business response. They remain the bedrock of what businesses should do first—ensure that their employees have access to HIV information, testing, treatment, and care, as well as a safe, confidential, and supportive work environment.

GLOBAL COOPERATION AND
INTERNATIONAL PARTNERSHIPS

Beyond pioneering a model corporate HIV/AIDS program for its own domestic employees, Levi Strauss participated in some of the earliest national and global programs on HIV/AIDS.

Levi's has participated in and supported activities surrounding World AIDS Day, which is observed on December 1 of each year, since it was launched in 1988. Created by two World Health Organization officials, World AIDS Day was sponsored by UNAIDS, the AIDS program of the United Nations, until 2004, when it became an independent organization. World AIDS Day came to sponsor the most important annual conference on HIV/AIDS and produced the most respected annual reports of HIV/AIDS statistics.

In 1997, the Global Business Council on HIV&AIDS, a peer advocacy organization, was established to encourage expanded and enhanced involvement of the corporate sector in response to HIV/AIDS.

Levi Strauss was deeply involved in the Global Business Council from its formation. After staging an unprecedented meeting of the United Nations Security Council to discuss AIDS in Africa in January 2000, UN Ambassador Richard Holbrooke joined the Global Business Council and led it. It was renamed the Global Business Coalition on HIV/AIDS, Tuberculosis and Malaria and expanded to include 225 members by 2010.

From its founding in 2000, the United Nations Global Compact, an initiative of former Secretary-General Kofi Annan, had urged companies to address the pandemic of HIV/AIDS. But in 2003, moved by the understanding that the pandemic had become a major threat to global development as well as a tragedy for individuals, families, and communities, the UNGC joined with the International Labor Organization and UNAIDS, an existing joint UN program on HIV/AIDS, to appeal for corporate leaders to take significant action to address the pandemic. Specifically, the joint appeal encouraged companies to adopt and implement fully the ILO Recommendation on HIV/AIDS and the World of Work and to join the Global Business Coalition on HIV/AIDS, Tuberculosis and Malaria. Levi's represented U.S. employers in these negotiations. The UNGC announced that it would use its Global Compact Learning Forum to focus on the development of examples and case studies on corporate action on HIV/AIDS. Since that time, the UNGC has developed and distributed an expanding library of training materials on HIV/AIDS and has convened seminars for business managers in many nations. As of 2011, there were forty-five case studies on effective programs on the UNGC website at www .gbchealth.org.

The United Nations Millennium Campaign, launched in September 2000 at a global gathering of world leaders, committed member nations to a new global partnership to reduce extreme poverty by setting a series of time-bound targets, with a deadline of 2015. These targets became known as the Millennium Development Goals (MDGs) and included the following goals regarding HIV/AIDS:

- Target 6a. Have halted by 2015 and begun to reverse the spread of HIV/AIDS.
- Target 6b. Achieve, by 2010, universal access to treatment for HIV/AIDS for all those who need it.

While the Millennium Campaign was primarily a partnership of governments, corporations were encouraged to work in partnership with the campaign. Companies such as Levi's participated in campaign conferences and developed global CSR (corporate social responsibility) programs to further the goals of the campaign.

Levi's also supported and participated in the global fund of Fight AIDS, Tuberculosis and Malaria, created in 2002 with broad support from the United Nations, the G8, victims groups, and other multinational organizations. By December 2010, the fund had given a total of $21.7 billion in grants to six hundred programs in 150 countries.

THE CHALLENGE OF CREATING A GLOBAL HIV/AIDS PROGRAM FOR EMPLOYEES

While these multinational coalitions represented a growing commitment of corporations to address HIV/AIDS, there remained many barriers to reaching all of a company's employees.

Levi's and other companies found that securing insurance coverage for their employees, including new hires who were already HIV positive, was often difficult. They also found that the stigma of HIV/AIDS was more powerful than they ever imagined, preventing effective education and other support efforts in some of their operations.

Levi's and other companies also increasingly realized that HIV/AIDS was a strategic issue for business. The epidemic imposed increased costs and decreased productivity if not managed effectively.

The first barrier was simply the global distribution of a company's employees. For some manufacturing and extractive firms, employees were concentrated in a limited number of locations and could be served by on-site health care clinics. Indeed, many of these firms already provided health care services to these employees. But for companies with more broadly dispersed employee populations, and for all companies whose sales and service offices were scattered across the globe, providing health, education, and services to all employees was far more difficult. The problems were all the more severe for apparel firms, particularly firms that had retail operations. These operations could be widely scattered, and employee turnover could be substantial.

The second barrier was that typical human resource mechanisms, such as benefit programs, insurance, and human resource policies were difficult and costly to harmonize and administer on a global basis. Individual national laws and regulations, local cultural and religious attitudes, and other factors could make human resource policies in general very difficult to manage. As a result, many companies did not achieve anything like standardization or universal coverage for employees on many benefits and policies.

Levi's found, for example, that HIV/AIDS testing, treatment, and care was not covered by local health insurance plans or national health services in many countries. Specifically, this was true in at least thirteen countries where Levi's had employees.

A third barrier was that in apparel, retail, and some other sectors of the economy, there had never developed as active a commitment to addressing HIV/AIDS globally as in other sectors. Global HIV/AIDS programs spread most quickly in manufacturing, mining, petroleum, and beverage industries, where workers were both concentrated and formally considered employees of the global entity. In the apparel industry, a complex web of independent firms produced the fabrics, sewed, and washed the garments. Similarly, retail outlets could be either independent or company-owned and in many countries was a mix of the two. Neither Levi's nor any of its apparel retail competitors had launched global HIV/AIDS programs to cover their retail employees in most developing countries.

Underlying many of these barriers was still the fundamental problem of *stigma*. Just as there was considerable fear and a stigma attached to those who suffered from HIV/AIDS in the 1980s in the United States, there was a strong stigma to having HIV/AIDS or even taking advantage of testing or other programs in many places in the 2000s. Global employers such as Levi's faced employee fear and community criticism if they openly addressed HIV/AIDS or openly provided health services related to the disease. Even some national political leaders continued to disseminate inaccurate information about HIV/AIDS and perpetrated the stigma attached. Employees were afraid to take advantage of a program's services, even simply to be tested. As a result, even a program that was widely available might not be successful.

The result of all these barriers was that, for many companies, it was much easier to contribute funds to NGO and national HIV/AIDS efforts than to try to reach their own employees with effective programs. Some questioned whether it was equitable if certain company employees, including ones most threatened by HIV/AIDS, did not have access to the same benefit and the same company programs as others.

LEVI'S COMMITMENT TO IMPROVE ITS GLOBAL HIV/AIDS OUTREACH

While Levi's continued to be recognized as a global leader in HIV/AIDS efforts, receiving dozens of notable awards, company leaders worried about the future. Its programs had begun in response to employee needs and drew on every corporate social responsibility (CSR) element in responding to the pandemic—employee efforts, public policy, marketing and consumer education, community programs, and reaching out to suppliers. In addition to its employee programs on HIV/AIDS, Levi's has contributed generously to public campaigns in response to the pandemic. These contributions had totaled more than $40 million since 1982. The company realized that, as a global employer, it was essential to revisit its response, clarify whether it was as supportive to employees as possible, and determine if it was meeting and crafting best practices for workplace HIV programs, particularly in the apparel sector.

In the early 2000s, it was clear that Levi Strauss & Co. had employees and operations in countries experiencing HIV/AIDS in different ways, each requiring attention. The company was seeking to ensure access to HIV/AIDS prevention, treatment, and care globally. It realized that it needed to return to its roots and revitalize its effort with employees. While addressing HIV/AIDS began by responding to employee needs over twenty-five years before, the company felt it had not kept up with reaching its employees worldwide.

In 2006, Levi's attended the Clinton Global Initiative, former U.S. President Bill Clinton's effort to inspire, connect, and empower a generation of global leaders to forge solutions to the world's most pressing challenges. In the spirit of the Clinton initiative, Levi's made a "commitment" to revitalize and expand its employee HIV/AIDS workplace policies, education, and benefits, with the goal of providing all of the company's employees and their families with access to HIV/AIDS counseling, preventive care, education, and access to antiretroviral treatment and drugs in all countries in which the company operated. Further, Levi's pledged to share its best practices in the development and implementation of HIV/AIDS workplace programs with other companies, particularly those in the apparel industry. This commitment was not made lightly but represented both the management's realization that it needed to revitalize its policies and its commitment to do so effectively. This launched a five-year development program, which was completed only in 2011.

Given this backdrop of building a global program that is unique and relevant to an array of local HIV epidemics and workforces, it was essential for Levi's to focus on key principles as it designed its new effort. The global HIV in the Workplace effort focused on creating a global HIV/AIDS workplace policy. Challenges included how to reach employees in a variety of work settings, including office and retail environments where clinical services are not offered on-site, and where employees are of different ages, educational levels, and part-time or short-term status. Levi's rarely delivered health care directly on-site with its own doctors, nurses, or clinical settings. While manufacturing environments in many locations might include clinical staff or facilities, Levi's did not have extensive clinical staff in its facilities, and therefore its employees were not receiving equitable access to HIV prevention, treatment, and care across work locations and countries.

As the company reviewed this situation, it was clear that the way that it could improve access to health services was via its partnership with the health insurance industry. Levi's explored whether its health insurance and benefit plans across countries offered coverage for HIV/AIDS services. It discovered that local insurance markets made it challenging to include HIV/AIDS in local health benefit plans. It was clear that the company had to engage in partnerships with local insurance providers to extend its benefits. Noting that changing local markets takes time, the company created a first-of-its kind global HIV/AIDS benefit plan to ensure that all employees in all locations had coverage.

A NEW GLOBAL HIV/AIDS PROGRAM:
DESIGNING SOLUTIONS

To design its global HIV/AIDS effort, Levi's looked toward firms that had already created truly global programs. Levi's managers considered that Chevron, Shell, and Rio Tinto had created the most comprehensive global programs, and Heineken, BMC, Coca-Cola, DeBeers, Anglo-Gold, and Unilever had created best practice programs in one region or country. As suspected, none of these firms faced the same challenges as those of apparel/retail firms needing to reach employees scattered in so many countries. Levi's managers found no apparel companies that had created truly global HIV/AIDS workplace programs.

In evaluating these programs, Levi's managers concluded that most protection, treatment, and care programs were offered "on-site" by company-employed doctors and nurses, and that most companies did not assertively use traditional human resource mechanisms (benefit and insurance programs, and the like) to provide these services. Most of the companies that stated they had "global" programs were focused primarily on areas and countries with high HIV/AIDS prevalence.

A company survey conducted in a high, a medium, and a low prevalence area indicated that 35 percent of employees knew someone with HIV/AIDS, over 40 percent had been tested for the disease themselves, but that half did not know where to go to receive information, testing, or other services. This survey also showed substantial fear of how becoming HIV/AIDS positive would affect their employment.

An internal analysis of insurance benefits and government-sponsored HIV/AIDS programs identified at least twenty-two countries where testing, treatment, and care were not adequate and would need a special Levi's corporate effort and funding. As noted earlier, Levi's managers were also aware that both managers and employees in many countries had little knowledge of the disease, and that this contributed to the problem of stigma for those who might seek testing, were HIV positive, or needed treatment or care.

Levi's managers believed it was critical for the company to commit to provide a core set of services in countries where insurance and government programs were inadequate. Levi's manager proposed that the company commit to providing to all employees worldwide:

- Coverage for all eligible employees and their legal dependents.
- Coverage for one HIV test per year.
- Coverage for HIV/AIDS treatment and care services.
- Administration and payments of HIV/AIDS treatment and care by a third party administrator either globally or regionally.
- Annual assessment of availability of local insurance and government services with transition to local programs when possible.

The Levi's proposal broke new ground in several ways. A commitment to cover all eligible employees and their dependents worldwide was, as Levi's research indicated, a first. Second, the development of a global third-party administration of claims would be a pioneer effort. The company believed the third-party administration was important for several reasons, not the least of which was that confidentiality could be more easily maintained. Managers would generally not be aware of which employees were seeking testing, were HIV positive, or were seeking treatment and care.

Finally, Levi's managers recognized that a truly global program could not be effective without a significant educational effort aimed at both company employees and managers. Employee and dependent education would focus on information about the disease and the services available from the company. Managerial education would focus on these, but also on the company's strategic stake in an effective HIV/AIDS program.

Levi's developed and piloted its new program in South Africa, Mexico, and the United Kingdom during 2008. It then adapted and expanded the program to the other twenty-two target countries in 2009–2011. As the program developed and expanded, Levi's corporate office funded the costs of program development and the costs of providing prevention, treatment, and care services where it was not available from insurance or the government. While initially corporate support would be crucial, it was hoped that the insurance markets and government programs would develop in the target countries and that necessary corporate support would decrease and plateau after 2011.

THE RESULTS: AN ENHANCED AND COMPREHENSIVE APPROACH

Levi's rededicated itself to a comprehensive approach to HIV/AIDS, reinforced by its soul-searching in 2006–2008. This comprehensive and truly global approach now includes:

- A global Employee HIV/AIDS Program that improves access to HIV/AIDS education, testing, treatment, and care services for employees and their dependents worldwide.
- Support for community organizations addressing HIV/AIDS, with a focus on addressing the stigma and discrimination, and educating workers in apparel manufacturing.
- Heightened awareness of HIV/AIDS prevention messaging with our consumers through retail marketing programs and World AIDS Day commemorative events.
- Engaged leadership in promoting effective global public policy.
- Promotion of best practices in the apparel industry.

During the reevaluation process, Levi's revised the principles that guided its HIV/AIDS programs. The company described the overall program's principles as "Our Compass: Principles that Guide Us" and listed them as:

1. Focus on affordability, availability, and/or acceptability to improve access of HIV/AIDS services.
2. Ensure equity based on program outcomes for all employees and dependents in all locations.
3. Deliver locally adaptable program offerings.
4. Address HIV/AIDS uniquely while integrating with wellness initiatives, as relevant and feasible.
5. Proactively manage expansion with keen focus on program results, financial implications, and sustainability.
6. Enforce progressive workplace policies and work practices that support a workplace free from stigma and discrimination, and ensure confidentiality in use of personal and health information.
7. Deliver employee education and benefits that serve employees infected and affected by HIV/AIDS.

8. Leverage partnerships to strengthen the local infrastructure needed to deliver program outcomes.
9. Capture lessons for use across Levi Strauss & Co. and with contractors and suppliers.
10. Determine the best practices to contribute to advancements in HIV/AIDS in the workplace.

The implementation of the revitalized global Employee HIV/AIDS Program consists of seven major components, designed to improve access to HIV/AIDS prevention treatment and care and to improve the work environment:

1. Worldwide HIV/AIDS Policy and Enhanced Leadership Communication. This commitment included:
    - The development of a Worldwide HIV/AIDS Policy anchored in Levi's Worldwide Business Code of Conduct.
    - A clear focus and emphasis on confidentiality, nondiscrimination, and anti-stigma in the policy and program.
2. The launch of the revised program in each location by the local leader.
3. A CEO message on December 1 every year—World AIDS Day.
4. An Employee Survey on HIV/AIDS in selected countries. This survey, administered annually, is administered to company employees in manufacturing, retail, and office locations, in both on-line and paper forms. Participation is voluntary and confidential, and an analysis of the results is used in trainings.
5. Enhanced HIV/AIDS Education for Management. This specialized training, conducted both for Levi's managers and for managers in partner organizations, helps managers effectively address human resource issues regarding HIV/AIDS in the workplace. It uses customized scenarios illustrating situations actually encountered in Levi's settings.
6. Enhanced HIV/AIDS Education for Employees and Dependents. This training, often conducted in partnership with a local NGO or community partner, is also offered electronically worldwide. Levi's is now piloting opportunities for dependents to take the training.
7. Provision of Testing, Treatment, and Care Services Worldwide. It is Levi's goal to have these services available globally to all its employees, regardless of whether local insurance and other programs exclude them. This part of the program involves annual monitoring of the availability

of services in local insurance plans and government HIV/AIDS programs and the creation of tailored programs for each company location. Levi's is committed to covering the full cost of testing, treatment, and care. The program is managed by a global third-party vendor to protect the confidentiality of the employees and dependents who use the services. Because country conditions and programs change rapidly, this part of the program must be tailored and rolled out individually to many of Levi's locations; this is currently being done.

LESSONS FOR OTHER COMPANIES

Levi's believes that its new global HIV/AIDS efforts have met company strategic and operational goals. Employee health needs are more effectively addressed, and anxieties over HIV/AIDS in the workplace have been lessened. Equity is achieved by making HIV/AIDS education, testing, treatment, and care available to all its global employees.

Levi Strauss's experience suggests at least ten lessons for companies that wish to create a truly global HIV/AIDS program. These include:

1. *Follow the Compass.* Align your program with the guiding principles of your HIV/AIDS effort. Occasionally, companies will fail to follow their own principles when the cost and effort to reach all employees are high.
2. *Work the Data.* Insurance claims tell only part of the story. Often, the insurance simply does not cover employees' needs and does not uncover their need for HIV/AIDS-related sources.
3. *Assume nothing.* Find a way to ask employees directly what they need, and assure them of confidentiality.
4. *Equity matters.* Don't let yourself off the hook because it is hard to cover some small groups. Find ways of covering even populations ineligible for local insurance.
5. *Focus on prevention.* Reaffirm the importance of prevention in any HIV/AIDS program by integrating HIV/AIDS education into wellness programs to avert future costs and lessen future suffering.
6. *Double-check coverage.* Clarify extent of coverage in existing health plans. Do not take the first report that "that will be covered" as the final answer. There are often hidden barriers to coverage.

7. *Align outcomes.* Make sure the bottom line of the company's program is access for *all* employees. Accept accountability for achieving this outcome.

8. *Ensure authenticity.* Make sure the company's commitment to dealing with HIV/AIDS is expressed both in employee benefit programs and in company corporate social responsibility programs for local communities. Demonstrate concern for employees, customers, and community.

9. *Use the brand.* Companies need to make HIV/AIDS efforts consistent with and an expression of the company's brand. There is always a temptation to give HIV/AIDS programs a generic and no-brand presentation.

10. *Embrace innovation.* To reach every employee, a company must be creative and innovative. Off-the-shelf solutions are not always available. Constant follow-up and creative solutions are necessary.

Finally, Levi's executives and managers (like those of other companies committed to comprehensive HIV/AIDS programs) believe strongly that their effort makes employees all the prouder of their company and pays dividends in employee loyalty and productivity.

NOTE

This chapter is developed from public sources and public presentations, including "Levi Strauss & Co.: HIV/AIDS," a Harvard Business School case that chronicles the early years of the Levi Strauss HIV/AIDS efforts, and Levi Strauss's excellent websites on its HIV/AIDS efforts at http://www.levistrauss .com/about/public-policy/hivaids and http://www.levistrauss.com/sustainability /people/hivaids. I am very grateful to Ms. Paurvi Bhatt, formerly Senior Director, HIV/AIDS Prevention, Treatment, and Care at Levi Strauss, for her counsel and her participation in the Notre Dame conference. I assume sole responsibility for the chapter as presented here.

Part II

SCHOLARSHIP ADVANCING THE
ROLE OF BUSINESS IN SOCIETY

8 | Some Ethical Explications of the UN Framework for Business and Human Rights

Georges Enderle

The UN "Protect, Respect and Remedy" Framework, proposed in 2008, arguably provides a thoughtful and solid structure on which the debate and action on business and human rights can be built. However, its ethical implications are barely articulated. This essay attempts to make this structure even stronger. It first points out some basic assumptions of the Framework. It then explicates several crucial ethical implications, in particular, the moral status of the corporation, the notion of moral responsibility, the distinction of different types of obligations, and the criteria of assigning these obligations to different moral actors. Finally, it examines if and to what extent this explication of corporate responsibility for human rights may conflict with the self-interest of business enterprises and how these potential conflicts can, at least in principle, be addressed.

INTRODUCTION

Since the turn of the millennium, the theme of "business and human rights" has been discussed with increasing urgency and in more and more circles. An important impetus was the launching of the United Nations Global Compact in 2000 by Kofi Annan,[1] along with the study "Human Rights—Is It Any of Your Business?" by Amnesty International and The Prince of Wales Business Leaders Forum in 2000.[2] In the intervening years, innumerable publications have appeared, among them, of particular significance, the reports of John Ruggie, the Special Representative of the Secretary-General of the United Nations for Business and Human Rights.[3] The title "Business and Human Rights" is quite catchy since it seems to combine two things that, for many, are a contradiction in terms.

The challenge for business and human rights arises from the drastic expansion and impact of global markets since the 1990s, on the one hand, and the lack of capacity of societies to manage their adverse consequences, on the other. As Ruggie reports in *Business and Human Rights* in 2007, this "fundamental institutional misalignment . . . creates the permissive environment within which blameworthy acts by corporations may occur without adequate sanctioning or reparation. For the sake of the victims of abuse, and to sustain globalization as a positive force, this must be fixed."[4]

In order to fix this fundamental institutional misalignment, the report states, transnational corporations and other business enterprises, along with other social actors, need to collaborate on the basis of an ethical framework that is built on a relatively broad, worldwide consensus. Today, such a framework is available, consisting of the human rights which, since the Universal Declaration of Human Rights in 1948, have been further developed toward a truly global support[5] and the acknowledgment of the "indivisibility, interdependency, and interrelatedness" of human rights, including both civil and political as well as economic, social, and cultural rights.[6]

This development is an undeniable fact and offers a unique opportunity for a contemporary business and economic ethics to embrace this global ethical framework. Securing all human rights to all people has become an extraordinarily important challenge. It concerns all levels of economic activities, that is, the formation and reform of the economic system (at the macro level), the activities of economic organizations (at the middle or meso level), and the economic activities of individual persons and groups (at the micro level). Within the scope of this essay, we can only focus on a few aspects of the responsibilities of corporations (i.e., at the meso level).

Indeed, it is relatively new that corporations are being held responsible for securing human rights. Until recently, it was primarily up to the states that had been assigned with the obligation to protect human rights. But it should not be overlooked that already in 1948 the Universal Declaration of Human Rights had called upon not only states but also "each individual and all organs of society" to promote human rights.[7] Hence, corporations as "organs of society" were already aimed to be responsible actors more than sixty years ago.

To illustrate the importance and timeliness of "business and human rights," one might recall a few cases that have caught public attention: Shell's alleged complicity in the death of Nigerian activist Ken Saro-Wiwa;[8] Google facing internet censorship in China;[9] investors asking companies in Sudan to respect human rights;[10] sweatshops and labor relations;[11] and access to basic medicines in developing countries.[12] An excellent online source of information is the Business & Human Rights Resource Centre with its website and Weekly Updates.[13]

In order to sort out the wealth of information about business and human rights, to clarify the human rights challenges transnational corporations face, and to provide guidance to meet those challenges, the United Nations "Protect, Respect and Remedy" Framework,[14] elaborated by John Ruggie, was developed and has, as Peter Davis writes, "provided a structure for the debate and action on business and human rights to be built on."[15] There is no doubt that this structure includes many important ethical implications. A case in point is the use of the term *responsibility*. However, these implications are barely articulated and most often remain hidden, perhaps in order to avoid philosophical controversies that might divert attention from action-taking.

On the other hand, philosophical reflection need not necessarily distract from action; rather, it can clarify key concepts and strengthen the structure of the UN Framework. Therefore, in this contribution, we attempt to point out some basic assumptions of the UN Framework and explicate several crucial ethical implications, in particular, the moral status of the corporation, the notion of responsibility, the distinction of different types of obligations, and the criteria of assigning these obligations to different moral actors. Moreover, with this explication of corporate responsibility for human rights, we examine if and to what extent it may conflict with the self-interest of business enterprises and how these potential conflicts can, at least in principle, be addressed.

BASIC ASSUMPTIONS IN THE UN FRAMEWORK FOR BUSINESS AND HUMAN RIGHTS

As a first step in our investigation, it is appropriate to point out a series of basic assumptions implied in the UN "Protect, Respect and Remedy" Framework. Given the current state of the discussion about human rights, these assumptions can be considered plausible and will not be explained here further, although, obviously, there are numerous dissenting views.

The UN Framework includes the following assumptions:

1. Corporate responsibility for human rights requires strategies and conduct that are ultimately oriented toward people (not things) and thus are "humanly just,"[16] aiming, for instance, at the expansion of "human capabilities."[17]
2. Human rights are universally valid moral norms, which, today, have been recognized worldwide, although not undisputedly.
3. Human rights comprehend all human rights: civil, political, economic, social, and cultural rights, including the right to development.
4. Human rights are minimal moral norms and do not encompass all moral norms and values that are relevant for business enterprises.
5. It is left open how the human rights can be justified, be it from a philosophical or religious perspective. (Possible approaches can be found, among others, in the work of Henry Shue,[18] Alan Gewirth,[19] Thomas Pogge,[20] and Florian Wettstein,[21] in the Protestant and Catholic Social Teachings, and in Judaism, Islam, Buddhism and Confucianism.)

MORAL OBLIGATIONS OF SECURING HUMAN RIGHTS

Starting from these five assumptions, we can summarize the human rights problematic as follows:

1. All human rights, as minimal norms, must be secured completely.[22]
2. Each individual and all organs of society must contribute to meet this norm, to the extent each is capable of.

The first proposition about the moral rights is relatively clear and does not need further explanation, if one can accept the assumptions mentioned above. The second proposition, however, is more difficult to understand and thus has to be investigated more closely. For this purpose, three aspects can be distinguished: (1) the subjects of obligations; (2) the types of obligations; and (3) the criteria on the basis of which the obligations are to be assigned to the various subjects. These three aspects can be presented with the help of a matrix, in which the rows indicate the subjects and the columns the types of obligations, while the filling of the cells marks the application of the selected criteria for assigning the obligations to the subjects (see table 8.1 and the list of criteria discussed below).

Subjects of Obligations

As the Universal Declaration of Human Rights states, in principle all human beings and all organs of society are obligated to contribute to securing human rights. The subjects of obligations include the

Table 8.1. Subjects and Types of Obligations for Securing Human Rights

	Respect		Protect	Remedy	Promote
	Direct	Indirect (no complicity)			
States					
Transnational corporations and other business enterprises					
Other organs of society					
Individuals					

states and their diverse organs, political and economic organizations, nongovernmental organizations, religious communities, international institutions, individuals, groups, and many more. It is important to distinguish between individuals and organs of society. Apparently moral obligations are being assigned not only to individual humans but also to the organs of society. Although the concept of the "moral actor" is not literally used, the Declaration of 1948 applies it substantively to the states, whereas large-scale enterprises, at that time, were not yet understood as "moral actors." However, for the current discussion about corporate responsibility for human rights, the concept of the moral actor is of fundamental importance and will therefore be explained later on.

Types of Obligations

Securing human rights involves not only a variety of subjects of obligations but also different types of obligations that depend on the ways these obligations can be fulfilled. Such a typology is crucially important in order to allocate human rights in a differentiated manner. Moreover, it helps to overcome the questionable, yet widespread dichotomy between "negative" and "positive" rights by locating the difference between avoiding action (noninterference) and taking positive actions not in rights but in correlative obligations. In line with Shue's pertinent work,[23] three types of obligations can be distinguished: (1) the obligation to avoid violations of human rights; (2) the obligation to protect human rights by demanding recognition of the first obligation and by establishing "institutional" provisions that prevent, as much as possible, the violation of this obligation through appropriate incentive systems; and (3) the obligation to provide the victims of human rights violations access to the remedy of their rights.

This triple distinction coincides, by and large, with the distinction made in the UN Framework, although the latter changed the order by placing "protect" (the second obligation) first, followed by "respect" and "remedy."[24] It assigns the obligation to protect exclusively to the state, calling it "the duty of the state"; the obligation to respect relates primarily to the corporation, calling it "the responsibility of the corporation"; and the obligation to remedy to both the state and the corporation.

Compared to the traditional understanding of the roles of the state and the corporation, the UN Framework offers considerable progress by significantly expanding and differentiating the responsibility of transnational corporations and business enterprises. This expansion and differentiation concerns not only the responsibility of the corporation to respect, but also the duty of the state to protect and the remedy obligations of both.

Nevertheless, the UN Framework does not go far enough for a number of authors. Because today's powerful transnational corporations should be understood as quasi-governmental institutions, their responsibility should also include the protection of human rights against third parties.[25] Moreover, transnational corporations should not content themselves with a defensive attitude but should adopt a proactive attitude to promote human rights.[26]

Criteria of Assigning Obligations

As becomes clear from the discussion of the subjects and types of obligations to secure human rights, the question arises about the criteria on the basis of which the different types of obligations should be assigned to the different subjects. According to a traditional understanding that prevailed after the Second World War until the end of the twentieth century, it was primarily the nation state and, internationally, the system of all nation states (along with their extraterritorial areas) that were responsible for securing human rights. In contrast, a cosmopolitical view identifies a power shift, caused by globalization in the last twenty years, from nation states to transnational corporations, and demands a redefinition and redistribution of their respective responsibilities.

In the literature, the following criteria are predominantly discussed:

1. The understanding of the roles of actors follows the strict separation of private and public interests: The state is responsible for public interests; the other actors for private interests.
2. The impact of the actor on the victims of violations of human rights: intentional, unintentional.
3. The complicity: direct, indirect, beneficial, silent, and structural.

4. The sphere of influence[27] of the actor on the victims and perpetrators of human rights violations: actual and potential influence.
5. The capability of the actor to respect, protect, remedy, and promote human rights, although the actor did not cause human rights violations directly or indirectly.

For all criteria, it is assumed implicitly or explicitly that the actor has a certain space of freedom (to a varying degree) to secure human rights in one or another way (by respecting, protecting, remedying, or promoting them).

Different authors employ different criteria. In the following, a short overview shows how selected authors apply the criteria to the matrix of subjects and types of obligations to secure human rights.

The Draft Norms of the United Nations[28] use the criteria "impact" (#2), "direct and indirect complicity" (#3), and "actual sphere of influence" (#4). They reject the strict separation of private and public interests (#1) and disregard the "capability of the actor." Furthermore, the Draft Norms focus only on economic, social, and cultural rights, while ignoring civil and political rights and the right to development.

In comparison, the UN Framework,[29] supported also by the Business Leaders Initiative on Human Rights,[30] comprehends, most importantly, all human rights. It assigns the exclusive duty of protection to the state but seems to decline a strict separation of private and public interests. The relevant criteria from the list above are "(direct) impact" (#2) and "complicity" (or "indirect impact") (#3). The criterion of the "sphere of influence" (#4) is criticized as "too broad and ambiguous" and rejected,[31] and that of the "capability of the actor" (#5) is deemed "confusing" and rejected as well.[32] In terms of the matrix above (table 8.1), the UN Framework criteria apply only to (1) the areas of respect, protect, and remedy for states and (2) the area of respect for corporations and other businesses.

Like the UN Framework, Florian Wettstein includes all human rights in the obligations of transnational corporations.[33] But unlike the UN Framework, he extends their responsibilities far beyond the scope defined by the UN Framework, using the criteria of "impact" (#2), "direct, indirect, beneficial, silent, and structural complicity" (#3), "actual and potential sphere of influence" (#4), and "capability of the actor" (#5). The strict separation of private and public interests is rejected.

The "hybrid model" of Wesley Cragg offers a practical proposal inspired by many initiatives, such as the Sullivan Principles, the Kimberly Process Certification Scheme, the Extractive Industries Transparency Initiative, and the Equator Principles.[34] It is about "specific rule systems" for selected human rights, based on the criteria of "impact" (#2) and the "specific setting" of an industry or a social conflict.

DETERMINING CORPORATE RESPONSIBILITY FOR HUMAN RIGHTS

After this short overview of several approaches to "business and human rights," we now attempt to determine the notion of the "responsibility" of the corporation. It implies that the corporation is conceived as a moral actor. What does this mean?

There are multiple ways of identifying the corporation; but not each and every way allows for conceiving it as a moral actor. For example, the notions of the firm as a production function, a nexus of contracts, a property, an economic mechanism, or an economic animal are inappropriate concepts to be associated with the status of a moral actor. Other notions may include this moral status, although it is not addressed explicitly. From the recent literature of business ethics we may mention Marvin Brown's categorization of the corporation and the understandings of citizenship and corporations discussed by various scholars. Brown distinguishes four categories: the corporation as property, as a community, as an agent, and as a provider.[35] Whereas the first category excludes moral agency, the other three categories can include it. Such an inclusion is also possible in various concepts of citizenship discussed by Andrew Crane, Dirk Matten, and Jeremy Moon.[36] Donna Wood and Jeanne Logsdon[37] elaborate more explicitly the concepts of corporate citizenship and business citizenship by referring also to the literature on corporations as moral actors by Thomas Donaldson,[38] Patricia Werhane,[39] and Richard De George.[40]

As Lynn Paine has convincingly showed in her analysis of the evolution of the corporate personality, "in today's society, the doctrine of corporate amorality is no longer tenable."[41] Hence it is astonishing that many authors still reject or are unaware of this notion of the moral actor. Among them, one can find renowned economists like Milton Friedman[42] and Robert Reich,[43] along with leading business magazines such as *The Economist* in its two surveys on Corporate Social Responsibility.[44] Moreover, this notion has not been recognized in documents of the Christian churches on ethics in business and economics (see the memorandum on entrepreneurial action by the Council of the Protestant Church in Germany[45] and the encyclical *Caritas in Veritate*[46]). Also the Manifesto for a Global Economic Ethic[47] remains silent on this point.

The concept of corporations as "moral actors" means that, as collective entities, they act with intention (or at least exhibiting intentional behavior) to achieve their goals and can be held morally responsible for their acts, which does not hold for value-free organizations and mechanisms. Because corporations are not ends in themselves, they are not moral persons; and because they are not human beings, they cannot claim the rights of human beings. Obviously, this concept of the moral actor indicates only the moral status of business organizations without assessing their moral quality. It is by no means a substitute for the responsibilities that individuals and groups carry in and for their organizations. But this concept is necessary in order to speak of "corporate responsibility" in a meaningful way.

Today, the term *responsibility* is very commonly used to express the moral obligation of an actor. As the German philosopher Walter Schulz writes, the concept of responsibility includes a polarity.[48] On the one hand, there is the inner pole or self-commitment originating from freedom. Responsibility thus rests on and requires an inner decision. On the other hand, this self-commitment originating from freedom has its point of departure and its point of destination in a worldly relationship (the outer pole). Responsibility is always "anchored" in one or several (also collective) subjects (i.e., who is responsible?), stretching to an authority toward whom one is responsible (for instance, stakeholders, courts, a life partner, or one's conscience) and relating to a very concrete matter for which one is responsible.

In applying Schulz's concept of responsibility to the corporation as a moral actor, one can gain three interesting insights.[49] First, "self-commitment originating from freedom" signifies a moral commitment of the corporation that transcends its sociological role and its legal definition. This moral "anchoring" is particularly important when, in the process of globalization, the sociological and legal environment of business is changing drastically. To fix the worldwide institutional mis-alignment mentioned above, not only law and regulations but also the ethical commitment of business is necessary.

Second, due to this moral anchoring, the decisive challenge for business has shifted: rather than only asking whether corporate social responsibility (CSR) should be mandatory or voluntary (as has been hotly debated in the European Union), the key question is now whether the corporation commits itself out of freedom and embraces the ethical imperative of securing human rights. Indeed, ethical responsibility is not limited to voluntary actions, as if mandatory actions were only a matter of legal responsibility. Even legal and regulatory requirements need the support of ethical responsibility, provided that one should pursue not only the letter but also the spirit of the law.

Third, in his reports, Ruggie emphasizes the far-reaching importance of due diligence for human rights to be exercised by corporations. It concerns corporate management in its entirety, taking seriously all actual and potential impacts on human rights. Therefore, due diligence demands (1) understanding the human rights context of the countries in which the corporation does or intends to do business; (2) assessing the corporation's own activities; and (3) analyzing the corporation's relationships with business and other entities. The manner of exercising due diligence becomes an important benchmark for assessing the company's commitment and credibility.

After clarifying the notion of the corporation as a responsible moral actor, we now turn to the question of its contents. Should corporate responsibility be limited to a subset of human rights (as in the UN Draft Norms and Cragg model), or should it extend, in principle, to all human rights? In agreement with the UN Framework, it is proposed here that all human rights be included in and subject to the due diligence exercise of the corporation. A principal limitation based on a kind of division of labor among different social actors cannot be justified, because a corporation can impact and violate any human right, not least because the different sectors of society (that is, the public and private as well as the political, economic, and cultural sectors) cannot be strictly separated from each other.

With regard to the question of assigning different types of obligations (namely, to respect, protect, remedy, and promote), the criteria of impact and complicity are relatively undisputed and can be justified with the direct and indirect causation of human rights violations, although one cannot deny that complicity can take on multiple forms, which are sometimes very difficult to assess.

However, as Ruggie criticizes, the criterion of sphere of influence is very ambiguous and thus cannot be applied in a satisfactory manner. This holds particularly with regard to the general definition of the sphere of influence (for instance, on the local and wider community) and to the perpetrators of human rights violations. Even if a corporation is able to exercise the protection of human rights similarly to a governmental organ, its capacity does not necessarily legitimize its exercise. Due to these difficulties, Ruggie correctly pleads for a systematic strengthening of the state duty to protect.[50]

It is much more difficult, however, to assess the relevance of the criterion of the actor's capability that goes beyond the causation of human rights violation. On the one hand, the capability is a necessary condition to protect against violations by third parties. On the other hand, it is not a sufficient condition because, in addition to the corporation, other capable actors (for instance, fairly well-functioning states) that are legitimized to exercise this protection can act as well. Admittedly, the situation is more complicated when the state actor possesses this capability only to a diminished degree or not at all.

Notwithstanding these difficulties, the UN Framework is a groundbreaking and very helpful contribution to the clarification of corporate responsibility with regard to human rights. This responsibility includes the following components: (1) Transnational corporations and other business enterprises have to "respect" all human rights worldwide. This means, they must not cause directly, or be involved as accomplices directly or indirectly, in human rights violations. (2) In order to perceive and fulfill these responsibilities, the companies have to exercise "due diligence" (that is, to be committed) to examine, on a regular basis, their corporate strategies and activities with regard to all potential and actual impact on human rights and to make sure that all human rights are "respected." (3) Therefore, companies are not responsible for all types of human rights violations, but "only" for "respecting" them, though in their entirety. This framework with its guiding principles for implementation[51] is of utmost practical importance for companies themselves and company-watchers alike, as is readily demonstrable on the extraordinarily informative website of the Business & Human Rights Resource Centre that is monitoring over five thousand companies.

DOES RESPONSIBILITY FOR HUMAN RIGHTS CONFLICT WITH THE SELF-INTEREST OF THE CORPORATION?

A multitude of objections has been advanced against the idea of a corporate responsibility to secure human rights. A first group of objections questions and rejects the general validity and binding force of human rights. On the basis of the assumptions made at the beginning of this essay, these objections are not pursued any further here. A second group conceives the corporation as an amoral economic organization that has to follow exclusively economic and legal imperatives. To the extent that human rights are not legally prescribed, they are supposedly irrelevant for the corporation. These objections, too, are not further discussed here because they have been dealt with on principle and refuted above.

A third group of objections acknowledges the general validity of human rights and recognizes the corporation as moral actor. But a variety of concerns are advanced when corporations are required to respect human rights as determined in the previous section. These concerns include many questions as to how those normative standards should be defined more precisely and how they can be integrated into concrete corporate policies.[52] In this section we focus on the question, What does corporate responsibility imply when it conflicts with corporate self-interest?

Self-interest of the corporation is a very strong motivation in the market economy and can, of course, take on very different forms: competitiveness, profitability, creation of wealth, reputation, and so forth. It can be understood in a narrow sense, in which only short-term and financial matters "count," or it can be defined as "enlightened" self-interest, which also includes a long-term perspective and the benefits of all (economic and other) factors for the corporation. Moreover, self-interest can be the only and exclusive motivation; or it can go hand in hand with other motivations, such as the willingness to contribute to the development of the country in which the corporation is doing business.

It is obvious that in many situations the responsibilities for human rights as defined above come into conflict with the narrowly defined self-interest of the corporation. If the corporation decides to pursue a narrow self-interest, it puts up with human rights violations when they conflict with its self-interest or it does not care about them at all. If, however, enlightened self-interest is the driving force of the corporation, the obligation to due diligence for human rights is taken very seriously and the potential human rights violations are examined carefully. In numerous cases, it then turns out that respecting human rights is actually compatible with enlightened self-interest. The preservation or restoration of a good reputation may play an important role here. In this situation, the exercise of due diligence allows it to make the so-called "business case" for human rights policy. The business case can be advanced by corporate management itself; or it can be stated in "proxy statements" of shareholders or demanded by other stakeholders (such as consumers and investors). The argument of enlightened self-interest for respecting human rights can go very far; it can include multiple perspectives and is, in the current human rights discussion, certainly far from being exhausted. But it comes to an end when the well-defined enlightened self-interest really conflicts with human rights policy.

With this conclusion, have we limited corporate responsibility definitively within the enlightened self-interest of the corporation? Doesn't the respect for human rights extend beyond it? Various reasons suggest that is not the case. On the one hand, in a state ruled by law, the corporation has not only a legal but also a moral obligation to comply with the laws and regulations, regardless of whether or not that obligation is in its enlightened self-interest. On the other hand, a strong argument can be made that the corporation—according to its power and capabilities—also bears a moral responsibility to contribute to the production and preservation of public goods: be it with regard to climate change, the protection against systemic risk in financial markets, or the creation of a level playing field in the global economy. It appears that, for this kind of commitment, aside from self-interest, other motivations are necessary to preserve and restore the interests of other actors and the common good. For instance, the creation of the wealth of a nation demands more than the strict pursuit of self-interest because it is a combination of both private and public wealth.[53] Not only self-regarding but also other-regarding motivations are required.[54]

According to the five assumptions stated above, human rights can be conceived as "public goods" because they meet the relevant criteria of a public good: First, one can enjoy (or "consume") human rights without violating the human rights of others (or reducing their "consumption"); that is, the criterion of nonrivalry. Second, no one should be excluded from the enjoyment of human rights: that is, the criterion of nonexclusivity.

What does this mean for the understanding of corporate responsibility? Because human rights are considered public goods, the relevant motivation of the corporation cannot be merely self-interest but has to include, in one form or another, the public interest of securing human rights. Having said this, one can leave it open whether corporate responsibility (as Ruggie postulates) consists of the respect and, along with state and international institutions, of the remedy of human rights or whether it also partially includes (as Wettstein and others suggest) the protection against third parties and the general promotion of human rights. In any case, corporate responsibility must go beyond self-interest.

IN THIS CONTRIBUTION I have attempted to strengthen the UN Framework for business and human rights by explicating several of its key ethical implications. Transnational corporations should be conceived as moral actors (but not as moral persons), if in any way they can be held publicly accountable according to their impact on and significance for society and nature. Moral responsibility includes both an inner pole of self-commitment originating from freedom (incorporated in corporate culture and policy and expressed through "due diligence") and an outer pole of a concrete relationship to the world (that is, the actual corporate impact on society and nature). Based on the criteria of impact and complicity, transnational corporations and other business enterprises have to "respect" all human rights worldwide; this means they must not cause directly, or be involved as accomplices directly or indirectly in, human rights violations. This explication of corporate responsibility for human rights does not necessarily conflict with the self-interest of the corporation. As far as it is enlightened, it can contribute to securing human rights. However, it must go hand in hand with a moral commitment that goes beyond self-interest in order to respect human rights as public goods.

NOTES

1. See the UN Global Compact website, http://www.unglobalcompact .org.

2. Amnesty International and The Prince of Wales Leadership Forum, *Human Rights—Is It Any of Your Business?* (London: Amnesty International UK and The Prince of Wales Leadership Forum, 2000).

3. Key United Nations documents are listed below:

United Nations, *Business and Human Rights: Mapping International Standards of Responsibility and Accountability for Corporate Acts*, Report of the Special Representative of the Secretary-General on the issue of human rights and transnational corporations and other business enterprises, John Ruggie (Human Rights Council, Fourth Session, A/HRC/4/35: 2007).

United Nations, *Promotion of All Human Rights, Civil, Political, Economic, Social and Cultural Rights, Including the Right to Development. Protect, Respect and Remedy: A Framework for Business and Human Rights*, Report of the Special Representative of the Secretary-General on the issue of human rights and transnational corporations and other business enterprises, John Ruggie (Human Rights Council, Eighth Session, A/HRC/8/5: 2008).

United Nations, *Promotion of All Human Rights, Civil, Political, Economic, Social and Cultural Rights, Including the Right to Development Clarifying the Concepts of "Sphere of Influence" and "Complicity,"* Report of the Special Representative of the Secretary-General on the issue of human rights and transnational corporations and other business enterprises, John Ruggie (Human Rights Council, Eighth Session, A/HRC/8/16: 2008).

United Nations, *Promotion of All Human Rights, Civil, Political, Economic, Social and Cultural Rights, Including the Right to Development. Business and Human Rights: Towards Operationalizing the "Protect, Respect and Remedy" Framework*, Report of the Special Representative of the Secretary-General on the issue of human rights and transnational corporations and other business enterprises (Human Rights Council, Eleventh Session, A/HRC/11/13: 2009).

United Nations, *Promotion and Protection of All Human Rights, Civil, Political, Economic, Social and Cultural Rights, Including the Right to Development. Business and Human Rights: Further Steps toward the Operationalization of the*

"Protect, Respect and Remedy" Framework, Report of the Special Representative of the Secretary-General on the issue of human rights and transnational corporations and other business enterprises (Human Rights Council, Fourteenth Session, A/HRC/14/27: 2010).

United Nations, *Guiding Principles on Business and Human Rights: Implementing the United Nations 'Protect, Respect and Remedy' Framework for Consideration by the Human Rights Council*, Report of the Special Representative of the Secretary-General on the issue of human rights and transnational corporations and other business enterprises, John Ruggie (Human Rights Council, Seventeenth Session, A/HRC/17/31: 2011).

4. UN, *Business and Human Rights: Mapping International Standards of Responsibility and Accountability for Corporate Acts* (2007), 3.

5. See R. Burke, *Decolonization and the Evolution of International Human Rights* (Philadelphia: University of Pennsylvania Press, 2010).

6. See D. J. Whelan, *Indivisible Human Rights: A History* (Philadelphia: University of Pennsylvania Press, 2010).

7. United Nations (UN), *Universal Declaration of Human Rights*, 1948; see http://www.ohchr.org/EN/UDHR/Pages/Introduction.aspx.

8. O. Balch. "Shell Shocked and in the Dock," *Ethical Corporation* (June 2009): 12–16.

9. G. G. Brenkert, "Google, Human Rights, and Moral Compromise," *Journal of Business Ethics* 85, no. 4 (2009): 453–78.

10. R. Kropp, "Investors Ask Companies in Sudan to Respect Human Rights," SocialFunds.com (November 8, 2010); see http://www.socialfunds .com/news/article.cgi/3076.html.

11. P. Hartman, D. G. Arnold, and R. E. Wokutch, eds., *Rising above Sweatshops: Innovative Approaches to Global Labor Challenges* (Westport, CT/ London: Praeger, 2003).

12. O. Balch, "Access All Areas," *Ethical Corporation* (April 2009): 12–16.

13. See the Business and Human Rights Resource Centre website, http:// www.business-humanrights.org.

14. UN, *Protect, Respect and Remedy: A Framework for Business and Human Rights* (2008).

15. P. Davis, "A Common Focus for Human Rights," *The Ethical Corporation* (February 2011): 43.

16. See A. Rich, *Business and Economic Ethics: The Ethics of Economic Systems* (Leuven: Peeters, 2006).

17. Three relevant works by Amartya Sen are *Development as Freedom* (New York: Knopf, 1999); "Human Development and Human Rights," in *Human Development Report 2000* (United Nations Development Programme, 2000), chapter 1; and *The Idea of Justice* (Cambridge, MA: Belknap Press of Harvard University Press, 2009).

18. H. Shue, *Basic Rights: Subsistence, Affluence, and U. S. Foreign Policy*, 2d ed. (Princeton: Princeton University Press, 1996).

19. A. Gewirth, *The Community of Rights* (Chicago: University of Chicago Press, 1996).

20. T. W. M. Pogge, *World Poverty and Human Rights: Cosmopolitan Responsibilities and Reforms* (Cambridge: Polity Press, 2002).

21. F. Wettstein, *Multinational Corporations and Global Justice* (Stanford: Stanford University Press, 2009).

22. Defined in UN, *Protect, Respect and Remedy: A Framework for Business and Human Rights* (2008), §52, the list of all human rights includes:

Labor rights: Freedom of association; right to organize and participate in collective bargaining; right to nondiscrimination; abolition of slavery and forced labor; abolition of child labor; right to work; right to equal pay for equal work; right to equality at work; right to just and favorable remuneration; right to a safe work environment; right to rest and leisure; right to family life.

Non-labor rights: Right to life, liberty, and security of the person; freedom from torture or cruel, inhuman, or degrading treatment; equal recognition and protection under the law; right to a fair trial; right to self-determination; freedom of movement; right of peaceful assembly; right to marry and form a family; freedom of thought, conscience, and religion; right to hold opinions, freedom of information and expression; right to political life; right to privacy; right to an adequate standard of living (including food, clothing, and housing); right to physical and mental health; access to medical services; right to education; right to participate in cultural life, the benefits of scientific progress, and protection of authorial interests; right to social security.

23. Shue, *Basic Rights*, 35–64.

24. UN, *Protect, Respect and Remedy: A Framework for Business and Human Rights* (2008), especially §§10–26.

25. Wettstein, *Multinational Corporations and Global Justice*, especially 305–11.

26. L. A. Tavis and T. M. Tavis, *Values-Based Multinational Management* (Notre Dame, IN: University of Notre Dame Press, 2009), 168.

27. The concept of sphere of influence was introduced into corporate social responsibility (CSR) discourse by the United Nations Global Compact and is also used by the United Nations Draft Norms (UN, *Draft Norms: Economic, Social and Cultural Rights: Norms on the Responsibilities of Transnational Corporations and Other Business Enterprises with Regard to Human Rights* [Commission on Human Rights, Sub-Commission on the Promotion and Protection of Human Rights, Fifty-fifth Session, E/CN.4/Sub.2/2003/12/Rev.2: 2003]). It is based on a model that consists of a set of concentric circles, mapping stakeholders in a corporation's value chain: with employees in the innermost circle, then moving outward to suppliers, the marketplace, the community, and the

governments. It is implicitly assumed that the "influence," and thus presumably the responsibility, of a corporation declines as one moves outward from the center. See UN, *Clarifying the Concepts of "Sphere of Influence" and "Complicity"* (2008), §§7–8.

28. UN, *Draft Norms* (2003).

29. UN, *Business and Human Rights: Further Steps toward the Operationalization of the "Protect, Respect and Remedy" Framework* (2010), §1.

30. See chapter 1 of Business Leaders Initiative on Human Rights, *Policy Report 4* (2009); available at http://www.ihrb.org/pdf/BLIHR_Human _Rights_and_MDGs.pdf (pub. 2010).

31. The concept of sphere of influence is questionable because it encompasses two very different meanings of "influence": the impact of the actor on the victim and the leverage of the actor on the perpetrator of human rights violations. Moreover, it includes several notions that should be distinguished: proximity (to the victim), causation, control, benefice, and political influence. Instead of using this concept, Ruggie proposes the concepts of "direct impact" and "indirect impact" or "complicity" and offers a precise and comprehensive definition of the "scope of due diligence." See UN, *Protect, Respect and Remedy: A Framework for Business and Human Rights* (2008), §§65–81; and UN, *Clarifying the Concepts of "Sphere of Influence" and "Complicity"* (2008).

32. "Such attributes as companies' size, influence, and profit margins may be relevant factors in determining the scope of their promotional CSR-activities, but they do not define the scope of the corporate responsibility to respect human rights" (UN, *Business and Human Rights: Further Steps toward the Operationalization of the "Protect, Respect and Remedy" Framework* [2010], §58). Also, companies' capacity, whether absolute or relative to states, should not, as a general rule, determine corporate responsibilities for human rights (§64).

33. Wettstein, *Multinational Corporations and Global Justice.*

34. W. Cragg, "Business and Human Rights: A Principle and Value-Based Analysis," in *The Oxford Handbook of Business Ethics*, ed. G. G. Brenkert and T. L. Beauchamp (Oxford: Oxford University Press, 2010), 267–304.

35. M. Brown, *Civilizing the Economy. A New Economics of Provision* (Cambridge: Cambridge University Press, 2010), 209–21.

36. A. Crane, D. Matten, and J. Moon, *Corporations and Citizenship* (Cambridge: Cambridge University Press, 2008).

37. D. J. Wood and J. M. Logsdon, "Business Citizenship: From Individuals to Organizations," in *Ethics and Entrepreneurship*, The Ruffin Series No. 3: A Publication of the Society for Business Ethics (Charlottesville, VA: Society for Business Ethics, 2002), 59–94.

38. T. Donaldson, *Corporations and Morality* (Englewood Cliffs, NJ: Prentice-Hall, 1982).

39. P. H. Werhane, *Persons, Rights, and Corporations* (Englewood Cliffs, NJ: Prentice-Hall, 1985).

40. R. T. De George, *Business Ethics*, 5th ed. (Upper Saddle River, NJ: Prentice-Hall, 1999).

41. L. S. Paine, *Value Shift: Why Companies Must Merge Social and Financial Imperatives to Achieve Superior Performance* (New York: McGraw-Hill, 2003), 91.

42. M. Friedman, "The Social Responsibility of Business Is to Increase Its Profits," *The New York Times Sunday Magazine* (September 13, 1970).

43. R. B. Reich, *Supercapitalism: The Transformation of Business, Democracy, and Everyday Life* (New York: Knopf, 2007), 12–14.

44. "The Good Company: A Sceptical Look at Corporate Social Responsibility," *The Economist* (January 22–28, 2005); and "Just Good Business: A Special Report on Corporate Social Responsibility," *The Economist* (January 19, 2008).

45. Rat der EKD, *Unternehmerisches Handeln in evangelischer Perspektive* (Gütersloh: Gütersloher Verlaghaus, 2008).

46. Benedict XVI, *Caritas in Veritate* (2009); available at http://www.vati can.va/holy_father/benedict_xvi/encyclicals/documents/hf_ben-xvi_enc_2009 0629_caritas-in-veritate_en.html.

47. H. Küng, K. Leisinger, and J. Wieland, *Manifest Globales Wirtschaftsethos: Konsequenzen und Herausforderungen für die Weltwirtschaft (Manifesto Global Economic Ethic: Consequences and Challenges for Global Businesses)* (Munich: Deutscher Taschenbuch Verlag, 2010).

48. W. Schulz, *Philosophie in der veränderten Welt* (Pfullingen: Neske, 1972), 629–840 (especially 632).

49. For more, see G. Enderle, "Corporate Responsibility in the CSR Debate," in *Unternehmensethik im Spannungsfeld der Kulturen und Religionen*, ed. J. Wallacher, M. Reder, and T. Karcher (Stuttgart: Kohlhammer, 2006), 108–24.

50. UN, *Business and Human Rights: Further Steps toward the Operationalization of the "Protect, Respect and Remedy" Framework* (2010), §§16–53.

51. UN, *Guiding Principles on Business and Human Rights: Implementing the United Nations 'Protect, Respect and Remedy' Framework for Consideration by the Human Rights Council* (2011).

52. Important information on these questions is available in UN, *Business and Human Rights: Further Steps toward the Operationalization of the "Protect, Respect and Remedy" Framework* (2010); UN, *Guiding Principles on Business and Human Rights: Implementing the United Nations 'Protect, Respect and Remedy' Framework for Consideration by the Human Rights Council* (2011); and Business Leaders Initiative on Human Rights, *Policy Report 4* (2009).

53. See G. Enderle, "A Rich Concept of Wealth Creation Beyond Profit Maximization and Adding Value," *Journal of Business Ethics* 84, supplement 3 (2009): 281–95.

54. See G. Enderle, "Whose Ethos for Public Goods in a Global Economy? An Exploration in International Business Ethics," *Business Ethics Quarterly* 10, no. 1 (2000): 131–44.

9 | The United Nations Global Compact and Human Rights

A Modest but Useful Niche

Douglass Cassel

My remarks concern the human rights principles of the United Nations Global Compact. Principles 1 and 2 are as follows:

Principle 1: Businesses should support and respect the protection of internationally proclaimed human rights; and
Principle 2: make sure that they are not complicit in human rights abuses.[1]

Principles 3 through 6 concern labor rights, which are also human rights. However, they raise different issues than do Principles 1 and 2. For example, the labor rights principles interact with the monitoring procedures of the International Labor Organization.[2] I do not address them here, and confine my remarks to Principles 1 and 2.

CRITIQUING THE GLOBAL COMPACT

It would be easy for critics to attack the Global Compact human rights principles.[3] They are open to the following charges:

Vague: What conduct must companies engage in if they are to "support and respect" human rights? Which human rights are "internationally proclaimed"?

Nonbinding: The principles state that businesses "should" support and respect human rights, not that they "must" do so.

Nonenforceable: The Global Compact has no mechanism, beyond self-reporting, to monitor or enforce compliance with its principles. Companies are asked to file annual "Communications on Progress," or "COP's." But no minimum progress is required or even monitored. The only sanctions are for a company to be designated "noncommunicating" if it fails to file a proper report, and to be expelled if it fails to do so two years running.[4]

Not Taken Seriously: Even this minimal reporting obligation is ignored by many companies. Of the over 11,000 companies who have signed on to the Global Compact as of 2013, over 4,000—about 35 percent—have been expelled for failing to file reports or proper reports.[5]

Relatively Few Members: While the Global Compact's 7,000 companies make it one of the largest global organizations of corporations claiming to make human rights commitments, its membership barely penetrates the universe of some 80,000 multinational corporations, ten times as many subsidiaries, and many more national companies.[6] In short, critics may say, the Global Compact human rights principles are at best meaningless, feel-good exercises in self-congratulation, and, at worst, misleading public relations gimmicks.

DEFENDING THE GLOBAL COMPACT

I do not share that critical view, mainly for three reasons.

First, the Global Compact is not the only corporate human rights game in town. There are other norms, instruments, and regimes with greater specificity and more teeth. For example:

Criminal Prosecution: Corporate executives, such as those who supplied Zyklon B to the Nazi gas chambers, were prosecuted at Nuremberg.[7] Although international law does not generally expose corporations to criminal prosecution,[8] corporations may be criminally prosecuted under national laws in many countries. For example,

Trafigura was fined one million Euros by a Dutch court for toxic dumping in Cote D'Ivoire.[9]

Suits for money damages: Corporate executives may be sued in U.S. courts under the Alien Tort Claims Act (ATCA)[10] for complicity in human rights violations. Whether they must have a *purpose* to aid and abet human rights violations, or merely *knowledge* that they are doing so, is currently in dispute among appellate courts.[11] Whether corporations (and not merely their executives) may be similarly sued under ATCA is also a question on which appellate courts currently disagree.[12] In 2013, after hearing argument on whether corporations may be sued, the Supreme Court in *Kiobel v. Royal Dutch Petroleum Company* nonetheless did not decide the issue, ruling instead that U.S. courts generally have no jurisdiction under ATCA over human rights violations committed in a foreign country.[13] *Kiobel* arguably leaves open several questions, including whether U.S. courts may hear ATCA cases against U.S. corporations (as opposed to the foreign companies sued in *Kiobel*) for violations overseas.

However, even if the court were to rule entirely against allowing cases against corporations under ATCA, suits against corporations for money damages can still be brought under state tort laws[14] and before courts of foreign nations.[15]

Human Rights Conditions on Project Finance: Under the "Equator Principles," more than seventy major private and public international banks require borrowers in project finance transactions, for projects whose total capital costs exceed $10 million, to conduct independent assessments of whether the projects meet certain social and environmental criteria, including human rights.[16] They must also adopt mitigating or remedial measures where feasible. If they fail to do so, they may be denied project financing by the lender.[17]

National laws: National laws regulate the human rights conduct of companies in regard to many human rights issues, such as nondiscrimination.[18]

OECD National Contact Points Mediation: The Organization for Economic Cooperation and Development (OECD) requires member states to establish "national contact points" to mediate disputes concerning corporate compliance with the OECD's Guidelines for Multinational Enterprises.[19] Some states—notably the United Kingdom and The Netherlands—utilize this authority to conduct and publish extensive investigations of the facts in dispute, together with company-specific recommendations.[20]

Marketplace discipline: Where human rights violations are publicized, companies may risk consumer protests, picketing, and even boycotts.

Industry codes: Many industries now have codes of conduct with human rights components.[21]

Second, in the context of this broad array of mechanisms to encourage corporate human rights responsibility, the Global Compact plays a helpful role as a start-up option. It offers a low barrier to entry. It puts human rights (and other Global Compact principles) on the agenda of the corporation, since the Chief Executive Officer must personally approve a company's joining the Compact. The Compact is thus a potential catalyst for corporate consciousness raising on human rights, as we have seen in this volume in the cases of Microsoft and Nestlé. The annual Communications on Progress serve to provide an annual reminder. In short, the Global Compact has developed its own niche in a broader array of corporate human rights mechanisms.

Third and finally, we are still very early in the game. Most major corporations have only joined the human rights bandwagon in the last decade or so. History teaches that human rights norms and regimes, once begun, tend to catch on and to expand and strengthen.

SUGGESTIONS FOR IMPROVED CORPORATE REPORTING UNDER THE GLOBAL COMPACT

This perspective leads to some suggestions for improved corporate reporting under the Global Compact, based on the history of reporting by states that are parties to the major UN human rights treaties.

The two major UN human rights treaties for states are the International Covenant on Civil and Political Rights and the International Covenant on Economic, Social and Cultural Rights. Both treaties were adopted by the UN General Assembly in 1966. It then took ten years to secure the minimum number of ratifications by states—thirty-five—for each treaty to go into force. Since then, more and more states have gradually joined the two treaties. As of 2013,, of the 193 UN member states, 167 are parties to the civil and political covenant, and 160 to the economic, social, and cultural rights covenant.[22]

The initial implementation mechanism under both treaties was self-reporting by states.[23] Originally this was done in much the same way as Global Compact reporting is done today—states filed reports, with little or no UN monitoring or feedback.

Over time, state reporting has gradually become more meaning-ful.[24] Today the treaty monitoring bodies issue detailed guidelines on the topics to be covered and data to be provided in the reports. They hold public hearings on the state reports. Many states send high-level delegations to present their reports. The treaty bodies send written questions to the states prior to the hearings. They invite shadow reports and proposed questions for the states from human rights NGO's (non-governmental organizations) who know the country concerned. They also meet with the NGOs. During the hearings there is an interactive dialogue with the state. After the hearings, the treaty monitoring body publishes its concluding observations, noting its positive observations as well as its concerns. States are expected to report back on those con-cerns in their next reports.

Now, I do not suggest that all of this be immediately replicated by the Global Compact with respect to corporations. Just as states were not ready to participate in such a process two decades ago, most corpo-rate members of the Global Compact are probably not ready today. The current situation—annual filing of reports, which are made public on the Global Compact web page—probably needs time to sink in.

But over time, the Global Compact should move to a more evolved reporting process, one that opens the door to dialogue and even to criti-cal engagement with representatives of stakeholders. Some companies are already taking steps in that direction. For example, Nestlé has an outside advisory group of experts for its "creating shared value" activi-ties in regard to nutrition, water, and rural development. Nestlé has also been in dialogue with Alliance Sud and Swiss NGOs over labor rights in Colombia.

Such initiatives are a start, but they need eventually to go further, and not just for Nestlé. The Global Compact might, for example, es-tablish an advisory body of experts to review and comment and pose follow-up questions to companies regarding their reports. It might organize some sort of public hearings, by country or by industry, or even for large transnational corporations, in which questions received from the public and affected stakeholders could be discussed with companies.

This need not and should not mean putting companies on trial, or even on the hot seat. It is difficult enough for companies to convince their lawyers to let them join the Global Compact without having to fear a trial-type cross examination. The dialogues between states and UN human rights treaty bodies are rather polite affairs. The dialogues on corporate reports should be the same. But these dialogues do raise issues, provide feedback, and allow some space for democratic participation, without degenerating into mud-wrestling.

So, in brief, Global Compact—good start. You fill a niche otherwise left unfilled. You raise consciousness and signal the respectability of human rights as an element of serious business practice. You may need some time to continue to recruit and consolidate at your current, relatively low level of corporate commitment. At the same time, you should begin to think about how best gradually to make your reports part of a more meaningful process of monitoring and participatory dialogue with stakeholders.

NOTES

1. See "The Ten Principles," at http://www.unglobalcompact.org.

2. For example, the ILO Freedom of Association Committee receives and processes complaints of violations of freedom of association. See information available at http://www.ilo.org/global/standards.

3. For a wide-ranging, well-informed critique, see S. Deva, "Global Compact: A Critique of the U.N.'s 'Public-Private' Partnership for Promoting Corporate Citizenship," *Syracuse Journal of International Law and Commerce* 34, no. 1 (2006): 107.

4. See *The Global Compact Policy on Communicating Progress*, available at http://www.unglobalcompact.org.

5. As of July 2013, the Global Compact web site claimed over 7,000 businesses as current members, compared with 4,000 members who have been expelled. It also claimed a total of over 10,000 "corporate participants," but these are presumably not limited to businesses.

6. UN, *Promotion and Protection of All Human Rights, Civil, Political, Economic, Social and Cultural Rights, Including the Right to Development. Business and Human Rights: Further Steps toward the Operationalization of the "Protect, Respect and Remedy" Framework*, Report of the Special Representative of the Secretary-General [J. Ruggie] on the issue of human rights and transnational corporations and other business enterprises (Human Rights Council, Fourteenth Session, A/HRC/14/27: 2010).

7. See, generally, M. Lippman, "War Crimes Trials of German Industrialists: The 'Other Schindlers,'" *Temple International Law and Comparative Law Journal* 9 (1995): 173.

8. *Kiobel v. Royal Dutch Petroleum*, 621 F.3d 111, 132–41 (2d Cir. 2010), *rehearing denied*, 2011 U.S. App. LEXIS, Feb. 4, 2011, *aff'd on other grounds*, 133 S. Ct. 1659 (2013).

9. R. Evans, "Trafigura Fined €1m for Exporting Toxic Waste to Africa," *The Guardian* (July 23, 2010).

10. 28 U.S.C. section 1350. The Act provides in full: "The district courts shall have original jurisdiction of any civil action by an alien for a tort only, committed in violation of the law of nations or a treaty of the United States."

11. Compare *Presbyterian Church of Sudan v. Talisman Energy*, 582 F.3d 244 (2d Cir. 2009), *cert. denied*, 131 S. Ct. 79, 122 (2010) (purpose test), *with Doe v. Exxon*, 2011 U.S. App. LEXIS 13934, at 79–80 (D.C. Cir. July 8, 2011) (knowledge test).

12. Compare, e.g., *Kiobel v. Royal Dutch Petroleum*, note 8 above (corporations cannot be sued under ATCA), with *Doe v. Exxon*, 2011 U.S. App. LEXIS 13934 (D.C. Cir. July 8, 2011) (corporations can be sued under ATCA), *Flomo v. Firestone*, 2011 U.S. App. LEXIS 14179 (7th Cir. July 11, 2011) (same), *and Romero v. Drummond Co.*, 552 F. 3rd 1303, 1315 (11th Cir. 2008) (same).

13. *Kiobel v. Royal Dutch Petroleum Co.*, 133 S.Ct. 1659 (2013).

14. E.g., William McCall, "Nike Settles Speech Case," *Deseret News* (September 13, 2003).

15. E.g., A. Hirsch and R. Evans, "Lawyers for Claimants in Trafigura case Seek £105m in Costs," *The Guardian* (May 10, 2010).

16. Equator Principles, Principles 2 and 4, available at http://www.equator-principles.com.

17. The introduction to the Equator Principles provides "STATEMENT OF PRINCIPLES: EPFIs will only provide loans to projects that conform to Principles 1–9 below." Ibid.

18. E.g., *Ash v. Tyson Foods*, 546 U.S. 454 (2006).

19. OECD Guidelines for Multinational Enterprises, updated May 25, 2011, Part II, Section I, available at http://www.oecd.org.

20. See Statements by National Contact Points for the OECD Guidelines for Multinational Enterprises, available at http://www.oecd.org.

21. See, generally, M. Wright and A. Lehr, *Business Recognition of Human Rights: Global Patterns, Regional and Sectoral Variations* (Corporate Social Responsibility Initiative, Working Paper No. 31 [December 2006]).

22. See table of states parties at http://treaties.un.org, "Chapter IV, Human Rights."

23. Civil and Political Covenant, art. 40; Economic Rights Covenant, art. 16.

24. See, e.g., *Report on the Working Methods of the Human Rights Treaty Bodies Relating to the State Party Reporting Process*, UN Doc. HRI/MC/2005/4, May 25, 2005.

10 | Integrative Social Contracts Theory and the UN Global Compact

Daniel Malan

In an era of political correctness and sophisticated communication, it would be unexpected to find any corporation today that would openly support the views expressed by Milton Friedman. In his famous article that was originally published in the *New York Times Sunday Magazine* in 1970,[1] Friedman argues that the only social responsibility of business is to increase its profits, and accuses those businessmen (*sic*) who argue that business has responsibilities to provide employment, eliminate discrimination, and avoid pollution as "preaching pure and unadulterated socialism." At the time, Friedman's views were echoed by a contemporary philosopher John Ladd, as quoted by Kenneth Goodpaster and John Matthews: "We cannot and must not expect formal organizations, or their representatives acting in their official capacities, to be honest, courageous, considerate, sympathetic, or to have any kind of moral integrity. Such concepts are not in the vocabulary, so to speak, of the organizational language game."[2] Implicit in Friedman's argument is the view that corporations could engage in some of these activities, as long as they do it because they believe that it will increase their profits and not because of a moral obligation. For example, he approves of a company that would spend money to provide amenities to a local community, but his approval is based on the belief that this will result in the attraction of more desirable employees, reduce the likelihood of sabotage, and possibly provide tax benefits.[3]

This type of argument resonates with the current risk-based approach to corporate responsibility. In terms of this approach, corporations should take their social responsibilities seriously because it will assist them to manage risks and exploit opportunities. Following a fairly scathing review of corporate social responsibility in 2005 by *The Economist*,[4] a new report was published in 2008 by the magazine, where it refers to the fact that the 2005 report "acknowledge[d], with regret, that the CSR movement had won the battle of ideas."[5] Whether this regret had anything to do with Friedman's views of CSR as unadulterated socialism is not clear, but the 2008 report—as indicated by the title "Just Good Business"—acknowledges, with no regret this time, that "clearly CSR has arrived."[6] It then proceeds to explain how companies should view this development: One way of looking at CSR is that it is part of what businesses need to do to keep up with (or, if possible, stay slightly ahead of) society's fast-changing expectations. It is an aspect of taking care of a company's reputation, managing its risks, and gaining a competitive edge. This is what good managers ought to do anyway."[7]

But there is a twist in the tale. Those who support corporate responsibility from a moral point of view increasingly support the "just good business" approach from an *operational* point of view. In other words, by integrating corporate responsibility into the strategic elements of the corporation instead of having a marginalized CSR department with a separate budget, the positive impact on stakeholders can be increased. This raises the question of intentionality—does it count from a moral point of view if your action is not based on a sense of moral duty? Kant would say no, but many beneficiaries of corporate responsibility will simply not care. Taking the nonmoral approach to its logical conclusion, one can move beyond doing something for enlightened self-interest to doing it because it is required by law.

The "enlightened self-interest" or "business case" approach to corporate responsibility is often used by corporations. It is problematic because it only works up to a point. There is always the realization that from time to time a corporation will have to make a decision that might conflict with either its own self-interest or that of its stakehold-ers. From a utilitarian perspective it works well to justify why bribery is wrong (even if you win the contract, you might go to jail) or why it is good to invest huge amounts of money in environmental technology not required by law (it will improve reputation and ultimately you will save money). It does not always work so well if you have to decide whether to retrench employees, close plants, or pay wages that do not conform to trade union demands. In short, this approach works well as long as there is alignment with ethical values, or when the issue at stake is a nonmoral one. But no company will want to produce a business case for child labor or corruption, even if the numbers will back them up in the short term. The reason is that the moral case can (and should) trump the business case, and clearly does when it comes to extreme examples of unethical behavior.

A FRAMEWORK FOR RESPONSIBILITY

It is important to spend a few moments to investigate the concept of responsibility. Consider the following statements:

- BP was responsible for the oil spill in the Gulf of Mexico;
- The responsible thing to do would have been honest communication to all BP's stakeholders from the very beginning;
- BP's response to accusations of irresponsible behavior has been in-adequate; and
- As the CEO of BP, Tony Hayward had to take ultimate responsibility for the oil spill.

These statements illustrate the different uses of the word "responsi-bility." Goodpaster and Matthews highlight three different meanings: to indicate that someone is to blame, that something has to be done, and finally that some form of trustworthiness can be expected.[8] It is in this last sense that the moral responsibilities of corporations are ad-dressed, and also where the link between individual actions and corpo-rate actions is clearly illustrated. Responding to Ladd's position (quoted above), they clearly state: "The language of ethics does have a place in the vocabulary of an organization. . . . Organizational agents such as corporations should be no more and no less morally responsible (rational, self-interested, altruistic) than ordinary persons."[9]

Goodpaster and Matthews argue further that corporations that monitor practices such as employment, health and safety, or environmental performance show the same rationality and respect that morally responsible individuals do.[10] We can therefore attribute actions, strategies, and also moral responsibilities to corporations just as we can to individuals.

The position of Goodpaster and Matthews that an organization reveals its character in the same way that an individual does provides a common sense approach to business ethics and corporate responsibility that remains attractive today to practitioners and lawmakers, that is, to those who do not necessarily have an interest in a theoretical grounding of moral responsibility. It is this approach, as well as the experiences—both the good and bad, but particularly the bad—of the impact that corporations can have on society that has resulted in what Oliver Williams[11] refers to as the growing consensus about the moral obligations and the emerging new role for the corporation in society.[12]

The framework shown in figure 10.1 can assist corporations to conceptualize, develop, and implement effective corporate responsibility programs. It is based on relevant and credible academic theory but presented in a user-friendly way that emphasizes practical application. The basic logic of the framework (read clockwise from the top left corner) is that companies need to go through a sequential process: first, of understanding corporate responsibility, then of taking responsibility, then

Figure 10.1. Dimensions of Corporate Responsibility

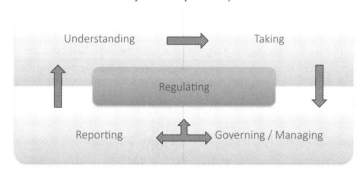

of ensuring that systems are in place to govern and manage, and, finally, of reporting on responsibility. This always takes place in a specific context with regulatory requirements, both voluntary and mandatory. Because the regulatory environment is pervasive, it informs all the other dimensions but specifically the activities of governing, managing, and reporting.

This chapter focuses mainly on the dimension of *understanding* responsibility, with specific reference to one voluntary corporate responsibility standard, the United Nations Global Compact (the Global Compact). The different dimensions of the framework are described briefly below.

Understanding responsibility is the crucial first step that many corporations miss by simply jumping on the bandwagon or joining an initiative such as the Global Compact without giving it proper and critical thought. Understanding responsibility implies thinking and debate about the moral responsibility of any corporation and taking a view on the link between the business case and the moral case for corporate responsibility. This is the dimension within which choices have to be made in terms of preferred moral theories. A detailed discussion of moral choices does not fall within the scope of this chapter—rather, a personal preference for the theory of Integrative Social Contracts Theory (ISCT) is presented. More detail on this approach is provided in the next section.

A conceptual understanding of moral responsibility does not necessarily translate into action on the side of companies. A conscious commitment has to be taken by companies to be moral actors. From a practical point of view, *taking* responsibility is crucial to ensure that appropriate programs are designed and implemented, and that the correct tone is set at the top.

The nuts and bolts of any corporate responsibility program are to be found in the way in which programs are *managed* and *governed*. The important distinction between management and governance is not discussed in detail here, but is critical to ensure effective implementation and management (by managers) as well as governance and oversight (by directors).

Reporting on responsibility closes the loop between performance, measurement, and stakeholder engagement. Although it is always a secondary activity, reporting is critical in an age of transparency and increased stakeholder interest in the activities of all companies. The reporting dimension is strongly influenced by regulation, since there are many voluntary and mandatory reporting standards in the world. From a voluntary perspective, the Global Reporting Initiative and the activities of the International Integrated Reporting Committee are probably the most significant at the moment.

Regulating responsibility is necessary because the role of corporations in society is so important that it cannot all be left to voluntary initiatives, and even those who make a voluntary and conscious commitment to take responsibility, will need some guidance. The debate about whether corporate responsibility should become a legal responsibility is a complicated one, and conventional wisdom suggests that a combination between minimum legal standards and innovation through voluntary initiatives should be encouraged.

As was mentioned above, the focus in this chapter is on understanding responsibility. The next section introduces a preferred theoretical approach, and the chapter concludes with an application of this theory to the UN Global Compact, arguably the most important corporate responsibility initiative in the world.

INTEGRATIVE SOCIAL CONTRACTS THEORY

In his earlier work, Tom Donaldson argues that morality should be applied to international affairs and—more specifically—international business.[13] According to him, this is the case whether morality is simply defined as enlightened self-interest or something more fundamental. He provides a detailed discussion of both cultural relativism and traditional Hobbesianism and illustrates how both these approaches fail to argue convincingly against the application of morality. Elsewhere, he discusses how morality can be applied to international business in a way that avoids both relativism and absolutism.[14] In this article, originally written in 1996, the basic outline of Integrative Social Contracts Theory (discussed below) is already present, and Donaldson proposes that companies must be guided by three principles:

- Respect for core human values, which determine the absolute moral threshold for all business activities.

- Respect for local traditions.
- The belief that context matters when deciding what is right and what is wrong.[15]

The core human values (also referred to as hyper norms) that Donaldson refers to are defined as respect for human dignity, respect for basic rights, and good citizenship.[16] Because these values are too vague to provide specific guidance, there is a requirement for companies to develop more specific codes: "Whenever intolerable business situations arise, managers should be guided by precise statements that spell out the behavior and operating practices that the company demands."[17]

The development and implementation of effective internal codes are not addressed in any detail in this chapter, but they remain among the biggest challenges for corporations around the world. In broad terms, there have been two main approaches: a compliance-based approach that provides detailed information and is usually more focused on the prevention of unethical behavior, and a values-based approach that encourages ethical behavior and allows employees to take a specific context into account when they make decisions.

Integrative Social Contract Theory (ISCT) was developed by Donaldson and Thomas Dunfee to provide guidance on ethical issues in international business and—as was explained above—suggests that there is an absolute moral threshold (hypernorms) that would apply anywhere in the world, but also that large corporations should have respect for local customs and traditions and can therefore negotiate microsocial contracts without transgressing this moral threshold. Companies are able to do this because context matters when deciding between right and wrong.

The basic message of ISCT[18] is that "implicit agreements constitute part of the basic software of business ethics."[19] As opposed to traditional social contract theory that investigates the contracts between citizens and governments, ISCT focuses on how economic participants will define business ethics. The veil of ignorance in ISCT is more revealing than the one suggested by Rawls.[20] The basic assumption is made that participants do not know their economic standing, for instance, which company they work for or what their personal wealth is. However, they are granted knowledge about their economic and political preferences, as well as a basic sense of right and wrong. Under these circumstances, participants are then hypothetically gathered for "a global congress to construct an agreement that would provide a fundamental framework for ethical behavior in economic activities."[21] The use of "integrative" emphasizes that "ISCT is based upon a hypothetical social contract whose terms allow for the generation of binding ethical obligations through the recognition of actual norms created in real social and economic communities. A hypothetical social contract is thereby integrated with real or extant social contracts."[22]

Donaldson and Dunfee argue that a hypothetical global congress for business ethics will not be able to agree on a detailed set of ethical rules and guidelines, but rather will agree on a process or broad framework. This framework of business ethics as social contracts is what they call the Global ISCT Macrosocial Contract for Economic Ethics:

1. Local economic communities have moral free space in which they may generate ethical norms for their members through microsocial contracts.

2. Norm-generating microsocial contracts must be grounded in consent, buttressed by the rights of individual members to exercise voice[23] and exit.

3. In order to become obligatory (legitimate), a microsocial contract norm must be compatible with hypernorms.

4. In cases of conflicts among norms satisfying macrosocial contract terms 1–3, priority must be established through the application of rules consistent with the spirit and letter of the macrosocial contract.[24]

Moral free space is defined as "[t]he freedom of individuals to form or join communities and to act jointly to establish moral rules applicable to the members of the community."[25] If a norm or a moral rule is generated within moral free space and has the support of the majority of the community, it is said to be "authentic." A community is defined as "a self-defined, self-circumscribed group of people who interact in the context of shared tasks, values, or goals and who are capable of establishing norms of ethical behavior for themselves."[26] Even though Donaldson and Dunfee make a distinction between their definition of community and the concept of stakeholders, I would argue that the concepts are sufficiently similar for ISCT to be interpreted as entirely compatible with stakeholder theory.

Members of a particular community have an ethical obligation to abide by the existing authentic norms, as long as these norms do not violate hypernorms. Hypernorms are defined as "principles so fundamental that they constitute norms by which all others are to be judged" and are "discernible in a convergence of religious, political and philosophical thought."[27] There are three distinct hypernorm categories:

- Procedural hypernorms—these stipulate the rights of voice and exit, and are defined as the conditions "essential to support consent in microsocial contracts";
- Structural hypernorms—principles "that establish and support essential background institutions in society"; these are necessary for political and social organization; and
- Substantive hypernorms—these are the fundamental "concepts of the right and the good."[28]

Donaldson and Dunfee include the following types of evidence in support of hypernorms—two or more of these would be sufficient for a "rebuttable presumption that it constitutes a hypernorm":

- Widespread consensus that a principle is universal;
- Inclusion in well-known global industry standards;
- Supported by prominent NGOs, regional government organizations, global business organizations, or an international community of professionals;
- Consistently referred to as a global ethical standard by the international media;
- Consistent with precepts of major religions and philosophies, as well as findings concerning universal human values; and
- Supported by the laws of many different countries.[29]

THE UN GLOBAL COMPACT

Today the Global Compact is the world's largest voluntary corporate citizenship initiative and describes itself as "a framework for businesses that are committed to aligning their operations and strategies with ten universally accepted principles in the areas of human rights, labor, the environment and anti-corruption." The ten principles were derived from:

- The Universal Declaration of Human Rights;
- The International Labor Organization's Declaration on Fundamental Principles and Rights at Work;
- The Rio Declaration on Environment and Development; and
- The United Nations Convention Against Corruption.

The Global Compact also emphasizes the strategic and risk-related benefits of participation (italics mine):

> The United Nations Global Compact presents a unique *strategic platform* for participants to advance their commitments to sustainability and corporate citizenship. Structured as a public-private initiative, the Global Compact offers a policy framework for the development, implementation and disclosure of sustainability principles and practices related to its four core areas: human rights, labor, the environment and anti-corruption. Indeed, *managing the enterprise risks and opportunities related to these areas is today a widely understood aspect of long-term "value creation"*—value creation that can simultaneously benefit the private sector and societies at large.[30]

This is an important point, and it links to the points raised earlier about normative and risk-based approaches to corporate responsibility. In its ten-year anniversary report of 2010, the Global Compact emphasizes this point time and time again. In his foreword, UN Secretary-General Ban Ki-moon states that "expanding markets and advancing the economic and social well-being of people and societies can be two sides of the same coin."[31] This is echoed by Global Compact Executive Director Georg Kell in his introduction: "Today, there is growing recognition from all corners . . . that when companies embed human rights, labor standards, environmental stewardship and anti-corruption measures throughout their organizations, it is good for both business and society."[32]

In July 2013 there were more than 10,000 participants in the UN Global Compact. This included more than 7,000 business participants, of which almost 6,000 were regarded as active participants.

Approximately 50 percent of all business participants come from Europe, followed by Latin America (22%), Asia (16%), Northern America (8%), and Africa (5%).[33] The leading countries in terms of participation are France and Spain (600 business participants each), followed by the United States (250), Brazil (200), and China (190).

The 2009 Global Compact Implementation Survey, conducted by the Wharton School at the University of Pennsylvania, highlighted the following issues:

- 65% of companies indicated that the Global Compact had significantly helped (24%) or moderately helped (41%) to advance corporate responsibility policies and/or practices;[34]
- 69% of companies indicated that corporate responsibility policies and strategies are developed and/or evaluated at the CEO level, while only 49% indicated that this happens at board level;[35]
- The top five most popular reasons for engagement in the Global Compact were (in order of preference): to increase trust in the company, to integrate sustainability issues, the universal nature of the principles, networking with other organizations, and to address humanitarian concerns;[36]
- 66% of companies indicated that they consider whether their suppliers comply with Global Compact principles, with 12% requiring compliance with the principles in order to be selected as a business partner. Compliance was measured predominantly by company audits (36%) and self-assessment questionnaires (35%), while only 12% used independent third party audits;[37] and
- Actions taken to spread the commitment to the Global Compact throughout subsidiaries included the creation of a corporate responsibility position in subsidiaries (47%), evaluation of subsidiary actions (43%), training and awareness-raising (41%), connecting the Global Compact principles to local issues (38%), partnerships at the local level (30%), and encouragement to join a Local Network (24%); and 20% indicated encouragement to join multi-stakeholder consultations.[38]

In terms of implementation of and/or compliance with the Global Compact Principles, the following information is highlighted, with specific reference to the area of localization of the Principles.

ASSESSING THE UN GLOBAL COMPACT

Williams has argued that the UN Global Compact is potentially the most effective instrument to gain consensus of the role of business in society.[39] This was at a time when there were just over a thousand business participants—certainly in terms of growth in numbers, the initiative has gone from strength to strength. In their ten-year assessment of the UN Global Compact, Macintosh and Waddock highlight three issues:

- New technologies and continually shifting boundaries make the UN Global Compact a "nested network," one network among others;
- The realization that global warming is happening and that there is a possibility of ecological meltdown increases the urgency of the initiative; and
- Since humans are inventive, creative, innovative and problem-solving creatures, we should be able to come up with solutions for the mess we created ourselves.[40]

By way of analogy, it would not be inaccurate to compare the UN Global Compact with a club—it is not too difficult to get into the club, and not too difficult to stay in the club. So, as opposed to sour grapes of people who do not qualify to get in and then criticize the club as being exclusive and elitist, some critics believe that it is too easy to get in and that the principles are too vague to be really useful. As Rasche points out, one "should not criticize the Compact for something it never pretended and/or intended to be."[41] Rasche explains the need for the principles to be filled with contextualized meaning—this is something that I will return to when I discuss the application of ISCT below.

Rasche also discusses the criticism that the UN Global Compact amounts to privatization of the UN. He points out that the global agenda is so demanding that partnerships are needed, and also that the UN has been in partnership with business associations for a very long time. This argument about the need for partnerships is particularly important in terms of the Millennium Development Goals, and is also reminiscent of Schwab's position on global corporate citizenship.[42]

In response to the criticism about lack of monitoring, Rasche retorts that "[t]he Compact was set up as a multi-stakeholder learning network based on dialogue and partnership between business, civil society and the UN system," and also explains how certification bodies like SA 8000 are challenged by blurred boundaries and therefore only certify single production facilities.[43] This is a legitimate response, but reputational issues related to the low entry barriers present some of the biggest risks to the future of the Compact. Certification or accreditation cannot be the answer to this problem—if the initiative itself can maintain its legitimacy, perhaps the focus of the press and other stakeholders should rather be to pressure companies who are guilty of what the UN Global Compact calls "systematic or egregious abuses" to step down voluntarily.

ISCT AND THE UN GLOBAL COMPACT

I argue here that an application of ISCT can assist a better understanding of the UN Global Compact and enable signatories to the initiative to respond to the formal and moral requirements of the Compact in such a way that it will strengthen their corporate responsibility programs and ultimately have a fundamental impact on how corporations deal with responsibility.

Donaldson states the following in support of his own view that self-interest is linked to the health of society: "When UN Secretary-General Kofi Annan in an address to The World Economic Forum on January 31, 1999, called upon global corporations to unite in affirming the principles of the UN Global Compact, he appealed not only to their moral idealism. He appealed also to their enlightened egoism."[44] This is in line with his argument that companies must take three steps to satisfy all conditions of the UN Global Compact: egoism, cooperative egoism, and corporate citizenship.[45]

- "Corporate egoism" provides the empirical no-brainer, where there is a direct short-term benefit to the company, for example, switching off the lights to save on the electricity bill;
- "Cooperative egoism" alludes to the efficiency hypernorm, where companies cooperate because it is in their collective self-interest to do so; for example, even though an individual bribe might result in an immediate

short-term advantage for a particular company, if all companies agree not to undermine the political and judicial systems through acts of bribery, the system will be more efficient and will be to everyone's advantage;

- "Corporate citizenship"—this is the third, and most difficult, rung of the ladder, because it expects companies to do something simply because it is the right thing to do, for example, to provide basic housing and health services in locations where these are not available.

Donaldson has not written extensively about the application of ISCT to the UN Global Compact, and that is what I would like to focus on in the remainder of this chapter. The basic argument proposed here is that the ten principles of the Global Compact can be regarded as substantive hypernorms. To qualify as hypernorms there are certain conditions that must be met—these have been discussed in the previous section, but broadly they relate to general consensus, alignment with existing standards, support by major stakeholder groups, consistency with major religions and philosophies, and incorporation into existing legal frameworks. It is clear that all ten Global Compact principles are supported by the majority of these types of evidence, although it should be noted that "alignment with existing standards" should be excluded to avoid a circular argument.

It is further argued that the way in which hypernorms limit moral free space can provide practical guidance to companies that have subscribed to the Global Compact, not only in how they need to adhere to the ten principles, but how they can structure and implement their broader corporate responsibility programs. In my view, the following statement by Donaldson and Dunfee supports this position: "Since such principles [hypernorms] are designed to impose limiting conditions on all micro contracts, they cannot be derived from a single micro contract, but must emanate from a source that speaks with univocal authority for all micro contracts."[46]

One potential difference in the application of ISCT is that Donaldson and Dunfee developed the theory as a guide for practical decision-making. In their very detailed examples of the application of ISCT, they always start with the need to "recognize the ethical problem." In other words, once faced by a practical decision, the decision maker proceeds to identify the appropriate hypernorms. Within the context of ISCT, I am therefore suggesting—to some extent—a reversal of the process. Viewing the UN Global Compact as a (nonexhaustive) set of substantive hypernorms, I suggest that decision makers can determine appropriate actions and programs from these norms and explore appropriate moral free space within them. This interpretation gives the UN Global Compact a certain dynamic power that is not present if it is merely seen as a voluntary code that confirms a set of static principles. Understood in this way, it could become a driving force for the design and implementation of effective corporate responsibility programs. Although Dunfee is circumspect in acknowledging that hypernorms alone may provide guidance to solve ethical dilemmas, I think it should be acknowledged that this could happen if the hypernorm is merely seen as a point of departure to explore moral free space. Out of this activity a practical guideline or solution could then be developed, which will apply at the level of the local community.

I am aware of the dangers of this process, as highlighted by Dunfee: "the search for hypernorms occurs in the context of decision-making, they are not to be fully 'discovered' *ex ante*."[47] However, if the ten principles are seen as a framework that can coordinate expectations,[48] this could be dealt with. Just as Donaldson and Dunfee refuse to suggest a finite list of hypernorms, because that would constitute moral absolutism,[49] the Global Compact should also not be regarded as a finite list that will provide an all-inclusive framework. The fact that the initial nine principles were later supplemented by a tenth (on anti-corruption), and the increasing convergence with the ideals of the Millennium Development Goals, illustrate this point clearly.

Let's look at a hypothetical example. Company A has decided to become a signatory to the UN Global Compact. It has a good reputation for corporate responsibility and wants to be part of the growing community of Global Compact signatories. The initial thinking to reach this decision probably went along the following lines:

- The Global Compact is the largest voluntary corporate citizenship initiative in the world—we want to be a part of this growing movement, and association with the UN will be good for our reputation;
- Since we are already a responsible citizen and implicitly support all the principles, the impact on our company would be minimal—we can

continue what we are doing in any case and must simply ensure that we
fulfill the technical requirements;

- The most onerous of these requirements (and the only one that is actively monitored and could lead to delisting) is the need to submit
  an annual Communication on Progress. We are already preparing a
  sustainability report according to the Global Reporting Initiative
  guidelines and we can therefore submit our existing report as our Communication on Progress.

I believe the above approach is indicative of how many companies
consider participation in the Global Compact. There is nothing inherently questionable in it from a moral point of view, and most of the
time this approach will probably not lead to any problems. It is in line
with the first two rungs in Donaldson's "ladder of justification": "corporate egoism" and "cooperative egoism" (supported by the efficiency
hypernorm). But it does not lead to the third rung of "citizenship": "The
Compact is asking companies to do many things simply because *they are
the right thing to do.*"[50]

So let's assume that Company A becomes a convert to ISCT and
accordingly reexamines its participation in the Global Compact. I believe it is likely that they will come up with the following approach:

- We support the Global Compact because it provides a *moral* framework of responsible corporate citizenship. We believe that the ten principles are in line with our own values as a company and we regard them
  as non-negotiable, even if this means that in some cases this support
  might not be in our own perceived self-interest;
- To prevent the Global Compact from becoming a list of empty and
  vague principles, we will actively investigate moral free space in all the
  communities and geographical locations where we operate around the
  globe. We will demonstrate fundamental respect for the ten principles,
  but also for local cultures and traditions, and we will implement the
  principles in such a way that it makes a real and positive difference at
  the local level;
- We understand that these activities that we will engage in have to be
  both authentic (i.e., supported by all our material stakeholders) and
  legitimate (i.e., in line with the substantive hypernorms of the Global
  Compact and other relevant hypernorms that we might identify).

An adapted version of the framework suggested earlier (fig. 10.1), with specific application to ISCT and the Global Compact, will look like figure 10.2. This flexible but context-specific approach will enable companies to make meaningful decisions at the local level without compromising the universal principles. It is also entirely compatible with the more recent UN Global Compact Management Framework, and could easily accommodate the framework's proposed activities of commit, assess, define, implement, measure, and communicate.

From an ethical perspective, moral free space allows contextualized and defensible choices. For example, it will allow companies to subscribe to the principle of nondiscrimination while at the same time supporting affirmative action in South Africa or localization in Botswana. One of the most striking examples of moral free space is that of Levi-Strauss in Bangladesh, where the company allowed two of its suppliers to employ children below the legal minimum age, sponsored their school education while they were working for the suppliers, and guaranteed them a full-time job once they reached the legal age.[51]

But moral free space also has boundaries. Therefore, it allows Nestlé to state categorically that they will apply the same waste water management standards in all countries where the company operates, regardless of local legal requirements. It also does not allow companies to engage in corruption in jurisdictions where its acceptance might seem to be the norm, because this would clearly violate the appropriate hypernorm.

A more challenging example is the case of Holcim in the Sudan, where, as a member of the International Committee of the Red Cross Corporate Support Group, the company became involved in the "Clean Water in Sudan Project." Is this simply a case of a valuable project that

Figure 10.2. Adapted Corporate Responsibility Framework

ISCT	CEO and Board Statement
UN Global Compact	
Communication on Progress	Mainstreaming and Alignment with Millennium Development Goals

takes the local context and needs into account, or is there a hint of non-adherence to one principle (protection of human rights) being hidden by support for another (care for the environment)?

CORPORATE RESPONSIBILITY SHOULD start with a moral choice. The business case can make this choice easier, but it should never become the main driver for responsibility. ISCT provides a moral framework that is particularly suitable for large, multinational corporations. The more general framework proposed in this chapter that incorporates the different dimensions of responsibility (understanding, taking, managing, governing, reporting, regulating) can guide any corporation, regardless of whether it is a signatory to the Global Compact.

As the world's largest corporate citizenship initiative, the Global Compact can make a significant contribution to strengthening and supporting global corporate responsibility initiatives. As the name suggests, the idea of a social contract is embedded in the initiative. Through initiatives such as local networks and collective action, further impetus is given to some of the fundamental tenets of ISCT, for example, contextualization and micro contracts. For *any* corporation, ISCT provides the opportunity to move away from lip service to a vague "business case" approach toward actions that can truly make a difference at the local and the global levels.

The application of ISCT to the Global Compact raises the bar in terms of all the dimensions of corporate responsibility. This has implications for the aggressive growth targets of the Global Compact Office. In terms of the views expressed here, less might be more. A smaller group of committed signatories that truly understand and support the moral case will be more effective and acceptable than a larger group of corporate egoists, both in terms of their own impact as well as setting a good example for others to follow.

NOTES

This chapter includes extracts from the author's unpublished PhD dissertation.

1. M. Friedman, "The Social Responsibility of Business Is to Increase Its Profits," *The New York Times Sunday Magazine* (September 13, 1970).

2. K. Goodpaster and J. Matthews, "Can a Corporation Have a Conscience?" *Harvard Business Review* 60, no. 1 (January–February 1982): 132–41. See p. 133 in particular.

3. Friedman, "The Social Responsibility of Business Is to Increase Its Profits."

4. C. Crook, "The Good Company: A Survey of Corporate Social Responsibility," *The Economist* (January 22, 2005).

5. "Just Good Business: A Special Report on Corporate Social Responsibility," *The Economist* (January 19, 2008): 4.

6. Ibid.

7. Ibid., 14.

8. Goodpaster and Matthews, "Can a Corporation Have a Conscience?" 133.

9. Ibid.

10. Ibid., 135.

11. O. Williams, "Responsible Corporate Citizenship and the Ideals of the United Nations Global Compact," in *Peace through Commerce: Responsible Corporate Citizenship and the Ideals of the United Nations Global Compact*, ed. O. F. Williams, C.S.C. (Notre Dame, IN: University of Notre Dame Press, 2008), 435.

12. In "The Purpose of the Corporation" (in *Peace through Commerce*, ed. O. Williams, 13–54), M. Smurthwaite provides a comprehensive overview of debates about the moral purpose of the corporation and summarizes the general trends and agreements in the relevant literature. She focuses on the nature of the corporation and the issue of corporate moral agency, as well the purpose and role of the corporation. The following is a very brief summary of her main findings:

- In terms of the nature of the corporation, it is something that exists in law, has a human element, and does not exist in a vacuum (19);
- There are three main approaches to corporate moral agency: first, that corporations do not have any moral responsibilities; second, that there is moral agency only insofar as this resides in the individuals who comprise the organization; and third, that the corporation itself is a moral agent (19–24)—as explained by Goodpaster above and supported by Donaldson, to be discussed below; and
- In terms of the purpose of the corporation, the two basic approaches are the classical liberal economic paradigm (the view that the corporation only has to make a profit) and the view that there is a broader purpose to the corporation, which includes corporate citizenship, a virtue ethics approach, and corporate social responsibility, as well as the social thought of the Catholic Church and other churches. These approaches suggest that the broader purpose of the corporation is not only to make

a profit but also to develop individuals and serve the common good, be a good citizen, contribute to the community as a whole, and be socially responsible (24–29).

13. T. Donaldson, *The Ethics of International Business* (New York: Oxford University Press, 1989).

14. T. Donaldson, "Values in Tension: Ethics Away from Home," in *Business Ethics: Readings and Cases in Corporate Morality*, 4th ed., ed. M. Hoffman, R. Frederick, and M. Schwartz (New York: McGraw-Hill, 2001), 475–83.

15. Ibid., 478.

16. Ibid., 479.

17. Ibid., 480.

18. This summary of ISCT is based on the original publication (T. Donaldson and T. W. Dunfee, *Ties that Bind: A Social Contracts Approach to Business Ethics* (Boston: Harvard University Press, 1999), as well as a précis provided by the authors for a special publication of "Business and Society Review" (Donaldson and Dunfee, "Précis for *Ties that Bind*," *Business and Society Review* 105, no. 4 [2000]: 436–43). It highlights the main components of ISCT, discusses the authors' response to some of the main criticisms levelled against the theory, and then proceeds to indicate how this could be applied to the Global Compact.

19. Donaldson and Dunfee, "Précis," 437.

20. The veil of ignorance was introduced in social contract theory by John Rawls to "[leave] aside those aspects of the social world that seem arbitrary from a moral point of view" (J. Rawls, "Justice as Fairness," in *Business Ethics: Readings and Cases in Corporate Morality*, 4th ed., ed. M. Hoffman, R. Frederick, and M. Schwartz [New York: McGraw-Hill, 2001], 55). These aspects include natural endowment or social circumstance: "Somehow we must nullify the effects of specific contingencies which put men at odds and tempt them to exploit social and natural circumstances to their own advantage. Now in order to do this I assume that the parties are situated behind a veil of ignorance. They do not know how the various alternatives will affect their own particular case and they are obliged to evaluate principles solely on the basis of general considerations" (Rawls, "Justice as Fairness," 55).

21. Donaldson and Dunfee, "Précis," 438.

22. T. Dunfee, "A Critical Perspective of Intregrative Social Contracts Theory: Recurring Criticisms and Next Generation Research Topics," *Journal of Business Ethics* 68 (2006): 304.

23. The right of voice is defined as "the right of members of a community to speak out for or against existing and developing norms" (Donaldson and Dunfee, *Ties that Bind*, 43).

24. Ibid., 46.

25. Ibid., 38.

26. Ibid., 39.

27. Donaldson and Dunfee, "Précis," 441.

28. Donaldson and Dunfee, *Ties that Bind*, 53.

29. Ibid., 60.

30. http://www.unglobalcompact.org/HowToParticipate/Business
_Participation/index.html.

31. United Nations Global Compact (UNGC), *United Nations Global Compact Annual Review—Anniversary Edition* (New York: United Nations Global Compact Office, 2010), 5.

32 Ibid., 6.

33. Approximate percentages based on a graph included in the Global Compact annual review (ibid., 11).

34. Ibid., 10.

35. Ibid., 13.

36. Ibid.

37. Ibid., 14.

38. Ibid., 15.

39. O. Williams, "The UN Global Compact: The Challenge and the Promise," *Business Ethics Quarterly* 14, no. 4 (2004): 755–74.

40. M. McIntosh and S. Waddock, "Introduction," in *The UN Global Compact: Looking Forward Ten Years After*, ed. McIntosh and Waddock (South Brisbane, Australia: Asia Pacific Center for Sustainable Enterprise, 2010), 1; available from the publisher at http://www.griffith.edu.au/__data/assets/pdf
_file/0003/287706/The-UN-Global-Compact.pdf.

41. A. Rasche, "The UN Global Compact: A Critique of Its Critiques," in *The UN Global Compact: Looking Forward Ten Years After*, ed. McIntosh and Waddock, 17.

42. K. Schwab, "Global Corporate Citizenship: Working with Governments and Civil Society," *Foreign Affairs* 87, no. 1 (January–February 2008): 107–18.

43. A. Rasche, "The UN Global Compact: A Critique of Its Critiques," 17.

44. T. Donaldson, "Steps for Global Transformation: The 2008–2009 Economic Crisis," in *The UN Global Compact: Looking Forward Ten Years After*, ed. McIntosh and Waddock, 9.

45. T. Donaldson, "De-compacting the Global Compact," *Journal of Corporate Citizenship* 11 (2003): 69–72.

46. Donaldson and Dunfee, *Ties that Bind*, 50.

47. Dunfee, "A Critical Perspective of Intregrative Social Contracts Theory," 308.

48. For a more detailed discussion of the coordination of expectation, see N. Hsieh, "Voluntary Codes of Conduct for Multinational Corporations: Coordinating Duties of Rescue and Justice," *Business Ethics Quarterly* 16, no. 2 (2006): 119–35.

49. Donaldson and Dunfee, *Ties that Bind*, 54.

50. Donaldson, "De-compacting the Global Compact," 71.

51. Donaldson, "Values in Tension," 483.

11 | The MDGs, Partnering for Results

The UK Government Perspective

Philip Parham

This brief essay will give an overview from a government perspective on "partnering to achieve the Millennium Development Goals." I plan to do three things:

First, to set out our perspectives on the September 2010 UN Millennium Development Goals Summit and how the United Kingdom government approaches development.

Second, to stress the vital role that the private sector plays in MDG achievement and to give you some examples of how the UK's Department for International Development (DFID) works in tandem with business.

And third, to outline the crucial role of civil society organizations in promoting the MDGs in developing countries, and how the United Kingdom works with them.

At that summit, over sixty world leaders came together at the United Nations in New York to reaffirm their commitment to the Millennium Development Goals and agree on an ambitious action agenda for achieving the goals by 2015.

During the summit, the UK focused its efforts on securing a major push on the most off-track MDGs, particularly women's and children's health. UN Secretary-General Ban Ki-moon's "Every Woman, Every

Child" event launched a global strategy aimed at saving the lives of more than 16 million women and children. At that event, the Deputy Prime Minister announced that the UK's contribution to this effort will lead to saving the lives of at least 50,000 women in pregnancy and childbirth and 250,000 newborns and will enable 10 million couples to access modern methods of family planning over the next five years. The event generated an unprecedented US$40 billion in resources for maternal and child health and convened a wide range of partners behind the global strategy. Significant commitments to action came from a number of developed and developing countries, as well as the private sector, charities, NGOs, and international organizations.

The UK also helped put a focus on combating malaria by co-hosting a high-profile side event that both raised awareness and generated significant new commitments from the international community. Deputy Prime Minister Clegg and International Development Secretary of State Andrew Mitchell announced our pledge of as much as £500 million per year by 2014 to help halve the number of deaths caused by malaria in at least ten African countries by 2015.

As the UK's Deputy Prime Minister set out in his address to the General Assembly at the summit, the United Kingdom takes extremely seriously the commitments it has made to the developing world. That is why our government has maintained its commitment to spend 0.7% of gross national income on overseas development assistance by 2013. By achieving this in 2013 we were the first G8 country to reach this target.

Increasing aid overseas is not an easy thing to do in a time of budget austerity, when UK taxpayers are feeling the pinch at home. But contributing financially to help developing countries achieve the MDGs is not merely altruism; it is also in developed countries' enlightened self-interest. Growth in the developing world means new partners with which to trade and new sources of global growth. When the world is less secure, all countries are less secure within it. The MDGs are the key to lasting safety and future prosperity for people right across the globe.

Given the economic challenges we face, there can be no stronger signal of the UK's commitment to the outside world, and we hope this provides additional encouragement to other donor countries to achieve their targets. It is vital that all countries stand firm by their commitments and make more efforts to help the poorest people in the world. Economic times are tough—but no one is suffering more than those already living in poverty.

We expect all countries to live up to the development commitments that they make. This applies not only to the financial commitments made by developed countries but also to the policy commitments made by developing countries.

We hope the United Nations will take the lead in following up on commitments made at the 2010 MDG Summit, both in the Outcome Document that 192 member states signed, as well as the many policy and financial commitments made in the various summit side events. It is vital both for achieving the MDGs and for the credibility of future United Nations summits that all governments are accountable for the promises they have made.

But it is also crucial that aid money is spent efficiently and effectively; it must achieve real results on the ground. That is why the United Kingdom's Department for International Development has completed a root-and-branch review of UK bilateral aid programs and also of the effectiveness of its funding through multilateral organizations. The UK's Secretary of State for International Development, Andrew Mitchell, announced the results of this review on March 1, 2011.

Using the results of the two reviews, DFID focused efforts where the need is greatest, and on the countries through the organizations where the UK is best placed to have a significant long-term impact on poverty. The UK is committed to the reform of multilateral institutions to ensure they are results-focused and offer excellent value for money. This will allow us to put more money behind strong performing organizations such as UNICEF and the GAVI alliance for vaccinations.

The Millennium Development Goals cannot be achieved by government efforts alone. All governments—both those in the developing world striving to meet the goals in their countries, and those in the developed world supporting their efforts—must work with partners outside government. The private sector and civil society organizations both play a critical role.

At the 2010 MDG Summit, world leaders agreed on the crucial role of the private sector for development and called on businesses everywhere to contribute to the MDGs.

The private sector is the engine of economic growth—creating jobs, increasing trade, providing goods and services to the poor, and generating tax revenue to fund basic public services such as health and education.

As well as stimulating growth, new thinking within the private sector, shaped by the market, can also offer insights into how to ensure better access to vital services or goods such as medicines or information.

With this in mind, in 2010 Andrew Mitchell announced that DFID would establish a new department to step up its engagement with the private sector. He expressed his intention to "recast DFID as a government department that understands the private sector, that has at its disposal the right tools to deliver and that is equipped to support a vibrant, resilient and growing business sector in the poorest countries."

The new Private Sector Department of DFID is now open. It will work on a large range of business-related issues, such as:

- Scaling up business models that enhance the contribution of firms to development
- Public-private partnerships
- Fair and ethical trade

As the UK's Ambassador in Tanzania, I saw firsthand the power of the private sector to deliver tangible benefits for the poor. In that country, DFID launched a £5 million call for proposals under the Africa Enterprise Challenge Fund seeking to support businesses in the agricultural sector to invest in new products and services or expand existing operations in a way that will be both profitable and reduce poverty.

The UK government is involved in a number of other initiatives across Africa aimed at harnessing the potential of business to promote the MDGs:

For example, Coca-Cola's Manual Distribution Centers (MDCs) model has brought hundreds of local entrepreneurs into their distribution networks across Africa. In so doing, they have tapped into dynamic new markets and created over 6,000 jobs in poor communities. (See the chapter on Coca-Cola in this volume.)

In Ghana, Cadbury is working with more than 40,000 cocoa farmers and their families to double cocoa production and improve incomes.

The Food Retail Industry Challenge (FRICH) encourages UK supermarkets and their suppliers to source more products from poor African producers. Through FRICH, Betty's and Taylor's of Harrogate are now sourcing their Yorkshire tea from smallholder farms in Rwanda. They have committed to purchase GBP 1 million of tea per year, leading to increased and more secure incomes for 17,000 poor smallholders and workers.

The United Kingdom government is proud to be a long-standing supporter of the UN Global Compact, the largest business membership organization working on responsible business in the world. The Global Compact's Executive Director, Georg Kell, has regularly met with senior officials in the UK Government, including the head of DFID's new Private Sector Department.

We are also pleased that the Global Compact has led the private sector track for the UN conference on the least developed countries, held in Istanbul in May 2012. This conference provided a blueprint for international cooperation to support the development of the world's poorest countries over the next decade. Enhancing the role of business in these countries is key to helping them to grow economically—and to meet the MDGs.

For lasting development and change, the UK government believes that a vibrant and active civil society is essential. Civil society organizations are an essential part of the global partnership to deliver the MDGs and public goods. Civil society is broader than the many diverse nongovernmental organizations (NGOs). It includes a wide range of non-state actors, including faith and diaspora groups, community-based organizations, and others. Some are large and established; others are small and informal.

Internationally, the role of civil society in development has become widely recognized. This was evident at the 2010 Summit, which called on "civil society, including non-governmental organizations, voluntary associations and foundations, the private sector and other relevant stakeholders at the local, national, regional and global levels, to enhance their role in national development efforts as well as their contribution to the achievement of the Millennium Development Goals by 2015." The governments present committed themselves to including those stakeholders in their planning.

Civil society plays a vital role worldwide in supporting citizens to improve their lives. Civil society organizations often provide support to disadvantaged groups and geographical regions that governments and official donors fail to reach. A review commissioned by the UK's Department for International Development showed that, in the fields of health and education, civil society organizations can often provide better results in areas where government provision of services is inadequate.

Civil society organizations have also piloted and mainstreamed development innovations such as micro-finance. By 2000, about 30 million poor families were receiving micro-credit from 1,580 nonprofit micro-finance institutions. Other civil society organization innovations increase the effectiveness of government or donor programs. For example, an NGO in India has increased vaccination rates by a factor of ten simply by giving a kilo of lentils to reward mothers when children complete their course.

Through its Civil Society Department, the UK's Department for International Development provides funding through a number of mechanisms that support civil society organizations to improve the lives of poor communities in developing countries, thus helping them to realize the MDGs. Let me give you a few examples of the sorts of programs that the UK funds.

In the Karamoja region of Uganda, we have supported young volunteers to implement activities in their communities to improve the health, skills, and livelihoods of their peers. The program has helped to raise awareness of the HIV/AIDS epidemic and increased access to health services.

In Southern Africa, we have supported the "Making Every Voice Count for Gender Equality" program. UK funding made it possible for a coalition of forty development organizations to campaign for a Southern African Development Community (SADC) Protocol on Gender and Development that set twenty-eight targets for the achievement of gender equality by 2015.

And in Peru, UK support has enabled CARE International to work with a local NGO, ForuSalud, to raise awareness about newborn health and maternal mortality. Around 160 women have been trained and accredited to monitor health facilities and service delivery. And citizens' monitoring has helped to combat violations of users' rights, such as poor treatment of indigenous women and attempts to charge for medicines that should be free.

I hope that these case studies help to illustrate the critical role of partnerships between governments, the private sector, and civil society in achieving the MDGs.

The UK—working with its partners in the developing world, business, and civil society—hopes to make those MDG goals a reality by 2015 and continue after 2015 with the broadened Sustainable Development Goals (SDGs) in the quest to overcome poverty.

12 | Business-NGO Collaboration on Peace Building

Patterns of Convergence

Hal Culbertson

Contemporary conflicts create significant challenges for meeting the Millennium Development Goals (MDGs). Since the end of the Cold War, most armed conflicts have been civil wars, in many cases involving influence or resources from neighboring states.[1] These conflicts are most severe on civilian populations, who have significantly higher fatalities than soldiers or members of militant groups.[2] Civilians also suffer from mass internal displacements or refugee flows; the recruitment, sometimes under duress, of militants and child soldiers from civilian populations; terrorism and gross human rights violations against members of opposing ethnic, religious, or political groups; and the entrenchment of animosity, discrimination, and intolerance in societal institutions, including educational, civil, legal, security, and commercial institutions. Frequently, conflicts lead to entitlement and market failures, as well as high costs that are unevenly distributed across groups in society, which in turn undermines progress on the development goals.[3]

The MDGs do not explicitly mention peace as a goal. The goals themselves hew much closer to orthodox development objectives of increasing incomes, expanding agriculture, and enhancing human flourishing.[4] Indeed, some have criticized the MDGs as providing incentives for quick fixes for problems of poverty without addressing the underlying social, political, and economic causes.[5] However, as the Millennium Declaration, which announced the MDGs, made clear, reducing conflict and building more peaceful societies is clearly an underlying agenda of the MDGs.[6] Furthermore, there are important links between development and conflict. Paul Collier and others dub conflict as "development in reverse," both because it pulls people away from more productive pursuits, and because of its destructive impact on human and physical resources.[7] As Humphreys and Varshney conclude, "The success of the MDG project will depend in large part on its success in countries in conflict or at-risk of conflict."[8]

Given the broad social, economic, and political destruction they cause, contemporary conflicts require equally broad and diverse interventions to build peace. As a result, a broad array of private actors, including religious groups, nongovernmental organizations, labor unions, educational institutions, health care institutions, and the business community, are increasingly recognizing the need to consider their role in peace building. This chapter will focus on the role of both businesses and NGOs in peace building, giving particular attention to the kinds of collaborative alliances that have formed between businesses and NGOs in this area. Business-NGO alliances have emerged in a wide variety of areas in recent years, from environmental and human rights issues, to poverty, health care, and emergency relief. After a preliminary consideration of some of the main conditions affecting business-NGO collaboration, this chapter will explore how both entities have understood their new roles in peace building and make some observations about emerging patterns of collaboration on peace building.

THE DYNAMICS OF BUSINESS-NGO COLLABORATION

Collaboration between NGOs and businesses is increasing.[9] Just a few decades ago, most interactions between businesses and NGOs were conflictual. NGOs criticized multinational companies for contributing to poverty, environmental degradation, and human rights violations, even as businesses sought to ignore or sideline the campaigns of NGOs against them. In the intervening years, NGOs have grown stronger in size, reputation, and influence, while the business community has increasingly recognized its responsibility to wider society and the need to work with a broader array of stakeholders.

This section will provide a framework for understanding business-NGO collaboration, which will be applied to collaborations on peace building later in the chapter. The framework focuses on different levels of collaboration between businesses and NGOs and gives attention to the significance of patterns of collaboration between particular industries and social sectors.

Levels of Collaboration

Many have begun to explore the dynamics that move business-NGO relationships from conflict to collaboration. As Bas Arts observes about environmental collaborations, NGOs and businesses have often moved from highly antagonistic relationships to more collaborative partnerships, sometimes in a fairly short time span. He points out that in 1995, Greenpeace decided to oppose the decommissioning and sinking of the Brent Spar, an oil platform in the North Sea, and launched a campaign against Shell, which owned the platform.[10] Greenpeace activists undertook a highly publicized occupation of the platform, creating a public movement that ultimately led Shell to scrap plans to decommission the platform. Greenpeace later had to admit that some information it provided about the amount of oil and toxic waste on the platform was dramatically overstated, leaving both Shell and Greenpeace with reputational damage. Arts observes that within six years of this incident, Shell and Greenpeace were each using a more collaborative approach to address environmental issues, and even working together on some projects.[11]

In examining the issues of business-NGO collaboration, it is important to recognize that the term *collaboration* can refer to a broad range of interactions. Austin has developed a framework for understanding different levels of business-NGO collaboration. At the lowest level is philanthropic collaboration, where the relationship between the business and the NGO is largely that of charitable donor and recipient.

At the next level is transactional collaboration, which involves the business and NGO working together on particular activities, such as cause-related marketing or contractual services. At the highest level, which Austin calls integrative collaboration, the joint work together involves the fundamental mission, core activities, and people at all levels of each agency.[12]

Austin's framework reflects some important distinctions in the kinds of relationships that have developed between NGOs and businesses. The distinction between philanthropic and transactional collaboration is particularly useful, because philanthropic activities of business are often commonly referred to as "partnerships" but involve little engagement with the core operations of the business beyond providing financial resources to the NGO. While NGOs certainly welcome corporate philanthropy, especially at a time when other sources of funding, such as government grants, are in decline, they also recognize that, to the extent they are seeking to leverage their relationship with a business to bring about wider change, philanthropy will not likely be the most effective form of collaboration.

Austin's use of the term "integrative" to describe highly developed collaboration between NGOs and businesses is more problematic, to the extent it suggests a merging of the organizations. While such a collaboration may, and often does, occur between business entities or between NGOs that merge to form a new joint entity, the different structure and nature of businesses and NGOs makes any kind of organizational integration unlikely and, in many cases, unworkable.

Covey and Brown propose a modified version of Austin's framework to better describe the complex cross-sectoral relationships that develop between NGOs and businesses. Their framework begins with the observation that conflicting and converging interests of both businesses and NGOs operate independently. Thus, an organization involved in a partnership may have strong converging interests, while having strong conflicting interests at the same time. They develop the concept of "critical collaboration" to describe situations where the parties have high levels of both converging and conflicting interests.[13]

By opening up Austin's linear framework to allow for critical collaboration, Covey and Brown provide a more nuanced tool for understanding the complex dynamics of NGO-business partnerships. The tool recognizes that cross-sector partnerships may involve more complex kinds of interaction than those between two similar entities. As they point out, the internal negotiation in which both NGOs and businesses engage when forming partnerships frequently involves finding an appropriate balance between converging and conflicting interests.

In deciding whether to join the Global Compact, for example, NGOs face the difficult question of whether they can be more effective in establishing new norms by their participation in the compact, or by keeping their distance and playing a role more akin to an external watchdog on the process. The different responses from the NGO community to this question in part reflect their differing assessments of their respective converging and conflicting interests, as well as different strategies for bringing about change. Both NGOs and businesses are familiar with these kinds of complexities as a result of their interactions with governmental institutions, which often involve both converging and conflicting interests.

Patterns of Collaboration

To better understand how converging and conflicting interests affect business-NGO collaborations, one important factor to consider is the particular industries and social sectors that are forming collaborative relations. By looking at which particular industries and social sectors are engaging in collaborative activities, and examining how these collaborative relationships are understood and communicated by each sector, one can see what kind of converging interests are motivating the collaboration, as well as how conflicting interests continue to play a role in the relationship.

Porter and Kramer observe that, from the corporate perspective, social issues fall into three categories. Generic issues are useful to society but have minimal relation to the company's operations or the long-term competitive environment. Value chain impacts are issues that are significantly affected by a company's operations. Competitive environment issues are social factors in the external environment that significantly drive competitiveness.[14] As Porter and Kramer point out, the assessment of which category an issue fits in will vary from industry to industry and even from firm to firm. "The AIDS pandemic in Africa may be a generic social issue for a U.S. retailer like Home Depot, a value chain impact for a pharmaceutical company like GlaxoSmith-Kline, and a competitive context issue for a mining company like Anglo American that depends on local labor in Africa for its operations."[15]

Drawing on Porter and Kramer's framework, Shumate and O'Connor examined 155 Fortune 500 companies and 695 NGOs for patterns of alliance formation between particular economic and social industries. Their study suggests that, in many cases, patterns of collaboration correspond to Porter and Kramer's framework by focusing on issues which have an impact on operations or the competitive environment of the company. For example, gas and electric utilities, chemical, mining, and crude oil production industries have a large number of alliances with environmental NGOs.[16] However, other alliances appeared to revolve more around generic support for social issues, such as the telecommunications industry's many alliances with NGOs in the fine arts and humanities.[17] They also argue that alliances can be fruitfully understood as part of the strategic positioning of both businesses and NGOs. As such, the communication of the alliance to each entity's constituency is a key dimension of the alliance itself.[18]

Alliance patterns also provide clues about the latent conflicting interests that continue to play a role in the interaction between businesses and NGOs. Where advocacy-oriented NGOs have targeted certain industries or particular businesses for negative publicity, the continuing possibility of such campaigns is a key threat that NGOs bring to the relationship. If the NGO perceives that the business is using the collaboration merely to bolster its public image, but not to make a real change in its behavior, sometimes called greenwashing in the case of environmental issues, the NGO's conflicting interest may override the collaborative, perhaps through leaving or criticizing the alliance. For NGOs that are less advocacy oriented, conflicting issues may involve questions of branding, sensitivity to local cultures, the pace of activities, or even power differentials between the business and the NGO.

Shumate and O'Connor's study did not consider peace building as a social industry category. While there is significant discourse, particularly in the academic literature, regarding business and peace issues and a growing array of case studies, businesses rarely discuss their involvement in peace-building or conflict issues in their annual or CSR (corporate social responsibility) reports,[19] which formed the basis of Shumate and O'Connor's data. This chapter will seek to fill this gap by exploring patterns of collaboration between businesses and NGOs on peace-building issues.

NGOS AND BUSINESSES AS PEACE-BUILDING ACTORS

The nature of contemporary conflict has significant implications for peace building. These implications can be seen in part through the lens of the expanding meaning of the term "peace building" itself. The term was first introduced by UN Secretary-General Boutros Boutros-Ghali in *An Agenda for Peace*.[20] In this document, which sought to lay out a comprehensive framework for UN responses to the growing number of conflicts in the post–Cold War environment, peace building was conceived of as a specific kind of activity which occurred during the post-violence phase of a conflict cycle. After fighting had stopped and an agreement between conflicting groups had been reached, the UN effort was seen as entering a peace-building phase when efforts would be made to rebuild institutions—the judicial system, security forces, schools, and the like—which had been ravaged by war.

Since this definition was first put forward, the concept of peace building has expanded to encompass any activity designed to strengthen cross-cutting ties, just institutions, nonviolent methods of conflict resolution, and equitable development.[21] Rather than describing a particular phase of a conflict, peace building is now understood more broadly to address issues surrounding past, present, and future conflicts.

In order to foster a more peaceful society, peace building requires attention to the many wounds brought about by previous violent conflicts.[22] These wounds include both injustices and human rights violations committed during the conflict through legal and political structures and also less direct but equally significant impacts, including conflict-related health issues (such as the prevalence of HIV/AIDS in war-affected regions), trauma or post-traumatic disorders, and the cultural acceptance of violence as a means of resolving conflict. One need only look to the way that trauma, which is often treated as an individual health concern, is now increasingly addressed as a public health issue, given that large percentages of the population in conflict-affected areas have experienced significant trauma.[23]

Contemporary peace building also addresses active conflicts using tools of conflict resolution and transformation, and continues to give attention to conflicts that emerge after an accord or cease-fire. In nearly 44 percent of the countries that sign a peace accord, violent conflict reemerges within five years.[24] As a result, a particular focus of contemporary peace building is to detect and address latent or expressed conflicts, which could quickly spread and destroy a fragile peace. This task is complicated by spoilers, who have an interest in conflict and as a result, actively seek to foment conflict during peace processes and in the period following an accord.

Finally, contemporary peace building also seeks to build more just institutions and societal relationships that will prevent the emergence of violent conflict in the future. While the primary aim of such interventions is often the state itself, private institutions and relationships that foster cross-cutting ties also have an important role to play. As Varshney's research has demonstrated, the single most important factor in determining whether rioting and civil conflict led to violence between major ethnic and religious groups in cities across India was whether the city had civil society organizations with strong cross-cutting ties.[25]

Peace building has also expanded beyond the confines of efforts by the UN or the international community to include efforts by a wide range of local and international actors. While the blue helmets of UN peacekeeping forces may have once been the focal point of international involvement in peace, peace builders now include a wide array of actors, such as youth groups, religious institutions, universities, NGOs, and businesses. The increased involvement of nonstate actors has resulted from many factors. Prime among these is the changing nature of contemporary conflict itself. Whereas proxy wars between superpowers were the dominant form of conflict during the Cold War, civil conflicts between groups defined by ethnic, religious, or other forms of identity are now much more common, often complicated by the involvement of external actors. The significant damage that such conflicts wreak upon societies include the divisions they create between families, clans, and ethnic and religious groups, the trauma of their tactics, and the significant ways in which these conflicts infect societal and international institutions.

Today's conflicts have deep and complex impacts on religious groups, educational institutions, the health care system, businesses, the judicial system, and many other societal institutions. While such institutions in the past may have understood their role as neutral bystanders, in fact they often have had to engage with conflict in complex ways, and it has engaged them, even if they did not support one group or another, either directly or indirectly. Identity-based conflicts easily replicate themselves within societal institutions in the affected society and beyond it, breeding intolerance, bias, or a defensive withdrawal.

With these changes in the nature of warfare and peace building as the backdrop, the following sections will focus on how peace building has emerged as an organizational mandate in two specific institutions: NGOs and businesses. In the final section I will then make some observations about the kinds of alliances that have emerged between NGOs and businesses to foster peace building.

NGO Peace Building

Peace building has grown as an NGO mandate over the past two decades. As is the case with the development of any new programmatic areas within NGOs, this has resulted from many factors, including their responses to experiences and needs on the ground in their working areas, the availability of funding, and the success of new models developed by other NGOs.[26] As Gerstbauer observes, the underlying mission of the NGO itself also has played an important role in whether the organization becomes involved in peace building. She notes how peace building has grown particularly in faith-based organizations, in part because of the importance of peace in their faith traditions.[27]

Specific issues, such as the environment, human rights, or corruption, often have NGO champions that take on the issue as their primary mandate and develop influential strategies and approaches specifically adapted to the needs of the issue. The NGO champions in these areas often become household names with wide recognition and respect, even as other NGOs seek to improve upon their approach. Greenpeace is widely recognized as a prominent environmental NGO. Amnesty International and Human Rights Watch are leaders in human rights advocacy, and Transparency International has developed a similar role in anticorruption efforts.

The field of peace building is more diffuse as an arena of NGO activity, with a variety of distinct methods and approaches being developed by NGOs working in different fields and contexts. NGOs with peace building as their primary mandate have emerged, but even these each have a distinctive operational approach. The International Crisis group provides high-level policy analysis, consulting, and advocacy to governments and international agencies on emerging and current conflicts.[28] The group Search for Common Ground works with local actors and particularly local media to promote collaborative problem-solving approaches to conflict.[29] International Alert combines grassroots work with affected populations with policy advocacy aimed at governments, the UN, and corporations.[30]

This diversity of approaches stems in part from the comprehensive nature of peace building itself. Peace building is not a narrow issue area, on a par with banning landmines or protecting endangered species. Rather, it is a broad area of involvement that potentially encompasses or overlaps with many other areas of practice, including relief, development, human rights, gender, the environment, and corruption. As a result, peace building has taken a variety of forms and approaches, even as it shares a common goal of reducing violent conflict and building societies that are more just, equitable, and peaceful.

Peace building has developed perhaps its most robust expression in connection with NGO work on human development. The signal event that led many development NGOs to consider giving more attention to peace building was the Rwandan genocide. Before the genocide, Rwanda had received significant development aid from the international community, and many NGOs had established operations there. As Uvin argues, despite a significant, long-term presence on the ground, many NGOs did not foresee the genocide, and, in some cases, their development work was conducted in ways that added fuel to the genocide. They then witnessed the destruction of their development efforts as the genocide unfolded over approximately one hundred days.[31] Some reacted by developing "conflict-sensitive" approaches to development, while others added peace building as a distinct programming area.

There are many similarities between development and peace building as areas of NGO involvement that have fostered the growth of peace building within the development sector. Both focus on working in fragile societies, many of which have significant experiences of conflict. Both take a long-term view, seeking to develop people and institutions that will foster peace and human flourishing, even as they seek to meet immediate needs, such as food, shelter, and livelihood. And both emphasize the importance of developing local capacities, rather than creating dependencies on external institutions.

But peace building also brought new emphases to NGO development activities. Peace building addresses politically sensitive issues, such as human rights violations, inequality between ethnic groups, and high-level peace negotiations, which were often carefully avoided by more traditional development programs, which focused on economic improvements. This difference has diminished somewhat in recent years, as development NGOs have increasingly adopted "rights-based" approaches to their work, which give more attention to human rights and justice concerns.[32] The peace-building agenda, while distinct from right-based approaches, shares with them its emphasis on the importance of improving public institutions and good governance as a central objective of development work.

Peace-building activities by development NGOs employ a similar funding structure to that of development programs, with substantial funding coming from official aid agencies, such as DFID, NORAD, SIDA, and USAID.[33] This funding structure differs from that for human rights NGOs, which typically do not accept any public funding for their work in order to maintain their independence. The funding structure also differs from environmental advocacy groups, such as the Sierra Club,[34] or human rights groups such as Amnesty International, which receive significant income from membership dues.

Beyond the development sector, many other NGO sectors have seen the emergence of peace building as a programmatic thrust. Organizations focusing on women and gender relations issues, such as Women for Women International and the Women Waging Peace Network, focus on the role of women in peace-building processes, particularly through building on international networks of women peace builders.[35] NGOs involved in the health sector, such as HEAL Africa, are considering how they can contribute to peace building when they intervene in countries torn by violent conflict.[36] Global Witness, which played a significant role in the Kimberley Process to regulate conflict diamonds, combines peace building and environmental concerns in its mission, which focuses on conflict and corruption related to natural resources and associated environmental and human rights abuses.[37]

Recent efforts to conceptualize the role that NGOs play in peace building underscore the diverse range of functions that NGOs can fulfill in peace processes. Paffenholz and Spurk identify seven distinct functions that civil society actors can perform: protection against armed actors; monitoring of potential conflicts and human rights abuses; advocacy and public communication at the local, national, and international level about particular conflicts and issues related to conflicts; in-group socialization to strengthen cultures of peace within particular communities or groups; social cohesion efforts to build bridges between conflicting groups; intermediation and facilitation of interactions between conflict groups; and service delivery to those affected by conflict.[38]

Van Leeuwen develops a more sectoral framework, which focuses on the complementary role that civil society can play in relation to international organizations and governments. Her analysis distinguishes various roles for NGOs in the areas of diplomacy and peace negotiations; military action; economic reconstruction and development; reforming governance; justice and human rights protection; and restoring the social fabric of society.[39]

These frameworks underscore the comprehensive character of the peace-building enterprise. Peace-building activities range from efforts to promote reconciliation, tolerance, and healing among victims of violent conflict to advocacy to UN agencies regarding policies affecting peace and conflict. They range from psychological interventions to address the trauma caused by war to diplomatic initiatives to prevent the outbreak of warfare. No single NGO is involved in all aspects of peace building. Actors, such as businesses, that form alliances with NGOs on peace-building initiatives should thus be aware of the particular focus of the NGO within the broader peace-building endeavor.

Business Peace Building

The idea that businesses would actively seek to play a role in peace building is a relatively recent phenomenon. As Nelson observed in her influential report *The Business of Peace* in 2000, "relatively little analysis has been carried out on the role of industries such as the natural resource and infrastructure sectors, travel and tourism, consumer goods and banking. In particular, there are limited examples available on the specific role that these industries can play in preventing, creating, exacerbating, or resolving conflict and how this differs from and relates to, the roles of government and civil society."[40]

Businesses working in conflict situations have historically viewed themselves as neutral or disinterested parties. Violent conflict was seen as a risk factor in the external environment and as a matter that should be handled by state institutions and the international community, not the business itself. Such a view was consistent with the dominant views of international relations and the view of conflict and peace building as a matter for governmental and intergovernmental actors.

Of course, business claims of neutrality have often been belied by their behavior in particular situations. During the colonial era, for example, state expansion and business profit-seeking were closely aligned, as the oft-cited example of the British East India Company's role in expanding the British Empire illustrates.[41] More recently, oil and gas companies have often been criticized for collaborating with states involved in human rights violations or environmental degradation.[42] Current legal regimes provide little basis for regulating business in conflict zones, although egregious behavior has sometimes been the subject of legal actions. However, in the last decade, voluntary efforts have emerged within the business community itself to reduce business contribution to violent conflict and to enhance its peace-building capacity.[43]

As was the case with relief and development NGOs, recent experiences on the ground in countries facing violent civil wars have played a significant role in reshaping business engagement with conflict and peace building. As international firms have increased their investments in emerging markets in the globalized economy, the civil wars and other conflicts that have taken place in some of these countries over the past few decades have forced businesses to face difficult issues about whether and how to engage in highly conflicted environments. Likewise, local and national businesses in areas of conflict have recognized that their operations may have an impact on violent conflict, and that they may have a role to play in building peace.

Businesses, and particularly multinational corporations, have also felt increasing external pressure to give more consideration to their role in fueling violent conflict. This has come in part from the expansion of global communications, which has heightened the reputational stakes for companies operating in these environments. NGOs, the Web, and the increased speed and scope of global communications have heightened public awareness of business activities around the world. At the same time, societal demands and expectations for business are changing. Peace is increasingly seen as an outcome that should result from ethical business behaviors.[44] Efforts to enhance corporate social responsibility have highlighted business involvement in zones of conflict as an area needing improvement. The UN Global Compact has given significant attention to this area through a number of publications discussing appropriate business behaviors in these contexts.[45]

Finally, business involvement in peace building is not entirely driven by external pressures. Internal changes in businesses, and particularly the internalization of the idea that the well-being of the surrounding society should play a role in business decisions and operations, play an important role in business involvement in peace building. As Sweetman observes, "This was especially evident in South Africa, where some companies were taking principled stands on apartheid that had to harm their business from a bookkeeping perspective."[46]

BUSINESS-NGO COLLABORATION ON PEACE BUILDING

Given the growing involvement and interest in peace building by both businesses and NGOs, collaborative efforts between them have begun to emerge. While businesses and NGOs certainly can and do engage in peace-building behaviors independently, such alliances have become a prominent means of achieving certain peace-building objectives. This section will explore emerging patterns of collaboration on peace building, with a view toward understanding the converging and conflicting interests of the actors involved.

Alliance Patterns

In the case of peace building, the industries most likely to become involved in alliances with NGOs have been those with operations in areas affected by conflict. As a result, the multinational extraction industry has played a particularly prominent role in collaborating with NGOs on peace-building issues. As Sweetman argues, "The companies most likely to become invested in business-based peacebuilding are those experiencing the highest costs and without exit options. Most of the companies examined that instigated their own efforts were in the extractive or agricultural sectors and could not pull out of the affected areas."[47] As the potential risk to businesses working in areas of conflict that their operations or reputation could be damaged by claims that they are fueling or exacerbating the conflict are potentially quite high, these industries have much to lose in terms of reputation and community value if they were perceived as benefiting from conflict. They also have much to gain from the stability of a more peaceful operating environment.

The Kimberley Process is perhaps the most prominent collaborative endeavor between NGOs and extractive businesses on peace building. Evidence that rebel groups in Angola and Sierra Leone were selling illicitly obtained diamonds to finance insurgencies was made public by the British NGO Global Witness and the Canadian NGO Partnership Africa Canada, and later confirmed by a UN report.[48] While the industry had previously ignored such claims, DeBeers, which controlled a significant proportion of the diamond trade, recognized that the industry was vulnerable to a global consumer campaign against trade in diamonds related to such conflicts.[49] As a result, DeBeers engaged with both governments and NGOs to develop the Kimberley Process for certifying diamonds as "conflict-free." The perceived success of this effort has led to further efforts to regulate industries involved in extracting resources such as coltan ore and timber, when they have strong connections to violent groups.[50]

The involvement of industries beyond the extraction industry in collaboration on peace building has been more mixed. Certainly, international businesses other than extractive industries operate in areas of conflict, by either necessity or choice. GM's local subsidiary in Colombia, GM-Colmoteres, partnered with Juan Bosco, an NGO involved in creating jobs for former militants in Colombia, to provide training for former militants in the auto industry.[51] The alliance, which won an award from the U.S. State Department, spurred other industries, such as Coca-Cola, to become involved in job training initiatives with Juan

Bosco.[52] International construction businesses have also partnered with NGOs to make their operations in areas of conflict more conflict sensitive, such as the use by the Swiss-Swedish construction company ABB of ethnically diverse employees for construction projects in the Balkans.[53] Sweetman chronicles several similar efforts by other industries.[54]

While there are many noteworthy examples of international firms beyond the extraction industry that are involved with NGOs in peace building, some studies suggest that responses to conflict by these industries can be quite limited. Jamali and Mirshak observe that several multinational corporations from the service sector, including financial, telecommunications, hospitality, and fast food industries, chose to continue operations as usual in Lebanon during the 2006 war with Israel. Interviews with managers at these firms indicated they took virtually no steps to address the conflict, besides protecting their employees and occasional individual humanitarian efforts, and all saw themselves as neutral, external actors in the situation.[55] While the political dynamics were certainly challenging in this situation, given the international character of the conflict, the highly limited response suggests that there is little incentive, both internal and external, for these industries to get involved in peace building.

Beyond multinationals, national and local businesses have sometimes played a significant role in peace building in ways in which international firms would not likely engage. National enterprises have played a role in peace negotiations and peace processes in a variety of settings. Given their deeper local roots and stronger ties with local constituencies, national firms often have more ingrained links to the conflict or to individual actors involved in the conflict. While this sometimes can compromise them politically, it can also present significant opportunities for business peace building.

These efforts often involve the creation of or affiliation with an NGO or nonprofit association of businesses that can take action in conjunction with or on behalf of the businesses. Rettberg documents the significant role that business leaders played in moving the peace process forward in El Salvador, contrasting this with the more mixed role of businesses in Guatemala and Colombia. She notes how the internal dynamics within the private sector, as well as its relationship with the government, affected its capacity to influence the peace processes in each situation.[56] Similarly, International Alert has drawn best practices from the private sector's involvement in peace building in Sri Lanka.[57] As these cases illustrate, because of their situation within a conflict, smaller, national firms may have potential significant capacities for peace building, distinct from multinationals.

From the NGO side, collaboration with businesses on peace building has occurred primarily with NGOs for whom peace building is a central or significant aspect of their organizational mission. International Alert, which defines itself as a peace-building organization, has been a leader in efforts to work with businesses, as has the Institute for Multi-Track Diplomacy.[58] Global Witness, which played a prominent role in the Kimberley Process, also regards peace building as a fundamental mandate, which it combines with a commitment to environmental concerns. Search for Common Ground has also engaged in collaboration with businesses, particularly through grassroots peace-building work with Chevron in Angola.[59] The nonprofit collaborative learning organization CDA, drawing on its role in helping NGOs working in conflict areas to "do no harm," has provided conflict assessments and consultations on making core operations more conflict sensitive.[60] Interestingly, involvement of businesses with large relief and development NGOs on peace building has been somewhat less common. There are a few exceptions, for example, Catholic Relief Services involvement in several local-level business initiatives, such as multiethnic banking in Bosnia-Herzegovina.[61]

Critical Collaboration

While both businesses and NGOs have discovered areas of overlapping interest that can form the basis of mutual endeavors, conflicting interests remain as part of the ongoing relationship. The Kimberley Process provides a useful lens for viewing both converging and conflicting interests. NGOs have given significant moral legitimacy to the process through their participation in its development and implementation. However, that legitimacy derives from their status as independent actors, who bring their own perspectives to bear on the process. Indeed, NGOs maintained public campaigns criticizing the diamond trade even as they participated in the development of the Kimberley Process.[62] In recent years, the process has failed to adequately regulate the diamond trade, particularly in Zimbabwe, and many NGOs have been critical of the process because of these failures. Ian Smillie, one of the leading NGO figures in the process, resigned in 2009, expressing his concerns over the failure of the process, and NGOs walked out of a meeting in protest.[63] As these events indicate, conflicting interests remain even in highly collaborative endeavors, and the conflicting concerns can override the collaborative in some situations.

Businesses have also maintained some distance in peace-building alliances. As already pointed out, businesses have given relatively little, if any, attention to peace-building initiatives in their annual CSR reports. In contrast, NGOs working with businesses on peace building often have significant public information on their webpages about the alliance.[64] This asymmetry in communication strategies is interesting. While it may reflect the different role of peace-building activities within the portfolios of the businesses and NGOs involved, it also may indicate some different perspectives and concerns about how peace-building activities will be seen by various constituencies.

Critical collaboration may also be seen in the tendency to form consortia or larger collaborative groups of NGOs and businesses instead of one-to-one initiatives on peace building. Collaborative arrangements with many members help spread both the costs of an initiative and the risks if an effort fails.[65] It may be easier in some cases to withdraw from a consortium of several peer institutions than to leave a one-to-one relationship. Furthermore, business associations working for peace often create their own NGO to carry out their peace-building work, rather than working with existing organizations. This reduces the independence of the NGO and therefore the potential for conflict, as the NGO is more or less under the control of the businesses involved.

While critical collaboration may be a general feature of business–NGO relations overall, it also reflects specific dichotomies within the practice of peace building itself. On the one hand, peace building is inherently a bridge-building endeavor. Peace building involves finding ways for two or more actors or groups in conflict to find a way to live together, through increasing mutual tolerance and respect, through establishing mechanisms, institutions, and spaces for nonviolently addressing differences that arise, or, at the very least, through agreements not to continue committing violence on one another. It may involve engaging in mutual economic, social, or political initiatives that build trust, or in making changes in the way structures in society operate. In all of these kinds of initiatives, changing the relationship between the conflicting parties is a central feature.

UN agencies, as well as scholars and practitioners of peace building, have all emphasized the need for coordination and collaboration between diverse actors, and not just the conflicting parties, as a key ingredient for peace building. As a result, peace-building efforts have increasingly focused on building relationships between groups beyond the protagonists themselves. Such efforts might seek to strengthen relations between religious organizations that have ties to opposite sides of a conflict, or to reestablish economic relations between members of different ethnic groups in a local market. This aspect of the peace-building endeavor clearly encourages diverse actors, including NGOs and businesses, working in areas of conflict to collaborate.

At the same time, peace building can present challenges for collaborative efforts, and particularly those between actors from different sectors. Peace building involves a complex and highly volatile form of political engagement. Missteps can quickly undermine years of effort. Peace building usually occurs in a social and political minefield, where any engagement with actors involved in the conflict will receive multiple interpretations from the opposing actors in the conflict and their supporters. Particularly when the conflict has been fierce, all sides will likely have committed atrocities or violations of human rights, thus making efforts to foster peace look like an attempt to downplay these violations or appease the violators. In such a climate, collaborating partners can be pulled in quite different directions by their various constituencies.

The fact that critical collaboration is the operative mode of interaction should not be seen as a threat to collaboration on peace building. On the contrary, the critical distance that NGOs must keep in these relationships is often what is needed to make the collaboration beneficial. NGO independence can give the collaboration a greater moral authority and power to legitimate, which is often one of the significant benefits to business of working with NGOs. Both NGOs and businesses have a long history of this kind of critical collaboration with governmental actors; however, until recently, they have not understood their relationship with each other in these terms.

THE ALLIANCE PATTERNS on peace building suggest that a primary reason businesses have become involved in collaboration on peace building is to address the value chain effects of their operations. The involvement of the extractive industries clearly fits this pattern, since it is motivated by their desire to address how their operations interact with the conflict and how these interactions are perceived by the local and international communities.

The recognition by businesses operating in areas of conflict that their operations may be having negative impacts on the conflict, and that they need to take concrete steps to avoid these kinds of impact, is itself a noteworthy achievement. The willingness of advocacy NGOs to collaborate with businesses, which the NGOs had previously seen as opponents, may stem in part from the NGOs' recognition that this is an important step in the right direction. In the case of conflict diamonds, for example, NGOs played a key role in pushing the diamond business toward a deeper recognition of its responsibilities in addressing conflict. Similar to business-NGO collaborations on the environment, which have a longer history than peace-building collaborations, the relationship moved from a highly conflictual one, where the NGOs had launched a negative publicity campaign, to collaboration on the issues raised.[66] It is interesting to note that the mission of Global Witness, a primary actor in the Kimberley Process, blends environmental and peace-building concerns. This blended mission may have influenced approaches and methodologies used in the collaboration.

However, this analysis also highlights some challenges facing business-NGO collaborations for peace building, particularly if these collaborations are to contribute to the MDGs. First, there is a significant need for more attention to collaborations that can foster positive peace building, particularly in post-accord situations. Many analysts of business involvement in peace point out different levels of engagement by businesses. Nelson, for example, develops a frequently cited pyramid that delineates three levels of involvement: compliance, risk minimization, and value creation.[67] She argues that businesses need to go beyond complying with legal mandates and reducing damage that is incurred from operating in conflicted environments and to develop strategies that foster the growth of peaceful human relations in the situations where they work. Such distinctions have parallels in NGO peace-building efforts, which often distinguish between the goals of reducing violence, often referred to as negative peace, and increasing peace and justice in society, or positive peace.[68]

As has already been noted, relapse into conflict following a peace accord is, unfortunately, a common occurrence, and is one of the most significant challenges to the achievement of the MDGs. Concerns about the slow pace of economic development or inequities in economic opportunities often play a role in such relapses. As Wennman notes, while peace agreements typically focus more on political and social dimensions, economic issues are increasingly addressed as part of peace negotiations.[69] Peace processes can be times of significant change in the political economy of a country. Often, one of the most significant needs in post-accord environments is job creation and employment, and these need to be addressed in ways that help ameliorate tensions between the social, ethnic, or political groups that caused the conflict.

International relief and development NGOs, which play a prominent role in the development of peace-building practice, have significant experience implementing reintegration and job training programs in this context. Significantly, these NGOs, while they are developing partnerships with business in other areas, have not developed substantial partnerships on this aspect of peace building. Further development of these relationships would hold the potential to expand the reach of these efforts and deepen the long-term potential for peace.

Second, while the extraction industry will likely continue to be a prominent player in peace-building efforts, other industries also need to consider their role in peace building, particularly in situations of post-accord peace building. As Bray notes, mobile phone companies are often some of the first to invest in post-conflict situations, since they have low costs of investment and quick returns. Engineering construction companies also often are among the first to begin operations in post-conflict situations to repair damage to the infrastructure.[70] Both of these industries have interests in peace building that go beyond a general interest in societal improvement. As the Arab Spring demonstrated, communications infrastructure can play a critical role in fostering nonviolent approaches to conflict in society. While the role of Facebook and Twitter may be overstated in the Egyptian and Tunisian revolutions, these technologies did play a facilitative role in disseminating information about government atrocities and organizing street protests. Similarly, efforts by engineering firms to rebuild infrastructure in ways that are sensitive to past, ongoing, and potential conflicts can help create a more stable society that continues to grow economically.

Collaborative relationships between NGOs and industries like these in post-conflict situations are not likely to emerge from the same dynamics that brought about the Kimberley Process. In collaborations between NGOs and the extraction industry, campaigns or threats of negative publicity by NGOs, coupled with corporate interests in minimizing risk in difficult environments, have played a significant role in the formation of collaborative alliances. However, in collaborations focused more on positive peace building and human development, the failure of corporations to engage in this kind of positive peace building is not likely to work well as the focus of a negative campaign by NGOs. In the absence of this kind of threat from NGOs, these kinds of collaboration will depend even more on the commitment of businesses to peace building.

To make headway in achieving the MDGs, collaborative relationships on positive peace building will need to go beyond philanthropic support to NGOs working on peace building in the environment. Businesses will need to engage in a deeper reflection on how their operations can contribute to the reconstruction of society, at the level of both infrastructure and social relations. The experience, expertise, and credibility that NGOs bring to these endeavors would make them useful partners in this process.

NOTES

1. Lotta Themnér and Peter Wallensteen, "Armed Conflict, 1946–2010," *Journal of Peace Research* 48, no. 4 (2011): 528.
2. Daniel Rothbart and Karina V. Korostelina, *Why They Die: Civilian Devastation in Violent Conflict* (Ann Arbor: University of Michigan Press, 2011), 16.

3. Frances Stewart, "Conflict and the Millennium Development Goals," *Journal of Human Development* 4, no. 3 (November 2003): 330–38.

4. See http://www.un.org/millenniumgoals/.

5. Paul J. Nelson and Ellen Dorsey, *New Rights Advocacy: Changing Strategies of Development and Human Rights NGOs* (Washington, DC: Georgetown University Press, 2008), 116–19.

6. United Nations Millennium Declaration, http://www.un.org/millennium/declaration/ares552e.pdf.

7. Paul Collier, Lani Elliott, Håvard Hegre, Anke Hoeffler, Marta Reynal-Querol, and Nicholas Sambanis, *Breaking the Conflict Trap: Civil War and Development Policy* (Washington, DC: The World Bank, 2003), 10.

8. Macartan Humphreys and Ashutosh Varshney, "Violent Conflict and the Millennium Development Goals: Diagnosis and Recommendations," paper prepared for the meeting of the Millennium Development Goals Poverty Task Force Workshop, Bangkok, June 2004, p. 2, at http://www.columbia.edu/~mh2245/papers1/HV.pdf.

9. Michael Yaziji and Jonathan Doh, *NGOs and Corporations: Conflict and Collaboration* (New York: Cambridge University Press, 2009), 123.

10. Bas Arts, "Green Alliances of Business and NGSs: New Styles of Self-Regulation or 'Dead-End Roads'?" *Corporate Social Responsibility and Environmental Management* 9 (2002): 26–27.

11. Ibid., 27.

12. James E. Austin, "Strategic Collaboration between Businesses and Nonprofits," *Nonprofit and Voluntary Sector Quarterly* 29, no. 1 (Supplement 2000): 71–76.

13. Jane Covey and L. David Brown, *Critical Cooperation: An Alternative Form of Civil Society-Business Engagement* (Institute for Development Research Reports, 2001), 2–3.

14. M. S. Porter and M. R. Kramer, "Strategy and Society: The Link between Competitive Advantage and Corporate Social Responsibility," *Harvard Business Review* 84, no. 12 (December 2006): 85.

15. Ibid.

16. Michelle Shumate and Amy O'Connor, "Corporate Reporting of Cross-Sector Alliances: The Portfolio of NGO Partners Communicated on Corporate Websites," http://www.ndsu.edu/fileadmin/communication/Corporate_Reporting_of_Cross-Sector_Alliances.pdf, p. 22. (Also available in *Communication Monographs* 77, no. 2 [2010]: 207–30.)

17. Ibid., 22.

18. Ibid., 23.

19. Charles P. Koerber, "Corporate Responsibility Standards: Current Implications and Future Possibilities for Peace through Commerce," *Journal of Business Ethics* 89 (2010): 473.

20. UN Secretary-General Boutros Boutros-Ghali, "An Agenda for Peace: Preventive Diplomacy, Peacekeeping, and Peace-Keeping." Available at http://www.un.org/ga/search/view_doc.asp?symbol=A/47/277.

21. Daniel Philpott, "Introduction: Search for Strategy in an Age of Peacebuilding," in *Strategies of Peace: Transforming Conflict in a Violent World*, ed. Daniel Philpott and Gerard Powers (New York: Oxford University Press, 2010), 8.

22. John Paul Lederach and R. Scott Appleby, "Strategic Peacebuilding: An Overview," in *Strategies of Peace: Transforming Conflict in a Violent World*, ed. Daniel Philpott and Gerard Powers (New York: Oxford University Press, 2010), 28.

23. See R. Srinivasa Murthy and Rashmi Lakshminarayana, "Mental Health Consequences Of War: A Brief Review Of Research Findings," *World Psychiatry* 5, no. 1 (February 2006): 25–30.

24. Collier et al., *Breaking the Conflict Trap*, 83.

25. Ashutosh Varshney, *Ethnic Conflict and Civic Life: Hindus and Muslims in India* (New Haven, CT: Yale University Press, 2003), 9.

26. Loramy Conradi Gerstbauer, "The Whole Story of NGO Mandate Change: The Peacebuilding Work of World Vision, Catholic Relief Services, and Mennonite Central Committee," *Nonprofit & Voluntary Sector Quarterly* 39, no. 5 (October 2010): 849.

27. Ibid., 859.

28. See http://www.crisisgroup.org/en/about.aspx.

29. See http://www.sfcg.org/sfcg/sfcg_home.html.

30. See http://www.international-alert.org/about-us.

31. Peter Uvin, *Aiding Violence: The Development Enterprise in Rwanda* (West Hartford, CT: Kumarian Press, 1998).

32. Nelson and Dorsey, *New Rights Adocacy*, 20.

33. Lorami Conrady Gerstbauer, "The New Conflict Managers: Peacebuilding NGOs and State Agendas," in *New Threats and New Actors in International Security*, ed. Elke Krahmann (New York: Palgrave Macmillan, 2005), 31.

34. Christopher J. Bosso, "Rethinking the Concept of Membership in Nature Advocacy Organizations," *Policy Studies Journal* 31, no. 3 (2003): 405.

35. See, e.g., Women for Women International at http://www.women forwomen.org/ and the Women Waging Peace Network at http://www.hunt alternatives.org/pages/82_women_waging_peace_network.cfm.

36. See, e.g., Nicole C. D'Errico, Christopher M. Wake, and Rachel M. Wake, "Healing Africa? Reflections on the Peace-building Role of a Health-based Non Governmental Organization Operating in Eastern Democratic Republic of Congo," *Medicine, Conflict and Survival* 26, no. 2 (2010): 145–59.

37. See http://www.globalwitness.org/.

38. Thania Paffenholz and Christoph Spurk, "A Comprehensive Analytical Framework," in *Civil Society and Peacebuilding: A Critical Assessment*, ed. Thania Paffenholz (Boulder, CO: Lynne Rienner, 2010), 67.

39. Mathijs Van Leeuwen, *Partners in Peace: Discourses and Practices of Civil-Society Peace Building* (Burlington, VT: Ashgate, 2009), 32–33.

40. Jane Nelson, *The Business of Peace: The Private Sector as a Partner in Conflict Prevention and Resolution* (The Prince of Wales Business Leaders Forum, International Alert, Council on Economic Priorities, 2000), 6.

41. Jennifer Oetzel, Michelle Westermann-Behaylo, Charles Koerber, Timothy L. Fort, and Jorge Rivera, "Business and Peace: Sketching the Terrain," *Journal of Business Ethics* 89 (2010): 351–73.

42. Ibid.

43. See Derek Sweetman, *Business, Conflict Resolution and Peacebuilding: Contributions from the Private Sector to Address Violent Conflict* (New York: Routledge, 2009), 12.

44. Oetzel et al., "Business and Peace," 360.

45. See the UN Global Compact's website at http://www.unglobalcompact.org/Issues/conflict_prevention/guidance_material.html.

46. Sweetman, *Business, Conflict Resolution and Peacebuilding*, 49.

47. Ibid., 53.

48. Ian Smillie, *The Kimberley Process Certification Scheme for Rough Diamonds*, Verifor Comparative Case Study 1 (Overseas Development Institute, 2005), 2.

49. Smillie, *The Kimberley Process*, 2.

50. Collier et al., *Breaking the Conflict Trap*, 143–44.

51. Oetzel et al., "Business and Peace," 356.

52. Sustainability Report 2009, Coca-Cola Latin Center Business Unit, at http://www.thecoca-colacompany.com/citizenship/pdf/sustainability_reports/2009_central_latin_english.pdf; see p. 13.

53. Sweetman, *Business, Conflict Resolution and Peacebuilding*, 40.

54. See ibid., chapter 3, for several examples.

55. Dima Jamali and Ramez Mirshak, "Business-Conflict Linkages: Revisiting MNCs, CSR and Conflict," *Journal of Business Ethics* 93 (2009): 459.

56. Angelika Rettberg, "The Private Sector and Peace in El Salvador, Guatemala, and Colombia," *Journal of Latin American Studies* 39, no. 3 (2007): 463–94.

57. Radhika Hettiarachchi, Lucy Holdaway, and Canan Gündüz, *Sustaining Business and Peace: A Resource Pack for Small and Medium Enterprises* (International Alert, 2009).

58. Sweetman, *Business, Conflict Resolution and Peacebuilding*, 29–30.

59. See Search for Common Ground at www.sfcg.org/programmes/sbp/programmes_sbp.html.

60. Zandvliet Luc and Mary B. Anderson, *Getting it Right: Making Corporate-Community Relations Work* (Sheffield, UK: Greenleaf Publishing, 2009).

61. Reina Neufeldt, *Catholic Relief Services Peacebuilding Activities* (Baltimore: CRS, 2006), online at www.crs.org/peace building/pubs/Peb0405_e.pdf (last accessed November 24, 2011).

62. Franziska Bieri, "The Roles of NGOs in the Kimberley Process," *Global Studies Journal* 20 (November 2010).

63. "Kimberley Process Derails over Zimbabwe," *Other Facets* 35 (Partnerships Africa Canada, August 2011).

64. See, e.g., the extensive resources in the "Economy and Peacebuilding" section of the International Alert website (www.international-alert.org) or the extensive set of cases studies and issue papers in the "Corporate Engagement" section of the CDA website (www.cdainc.com).

65. Jennifer Oetzel, Katheen A. Getz, and Stephen Ladeknnn, "The Role of Multinational Enterprises in Responding to Violent Conflict: A Conceptual Model and Framework for Research," *American Business Law Journal* 44, no. 2 (Summer 2007): 342.

66. Arts, "Green Alliances of Business and NGOs," 27–28.

67. Nelson, *The Business of Peace*, 7.

68. Mary B. Anderson and Lara Olson, *Confronting War: Critical Lessons for Peace Practitioners* (Cambridge, MA: Collaborative for Development Action, 2003), 12.

69. Achem Wennmann, *The Political Economy of Peacemaking* (New York: Routledge, 2011).

70. John Bray, *Practice Note 3: Foreign Direct Investment in Conflict-Affected Contexts* (International Alert, 2010), 6.

13 | Putting Reputation at Risk

The Seven Factors of Reputational Management

James S. O'Rourke, IV

INVESTING IN REPUTATION MANAGEMENT

Wise managers know they must invest in structures that will grow and protect their corporate reputation. They understand that corporate reputation—apart from brand and product reputation—is a manageable strategic asset. Those managers also know that, on very little notice, they may be required to withdraw that investment and redeploy it elsewhere. Limited resources mean limitations on where, when, and how to invest, and, at key moments in the history of their organizations, they may have to sacrifice some aspect of corporate reputation to protect another.

"Every individual, every company, every organization develops a reputation," according to business journalist Ronald Alsop.[1] And, while it may take many years to form and is usually quite durable, a company's reputation can be undone in fairly short order. Examples include names as famous as Enron Corporation, Bankers Trust, and Arthur Andersen, and as obscure as Odwalla, Inc., a California-based fruit drink producer, or ValuJet, a discount airline that never recovered from a disastrous crash in the Florida Everglades in 1996.

Reputation is more than just a company's good name, of course. It is a composite of those factors affecting how others, particularly those outside of the organization, view the company. Issues affecting an entire industry can taint the name of a company not responsible for any of the publicized misdeeds. When a second officer drove the *Exxon Valdez* into Bligh Reef in Alaska's Prince William Sound on March 24, 1989, the image of every petroleum company in the world, particularly those in the United States, took a hit, as well. When Northwest Airlines left hundreds of passengers stranded aboard airliners on the ramp at Detroit Metro Airport during a snowstorm in January of 1999, every other airline suffered. Congressional critics began hearings on a "Passenger Bill of Rights" that would affect all commercial carriers in the United States.

Whether the cause of reputational damage is spread across an entire business sector, the result of economic or cyclical factors, or the fault of individual managers who miscalculate the impact of their actions, corporate reputation is among the most valuable and volatile of a company's assets.

Numerous polls and surveys of executives, investors, analysts, and others have turned reputation management into a competitive sport, focusing on annual rankings and lists of most and least admired firms. Tracking services now permit managers to examine what's being said about them, as well as their competitors, on a real-time basis, 24/7. Investment in the creation, development, and protection of a company's good name is no longer the province of a small group in the corporate public relations department. It is a key factor in every organization's long-term strategic planning, and executives in virtually all industries are now held accountable for the results.

A FEW IMPORTANT DISTINCTIONS

It may help if we separate a few terms commonly used as synonyms. Corporate *reputation* is most often thought of as an organization as seen by outsiders, while corporate *identity* is an organization as seen by insiders. And corporate *image* is the tangible appearance of an organization to all. So, while the *reputation* of United Parcel Service is one of a low-cost, reliable, overnight package delivery service, as seen by its customers and the general public, the company's *identity* is the view that insiders have of a privately held firm that went public and shared the wealth with its employees. And of course the *image* of the firm is sparkling clean brown trucks, efficient package handlers in brown shirts and shorts, and an advertising campaign that asks, "What can Brown do for you?"

Corporate reputation, obviously, is composed of numerous key attributes, including the firm's capacity for innovation, the quality of its management and employees, and the perceived quality of its products and services. Reputations are also built on a company's long-term investment value, which explains consistently high reputational rankings for firms such as McDonald's Corporation, Johnson & Johnson, and Berkshire Hathaway. Financial soundness, social responsibility, and the use of corporate assets are also factors affecting how everyone from employees to corporate directors view an organization.[2]

While reputation is composed of many such attributes, it is also relative to the reputation of others, particularly those in the same industrial sector. And, as we have said, with some notable exceptions, it is also usually quite enduring. Research conducted by Kevin Keller of Dartmouth's Tuck School of Business documents the characteristics of strong brands and explains why they include a forgiveness factor: customers, investors, employees, and other stakeholders are more than willing to forgive a strong company with a solid reputation because they know that performance failures, product recalls, and management missteps are really aberrations from the norm, rather than business as usual.

The Coca-Cola Company's mishandling of a product contamination crisis in Europe during the summer of 1999 is a case in point. A bad batch of CO_2 found its way into Coca-Cola products bottled in Belgium and onto grocery store shelves in the cities of Bornem, Lochristi, and Kortrijk. When reports of school children feeling nauseated and seeking hospital treatment after consuming Coca-Cola products hit the local press, company executives dismissed the incidents as overblown and "hardly a health hazard." CEO Doug Ivester, in fact, was in Paris at the time of the incident, yet chose to fly back to Atlanta rather than address it directly. He not only misread local sentiment regarding the company's obligations but also failed to grasp the larger cultural implications of the crisis. Belgian Prime Minister Jean-Luc Dahaene had been forced out of office because of a scandal involving contamination of the food supply, and others seized the opportunity to take cheap shots at the American soft drink giant. Sweden's *Svenska Dagbladet* proclaimed, "200 Poisoned by Coca-Cola," and Italy's *La Stampa* declared, "Alarm Across Europe for Coca-Cola Products."[3]

Following a recall of the company's products, which cost $103 million over a six-week period and resulted in a drop of more than twenty points in Coca-Cola's share price, the brand did recover. It took just less than a year for consumers in Europe to resume their pre-crisis consumption patterns, and for the company's stock value to return to the level of $75 per share. The damage to the company's reputation cost Doug Ivester his job, however, since key investors lost confidence in his ability to protect the brand.

SEVEN FACTORS GOVERNING REPUTATIONAL RISK MANAGEMENT

While events that are entirely unforeseen may affect how key stakeholders view a company, reputation management is not simply a reactive enterprise. Seven key factors govern how any organization can manage reputation.

1.   Corporate reputation is a manageable, strategic asset.

The belief that corporate reputation is so widespread among so many stakeholders, or that most of the factors affecting what those groups think of a company are too numerous to count, has led some managers to believe that corporate reputation is essentially unmanageable. Nothing could be further from the truth. Consider the case of a company whose reputation is almost entirely dependent on the image of its founder and chief executive.

Martha Stewart Living Omnimedia, Inc. In the pre-dawn darkness of October 8, 2004, celebrity homemaker and domestic lifestyle icon Martha Stewart reported to the Federal Correctional Facility in

Alderson, West Virginia, to begin serving a five-month prison sentence for lying about a stock sale. Stewart was convicted in March 2004 of lying to federal investigators about why she sold ImClone stock in December 2001, just before the stock price plunged. She had claimed she had no inside information and that her transactions were entirely lawful, but her actions before and during the investigation suggested otherwise.[4]

Stewart had been free on bail following her March 5, 2004, conviction on conspiracy, obstruction, and perjury, proclaiming her innocence and her intention to appeal the verdict. ImClone CEO Samuel Waksal was already in jail on a stock fraud conviction related to the sale of his shares of the company, and Martha's broker, Peter Bacanovic, was awaiting sentencing on charges nearly identical to those for which she was convicted.

Why would a woman worth hundreds of millions voluntarily surrender to federal authorities and undergo the humiliation of strip searches and complete loss of privacy? Why not simply wait for the appeals court to review her claims of judicial error in the trial courts? The answer has more to do with Ms. Stewart's company, Martha Stewart Living Omnimedia, Inc. (NYSE: MSO) than it does with her personal freedom. From the day of her indictment in June 2003, her company had sustained a relentless beating in the press, in the stock market, and in topline revenues. In the second quarter of 2004, MSO reported an operating loss of $19.3 million on sales of $44 million, down from a profit of $1.5 million on $65.8 million in operating income the year before. Those losses were more than one-third higher than analysts had predicted, with income falling in every area, from publishing to television to merchandise sales. While corporate expenses continued to rise, payroll was cut from 558 to 450 employees. Advertisers, readers, and business partners were fleeing in droves. To stem the losses, the company shut down its mail-order catalogue business and began spending cash reserves.[5]

Those problems would not necessarily go away even if Stewart had managed to clear her name quickly and reverse the conviction on appeal. "The protracted scandal," according to *Business Week*'s Diane Brady, "took its founder and one-person publicity machine out of commission at a crucial time in MSO's growth."[6] Following her tearful speech to the press on September 15, in which she announced that she would surrender to federal authorities and begin her five-month prison term, to be followed by a similar period of home confinement, her company's stock price rose 3 percent, closing at $11.26. While that is far from the $20 highs her stock reached a year earlier, it may be a harbinger of things to come.

Martha Stewart's choice to put her own reputation (and personal comfort) at risk was unquestionably the smartest move she could make in support of her company. Granted, she owned 100 percent of the Class B shares and would benefit from a rising stock price, but she would forego nearly half of her $900,000-a-year base pay and lose control of the company, perhaps permanently. Most public relations experts, including the legendary Howard Rubenstein, think it was a shrewd move. "I thought she was brilliant. It took a lot of courage. . . . But if she had lingered during her appeal, the damage would have continued. Now . . . she will be past this and she can start to do new things."[7]

Many factors can affect corporate reputation, including the behavior of executives responsible for the company's image. While it is clear that no post-conviction maneuvering could do much to salvage the reputations of Tyco, Enron, WorldCom, Adelphia, and others, it is equally clear that key stakeholders—including investors, customers, suppliers, employees, regulators, and others—closely follow the behavior of corporate executives, looking for signals that will indicate the depth and sincerity of the company's intentions.

Public relations consulting firm Burson-Marsteller has data from a series of surveys indicating that the stakeholders who matter most to a firm will link a company's reputation directly to that of its chief executive. "Although their reputations can rise and fall dramatically," says Leslie Gaines-Ross, "CEOs remain the designated guardians of their company's reputation. The direct relationship between CEO performance and a company's reputation is stronger than it was during the pre-Enron and Internet-boom days." Gaines-Ross, chief Knowledge and Research Officer for Burson-Marsteller, added: "The importance of this relationship has grown 25 percent since our first survey was conducted among influential stakeholders in 1997. CEOs are now called upon to make far more difficult decisions, are held accountable for any transgressions and remain the organization's public face and ethical compass."[8]

2. Reputation management requires regular, sustained investment.

If corporate reputation is manageable, then regular investment in the structures, activities, staff, and tools of reputation management is essential. Very few business activities are managed without some form of sustained, serious investment, including annual balance sheet entries devoted to the people and processes needed to make them successful.

McDonald's Corporation. As an icon brand, McDonald's can be interpreted in a variety of ways. Thomas L. Friedman sees the golden arches as a vehicle of world peace.[9] Others have argued that McDonald's is a metaphor for the source of all that is wrong with the modern world since World War II.[10] The reality, of course, is somewhere between those two extremes, and the corporation has been mindful of the attitudes of its customers, mirroring their preferences and responding to the dynamics of the marketplace.

During the late 1970s, McDonald's became the target of environmental activists who opposed the use of chlorofluorocarbons (CFCs) in the packaging used to keep hamburgers, breakfast sandwiches, and other foods warm prior to serving. Preliminary but inconclusive evidence pointed to various environmental harms, so the company voluntarily removed CFCs from their packaging, using a recyclable, inert foam to keep sandwiches warm. The move was seen as a victory for environmentally responsible behavior within the company, but it had little effect on the company's public reputation.[11]

"We removed the CFCs," said former McDonald's vice president for corporate finance, Jerry Langley, "we recycled the foam packaging into benches, serving trays, and other durable, high-impact fixtures, and were convinced we were doing the right thing." When news reports and survey data indicated that elementary school teachers were telling their students not to eat at McDonald's because "they used packages that harm the earth's ozone layer," senior management responded. Ed Rensi, president of McDonald's USA, said, "We're going back to paper. I can't live with the impression that we're harmful to the earth, even if it isn't true." The world's largest restaurant chain began serving its trademark food in light cardboard containers and paper wrappings within days of that decision.

The company deliberately put its reputation for hot, tasty food products at risk in order to address the larger issue of environmental responsibility and its image as a responsible corporate citizen. "We never gave it a second thought," said Langley. "First, it was the right thing to do. And, second, we knew that any damage to our global reputation as a responsible organization would be extremely difficult to undo."[12]

During 2003 and 2004, Jack Daly, corporate senior vice president and chief communication officer for McDonald's, moved the handling of fat and sugar-content issues to the top of his team's list of concerns, noting that consumer perceptions of "quality" were shifting away from the company's traditional menu offerings. A new range of salads, bottled water, and reduced carbohydrate items, along with the disappearance of "supersized" menu items, has led the company's return to profitability.

Daly's handling of the explosive backlash of anti-American sentiment and the risks involved for the company's franchisees and partners is now seen as a "best practice" for other icon brands to emulate. The *New York Times* described McDonald's as having been largely unaffected by a rising tide of negative attitudes toward American products and brands following the U.S. invasion of Iraq in 2003.[13]

McDonald's menus in India, Russia, New Zealand, and the UK continue to reflect the taste and culture of the local community. The company has insisted for years that local franchise operators have a substantial stake in the operation and execution of McDonald's strategy worldwide. The country of origin of the corporation is downplayed in every instance in favor of the company's contribution to the local community. Few are aware, for example, that the Pushkin Square restaurant (the company's largest retail outlet anywhere) is owned and operated by the partners of McDonald's Canada.

At the urging of public relations advisor Al Golin, McDonald CEOs Ray Kroc and Fred Turner began investing in what they called "the community goodwill bank." The company founder, Ray Kroc, took Golin's advice to "invest early and often in those issues, activities, and causes that each community cares about most." And they should do this, he said, with no expectation that they would "ever need to make a withdrawal." When the time comes to withdraw, or depend on the goodwill of the community to survive some crisis, it's too late to begin thinking about which causes or issues to support.[14]

Golin's advice has paid off handsomely over the years for McDonald's, perhaps never more vividly than on June 18, 1984, when James Alan Huberty walked into a McDonald's restaurant in San Ysidro, California, and opened fire with a semi-automatic assault rifle on a lunchtime crowd, leaving 21 dead and 19 injured. The company's senior leadership responded by closing the store after the police had processed the crime scene, then bulldozing the building and transforming the site into a park, which they donated to the City of San Ysidro. Memorial scholarships were established to honor those who had lost their lives in the incident, and direct assistance to their families became a priority for McDonald's. The franchisee, with the company's help, built another restaurant less than three miles away. Rather than dwell on the horror of what had happened, the community offered sustained accolades for the way in which McDonald's had responded to the tragic event and its incredibly sad aftermath.[15]

3. To manage reputation, you must first analyze risk.

Allstate Insurance Company. "We face real reputational risk daily," said Peter Debreceny in 2005. "We insure 20 million households, handle $25 billion annually in claims, employ 40,000 people, and contract with an additional 30,000 independent agents who write policies." Debreceny was then vice president for corporate relations for the firm based in Northbrook, Illinois, and nominally responsible for managing the company's reputation. What sort of risk did he envision? "Well, following the recent hurricanes in Florida, we found a few people with whom we had contractual relationships overstating claims expenditures and providing kickbacks to homeowners. That's clearly illegal, but where substantial sums of money are involved, temptations can be great."[16]

The company faces reputational risk of many sorts, most of them related to delivering on the company's well-known brand promise, "You're in Good Hands." The question is how to properly analyze that risk so that the company can prepare for it.

Following Hurricane Andrew in 1992, the company clearly concluded that they had too much exposure in Florida. To reduce that exposure, all homeowners' policies were reassessed; many were subject to steep rate increases, while others were not renewed. Allstate executives knew that they would anger a number of policyholders, many of whom also held highly profitable automobile coverage with Allstate. "We knew," said Debreceny, "that we'd lose some policyholders with our rate increases and underwriting decisions, but we felt if we analyzed the risk carefully, it was one we would be willing to take."[17]

No one foresaw the hurricane season of 2004. "Two things occurred," Debreceny said, "which no one expected. First, we experienced four hurricanes, category three or greater, in one season, two of them on precisely the same track. Second, everyone thought the real risk was on the coastline, yet areas inland, near Orlando, were among the hardest hit." Quite literally, all of the money Allstate had made in the state of Florida during the previous decade had been wiped out.

So how does his company go about analyzing such risk? "We had to find additional solutions," he said, "that don't involve nonrenewal. We could run down the book," he said, meaning that they would simply write fewer policies in Florida, while allowing a large number to lapse. The company could also reinsure their risk with other companies or with the state government. "Low-severity, high frequency events [such as auto accidents] can spread risk and increase both profit and stability," he noted, "while high-severity, low frequency events are impossible to guard against."[18]

The real problem, he acknowledged, is that media coverage of such events and the industry's reaction to them can lower esteem for a brand. "It takes a long time to regain that esteem," he said. Allstate's retention ratio for policyholders was 91 percent in early 2005, with satisfaction rates very close to its competitors GEICO and USAA. "Between 2001 and 2002," said Debreceny, "we dropped 6.2 points in image measurement, while the industry itself was down 4.0 points. After considerable hard work, we've gained back two-thirds of that and are now 2.5 points ahead of where we were 12 months ago."[19]

Debreceny's team at Allstate made reputational risk analysis a daily part of their corporate communication routine. "One story can't drive a trend," he said, "but we must be rational in our approach. Every story is accompanied by actions the company or [the industry] have taken, and we have to be cognizant of public reaction." What sort of things did his team worry about? "Well," he said, "five things, basically. First, an employee who might garner negative publicity. Second, of course, necessary business decisions, such as price increases. Third, I think we worry about state insurance commissioners who might take independent action and garner publicity. Beyond that, just two things: an inadvertent transgression of regulatory or legal issues, and then normal corporate issues that might affect any company."[20]

Continual analysis of those and other problems directly affected how Debreceny and his communication team planned, budgeted, invested, and acted. "The most successful use of communication," he notes, "is in the business decisions themselves. We first need sound policies in the public interest. Then, disciplined execution. And, finally, clear, continuous communication."[21]

4.   Careful planning follows risk analysis.

Reputational risk management, although volatile from day-to-day in a global organization, involves long-term strategic considerations. As a result, reputational standing with various stakeholders is directly affected by the planning processes a company establishes to deal with such issues. The companies we have examined thus far have all occupied favorable positions in highly competitive industries. What happens when a virtual monopoly begins to erode?

De Beers, Ltd. On July 9, 2004, De Beers, the world's largest diamond producer, agreed to plead guilty to criminal price fixing. That move ended a decade-long case against De Beers and paved the way for them to return to the United States after an absence of nearly half a century. The direct result of the plea was a fine of $10 million, but the indirect outcome was that De Beers was able to reestablish itself in the United States, the world's most lucrative market for diamonds, as it looked to new markets and shifted its business focus in response to a declining grip on the production of rough diamonds.

Although the United States remains De Beers's biggest market for diamond jewelry worldwide, the South African-based company has historically sold to the United States only through intermediaries. De Beers pulled out of the U.S. market shortly after World War II, when the Justice Department alleged it had fixed the price of industrial diamonds. Federal antitrust enforcers filed criminal charges against De Beers again in 1994 but had trouble prosecuting the elusive De Beers executives, who avoided U.S. soil for fear of detention.[22] With plans to develop a direct retail presence in the U.S. and implement several new global brand-building initiatives, Nicky Oppenheimer and his senior team were faced with an unpleasant choice: plead guilty to criminal charges or forego the North American marketplace.

Antitrust issues were not the only obstacles De Beers would encounter in the United States. Federal officials were reluctant to facilitate De Beers's entry into the United States in light of the company's history of harsh labor conditions and support for South Africa's apartheid regime. De Beers's attempts to have the U.S. price-fixing charges dropped were unsuccessful with the Clinton, Bush, and Obama administrations, and the company will likely face additional private lawsuits and antitrust enforcement once they are established in the United States.[23] Additionally, negative publicity surrounding a European Union investigation into De Beers's new "Supplier of Choice" system in 2004 meant that the company would be under even closer scrutiny.[24]

Most significantly, De Beers must carefully manage its image in the eyes of the American public. The diamond industry has become a target for activist groups worldwide because of unchecked illegal mining and the trading of so-called "blood diamonds." That term is used to describe diamonds illegally traded to finance rebel factions and terrorist activities that have been linked to the death, maiming, and displacement of millions of South Africans, and this trade remains a pressing global concern. Though De Beers has undertaken steps to filter out any blood diamonds from their own stockpile, their methods have been far from foolproof. Numerous human rights groups continue to claim that De Beers is responsible for the proliferation of the blood diamond trade.[25]

How can De Beers demonstrate their commitment to eradicating the blood diamond trade and keep their brand from being tarnished by associations with war-torn Africa and terrorist regimes? From CEO Nicky Oppenheimer's perspective, the guilty plea in U.S. Federal Court was just the first step. It represented an important acknowledgment, however, that a virtual monopoly over raw materials and the means of production will not guarantee a long-term favorable position in the marketplace. Corporate reputation and the sensitive, potentially volatile views that the public holds about the company are among De Beers's most precious, and difficult to manage, assets.

5.   To manage reputation, you must measure reputation.

How do managers plan as they review the landscape of choices? Is there a formula? British poet John Milton wrote in the seventeenth century, "If we are unable to measure that which is important, we will ascribe importance to that which we can measure." So, what should a conscientious manager measure, and what should she do with the information once she has gathered it?

Genentech, Inc. Since 1976, Genentech has been a leader in the biotechnology industry, translating innovative science into commercially viable medicines. Genentech was the first company to bring a biotechnology drug to market and the first to become profitable. With a corporate culture grounded in scientific research, meaningful data for decision-making is held in the highest esteem. According to Debra Charlesworth, director of corporate relations at Genentech, "Here we're inclined to say, 'In God we trust; everyone else must bring the data.'" Every aspect of the company is influenced by this data-driven culture, including the measurement of Genentech's reputation.[26]

The mission of the Corporate Relations Department, as with similar departments in other companies, is to communicate key corporate messages to the company's various target audiences. When Charlesworth joined Genentech, she observed that her group needed better data to carry out their work, but she concluded that traditional public relations methods offered inadequate tools for collecting and analyzing data.

"We began looking at our data needs in a holistic manner," she said. "How does one data stream relate to another, and how are the needs of the entire organization served by the way we gather, analyze, and organize that data?" Charlesworth and her team were determined not to create data solely for its own sake. Instead, they sought to design measurement systems that captured and analyzed the data that would be useful for executing the group's strategic mission.

The department's first project under her guidance was to overhaul the process for tracking media inquiries. The immediate task was to convert the group's inefficient, paper-based system into a fully functional database that would ensure that someone from the department handled every media inquiry promptly. As the group considered this process, they realized that they could also capture additional information that would be of broader strategic interest. For example, by looking at the inquiry topics, key media issues could be categorized and tracked over time. Which questions were reporters asking the company? Was the company adequately prepared to address those recurring questions? If not, why not? Was it a communications issue, or did management need to articulate a policy position?[27]

The department's second project was to upgrade its processes for analyzing media content. The department's team members managed most of the media inquiries but lacked a uniform system for evaluating the final media stories. Charlesworth also saw that Genentech, like so many companies, used different PR agencies to work on various communication programs. Rather than relying on each agency's individual measurement system, Charlesworth and her team wanted a single measurement method. The answer was to bring media measurement in-house by purchasing a software package from a third-party vendor. The software ensured that all media coverage would be measured according to the same criteria, and the resulting data could be systematically analyzed. Her department could execute searches on the coverage, count placements, and measure tone in a consistent way. The new software package, supplied by Biz360 of San Mateo, California, allowed the department to remove many of the variables in audience measurement and tone, giving a more accurate view of Genentech's media coverage.

Charlesworth's relentless pursuit of consistency, accuracy, and immediacy have given her communications team a data stream that provides consistent insight into the company's execution of its communication strategy. By measuring what people say about them, their competitors, the industry, and more, they are not only more efficient in responding to press queries, they're smarter about a broad spectrum of the company's other public relations activities. Armed with specific data each morning, the department can engage in substantive conversations with Genentech's senior management about the company's reputation and the investment they are making to improve it.

6.   Accountability for reputation is a senior management function.

Claims from chief executives that corporate reputation is "everyone's responsibility" mean, essentially, that no one is accountable for what happens to the corporate brand. And while it is clear that the chief executive is ultimately accountable for organizational performance, it is equally clear that the CEO cannot monitor dozens of factors across multiple audiences, 24/7. At best, a chief executive can pay close attention to share price and projected earnings each day, but tracking those issues that may explode on the front page of the *Wall Street Journal*, *New York Times*, or the cover of *Business Week* is nearly impossible for the top officer in an organization. The answer is to invest a chief communication officer with the responsibility of planning, monitoring, measuring, and alerting others to issues most likely to affect the corporation's social standing among key stakeholders.

Great West Casualty and Old Republic International. A. C. Zucaro, chairman and CEO of Old Republic International Corporation, arrived at work in Chicago on a January morning in 1999 and picked up the *Wall Street Journal*, as usual. As he worked deliberately through his first cup of coffee, his business instincts told him this would be a good day: interest rates were down, the market was up, and the many subsidiaries of Old Republic were performing well. For the moment, Mr. Zucaro was a happy man.

As he moved to section two of the *Journal*, his optimism sank. On the front page of the "Marketplace" section was an article discussing a lawsuit involving a subsidiary of Old Republic, Great West Casualty Company. This was nothing new for a company with $2 billion in revenues and nine operating subsidiaries. But Zucaro knew from the headline that this Friday morning would be less pleasant than most: "An Old Woman Crossed the Road, and Litigiousness Sank to New Low."

On her way to work at 4:30 a.m. on July 1, 1998, eighty-one-year old Gertie Witherspoon blew out a tire and careened into a roadside ditch. With her automobile disabled, Mrs. Witherspoon left her car and began walking along U.S. Route 71 near Adrian, Missouri. Still dazed from the accident, she attempted to cross the highway to reach help. At just that moment, two semi-trucks traveling almost side by side, spotted the small figure in the road as they passed under a bridge. Traveling nearly 70 miles per hour, the truckers were unable to avoid hitting her. According to the police report, the driver of the rig slammed on his brakes and skidded more than 100 feet. Mrs. Witherspoon was pronounced dead at the scene.

Friends and relatives were stunned and saddened, particularly at Dave's Wagon Wheel Restaurant, where Mrs. Witherspoon worked fifty hours a week as a waitress. No one took the news harder than Joyce Lang, Mrs. Witherspoon's only daughter. "The family was crushed," she said, "and I was determined to find out more about what happened that morning." In the days and weeks following the accident, Ms. Lang, sought more information about the accident. She received only indifferent statements from the Missouri Highway Patrol and the truck owner, Rex Williams of Vernon County Grain & Supply. Frustrated in her attempts to learn more about her mother's death, Ms. Lang telephoned a claims adjuster at Great West Casualty Company to ask a few questions.

The adjuster at Great West Casualty explained that the police report and witness statements showed no fault on the part of the truck driver. "Is that all you can tell me?" she asked. "The case is closed," the adjuster responded. "Well," said Ms. Lang, "I can open it." Believing that the family was preparing legal action against Great West Casualty Company, the claims representative moved to file suit on behalf of his company against Gertie Witherspoon's estate. "It was never my intention to sue the company." Ms. Lang said later. "I did contact an attorney, but it was only to find out what our rights were. We filed no claims or lawsuits."

About five months later—just a few days before Christmas, on December 18, 1998—Joyce Lang received notice of a legal claim filed against the Witherspoon estate for damages to the truck that struck her mother. Specifically, the claim sought $2,886 "on account of property damage caused to a vehicle due to the negligent actions of Gertie Witherspoon on July 1, 1998." The Kansas City press had only reported the accident in which Mrs. Witherspoon died on September 4 of that year, when Barbara Shelly, a reporter for the *Kansas City Star* and an acquaintance of Ms. Lang, wrote a brief article elaborating on the life of Gertie Witherspoon. By coincidence, Ms. Shelly happened to be speaking with Ms. Lang on the day the claims notice arrived. "Seeing my mother's name in print like she was a criminal," said Ms. Lang, "I was devastated." Ms. Lang received the notice because she was serving as executor of her mother's estate. "I'm not paying them for killing my mom," she said. "I'll sit in jail first."

Amazed by the insurance company's actions, Ms. Shelly wrote a second article discussing the accident and the insurance company's response. Details in the second article appeared in the January 8, 1999, edition of the *Kansas City Star*. The story was picked up a week later by the *Wall Street Journal*. It was at that moment that A.C. Zucaro sensed trouble. Covering the claim filed by Rex Williams was a fairly small matter. The more immediate problem for him would be the company's response to the storm of media criticism.

Zucaro's principal problem was not the lawsuit, nor was it the *Wall Street Journal* article. The more serious underlying issue was that he had no one—in a company with more than $9 billion in assets under management, and thousands of employees in four major insurance groups—designated as monitor and guardian of the company's reputation. With a senior official acting as chief communication officer, that story would have been an unlikely candidate for national news, because the Great West Casualty subsidiary would not have responded as it did without considering the reputational consequences of its actions.

Corporate attorneys, seeking to limit liability exposure and head off litigation, were charged with the responsibility of replying to Joyce Lang and issuing a statement to the news media. In each instance, the company's official response made matters worse, largely because the firm's executives appeared insensitive to the human issues in the case. As a result, everyone from investment analysts to corporate watchdogs took notice, prolonging the agony for the company and pushing corporate financial performance under the microscope. Perhaps coincidentally, ORI's stock price began a sustained slide from $20 a share to less than $8.

7.   Withdrawal or retreat may be your best option.

The history of corporate reputation management is replete with examples of companies that have decided to withdraw from a market, retreat from a business position, or regroup in order to salvage a more important portion of the business. Coca-Cola dumped its ill-fated effort to launch a reformulated "New Coke" when loyal consumers told the company that they strongly preferred the taste of "Classic Coke." Charles Lazarus opened a chain of discount stores in 1948 known as

"Children's Supermarts." A decade later, the company rebranded as Toys R Us and became a $12 billion powerhouse in the retail toy business. And more than fifty years later, CEO John Eyler stated that the company whose name is synonymous with toys might exit the toy business entirely to focus on children's clothing and furniture.

Delta Airlines CEO Richard H. Anderson, following the lead of his predecessor, Gerald Grinstein, did what many airline executives had contemplated for years: he cut costs, transformed the company's retirement system from a defined-benefit plan into an employee-managed 401k, unloaded expensive leased aircraft, and negotiated pay and benefit concessions out of pilots, machinists, and flight attendants. Thus far, that strategy has helped Delta avoid Chapter 11, or worse, as the economy improves and business travel increases.

Anderson did more, however. In a deliberate move designed to segment passenger traffic, the company eliminated first-class seating in overseas flights, expanded Delta's Business Elite service, and worked very hard to attract the industry's lowest-paying passengers from discount carriers such as JetBlue, Southwest, Midwest Express, Spirit, Allegiant, and others, while retaining the number of more profitable business travelers. Pulling out of the pricey, first-class overseas market was a calculated risk, as well, but it's one that Delta's leadership felt comfortable with, since most of those seats were upgrades or free tickets earned though the airline's frequent flyer program.[28] In 2010 the company also sold two of its regional carriers that operate as Delta Connection for a total of $82.5 million. Anderson sold Mesaba Airlines to Pinnacle Airlines Corporation for $62 million and Compass Airlines to Trans States Holdings, Inc., for $20.5 million.[29] The withdrawal from an ownership position in its key business partners would represent another substantial risk to Delta's reputation for dependable, reliable service, but company spokesmen say it's one they're now willing to consider.

As bold as those moves have been, however, very little compares with what happened to Sears Roebuck & Company, formerly America's largest retailer. While Sears' troubles can be traced back decades or more, it was a little more than ten years ago that the company's highly profitable credit business began to imperil the structure and survival of the entire company.

Sears Roebuck & Company. It was just 8:30 a.m. on a Sunday morning in the spring of 1997, while most of Chicago was either still asleep or out retrieving the morning paper. Arthur C. Martinez was meeting with a dozen of his company's top executives at their headquarters building in suburban Hoffman Estates. For a few moments, the room grew quiet as Martinez tried to digest what he had just been told. Lawyers for Sears Roebuck & Company were explaining how employees had secretly violated federal law for nearly a decade.

Martinez couldn't believe what he was hearing: Sears attorneys and credit employees, according to a bankruptcy judge in Boston, had for years been dunning delinquent credit-card holders who had filed for—and had been granted—bankruptcy protection. The newspapers and cable television news channels didn't have the story yet, but it would only be a matter of hours before they would. The company that Martinez, a former Saks Fifth Avenue executive, had struggled to turn around would quickly be mired in the worst legal and ethics scandal in its 111-year history.

The United States Department of Justice was already considering not only civil penalties but criminal prosecution. Worse, this was not simply a rogue operation or an honest misinterpretation of the law: Sears appeared to have been violating the rights of many of its customers systematically and intentionally. The company, the lawyers were suggesting, may even have put the illegal practice into its procedures manual.[30]

How could such wrongdoing have gone unchecked for years? Martinez wanted to know. "Not one phone call about this? Ever?" he demanded. According to at least one participant in the meeting, it was a "sickening moment." An extensive investigation would later reveal an ethical lapse that cost the company more than $500 million. According to Sears Senior Vice President Ron Culp, the collection scheme began to unravel in November 1996, when Francis Latanowich, a disabled security guard, hand-wrote a letter on a yellow legal pad, begging the Boston Bankruptcy Court to reopen his case. Although Judge Carol Kenner had wiped out his debts, Sears later asked Latanowich to repay the $1,161 he owed for a TV, an auto battery, and some other merchandise. But the monthly payment, he wrote, "is keeping food off the table for my kids."[31]

Sears, it turned out, had mailed Latanowich an offer. In return for $28 a month on his account, the company would not repossess the goods he had bought with a Sears charge card before he went bankrupt. The practice of urging debtors to sign such deals, called reaffirmations, is legal and relatively widespread in the retail credit business, but many judges view them as unethical practices that keep people from getting a fresh start. Moreover, every signed reaffirmation *must* be filed with the court so a judge can review whether the debtor can handle the new payment. Sears Roebuck & Company had not filed this one with the court, and Judge Kenner wanted to know why not.[32]

During a January 29, 1997, hearing, a Boston attorney working for Sears offered a convoluted technical excuse for not filing. Kenner's response: "Baloney." There were hints from prior cases that Sears, both praised and feared nationwide as the most aggressive pursuer of reaffirmations, was not filing many of them with the court. Sears, in fact, was using unenforceable agreements to collect debts that legally no longer existed: the company had apparently ignored the law nearly 2,800 times in Massachusetts alone.

Between 1994 and 1998, personal bankruptcies in the United States rose from 780,000 to more than 1.3 million, leaving many retailers and credit card issuers awash in bad debt. Sears, as the nation's second-largest retailer, was in a particularly vulnerable position. That year, the company earned 50 percent of its operating income from credit, including charge cards held by more than 63 million households with Sears credit cards.

The problem, as Martinez would come to discover, was that too many of those new card-holders barely qualified for credit. In its zeal to attract new business, Sears became a lender to its riskiest customers. As the number of bankruptcies rose nationwide, so did the number of unpaid accounts at Sears. By 1997, more than one-third of all personal bankruptcies in the United States included Sears as a creditor. Companies heavily dependent on income from their credit cards chose to aggressively pursue bad debts, and Sears was just one of many to do so. The list included such prominent creditors as Federated Department Stores, the May Company, G.E. Capital, Discover Card, and AT&T.

As Martinez would also come to discover, the problem was neither isolated nor small. During the previous five years, some 512,000 customers had signed reaffirmation agreements with Sears, pledging to repay debts that totaled $412 million. Martinez suspected that his company's transformation from an exhausted, defeatist bureaucracy into "an aggressive, can-do company" had an unanticipated consequence: managers simply would not send bad news up the chain of command.[33]

A culture of aggressively pursuing bad debts while filtering out bad news from top management had become part of the company's culture and official policy. Michael Levin, chief of Sears' law department, explained to his CEO that at least one outside law firm had told someone in the company that Sears' policy was questionable. But word of the alert, which might have triggered a broader investigation within the company, somehow never worked its way up through the bureaucracy.

Sears' credit woes were not confined to those reaffirmation agreements, however. When the company launched its own Gold Master-Card in 2000, the strategy seemed fairly straightforward. Sears would roll out a multipurpose card to retain the business of Sears store-card customers, who were flocking to lower interest rate offers on other bank cards. Yet by the end of 2002, Sears reported a 28 percent decline in profits and its stock tumbled by 32 percent. The main problem, according to company executives, was the MasterCard division. Sears was forced to raise its bad-debt reserve by $189 million, largely to cover charge-offs on the card, which management had said would be less risky than the Sears store card.[34]

"The MasterCard program was clearly ill-conceived," according to Richard Church, managing director at Shumway Capital Partners. His greatest concern was that the card appeared to run counter to the needs of those who shopped in Sears' 870 stores.[35] Joining forces with MasterCard looked like a smart way to protect their huge credit business, which accounted for 60 percent of Sears' profits at the time. The reality was that their most credit-worthy customers were fleeing in large numbers for lower-interest bank cards, leaving Sears with the highest-risk, least desirable credit customers.

By October 2002, Sears had doubled its credit-card balances to $10.8 billion, or 37 percent of its $29 billion in total credit receivables. Not long after that, default rates began rising, leading to a steady erosion of Sears' profits. By July 2003, CEO Alan Lacy decided that Sears could no longer effectively manage credit card operations and put the credit division up for sale. Sears' 59 million credit card accounts went to Citigroup for about $32 billion in cash and stock. The deal immediately saved the company about $200 million in operating costs and resulted in another $200 million in annual performance payments from Citigroup.[36]

For years, people had come to Sears because credit was easily available. Quality Craftsman tools and Kenmore appliances drew people into the stores, but none of the "softer side" merchandise, including a dowdy, downscale apparel collection, had ever proven profitable. Lacy knew that he had to move and move fast, if he were going save what once was America's largest retailer from the same fate that befell Woolworth's, Montgomery Ward, and Kmart. The sale of the credit division permitted him to write off the $1.9 billion debt he had incurred to acquire catalogue and Internet powerhouse Land's End, and made possible a thorough revamping of Sears stores nationwide. Putting the reputation of Sears as a friendly, cooperative retail creditor at risk made it possible for Alan Lacy to reinvest in other portions of the business, which, in turn, boosted the reputation of the company as a whole.

THIS IS NOT simply public relations as an afterthought to corporate brand management. This is corporate strategy that begins with key stakeholders and concludes with careful measurement and agreed-upon metrics for managing reputation. Communication, thus, becomes the driver for corporate strategy. To do that effectively, communication must become a strategic partner in the corporate planning process. This means, of course, that reputation management must become a priority for the company and must be led by a senior member of management, preferably at the executive or senior vice president level.

It means, further, that adequate staff, budget, and access to the chief executive must become priorities for the firm, as well. In the last analysis, managing the company's good name may be more important than any of the other, more traditional responsibilities of a chief executive. "Who steals my purse steals trash," Shakespeare's Othello tells us. "'Tis something, nothing; / 'Twas mine, 'tis his, and has been slave to thousands; / But he that filches from me my good name / Robs me of that which not enriches him, / And makes me poor indeed."

NOTES

1. R. J. Alsop, *The 18 Immutable Laws of Corporate Reputation: Creating, Protecting, and Repairing Your Most Valuable Asset*, Wall Street Journal Books (New York: Free Press, 2004).

2. C. J. Fombrun, *Reputation: Realizing Value from the Corporate Image* (Boston: Harvard Business School Press, 1996).

3. H. Smith and A. Feighan, "Coca-Cola and the European Contamination Crisis (A), (B)" (Notre Dame, IN: Eugene D. Fanning Center for Business Communication, Mendoza College of Business, University of Notre Dame, 2000).

4. M. Newman, "Eluding Press, Stewart Slips into Prison before Dawn," *New York Times* (October 9, 2004), B3.

5. C. Hays, "Stewart's Woes Hurt Company; Losses Expected through 2004," *New York Times* (August 4, 2004), C1, C3.

6. D. Brady, "For Martha, It's Time to Do Time," *Business Week Online* (September 16, 2004).

7. B. White, "Martha Stewart Begins Her Makeover: Image Experts Praise Stewart's Decision," *Washington Post* (September 16, 2004).

8. L. Gaines-Ross, Chief Knowledge and Research Officer, Burson-Marsteller, personal interview, New York (October 16, 2004).

9. T. Friedman, "The Golden Arches Theory of Conflict Prevention," *The Lexus and the Olive Tree* (New York: Anchor, 2000), 248–75.

10. G. Ritzer, *The McDonaldization of Society*, Rev. New Century Ed. (Thousand Oaks, CA: Pine Forge Press, 2004).

11. J. Langley, former vice president, Corporate Finance, McDonald's Corporation, personal interview, Notre Dame, IN (October 18, 2004).

12. Ibid.

13. "War and Abuse Do Little Harm to U.S. Brands: Most Products Escape Rising Anger Abroad," *New York Times* (May 9, 2004), 1.

14. A. Golin, personal interview (September 17, 2004). Supplemental interviews with Richard A. Starmann, former McDonald's senior vice president for corporate communication (October 15, 2004).

15. R. G. Starmann, "Tragedy at McDonald's," in *Crisis Response: Inside Stories on Managing Image under Siege*, ed. J. Gottschalk (Detroit: Gale Research, 1993), 309–21.

16. Debreceny, P.D., Vice President for Corporate Relations, Allstate Insurance Company, personal interview, Northbrook, IL (February 17, 2005).

17. Ibid.

18. Ibid.

19. Ibid.

20. Ibid.

21. Ibid.

22. J. R. Wilke, "DeBeers Is in Talks to Settle Price-Fixing Charge," *Wall Street Journal* (February 24, 2004), A1, A14.

23. Ibid.

24. V. Knight and J. Range, "EU is Looking Into Complaints Involving De Beers," *Wall Street Journal* (March 18, 2004), A12.

25. A. Davgun, H. McDaniel, and M. Thomas, "De Beers, Ltd.: Polishing Up Its Brand Image for the U.S. Market," ed. J. O'Rourke (Notre Dame, IN: Eugene D. Fanning Center for Business Communication, Mendoza College of Business, University of Notre Dame, 2004).

26. D. Charlesworth, telephone interview, from Genentech Headquarters, South San Francisco (January 6, 2005).

27. Ibid.

28. E. Perez, "How Delta's Cash Cushion Pushed It onto Wrong Course," *Wall Street Journal* (October 29, 2004), A1, A11. See also M. Maynard, "Billion-Dollar Ball in Delta Pilots' Hands," *New York Times* (October 29, 2004), C1, C8.

29. S. Bomkamp, "Delta Sells Two Regional Carriers for $82.5M," Associated Press (July 1, 2010).

30. J. B. Cahill, "Sear's Credit Business May Have Helped Hide Larger Retailing Woes," *Wall Street Journal* (July 6, 1999), A1, A8.

31. J. McCormick, "The Sorry Side of Sears," *Newsweek* (February 22, 1999).

32. E. R. Culp, former senior vice president, corporate communications, Sears Roebuck & Company, personal interviews (November 1, 1999, to January 15, 2000).

33. "Sears to Pay Fine of $60 Million in Bankruptcy Fraud Lawsuit," *New York Times* (February 10, 1999), C1.

34. R. Berner, "How Plastic Put Sears in a Pickle," *Business Week Online* (October 30, 2002).

35. Ibid.

36. A. R. Sorkin, "Sears to Sell Card Portfolio to Citigroup for $3 Billion," *New York Times* (July 16, 2003), C1, C2.

14 | The UN Global Compact

Forum for Environmental Leadership

Deborah Rigling Gallagher

> *The Global Compact's strengths and weaknesses both stem from its having adopted a model that promotes learning by recognizing and reinforcing leadership.*
>
> —John Ruggie[1]

In the spring of 2000, business, labor, and civil society leaders joined with United Nations representatives to develop a framework to serve Secretary-General Kofi Annan's 1999 call at the World Economic Forum in Davos, Switzerland: "I call on you—individually through your firms, and collectively through your business associations—to embrace, support and enact a set of core values in the areas of human rights, labor standards, and environmental practices." Ultimately, the United Nations Global Compact was organized as a broad network of business leaders, nongovernmental organizations, and labor organizations who would "embrace, support and enact, within their sphere of influence, a set of core values in the areas of human rights, labor standards, the environment and anti-corruption."[2] It is important to note that while the Compact's builders initially sought private sector representation via business associations, a decision was made early on to "seek greater involvement and leadership directly from CEOs."[3]

Much has been written about the development of the UN Global Compact and the negotiations surrounding its configuration and operational goals.[4] Clearly, however, designers stipulated that it be a network of organizational *leaders*, focused on using tools of partnership, dialogue, and learning to support and promote the Compact's principles. From its inception in 2000, leaders of businesses were asked to commit to three activities as members: publicly promote the UN Global Compact's mission, engage in dialogue about accomplishments and lessons learned, and partner with other members to benefit the greater good.[5]

This chapter examines how the tools of organizational leadership, and more specifically business environmental leadership, were leveraged in two UN Global Compact learning network initiatives—Caring for Climate and the Environmental Stewardship Strategy—to address environmental challenges by promoting a shared understanding of high-level environmental management practices. I first reflect on the art and practice of environmental leadership in a private sector context and examine how the UN Global Compact can be considered a vehicle for environmental leader firms to exercise institutional entrepreneurship. I then describe how the UN Global Compact's learning network platforms facilitate entrepreneurial firms' practice of environmental leadership. Finally, I examine the Environmental Stewardship Strategy in detail to show how corporate leaders engage with the UN Global Compact's voluntary code of conduct to learn about, implement, and promote beyond-compliance environmental management practices. Interview data from participants in the development of the Environmental Stewardship Strategy are analyzed to provide a ground-level understanding of business leaders' participation in one of the UN Global Compact's signature environmental leadership initiatives.

ENVIRONMENTAL LEADERSHIP

Environmental problems are intractable; they come in the form of critical global challenges, such as climate change, resource scarcity, habitat loss, and diminished biodiversity. They cross political and geographical boundaries and transcend human time scales. Scientists, policy makers, and business leaders each have a role to play in addressing these problems. In their roles as environmental leaders seeking to address these crises, their application of personal leadership skills is critical.

Researchers have long noted that private sector managers who act as environmental leaders take on roles as change agents within their organizations,[6] work collectively with leaders in other organizations,[7] act as champions for environmental initiatives,[8] and emphasize the use of higher-order environmental management tools.[9] Environmental leadership has thus been defined as "the ability to influence individuals and mobilize organizations to a vision of long-term ecological sustainability."[10]

Researchers studying leadership as applied to promote environmental sustainability have suggested that complex, global environmental challenges require leadership approaches that recognize contradictions, integrate different perspectives, and focus on high-impact change.[11] Others have asserted that such leaders must apply systems thinking, focus on spiritual approaches, and engage in collaboration.[12]

As important as individual leadership is to confronting environmental problems, perhaps equally important is the leadership role that organizations themselves play. There is evidence that in the face of such complexity, leader organizations do step up to address environmental problems. For example, the Association of Climate Change Officers, whose public and private sector members share information about strategies to address climate change, and the World Mayors Council on Climate Change, convened to advocate for local actions on climate change, both play key roles in efforts to confront climate change impacts. And the United Nations Global Compact plays a crucial role in promoting business behaviors to address a variety of critical social and environmental issues.

Leader businesses take on multiple challenges. In addition to meeting their required responsibilities to comply with a variety of environmental regulations, they increasingly act as prime movers and early adopters of beyond-compliance environmental management practices. They voluntarily participate in initiatives such as the third-party certified management system, ISO 14001, or work with the Carbon Disclosure Project to report carbon emissions. Early adopters of advanced

environmental management practices are role models who use their social influence to encourage other firms to explore new, more advanced
modes of environmental management behavior. By doing so they are
participating in the diffusion of critical practices; thus they can be
seen as institutional entrepreneurs.[13] These early adopter firms leverage newly constructed policy tools, such as the voluntary environmental
programs described above, to obtain competitive advantage while promoting cutting-edge environmental practices. Participation in voluntary environmental programs provides opportunities for entrepreneurial
firms to network with global governance organizations and regulatory
agencies to set standards for follower firms.

Institutional entrepreneurs use strategic resources such as scientific
acumen, broad supply chain management capabilities, and critical relationships with regulatory agencies and global governance organizations
to advance their positions as market leaders.[14] Research has shown that
firms adopt advanced environmental management practices to achieve
competitive advantage.[15] While these firms act as environmental leaders
and mobilize firm capabilities to advance long-term ecological sustainability, they are necessarily focused on promoting economic interests.

Institutional entrepreneurs seek to create structures in which the
practices and processes they respect are regularized and diffused.[16] They
strive to create new institutional forms and practices that advance specific behavioral norms.[17] Firms seeking to exercise leadership in service of advancing a particular normative vision, such as the practice of
advanced environmental stewardship to address global environmental
crises such as climate change, are values-based institutional entrepreneurs. They are motivated to accelerate the diffusion of these practices
by acting first as values-based institutional entrepreneurs. These firms
partner with organizations like the UN Global Compact, which are
grounded in promoting the overarching role of business in addressing
global problems such as poverty, inequality, and climate change.[18] The
values-based institutional entrepreneurs who join the United Nations
Global Compact sign on to its core principles and pledge to engage in
a variety of activities geared toward fostering business behaviors that
advance progress toward the United Nations Millennium Development
Goals.[19] In partnership with the UN Global Compact, member firms
assert and promote their values as environmental leaders to change environmental institutions. They seek to diffuse the advanced practices

[handwritten marginalia:] How can they simultaneously seek advantage + seek to promote diffuse new normal?

But maybe not by giving away / Patents etc? Ask his opinion on Tesla.

they voluntarily execute, by promoting the Compact's environmental principles summarized below through participation in platforms such as those detailed later in this chapter.

THE UN GLOBAL COMPACT AND ENVIRONMENTAL LEADERSHIP

Three of the nine principles initially declared by the UN Global Compact's originators were dedicated to business support and promotion of environmental leadership behaviors:

Principle 7: Businesses should support a precautionary approach to environmental challenges. This principle calls on environmental leaders to take preventive actions to address environmental management challenges even in the face of scientific uncertainty.

Principle 8: Businesses should take initiatives to promote greater environmental responsibility. This principle calls on environmental leaders to adopt and promote practices that fully integrate environmental considerations into business planning and decision-making.

Principle 9: Businesses should encourage the development and diffusion of environmentally friendly technologies. This principle calls on environmental leaders to develop technologies to minimize pollution, reduce waste and material inputs, improve the efficiency of manufacturing processes, and develop communication strategies to disseminate best practices.

The UN Global Compact is a voluntary code of conduct[20] with a significant focus on its ability to serve as a global learning network.[21] As an institution created to influence member organizations to enact management practices that produce global solutions to critical environmental problems, the UN Global Compact seeks to bring member organizations into closer affinity with each of the three environmental principles described above. Thus its initiatives must be designed to both actively engage the imagination of member organizations and catalyze subsequent commitment of valuable time and effort to promote environmental leadership principles and practices.

The UN Global Compact's learning network approach seeks to engage the participation of its members, who are playing many different organizational roles in a broad range of cultural and political settings and are responsible for the production of a variety of products and services. These membership dynamics emphasize the need for the UN Global Compact's learning networks to be highly innovative. The structure of the UN Global Compact's learning networks and the content to which they provide access must support professional relationships engaged in innovation, learning, and implementation.[22] Accordingly, the UN Global Compact's learning networks "aim to reach broader, consensus-based definitions of what constitutes good practices than any of the parties could achieve alone. These definitions together with illustrative case studies are then publicized in an on-line information bank, which will become a standard reference source on corporate social responsibility."[23]

Learning network-based initiatives, which incite members' active participation and also spur their creativity, have long served as the foundation of the UN Global Compact's environmental leadership efforts. The learning network initiatives, which enable members to share expertise and experience and to learn from each other, are by design a platform for firm social engagement and also a tool for values-based institutional entrepreneurs seeking to broadly diffuse new norms for business environmental management practice. In the following sections I focus on two such initiatives: Caring for Climate, a firmly institutionalized initiative designed to engage significant numbers of member firms in a broad-based effort to confront the impacts of global climate change, and the more recent Environmental Stewardship Strategy, which focuses on leveraging leader firms' expertise in employing advanced strategies to address critical environmental issues. In the closing sections I present a detailed examination of the design and implementation of the Environmental Stewardship Strategy learning network, including an analysis of participant firm perspectives.

CARING FOR CLIMATE

Caring for Climate was established in 2007 by UN Secretary-General Ban Ki-moon as an initiative for UN Global Compact member organizations to demonstrate leadership on the issue of climate change. Participants in the learning network initiative support ongoing efforts to identify and disseminate practical solutions to climate change challenges, set organizational goals for emissions reductions, and publicly declare progress toward those goals. The network framework, in which members share ideas and strategies on issues, such as promoting efforts to achieve carbon neutrality and understanding the impact of climate change on global development and poverty reduction efforts, enables business leaders to collaborate to advance technical and management solutions and to help shape public policy and public attitudes related to climate change. The initiative is guided by the efforts of a fourteen-member steering committee composed of senior corporate environmental officers from firms across the globe. Caring for Climate signatories have regularly gathered in advance of international climate change negotiations to lend a business perspective to these negotiations. Recent discussions have centered on redesigning products, investing in renewable energy, and technologies for carbon capture, storage, and sequestration.

Member CEOs who support Caring for Climate develop and expand on firm- and enterprise-level strategies for addressing climate change, and publicly disclose data on greenhouse gas emissions as part of their disclosure responsibility commitment within the UN Global Compact framework, namely, the annual Communication on Progress. The global and economic reach of Caring for Climate signatories is as significant as the issues they confront and the solutions they promote. The approximately four hundred companies that participate in Caring for Climate originate in about sixty-five countries with both developed and emerging economies. Specific issues on which they focus include low-carbon innovation and climate change adaptation. Participating companies share information on their challenges and successes in online learning forums, research publications, and in face-to-face annual meetings.

THE ENVIRONMENTAL STEWARDSHIP STRATEGY

In 2009, when member companies of the UN Global Compact indicated that a standard framework would help improve their approach to environmental management, UN Global Compact managers convened a working group on environmental stewardship to explore best practices. Building on the Compact's successful Caring for Climate leadership initiative, the project was designed to promote a model for strategic environmental stewardship. Initially termed the supra-environmental stewardship strategy, the project focused on explicating and sharing innovative corporate environmental policies, programs, and strategies to address issues such as climate change, water, energy, and ecosystems throughout organizational value chains. The working group, a partnership between the UN Global Compact, seventeen companies, and Duke University, began by identifying the environmental management and sustainability practices that group members most frequently used. The group first shared these practices through an initial web-based meeting. Attendees recognized that the information presented about the challenges of environmental stewardship was sufficiently compelling to decide to develop an Environmental Stewardship Strategy (ESS), to be provided to all UN Global Compact members at the tenth anniversary meeting of the Global Compact in June 2010.

The goal of the ESS was to expand the UN Global Compact's influence by leveraging its members' organizational leadership and institutional entrepreneurship behavior to influence the creation of behavioral norms that incorporate high-level environmental stewardship practices. ESS developers acknowledged that businesses engaged in environmental stewardship work to address environmental problems by creating effective management solutions. ESS designers recognized that the environmental leader organizations acting as institutional entrepreneurs through membership in the United Nations Global Compact not only identify and implement advanced environmental management practices on an ongoing basis, but also continually seek to share and promote them to global colleagues, who may be customers, suppliers, or competitors.

Interviews with leading and learner firms, analysis of webinar content, focus group discussions with member firms, and broad-based research on best practices informed the development of the ESS. In anticipation of the development of the strategy, a learning network was built around a series of webinars with working group members, UN Global Compact members and staff, researchers, and other interested parties. Each webinar confronted a specific environmental issue, such as water resource management or climate change adaptation. Working group members and other participants shared information about best practices in environmental stewardship. Webinar content was summarized and PowerPoint presentation materials were made available to all attendees.

Senior managers responsible for overseeing environmental sustainability efforts were then interviewed to learn about their internal efforts to develop an advanced environmental stewardship strategy, to work within their supply chain, and to engage in environmental public policy development. Issues such as what differentiates leader firms from follower firms and how firms track future environmental challenges were explored. Questions examined the level of involvement by CEOs and boards of directors in strategic environmental stewardship.

A common definition of environmental stewardship was developed, as follows: "a comprehensive understanding and effective management of critical environmental risks and opportunities related to climate change, emissions and waste management, resource consumption, water conservation, biodiversity protection and ecosystem services."[24] Research on leader firms revealed that when initiatives were successful, CEOs and boards of directors were engaged with company managers in applying four principle approaches to environmental stewardship across organizations:

1. Environmental stewardship is *embedded* into all facets of the organization.
2. Short-term targets are *balanced* against long-term goals.
3. Best practices are *diffused* throughout value chains and business networks.
4. Best practices are *translated* into processes and practices across firm geographies.

Using the principles as a framework, working group members developed a "straw man" model of the ESS. This model was based on the newly developed UN Global Compact Management Model, a standard, five-step continual improvement framework designed to assist UN Global Compact members develop operational strategies congruent with the UN Global Compact's ten principles. Focus group participants critiqued the ESS straw man model and offered suggestions for improvement. Ultimately, the centerpiece of the UN Global Compact's ESS became an eight-step continuous improvement process, which directs organizations on an annual basis to carry out the following:

1. *Recommit* to the UN Global Compact's environmental principles.
2. *Assess* the landscape of environmental performance by conducting external benchmarking activities.
3. *Declare* specific intentions to improve firm performance in a public forum such as an organizational website.
4. *Engage* with individual and institutional stakeholders by participating in efforts to promote pro-active environmental policies.
5. *Perform* according to declared environmental improvement intentions.
6. *Evaluate* performance against intentions by comparing year-to-year accomplishments.
7. *Disseminate* results of environmental performance through the UN Global Compact's annual Communication on Progress (COP) process.
8. *Anticipate* future environmental challenges by engaging in collaborative research and dialogue with leading and learning firms and experts.

The strategy was designed to help business leaders generate social and economic value from successful management of their organizations' relationships with the environment. The ESS, initially conceived as a stand-alone tool to be documented in a research report, was eventually constructed as a web-based social networking platform. Member companies and others could visit the website home of the ESS to learn about advanced environmental stewardship practices, view case studies submitted from leader firms, and engage in discussions about critical environmental issues. The website, hosted by Duke University's Nicholas Institute for Environmental Policy Solutions, served as a learning network platform for environmental leaders and learners. The eight steps of continuous improvement were represented visually as a wheel with the segments "Recommit," "Assess," "Declare," and so forth.[25]

THE ENVIRONMENTAL STEWARDSHIP STRATEGY RESEARCH STUDY

Concurrent with the development of the ESS tool, independent research was conducted to discern the motivations and examine the behavior of working group members. Past quantitative empirical research on the UN Global Compact has focused on issues such as overall motivations to become members and market responses to membership. For example, Cetindamar and Husoy, employing a survey of twenty-nine Compact members to investigate both member motivations for joining and the influence of UN Global Compact participation on firm performance, showed that while members were not motivated to participate in UN Global Compact initiatives to further economic goals, both ethical and economic benefits were realized.[26] Janney and others conducted a series of event studies to show that investors respond positively to a firm's decision to participate in the UN Global Compact.[27]

In contrast, the study of the ESS working group members used qualitative data analysis to present a picture of the viewpoints and behaviors of an elite group of member companies, self-described environmental leaders, who took part in the development of the ESS initiative. The study sought to understand how these UN Global Compact members would differentiate between environmental leader and learner firms and to uncover their motivations to apply advanced environmental stewardship practices. Additionally, researchers were interested in exploring leaders' perspectives on methods that could be employed to engage a wide range of small businesses, learner firms, and other stakeholders in advancing critical environmental stewardship practices. Finally, the study was focused on identifying the critical environmental stewardship issues that the ESS tool should address and on determining participants' expectations of it as a partnership, dialogue, and learning network tool.

Interviews were conducted with a subset of working group senior managers and other participants. Interviewees held senior corporate level positions as directors of sustainability, industrial ecology, environmental health and safety, sustainable development, corporate social responsibility, or climate change. Participant firms and their industry sector and primary location are shown in table 14.1.

An interview guide, jointly developed by Duke University researchers and UN Global Compact staff (see appendix), was used to frame open-ended conversations with participants.[28] The open-ended interviewing process enabled researchers to collect data and gain insight into underlying meanings by probing answers and asking follow-up questions. Interviews were recorded and transcribed. Qualitative data were compiled into an interactive data base using NVivo software.

Table 14.1. Participant Firms

Firm	Industry Sector	Location
**Cosco	Industrial Transportation	China
**Deutsche Telekom	Fixed Line Communications	Germany
**Dow Chemical	Chemicals	USA
**DuPont	Chemicals	USA
**Ericsson	Fixed Line Communications	Sweden
**Eskom	Gas, Water & Multiutilities	South Africa
**Holcim	Construction & Materials	Switzerland
**Infosys	Software & Computer Services	India
**Intel	Technology, Hardware, Equipment	USA
**Novo Nordisk	Pharmaceuticals & Biotech	Denmark
**Ricoh	Industrial Engineering	Japan
**SAP	Software & Computer Services	Germany
**Swiss Re	Financial Services	Switzerland
**System Capital Management	General Industries	Ukraine
**Titan Cement	Construction & Materials	Greece
**Vestas	Technology, Hardware, Equipment	Denmark
**Westpac	Financial Services	Australia
Baosteel	Industrial Metals and Mining	China
China Minmetals	Industrial Metals and Mining	China
Coca-Cola Hellenic	Beverages	Greece
Cool House	Cement	UAE
Deloitte	Support Services	USA
Fuji Xerox	Technology, Hardware, Equipment	Japan
H&M Hennes & Mauritz AB	Personal Goods	Sweden
Levi Strauss & Co	Personal Goods	USA
Nokia	Technology, Hardware, Equipment	Finland
Novartis	Pharmaceuticals & Biotechnology	Switzerland
PepsiCo	Food Producers	USA
Reed Elsevier	Media	United Kingdom
Saint-Gobain	Industrial Metals & Mining	France
SEKEM Group	Food Producers	Egypt
Sustainable Living Fabrics	General Industrials	Australia
Tata Consultancy Services	Software and Computer Services	India

** Denotes Working Group Member Firm

Qualitative data were examined using constant comparison methods. In this method, data "bits" are grouped into roughly equivalent categories to discern common cross-case patterns. Individual firm spokesperson responses to interview questions were synthesized into a series of firm-based case studies. These cases were then examined and compared to elucidate cross-cutting themes and ideas. While constant comparison methods are often used to develop theory, the goal of this study was purely to uncover broad themes and sort information about common behaviors, opinions, and motivations of participants in the UN Global Compact's ESS partnership. Ongoing research explores the data using grounded theory methods in consultation with theories of leadership, learning networks, and institutional entrepreneurship and is focused on generating and testing hypotheses.

Several critical themes were uncovered during cross-case comparisons. First, ESS participants had much to say about the characteristics of environmental leaders. The importance of top management commitment to diffusing values throughout the company and transparently sharing results with a wide range of stakeholders was echoed by many interviewees. For example:

> I think firstly it is top management commitment that is crucial. Having the ability to take a vision of the top management, cascading it down through the shop floor, having every employee of the company understanding his or her role in fulfilling that vision, that is what it takes to realize environmental progress.

> Some of the key characteristics of the leaders are that they identify emerging trends and have an in-depth understanding of the long-term characteristics of the implications of the issues. . . . They tend to be good at broad stakeholder engagement so they have good relationships with stakeholders in the environmental space, whether it be an NGO or the scientific community or specific government agencies in the area. . . . They try to participate in collaborative activities based on their relationships before working on projects.

> Our experience is that it is very fruitful to have an open discussion with different stakeholders going forward. And very often we feel that

having the experience of having been in the business for a very long time and in very many different countries, having a global view, we could add perspective to finding sustainable solutions.

Interviewees' ideas about what differentiates leaders from learners informed their recommendations on how a learning network might be designed to benefit learner firms and what environmental stewardship practices should be emphasized. The primary distinction they made between leaders and learners was that leaders go well beyond what is generally expected and have a bias for transparency. Two comments were worth noting:

But a leading company will not only measure but will then have ambitious targeted goals. . . . [They include] making what you are doing publicly available, because that shows accountability to all stakeholders, external and internal. And I think without these elements, without the leadership, without the vision, without the measurement, without the ambition, and without the disclosure you could never be a leading firm.

So it's really important for a leading firm to think outside of the most obvious, to challenge the scope of responsibility, to look in many dimensions.

Participants noted that in their experience, the UN Global Compact does not reach a significant number of small and medium-sized businesses, who are most often characterized as learner firms. They agreed that efforts should be taken to reach out to these businesses and offered recommendations for promoting engagement of small businesses, learner firms, and other stakeholders in environmental stewardship. They emphasized the importance of leaders sharing knowledge with learners and providing opportunities for learners to influence policy-making. As several commented,

I think there really needs to be some sort of grassroots program that is driven by environmental agencies and environmental NGOs or perhaps even the UN Global Compact in countries where they are present by giving examples and sharing experiences of specifically what small to medium businesses have been able to do.

I think that small and medium sized enterprises really should be engaged in the organizations that have the standouts on both the national and international level. I think that is the way for them also to make their voice heard, to put their points forward.

[It is important] to have either cross-function industry specific or cross-industry specific work groups on specific areas where you can actually talk with the leading firms about different aspects. And then, using the best of the best and together going forward and presenting knowledge to government bodies, local governments, etc.—that is one way you can be very visionary.

Participants acknowledged that climate change is a primary focus of their company efforts and thus should be afforded a prominent position within the ESS tool. While individual firms expressed interest in addressing environmental issues of particular importance in their geographic settings and to their core businesses, several critical environmental stewardship issues were found to be of common concern to participants. Members emphasized that issues such as water scarcity, managing community concerns, resource conservation, and waste management are also at the forefront of their work. For example, from our interviews:

Twenty-five years ago nobody thought that carbon dioxide would be the issue that it is today. Water scarcity, we know, is going to become an issue, because with rising population and living standards, it will obviously become a key thing for the future.

We are . . . large and visible, in the small community we operate. We have a number of environmental and social issues that our strategy aims to address, for example: climate change; our carbon footprint; eco-efficiency; conservation of nonrenewable resources; recycling of secondary materials; and community engagement.

Considering the breadth of critical environmental issues that participant firms confront daily, and the variety of internal company approaches employed to address these concerns, the challenge of delivering a tool for sharing environmental stewardship strategies is predictably complex. Member expectations of the ESS to serve as a partnership, dialogue, and learning network platform to reach both leaders and learners alike varied considerably, confirming the need to design a flexible and evolving tool or set of tools. For example:

> It would be very helpful if our company could network with experts to address key strategic carbon abatement strategies [and] also enable them in developing critical sustainability management skills. It would also be useful if we could have access to the best practices industry benchmarks on sustainability.

> Continue to build best practices and leaders. Encourage all companies to learn from each other. Learning what works and providing venues for collaboration within and across industries will be critical.

> We would very much appreciate . . . focusing on the leadership skills required, challenging activities like transformative work, and . . . supporting cross-sector activities. These would include, for example, . . . doing a cross-sector global profile on environmental, energy, and climate activities.

Finally, when members reflected on the importance of participating in the ESS development project, it was clear that the overarching benefit of engagement, even for leader firms, was learning from each other. As one commented, "I think the most useful part of this project for us is learning from others. . . . I think many of us are both leaders and learners."

THE UN GLOBAL Compact members who participated in the design of the Environmental Stewardship Strategy indicated that participation was beneficial on several fronts. They learned a great deal from each other about how to enact advanced environmental stewardship practices to address critical issues such as climate change and biodiversity protection. They committed to fostering the development of the ESS tool as a means of reaching out to other leaders while engaging with learner firms. Participation in the ongoing development of the ESS tool offered an opportunity to fulfill these leaders' roles as institutional entrepreneurs, by fostering diffusion of advanced environmental stewardship strategies through an innovative web-based learning network tool.

Their experiences highlight the promise of the UN Global Compact organization, with its learning network platform. The ESS platform, like all influential learning networks, provides its users with opportunities to share critical information such as case studies of exemplary practices and to engage in dialogue. The UN Global Compact's ESS offers users of the learning network opportunities to confront problems, consider solutions, and come to a general consensus about the way forward. However, as participants in the ESS development recognized, efforts to reach out to small and medium businesses, which make up over 75 percent of the global economy, must be undertaken so that its significant promise will be realized and both leaders and learners alike regularly participate in the dialogue it supports.

APPENDIX: INTERVIEW GUIDE

1. Does your firm have a corporate environmental strategy? If so, what challenges does the strategy hope to confront? What issues served as a catalyst to the strategy's development and why? What are the most important issues or challenges in making your company more sustainable? How is progress toward fulfilling your strategy measured and reported? If no strategy exists, why not?

2. If your firm has a corporate environmental strategy, what role does the CEO/Board have in shaping or managing environmental policies and strategies? How much of the strategy is guided or controlled by top management?

3. For this study, we hope to note differences between how "leading" and "learning" firms approach environmental strategy. Based on your experience, what differentiates a firm "leading" on environmental management from one "following" environmental management initiatives?

4. Does your current environmental management strategy incorporate a value chain and/or life cycle approach? If so, how? If not, how would you restructure your strategy to incorporate a value chain or life cycle approach?

5. What types of government policy (local, national and international) have had the greatest impact in transforming your environmental management practices in the past?

6. How do you think more firms, including small and medium-sized enterprises, can be engaged with applicable local, state, federal and international governance institutions to develop proactive environmental policies and guidelines?

7. Is your firm aware of state/regional/national environmental regulations? If so, do you in any way go above and beyond what is required by the law? Why or why not?

8. Does your strategy incorporate a specific plan for involvement in environmental public policy or does your engagement follow a broader company policy? If so, what forms does this engagement take (lobbying? advocacy? board membership?)?

9. Does your firm track upcoming environmental management issues and challenges? If yes, what approaches are employed?

10. How do you envision using this framework for the development of a surpra-environmental stewardship strategy in your company? What resources would assist your firm in reaching a new level of environmental management? What could we provide as an interim deliverable as an incentive to participate in a follow-up online survey?

NOTES

I am indebted to the seventeen members of the Environmental Stewardship Strategy working group and affiliated UN Global Compact member companies who participated in the development of the Environmental Stewardship Strategy, and especially those who were interviewed for the research study. Without the assistance and support of the UN Global Compact environmental issues team, led by Lila Karbassi, this research would not have been possible.

1. The epigraph is taken from J. Ruggie, "Global_governance.net: The Global Compact as a Learning Network," *Global Governance* 7 (2001): 371–78.

2. UN Global Compact, at http://www.unglobalcompact.org/About The GC/TheTenPrinciples/index.html.

3. G. Kell and D. Levin, "The Evolution of the Global Compact Network: An Historic Experiment in Learning and Action," in *Building Effective*

Networks (The Academy of Management Annual Conference, Denver, CO, 2002), 7.

4. See Kell and Levin, "The Evolution of the Global Compact Network"; G. Kell, "The Global Compact: Selected Experiences and Reflections," *Journal of Business Ethics* 59, no. 1/2 (2005): 69–79; O. F. Williams, "The UN Global Compact: The Challenge and the Promise," *Business Ethics Quarterly* 14, no. 4 (2004): 755–74; and A. Rasche, "A Necessary Supplement: What the United Nations Global Compact Is and Is Not," *Business and Society* 48, no. 4 (2009): 511–37.

5. Ruggie, "Global_governance.net," 372.

6. B. L. Flannery and D. R. May, "Prominent Factors Influencing Environmental Activities: Application of the Environmental Leadership Model (ELM)," *The Leadership Quarterly* 5 (1994): 201–21.

7. A. E. Feyerherm, "Leadership in Collaboration: A Longitudinal Study of Two Interorganizational Rule-Making Groups," *The Leadership Quarterly* 5 (1994): 253–70.

8. L. M. Andersson and T. S. Bateman, "Individual Environmental Initiative: Championing Natural Environmental Issues in U.S. Business Organizations," *Academy of Management Journal* 43, no. 4 (2000): 548–70.

9. P. Bansal and K. Roth, "Why Companies Go Green: A Model of Ecological Responsiveness," *Academy of Management Journal* 43, no. 4 (2000): 717–36.

10. C. P. Egri and S. Herman, "Leadership in the North American Environmental Sector: Values, Leadership Styles, and Contexts of Environmental Leaders and Their Organizations," *Academy of Management Journal* 43, no. 4 (2000): 571–604.

11. O. Boiral, M. Cayer, and C. M. Baron, "The Action Logics of Environmental Leadership: A Developmental Perspective," *Journal of Business Ethics* 85, no. 4 (2009): 479–99.

12. L. W. Fry and J. Slocum, "Maximizing the Triple Bottom Line through a Strategic Scorecard Business Model of Spiritual Leadership," *Organizational Dynamic* 31, no. 1 (2008): 86–96; and B. Redekop, *Leadership for Environmental Sustainability* (New York: Routledge, 2010).

13. T. B. Zilber, "Stories and the Discursive Dynamics of Institutional Entrepreneurship: The Case of Israeli High-Tech after the Bubble," *Organization Studies* 28, no. 7 (2007): 1035–54.

14. I. Montiel and B. W. Husted, "The Adoption of Voluntary Environmental Management Programs in Mexico: First Movers as Institutional Entrepreneurs," *Journal of Business Ethics* 88 (2009): 349–63.

15. Bansal and Roth, "Why Companies Go Green"; and Stuart L. Hart and Mark B. Milstein, "Creating Sustainable Value," *Academy of Management Executive* 17, no. 2 (2009): 56–69.

16. S. N. Eisenstadt, "Cultural Orientations, Institutional Entrepreneurs, and Social Change: Comparative Analysis of Traditional Civilizations," *American Journal of Sociology* 85, no. 4 (1980): 840–69.

17. P. J. DiMaggio, "Interest and Agency in Institutional Theory," in *Institutional Patterns and Organizations: Culture and Environment*, ed. L. G. Zucker (Cambridge, MA: Ballinger, 1988), 3–22.

18. K. A. Wade-Benzoni, A. J. Hoffman, L. L. Thompson, D. A. Moore, J. J. Gillespie, and M. H. Bazerman, "Resolution of Ideologically Based Negotiations: The Role of Values and Institutions," *Academy of Management Review* 27, no. 1 (2002): 41–58; and N. Phillips, T. Lawrence, and C. Hardy, "Inter-organizational Collaboration and the Dynamics of Institutional Fields," *Journal of Management Studies* 37, no. 1 (2000): 23–44.

19. As stated by UN Secretary-General Ban Ki-moon in 2010: "The Millennium Development Goals set timebound targets, by which progress in reducing income poverty, hunger, disease, lack of adequate shelter and exclusion—while promoting gender equality, health, education and environmental sustainability—can be measured. They also embody basic human rights—the rights of each person on the planet to health, education, shelter and security. The Goals are ambitious but feasible and, together with the comprehensive United Nations development agenda, set the course for the world's efforts to alleviate extreme poverty by 2015." Available at http://www.un.org /millenniumgoals/bkgd.shtml.

20. D. Vogel, "Private Global Business Regulation," *Annual Review of Political Science* 11 (2008): 261–82.

21. See Ruggie, "Global_governance.net."

22. F. Van der Krogt, "Learning Network Theory: The Tension between Learning Systems and Work Systems in Organizations," *Human Resources Development Quarterly* 9, no. 2 (1998): 157–77.

23. J. Ruggie, "The Theory and Practice of Learning Networks: Corporate Social Responsibility and the Global Compact," *Journal of Corporate Citizenship* 5 (2002): 27–36, especially 29.

24. See D. R. Gallagher, "The UN Global Compact Environmental Stewardship Strategy," Research Report and Recommendations Prepared for the United Nations Global Compact Leaders Summit, New York City, June 24–25, 2010. Available as "Environmental Stewardship Strategy: Overview and Resource for Corporate Leaders," at http://www.unglobalcompact.org /docs/issues_doc/Environment/Environmental_Stewardship_Strategy.pdf.

25. For a visual representation of the wheel, see http://www.unglobal compact.org/docs/issues_doc/Environment/Environmental_Stewardship _Strategy.pdf, p. 14.

26. D. Cetindamar and K. Husoy, "Corporate Social Responsibility Practices and Environmentally Responsible Behavior: The Case of the United Nations Global Compact," *Journal of Business Ethics* 76, no. 2 (2007): 163–76.

27. J. J. Janney, G. Dess, and V. Forlani, "Glass Houses? Market Reactions to Firms Joining the UN Global Compact," *Journal of Business Ethics* 90, no. 3 (2009): 407–23.

28. R. Weiss, *Learning From Strangers; The Art and Method of Qualitative Interview Studies* (New York: Free Press, 1994).

15 | Pursuing Purposeful Profit

Mark R. Kennedy

After observing business from both a business executive suite and the halls of Congress, both in America and around the world, I am convinced that the greatest untapped profit opportunity available to businesses today is having a *purpose* that benefits both society and the bottom line.

That's not just a truism. As I will show, the particular features of the modern economy mean that rewarding returns are best achieved by orienting your business along parallel goals of business profit and the social good.

While I was in Congress, Paul Neaton, a local farmer, challenged me to focus, as he put it, on "the left side of the decimal point"—not on actions that change the price of corn by pennies per bushel but those that change the price by dollars.

In today's competitive marketplace, it is hard to find unexploited prospects for gaining incremental advantages over your rivals. Businesses invest enormous effort to improve their marketing, operations, or logistics. But, partly because their competitors are making similar expenditures, these efforts rarely contribute more than pennies a share to a company's incremental profit. That's the wrong side of the decimal point. This prevailing preoccupation with functional effectiveness reflects an incomplete understanding of the nature of business.

According to a 2008 McKinsey global survey, only 12 percent of business executives believe their companies do a good, or even adequate, job anticipating societal needs and pressures.[1] This shows that businesses are not serious enough about developing strategies for the so-called *nonmarket*—the broader societal forces, in politics, regulation, and activism, that shape the market from the outside. And that's a shame for society and for business, because the best way to add dollars—rather than just cents—to your profit per share is to identify and truly appreciate society's needs and direct your company's energies to profitably meeting them.

Too few businesspeople have studied Plato, who wrote, "Good actions give strength to ourselves and inspire good actions in others." He understood millennia ago that good actions benefit the good people who do them—that advancing society's interests could advance one's own interests. Many businesspeople don't understand that.

The recent McKinsey survey also found that approximately two-thirds of all CEOs thought corporations should "balance generating high returns to investors with making contributions to public good." Of that subgroup, more than half said that they reached this conclusion because they believed it was the right thing to do. While one should applaud these executives for their good intentions, their response misses what Plato observed so long ago—that good actions could benefit them directly, too.

Another third of those executives who believed in contributing to the public good responded that corporations should do so in order to gain competitive advantages. That is closer to the mark. Yet, they identified those advantages as "customer loyalty, a better ability to attract or retain talented employees, and positive media coverage." In other words, they thought the advantage was that doing good would inspire others to do good for them. These executives got *a part* of Plato's insight but missed many of the other ways in which good actions can make a business stronger.

The idea that you can raise your profits by improving society is not new. In 1953, Charles Erwin Wilson, then president of General Motors, was appointed secretary of defense by President Eisenhower. During his hearing before the Senate Armed Services Committee, he was asked if, were he secretary of defense, he could make a decision averse to the interests of General Motors. Wilson said he could but added that he could not imagine such a situation, "because for years I thought what was good for the country was good for General Motors and vice versa." (Wilson is frequently misquoted as saying, "What's good for General Motors is good for the country.")[2]

The idea itself has stuck around, though it isn't always put into practice. In a recent *Harvard Business Review* article, Michael Porter and Mark Kramer observe that executives fail to understand the full benefits of good acts. According to them, "most companies remain stuck in a 'social responsibility' mind-set in which societal issues are at the periphery, not the core. The solution lies in the principle of shared value . . . which involves creating economic value in a way that also creates value for society by addressing its needs and challenges. Business must reconnect company success with social progress. Shared value is not social responsibility, philanthropy, or even sustainability, but a new way to achieve economic success. It is not on the margin of what companies do but at the center."[3]

That's more like Plato.

The Economist, too, once observed that "managing in a time of turbulence requires . . . a sense of purpose, a reason for existence, and a guiding philosophy that will motivate and unify a scattered workforce and make it more competitive."[4]

And this is not just theory. It is proven in practice. Specifically, Apple's astounding success is largely attributable to Steve Jobs's exhilarating purpose—to, as he put it, "make a contribution to the world by making tools for the mind that advance humankind." That's true of many other companies, too. Two Stanford University Business School professors, James Collins and Jerry Porras, have researched this thoroughly. They compiled a list of 179 corporate CEOs who were identified by their peers as those with the clearest sense of purpose. From 1920 to 1990 the companies of these CEOs outperformed the stock market by a factor of 50.[5]

In short, finding and pursuing a purpose for your business that maximizes both profits and the social good is the new frontier of dynamic performance.

Why is this the case? There are many reasons—some of them unique to our times.

ENGAGE OR ENRAGE

The financial crisis and the prolonged economic slump that followed have reignited the debate over whether business should "do good by doing well" or "do well by doing good." The classic expressions of the first view come from Milton Friedman, who said that "the business of business is business" and "the social responsibility of business is to increase its profits."[6] Friedman didn't say that because he didn't care about society. Rather, he believed that society was best improved by individuals freely pursuing their own interests in a competitive market. So he argued that, rather than compel corporate boards to hand over profits to charity, we should let shareholders choose how they, as individuals, wanted to do good with that money. Friedman advocated prioritizing doing well, and letting individuals choose how to use their own money to do good—in a phrase, "doing good by doing well."

The opposite view, the stakeholder approach, has long been advocated by organizations such as the Business Roundtable. They maintain that businesses must attend to the interests of more than just their shareholders. Businesses, they say, should consider all their stakeholders, including employees, suppliers, and the communities in which they operate.

The debate welled up at the 2008 annual meeting of the World Economic Forum in Davos, Switzerland. Bill Gates advocated the stakeholder view. He called for a "creative capitalism," in which big corporations would integrate doing good into doing business. Lawrence Summers retorted in Friedmanesque fashion. He said, "It is hard in this world to do well. It is hard to do good. When I hear a claim that an institution is going to do both, I reach for my wallet. You should too."[7] Summers, just as Friedman before him, was critical of the idea that a company should do good simply for the sake of doing good. The debate never really changes.

But the modern economy has made the debate obsolete.

Neither Friedman nor Summers fully considered the development of what my friend Nate Garvis calls the "outrage industry that can't take yes for an answer and gets paid by the fight" (that is, those people whose jobs are dependent on outrage over specific problems and would need to find new careers if the problems were solved). The phrase does not refer to the entire activist community, which includes many very different organizations with wide-ranging focuses and approaches. For simplicity's sake, let's divide them into carrot and stick groups. Many carrot activist groups have a track record of partnering with companies to make progress on key issues. Stick activist groups sometimes only seem interested in stirring up trouble, not solving problems. The legitimacy of their causes and techniques is sometimes questionable, though their actions can sometimes lead to positive change. (Notably, in his landmark book, *Capitalism and Freedom*, Friedman makes no mention of these groups in his list of forces that affect how a company thinks about social responsibility.)[8]

The effects of being placed in either type of activist group's spotlight can be long-lasting and severe. Even though Nike has behaved admirably in the two decades since it became the symbol of child labor, people young and old around the world can immediately recall this unfortunate chapter in Nike's history. And the activists who defined Nike so negatively managed to do so in a time when the world was much less wired than it is today. Today, activist groups have many more, and more powerful, tools at their disposal.

In our wired and hyper-networked world, businesses operate in a fishbowl. An activist group can go viral around the world with an iPhone video showing, say, how one company employee acted in Nigeria. The activist group can claim that that employee is representative, and can use that video to define the company as a whole or place it in a very unfavorable light. This will affect how a company is perceived by its prime customers, or by voters who might consider a new way to restrict its activities. Sometimes, this scrutiny is well-deserved—some bad business operators deserve to be demonized. Yet even good, reputable companies and organizations must be prepared to respond to alleged offenses that are aberrant from their normal conduct or are a derivative result of their operations.

What this means, now that we're all so connected, is that the contentious "Friedman vs. Stakeholder" debate is obsolete. I maintain that in today's politically charged environment, even those who embrace Friedman's philosophy—namely, that profits are a company's highest priority—must recognize that companies need to "do good" *in order to* be permitted to continue to "do well." Again: Businesses must strategically "do good *to* do well." This is required both to reduce the disruption of profitable activities and because, today, good works are tools for increasing shareholder value.

Let me explain why.

Because society is now so global, pluralistic, and tightly linked together by Twitter and Facebook, different people are more connected than ever. Everybody is involved with everybody else's business. And so we can have—in fact, we need to have—more partners and more teammates to achieve our goals. Business is no exception. Businesses everywhere need to have a record of success in working with carrot activist groups, in order to effectively rebuff the political, public-relations, and regulatory assaults of stick activist groups. The more good a business does, the bigger, the stronger, and the more loyal the team of people with common interests it can rely on to defend it. It's just what Plato meant when he said, "Good actions give strength to ourselves and inspire good actions in others."

That is the paradox of modern business. If your goal is to maximize profit for your shareholders, as Milton Friedman advocated, you must pursue this goal in parallel with benefiting society as a whole. This will, indirectly and over the long-term, boost your bottom line. The optimal way to do this is to align your public engagement and good works—your nonmarket strategy—with your market strategy. This is what I call *purposeful profit*.

Purposeful profit, I claim, is an evolution in thinking that moves beyond corporate social responsibility (CSR) and is even more beneficial to society than pure altruism. Currently, CSR is viewed as an appendage, or an expense item. During times of economic stress, as we just experienced, it is considered incidental—not essential—to the company's strategy, and is thus quickly trimmed back.

Pursuing purposeful profit doesn't just improve a company's standing with political, regulatory, and activist forces. It does what Porter and Kramer have identified as creating shared value (CSV).[9] CSV is a step beyond CSR. While CSR activities are supplementary to a company's primary business, CSV activities emerge from the core of the company, support the company's strategy, and offer opportunities to improve company profitability. This means that a company that organizes its good works around a CSV model is less likely to cancel them when times are tough. If anything, a company that is oriented toward fixing social problems can expand in challenging times.

In my purposeful profit schema, each business has a unique purpose that lies at the intersection of its market strategy and the social good. A company can benefit from fleshing out its purpose by specifically articulating how it relates to human rights, workforce standards, the environment, corruption, and poverty mitigation. This will not only benefit the company's profits and society now, but will also increase the likelihood that its future profits will not be disrupted.

WISDOM OF AN EGYPTIAN TAXI DRIVER

I often see similarities between the two worlds in which I have worked—business and politics. There are many events in the two that, although much different in scale, parallel each other in instructive ways. The fate of Hosni Mubarak, for example, is a powerful lesson about how leaders need a purpose that benefits others. His fall from the presidency of Egypt exemplifies what happens to those who seek to succeed personally with too little regard for the common interest. Mubarak's downfall was inevitable, as was clear to me ever since a memorable taxi ride on September 2, 2004—years before the recent Arab Spring. I was on my way to the last night of the Republican National Convention in New York City. My driver was Egyptian, and he was happy to discuss his views.

I asked him whether America should have gone into Iraq. His reply was quick and passionate: "Of course America should have gone into Iraq. And next it should go into Egypt, then Syria, and then Saudi Arabia." He went on to say that Mubarak had done little for the Egyptian people during his tenure and allowed little political freedom.

My taxi driver had a degree from a university in Egypt. But, he said, there were no jobs in his home country. He expressed frustration with the region's economic stagnation. He said he probably made more money driving a taxi in New York than most of those who put their college degrees to use in Egypt. He argued that the Arab world needed to be shaken up so that its oppressive rulers allowed more economic and political freedom, and therefore opportunity, for the Arab people. He believed that this was necessary to end the hopelessness that drives terrorism.

Given the bleak prospects for young people in his home country, it's no wonder the Egyptian people rose up against Mubarak. Of course, it remains to be seen how soon Egypt can develop leaders who can create economic and political freedom and opportunity.

If the purpose of your business is all about you and not about helping others—which was my taxi driver's assessment of Mubarak's presidency—it may be only a matter of time before protesters show up at your doorsteps. If you don't engage with others in society with common interests, you will certainly, eventually, enrage some. And then you might find yourself without many allies to defend you against the enraged. That is why it is so important to establish a purpose for your business that benefits both your bottom line and society.

DO GOOD TO DO WELL: A CASE STUDY

Consider an example that illustrates how a company's purpose can align with its market strategy. It involves a logistics company whose market strategy is to be the best in the world at affordably delivering freight—rain or shine—in a timely manner. Society benefits from the low costs and more reliable access to goods and services that this company provides. So, the company defines its purpose as "improving people's lives through affordable and timely freight delivery."

Suppose an association brought together businesses, including this logistics company, and nongovernmental organizations (NGOs) to map out a strategy for helping people in need during natural disasters. Suppose, then, that the logistics firm agreed during the meeting that it would help streamline the relief process by optimizing the logistical flow of relief through any available airports and roads—even when these are damaged or of insufficient scale. By applying its expertise in this area, the logistics firm could bring more aid to more people, undoubtedly saving lives.

But then suppose that, even though the logistics firm had agreed to help, a representative from an NGO was angry with the logistics firm because it would not embrace the philosophy that the firm's sole purpose was to save lives. In other words, the firm would not agree that it should only "do good to do good." This actually happened. And the

NGO rep got so incensed that she stalked out of the discussions. Witness the contention that disagreements over Friedman's assertion can still evoke.

This example highlights the path to less conflict and more progress. Here's what I mean: The logistics company was obviously happy to save lives, but there are many other ways the firm could work toward that goal—funding food for starving children, providing clean water for those without it, or supplying maternal care in impoverished regions. If the firm were to define its purpose as "saving lives," it would logically be obligated to contribute its resources to every such proposal, even if the effort did not have even a remote connection to the company's market strategy. It makes sense for a food company to have a purpose that includes feeding starving children; for a company that builds water systems to have a purpose that includes providing drinking water to all; and for a health care provider to have a purpose including bringing maternal care to impoverished regions. But it doesn't make sense to expect a logistics company to be involved in all of these different tasks.

Rather, the logistics firm's aim should be to engage with society in ways that mesh with and support its market strategy and purpose. It can improve people's lives by delivering freight (relief) in a timely manner (saving lives) during disasters. And because this activity also is consistent with the firm's market strategy, it allows the firm to keep its sources affordable for other customers, while keeping its shareholders (and Friedman!) happy with increased profits.

The logistics firm would, as Plato foresaw, "inspire good actions in others," in at least four different ways:

1. Good press highlighting the company's core capability would ultimately lead to more sales.
2. Improved employee engagement would lead to lower turnover.
3. Improving its standing with members of society would help it partner with carrot-style NGOs with a common interest and receive the benefit of the doubt from stick-style NGOs and governments in various circumstances—approvals for construction of logistics facilities, and so on.
4. And, finally, the aid would engender greater brand loyalty, especially with those prospective future customers in the disaster region where the firm had helped.

These would all "give strength" to the logistics company and to their employees, who would gain experience in high-stress conditions that would prepare them for doing their normal jobs with even higher productivity.

All these by-products lead to higher profits, the aim that Friedman defined for businesses. So, this example shows how a company can, as I said, "do good *to* do well." It is a true win-win, in which both the company and society benefit.

And here's the best part: Society as a whole is better off when each company does good within its own market. This is basic economics—the law of comparative advantage. Each company has specific, local knowledge of its market that other companies, working in other markets, don't have. That knowledge allows it to "do good" more effectively and more efficiently in its area of expertise. So the greatest good will be accomplished when each company focuses its "do-good" efforts on its own market. Why should each company get caught up in everyone else's business?

Imagine if the logistics firm representative had explained this to the NGO executive—their meeting would have had a better end.

EMBRACE A PURPOSE FOR YOUR BUSINESS— OR ELSE

You might say, "That's all well and good, but I'll pass on any such 'do good' activities and focus on my core business. It's a pleasant thought, but not very practical—certainly not optimal." But it's not up to you anymore. Today, you have no choice but to embrace the idea of purposeful profit for your business, for five reasons.

First, in democracies, the majority rules, not Milton Friedman. In 2011, Edelman, an American public relations firm, conducted a global poll of the "informed public" (defined as people with university degrees and in the top quarter of wage-earners in their age groups and countries). The results were striking. They revealed wide disagreements on Milton Friedman's famous statement that "the social responsibility of business is to increase its profits."[10] The proper role of business, the poll showed, not only divides people within countries but varies *between* countries as well. For example, 84 percent of those polled in the United Arab Emirates agreed with Friedman's statement, compared with less than a third in Spain.

The Edelman poll placed America in the middle, in terms of support for Friedman's view—Europe was generally less supportive, while Asia was more supportive. America's informed public was split, with 56 percent agreeing with Friedman's assertion. In contrast, in nearly all European countries, far fewer people agreed with Friedman. The notable exception was Sweden. (Perhaps this Nordic country accepted Friedman's view because the government does everything else for Swedish citizens, leaving businesses with no role other than making money.) In nearly all Asian countries, a higher portion of the informed public agreed with Friedman than in America. The notable exception was China—however, based on my experiences in China, I suspect that this finding reflects more of a hesitancy to disagree with the Communist Party ethos than true feelings about the role of business.

If you carefully observe the interests and views expressed by other cultures, these differences are evident. Europeans' relative suspicion of the profit motive became clear to me when I studied at the Rotterdam School of Management at Erasmus University in the Netherlands in 1982. They had a guilder beer night back then. Guilders were the Dutch currency before the euro, and they were worth about 33 U.S. cents at the time—a pretty good deal for a glass of Heineken or Grolsch. On one such night, I was standing at the bar getting another pint when the Dutch student next to me, a total stranger, taunted me by calling me a capitalist. I replied by saying, "This might come as a surprise to you, but where I come from that is a compliment."

And I encountered another, and equally telling contrast, while traveling through Dubai recently. I saw something I have not seen in America for decades—an advertisement for cigarettes. Maybe I shouldn't have been surprised. If 84 percent of your population believe that the corporate responsibility of business is to increase profits, and if advertising smoking increases profits, then why not? The ad promised that if you smoked its brand of cigarettes, you would "enjoy true quality." I wanted to ask, "True quality what?"

The point of this is that a business's strategy must conform to its social context. Advertising cigarettes may be acceptable and profitable in Dubai, but in a country like Spain it would incite the democratic majority to find ways to stop the advertisements and further restrict its business.

The wide divergence in views regarding the role of business has serious consequences for how a business can and should act. In a democracy, the views of the majority trump those of Milton Friedman—regardless of how sound his thinking may be. In Europe, Friedman's view is held by only a small minority. So European voters and their political representatives won't be happy with a business that pursues only profit. And if the powerful politicians aren't happy with a business, they can enact policies that will make that business unhappy, too.

Unless a company cultivates a strategy for engaging and satisfying nonmarket actors, such as activist groups and governments, in ways that are mutually beneficial, it could find itself on the outside looking in. Ideally, as in the example of the logistics company, those mutually beneficial activities should align with and support the company's overall strategy. But it is imperative for companies to positively engage society—they don't have a choice in a democracy.

As a result, most companies find their profits are more sustainable if they focus on doing good *to* do well in pursuit of purposeful profits.

Second, in high-growth markets, you beat corruption or corruption beats you. The best growth opportunities available today are in areas that suffer from high levels of corruption. When a company moves into these markets, it will generally employ people with a wide range of cultural norms. If the company does not set its own norms that severely discourage illegal acts, it can expect illegal acts to follow—and its bottom line to hurt. This is where purposeful profit is needed. If a company's stated goal and sole corporate culture is the pursuit of money, and if corruption pays out more to employees than doing business legally, the employees, logically, will be more susceptible to corruption. A profit motive that is unmatched with purpose can actually leave a company more vulnerable to corruption in these markets. In order to innoculate your company, you need to have and promote a company ethos of devotion to a social purpose.

Third, without purpose, stakeholders will be in conflict. To be successful, a business must have a tight focus on a goal that makes it special and aligns its stakeholders. The profit motive, by itself, is insufficient in doing either. But a clearly defined purpose that is good for society as a whole—and is *distinct*—can keep employees, suppliers, communities, and stockholders unified in a common effort. Defining a purpose aligns the parts of a company's team in the same direction. It makes employees more likely, as it were, to sing from the same songbook.

Fourth, employees without purpose will disengage. Today's workers—especially younger workers—yearn for meaning. Giving it to them won't just protect against corruption but will also improve worker attraction, retention, and motivation. A worker who thinks about her job's contribution to the improvement of society will feel personally invested in the company's activities, making her more enthusiastic and attentive to her work and more likely to stick with the company during times of difficulty. A worker who thinks about nothing but his paycheck is more likely to get bored and watch the clock, his eyes glazing over.

Many of our brightest young people today want to be a part of something bigger. If your company is not, you won't be able to attract the best.

Fifth, intellectual property is either used for the good or else threatened with theft. We all know that some countries don't always respect intellectual property (patents, trademarks, brands). A high-income company from a high-income geography that pursues only profit in a low-income country is likely to face resentment from the local population. If the locals don't see the company using its intellectual property for good, they will want to take it for themselves, for their own use. But if the company is using its intellectual property to promote their well-being, it will have more allies helping to enforce its rights. Without society's approval, it has no intellectual property to enforce.

MARKETING YOUR PURPOSE: THEORY AND PRACTICE

Many companies already have statements that describe either their market strategy or their benefits to society. Too few companies today have a mission, a purpose, that unifies the two. Doing so is an essential first step to achieving purposeful profit.

Defining a purpose is a three-step process:

First, make sure you have a clearly defined market strategy. This is a vitally important step.

Second, list all of the positive and negative impacts that achievement of your business strategy has on society, and delineate how you can maximize the benefits and minimize the detriments. (For a few companies, finding a societal benefit may be impossible. Some have to really reach. I saw a humorous example of this in the Denver airport with an advertisement for the Coor's Museum. The billboard read, "Hey, it's educational." But most companies can develop a long list of benefits more easily, if less humorously.)

A startling recent survey of executives showed that little more than half believed that large corporations made a positive contribution to the public good. The other half was divided between believing that big companies' impact on the public good was neutral and believing that it was negative.[11] This starkly demonstrates that companies need to do better in identifying and advertising their societal benefits.

Third and finally, reach consensus on which purpose that maximizes societal benefits best aligns with your market strategy. That's your purpose statement.

Once you have the substance of your purpose, you need an effective presentation of it. I am constantly looking out for real-world examples of organizations proclaiming a purpose, and I have observed four types: (1) platitudinal, (2) pedestrian, (3) "a bridge too far," and (4) differentiating. It reminds me of Goldilocks trying out the bear's chairs: platitudinal and pedestrian purposes are *too small*, a-bridge-too-far purposes are *too big*, and differentiating purposes are *just right*. Here's what I mean:

1. Platitudinal: These purpose statements are either unachievable, outside the influence of the company, or both. They are of little value. While recently dining at the Hard Rock Café in Shanghai, I noticed that the slogan "No Drugs or Nuclear Weapons" was emblazoned on the wall. These are worthy goals but perhaps not achievable—certainly not by Hard Rock Café.

2. Pedestrian: These purpose statements are less lofty but more easily understandable, achievable, and aligned with the business strategy. Hence

they more directly benefit society, even if they are less profound. This may be the best a company can do, depending on its business activities. But too often they are little more than advertising slogans, rather than truly differentiating purposes. I've seen four examples recently: (i) a Sealy mattress truck in Chicago reading, "We support the backbone of America"; (ii) a Pepsi billboard in Hollywood reading, "Every Pepsi refreshes the world"; (iii) a UPS truck in Paris reading, "Synchronizing the world of commerce"; and (iv) a Directski.com advertisement in London reading, "I want to bring affordable skiing to the people . . . the rest of the world is Bono's problem," a quote attributed to founder Anthony Collins.

3. A bridge too far: These purpose statements are extremely hard to achieve, and they leave the company open to accusations of being insincere, such as "greenwashing." If you use it as a statement, you better be able to achieve it—or else you're welcoming activists to come after you. One example of this stands out—the London billboard for British Petroleum reading, "BP: Beyond Petroleum."

4. Differentiating: These purpose statements hit the sweet spot—they articulate a goal of expanding the social benefits that come from achieving your market strategy.

And it's essential to choose your presentation to the public—your advertisement—of your purpose carefully. When I travel, I always look out for good examples. Some of the best I have recently seen include these, which could be fine models for your own purpose advertising campaign: (i) NBC 4's advertisement on a Washington, DC, bus, which shows a reporter in protective gear saying, "I am protecting the community"; (ii) an ExxonMobil billboard in Brussels airport reading, "Taking on the world's toughest energy challenges"; (iii) ABB's campaign to make sustainability into a competitive advantage, including a Frankfurt billboard reading, "Cut CO_2 emissions by 180 tons a year? Absolutely," and a London airport billboard reading, "Cities that consume 30% less energy? Certainly"; (iv) GE's "eco-magination" campaign, including a locomotive advertisement in the Dubai airport proclaiming "less fuel, fewer emissions, more reason to celebrate"; and (v) Starbucks' Shared Planet commitment to purchase only the highest quality, ethically sourced, and responsibly grown coffee, to reduce their environmental footprint and fight climate change.

Also consider the advice of speechwriter Steve Moore, the Communications Assistant at the National Conference of Democratic Mayors. To persuade the public, he focuses on the two middle attributes of the famous Meyers-Briggs personality evaluation method, articulating the benefits of what he is advocating in a way that appeals to both the five-sense and intuitive perspective—as well as incorporating both logical and emotional arguments. Doing the same for your purpose statement will help you communicate your purpose to multiple constituencies with widely different perspectives.

EMBRACING THE UN GLOBAL COMPACT AND MDGS

A good way to start on both (1) finding a suitable purpose and (2) presenting that purpose effectively to diverse constituencies is to look at the standards of international institutions. There are two main benefits to embracing the United Nations Global Compact.[12] First, the Compact is based on fundamental principles that you should incorporate into your purpose; and second, the Compact is itself shorthand for commitment to globally recognized standards in human rights, labor rights, environmental treatment, and combating corruption. Accepting the Compact helps you do good—and lets others know about it, too.

Embracing the United Nations' Millennium Development Goals (MDGs) can align your company's activities with goals that are considered a global priority. Your employees and stakeholders can more readily understand these goals, defined by international institutions, than goals emerging from any one culture.

And these goals can boost businesses' bottom lines, too. (Do you see a pattern?) International business requires universal understandings about what each party can expect from each other. When a merchant in Qatar contracts with a supplier to Japan to supply the French marketplace, participants in all three locations need to be able to rely on each other to meet expectations. The power of the Global Compact, with over 10,000 signatories, including over 7,000 businesses in over 135 countries as of 2013,[13] makes it a credible starting point on which to build acceptable global standards that can increase business efficiency in the long run.

And there's an immediate benefit, too. Many of a company's most important prospective allies do not think like MBAs. Many of them reside in places like Europe, whose denizens have far higher regard for the United Nations than many Americans do. An important value of embracing the Compact and efforts that address the MDGs is that doing so helps a company direct its activities in ways that appeal to a broader audience.

PUT YOUR PURPOSE CENTER STAGE

A purpose is of no value unless you truly and publicly embrace it—it will not provide value if hidden under a basket. You can give meaning to all of your activities by connecting them to your purpose; this will also help people form a lasting impression of your company, an impression that connects your company with good works.

Procter and Gamble is considered one of the world's foremost marketers, so their actions are worth considering. P&G understands that there is more to its business than hawking soap. To help Tide and its other products stand out, P&G commits to a unifying purpose that inspires employee commitment, brand loyalty, and good will. Financial tear sheets list the most significant lead underwriter in the upper left hand corner. But when you go to the upper left hand corner of Procter and Gambles' website home page, you will see what gives P&G legitimacy, the heading "Inspired by Purpose."[14] When you click on the link "Power and People," you read: "Companies like P&G are a force in the world. Our market capitalization is greater than the GDP of many countries, and we serve consumers in more than 180 countries. With this stature comes both responsibility and opportunity. Our responsibility is to be an ethical corporate citizen—but our opportunity is something far greater, and is embodied in our Purpose."[15]

P&G commits to ethics right up front and rightly identifies its purpose not as a responsibility but as an opportunity. It describes its purpose as follows: "We will provide branded products and services of superior quality and value that improve the lives of the world's consumer, now and for generations to come. As a result, consumers will reward us with leadership sales, profit and value creation, allowing our people, our stakeholders and the communities in which we live and work to prosper."

An opportunity, indeed. P&G's purpose, in short, is to "improve the lives of the world's consumer, now and for generations to come." The opportunity this commitment provides includes more engaged employees, more brand loyalty, and more receptive public officials. Procter and Gamble could not be clearer on its purpose. It sets the standard in this regard (and many others). Other organizations would be wise to follow.

And, indeed, those companies that have put purpose center stage have reaped the benefits. For example, because the design of the Prius shouted out that it was a hybrid, it sold significantly better than the Honda Civic hybrid. Many consumers want to be conspicuously environmentally friendly, and they were attracted to the Prius for this reason.

Embrace your purpose and others who share that purpose will embrace you.

IN TODAY'S DIVERSE and hyper-connected world, the debate over whether to "do good to do well" or to "do well to do good" has dissolved. We all must now pursue purposeful profit. Doing otherwise is unsustainable. To succeed in the long term, companies must engage and benefit society in a manner that complements and supports its overall strategy. Only this enlightened approach will allow companies to achieve Friedman's endorsed goal of "maximizing profit" over the long run.

A purposeful profit approach pays many dividends. More carrot activist groups will partner with a purposeful company. Stick activist groups are less likely to attack one. A purposeful company will have more stakeholders who are more aligned, and its employees will be more engaged. It will be able to navigate the treacherous waters of corruption. It will find more partners willing to defend its intellectual-property rights around the world, if it has used what makes it unique to benefit others. It will be more likely to receive the benefit of the doubt from governments. Most exciting, maintaining a razor-sharp focus on society's real needs will help it uncover new, unexploited opportunities for profitable growth.

My service as a United States Congressman and a Fortune 100 senior executive has convinced me that both politics and business really are noble professions. Gridlock has disabled the former, while acts of corruption have tarnished them both. But faithfully fulfilled, both can make enormous contributions to the solution of society's greatest and most intractable problems. And businesses can do that while also contributing to their own bottom line.

We're lucky to live in a world where private interests and the social good so frequently align. Businesses should make the most of the opportunities that provides.

NOTES

1. Survey data can be found in "From Risk to Opportunity: How Global Executives View Sociopolitical Issues," *McKinsey Quarterly* (September 2008).

2. "History of General Motors," at http://en.wikipedia.org/wiki/History _of_General_Motors.

3. M. Porter and M. Kramer, "Creating Shared Value," *Harvard Business Review* 89, no. 1 (January–February 2011): 62–77.

4. "The Vision Thing," *The Economist* (November 9, 1991): 81.

5. A. A. Marcus, *Business and Society: Strategy, Ethics, and the Global Economy*, 2nd ed. (Chicago: Irwin, 1996), 13.

6. Friedman's most famous articulation of this view is found in "The Social Responsibility of Business Is to Increase Its Profits," *New York Times Sunday Magazine* (September 13, 1970).

7. M. Kinsley, *Creative Capitalism: A Conversation with Bill Gates, Warren Buffett, and Other Economic Leaders* (New York: Simon & Schuster, 2008).

8. M. Friedman, *Capitalism and Freedom (40th Anniversary Edition)* (Chicago: University of Chicago Press, 2002).

9. Porter and Kramer, "Creating Shared Value."

10. "Milton Friedman Goes on Tour," *The Economist* (January 29, 2011): 63.

11. "From Risk to Opportunity," *McKinsey Quarterly*.

12. See the UNGC website at http://www.unglobalcompact.org.

13. See http://www.unglobalcompact.org/AboutTheGC/index.html.

14. Available at http://www.pg.com/en_US/index.shtml.

15. Available at http://www.pg.com/en_US/company/purpose_people /index.shtml.

16 | Employee Engagement through Social and Environmental Responsibility

Ante Glavas

Studies in the last decade of the work force in the United States painted a very bleak picture. Only 29 percent of the workforce was engaged,[1] and an estimated $300 billion was lost per year in the United States due to decrease in productivity from disengaged employees[2]— and these studies were conducted at a time when the job market was better than it is today. Furthermore, work is not one of the top eight reasons that make people happy in the United States.[3] Yet work is becoming even more central to the lives of many employees.[4] Employees are living lives that are becoming faster and more efficient but doing work that does not fulfill them, with little time left to find fulfillment outside of work. This is an issue not only for employees but also for employers. A disengaged workforce is a huge loss in profitability.

On the other hand, employees seek increased meaning in their work,[5] which is why engaging in social and environmental responsibility activities can be appealing to them. As such, the impact of companies committed to the ideals of the UN Global Compact might have a positive influence on the engagement, productivity, and well-being of employees. While most of the discourse in social responsibility and sustainability is conducted at a macro level,[6] it is important for organizations to understand how and why employees are affected by working for the greater good. Doing so has important implications in three areas:

1. Moving beyond being solely a CEO agenda: by understanding the mechanisms that best motivate employees to engage in social and environmental responsibility, organizations can craft strategies that engage employees organization-wide.
2. Profitability: the engagement, intrinsic motivation, and satisfaction of employees lead to better performance, increased creativity, and greater retention rates.
3. Well-being: creating a more humane work environment is in and of itself a goal of the UN Global Compact.

Therefore, the purpose of this chapter is to outline how employees are affected by working for companies that aspire toward the ideals of the UN Global Compact (UNGC) and its ten principles. I begin by briefly outlining the business case, then explain some of the potential underlying mechanisms, and conclude with directions for implementation.

BUSINESS CASE

An argument can be made that for many companies, the business case for social and environmental responsibility is not important. While we in academia are spending time trying to prove the business case, companies are moving ahead; what organizations need is more help on the *how* of implementing ideals of the UNGC. It is as if academia and business sometimes live in two parallel universes.[7]

Furthermore, the business case has been extremely difficult to prove, with inconclusive evidence.[8] There are too many variables that influence financial performance, which makes it difficult to tease out the impact on the bottom line of social and environmental responsibility. Perhaps that is why there has been so much focus on cost-savings; it is easy to measure the impact on the bottom line of "turning off light bulbs." However, a more robust and straightforward case can be made for the impact on individual employee variables. Doing so would not only provide a powerful business case but also free up the time of scholars and managers to focus on the challenging questions of implementation and *how* to engage employees.

Although more work is needed to create a compelling business case with robust metrics, there are encouraging studies that show the positive impact of social and environmental responsibility on the following employee variables:

- Performance[9]
- Engagement[10]
- Retention[11]
- Creative involvement[12]
- Commitment[13]
- Attractiveness to prospective employees[14]
- Identification with the organization[15]
- Organizational citizenship behaviors[16]
- Employee relationships[17]

UNDERSTANDING THE UNDERLYING MECHANISMS

Before exploring the underlying mechanisms, it is important to take a humbling step backward and assess what we do know about employee workplace performance and attitudes. A possible conclusion is that our current management models of employees might not be as good as we think they are. Granted, both business practice and academia have come a long way in the last century in terms of understanding what drives employee behaviors and outcomes; however, Humphrey, Nahrgang, and Morgeson, in a meta-analysis of all of the studies on work design to date, found that our current models explained only 43 percent of the variance in employee outcomes.[18] Furthermore, Morgeson, Dierdorff, and Hmurovic state that "despite nearly 100 years of scientific study, comparatively little attention has been given to articulating how the broader occupational and organizational context might impact work."[19] Such broad contexts include the state of the environment and society as a whole.

To further the point, we also know that money influences the well-being of people, but only up to the threshold of meeting basic needs.[20] As the previously mentioned meta-analysis has shown, much more drives employees than what is explained by our current models. Our management models are primarily driven by financial metrics, ignoring other aspects of what drives employees. Furthermore, what we measure and reward is often what we get.[21] We also know that emotions play a key role in business decision-making.[22] However, the culture of work is such that we pretend that everything should be rationally argued because humans will always cognitively make the best informed decision. We know that values alignment is important for employee motivation.[23] Yet we often focus on a one-way alignment with corporate values—which are often solely profit-driven—without trying to truly tap into the core human values of employees.

If our management models are incomplete, then it does not make business sense to cling to them; an incomplete model is not only failing to account for a portion of workplace performance but could actually be leading to the current level of workforce disengagement. This is not to say that we should do away with the great progress we have made, but rather we need to explore what else also drives employees. Therefore, exploring the mechanisms of why and how employees engage in social and environmental responsibility is crucial.

Some of the potential underlying mechanisms for socially and environmentally responsible organizations are as follows:

1. Values alignment: Such organizations align with the values of caring in their employees, which then leads to greater caring for key stakeholders and profit as a result.[24]
2. Whole self: The more employees can show of their whole selves at work, the more (a) engaged they will be[25] and (b) the greater the quality of relationships at work because they engage with their whole selves, as opposed to an exchange-based paradigm.[26]
3. Intrinsic motivation: Intrinsic motivation leads to numerous outcomes, such as creativity,[27] which is manifested in the desire and ability to create win-win solutions for society, the environment, and society.[28]

Another, fourth, underlying mechanism that deserves detailed attention is meaningfulness at work. First of all, it potentially is the underlying mechanism behind the above three underlying mechanisms. Meaningful work allows us to feel more whole, be more motivated, and feel a greater values alignment. Also, as will be explained in the following section on implementation, the theory behind meaningful work lends itself to models of implementation.

From the literature on meaningfulness in work, we know that there are different kinds of meaning and that employees care about different things. The literature primarily defines three kinds of orientations toward work, based on the meaning that employees find in work.[29] The first is *job orientation*, where the meaning of work is based primarily on the material benefits. The second orientation is *career orientation*, where the focus is on advancement in work and the ensuing rewards. Such benefits satisfy higher-order needs, such as self-esteem.[30] The third orientation is a *calling orientation*, in which work is seen as making the world a better place. As Wrzesniewski describes it,

> it is the individual doing the work who defines for him- or herself whether the work does contribute to making the world a better place. For example, a schoolteacher who views the work as a Job and is simply interested in making a good income does not have a Calling, while a garbage collector who sees the work as making the world a cleaner, healthier place could have a Calling.[31]

Accordingly, work design theory could take different kinds of work meaningfulness into account. As work design is currently constructed, work meaningfulness assumes that all employees have the same orientation in that all employees care about the same things. By introducing a model in which work meaningfulness is broken into a job, career, and calling orientation, it is quite plausible that different relationships and effects might be found between work design characteristics and work outcomes. For example, those with a job orientation who value material benefits might be most influenced by pay compensation. Those with a career orientation could be more influenced by fairness of pay and by the ability to perform to their maximum capabilities, implying that they value greater autonomy and variety in skills and tasks, so as to be able to show themselves in the best light. Those with a calling orientation might be more influenced by task significance. In practice, it is most likely that a combination of all three orientations exists in a given individual. Such implications are important for understanding how to communicate and motivate employees. Currently, our performance management systems only account for a job and career orientation.

Meaningfulness is also neither static nor a fixed property of a job or organization; rather, it is subjective and is a subset of sensemaking.[32] As such, meaningfulness can be interpreted through two lenses (see table 16.1):

1. Meaningfulness at work: meaningfulness stems from membership in the organization and not necessarily from what one does (e.g., my organization is committed to the principles of the UNGC, but my job does not directly contribute to implementing them).
2. Meaningfulness in work: meaningfulness stems from what one does (e.g., my organization is not really socially or environmentally responsible, but my job contributes to the greater good).

Such a distinction is important for employees working in socially and environmentally responsible organizations. Often an organization can be considered socially and environmentally responsible at a macro level, while individual jobs may not directly contribute to bettering society and/or the environment. In such organizations, the social and environmental responsibilities are often confined to a small group of individuals or a specialized department. But employees might still find pride working for such organizations, due to sharing an identity no matter what their individual job involves.[33] This would correspond to meaningfulness at work as described by Pratt and Ashforth.[34] For purposes of work

Table 16.1. Models of Meaningfulness at/in Work

		In Work	
		Low	**High**
At Work	**High**	**Peripheral:** Employee loves company but is not inspired by what they do each day.	**Embedded:** Completely engaged employee who loves the company and what they do.
	Low	**Disengaged:** Completely uninspired employee.	**Lone Ranger:** Employee enjoys functional tasks but is not engaged by the company mission.

Note: The above model builds on Pratt and Ashforth's meaningfulness model (2003).

design theory, it would be interesting to explore differing impacts in work design depending on meaningfulness at work and meaningfulness in work. The calling dimension of meaningfulness could potentially be experienced both in and at work. For example, certain employees' jobs might not directly contribute to society or the environment, but they might feel that they are contributing to creating a better world because they are working for an organization that is creating a better world. The distinction between meaningfulness at work and meaningfulness in work is important for work design, which has primarily focused on the design of the job irrespective of the organization or context.[35]

In practice, it might be difficult to achieve complete meaningfulness at and in work. Rather, just like the principles of the UNGC, it is a journey toward which organizations can aspire.

IMPLEMENTATION

Research has helped us identify critical success factors for employee engagement. The following is a brief but useful list of factors, with corresponding studies identified in the notes:

- Importance of top management and supervisor commitment.[36]
- Aligning with employee values.[37]
- Training, attending conferences, and employee awareness.[38]
- Influence of pay structure.[39]
- Difference in personality traits.[40]

These are key elements for engaging employees. But what is perhaps more important is the overall strategy of implementation. Too often, organizations simply create social and environmental initiatives for employees, without thinking through the impact on the organization and employees. As one result, we often see glossy corporate responsibility and sustainability reports that look nice, but when one digs beneath the surface, one merely finds a group of fragmented and disparate initiatives.

In order to help guide strategy for engaging employees, it is useful to expand table 16.1 into different strategic models. Neither of the below presented models is necessarily better, and certain models might make more sense for an organization depending on the nature and situation of the organization:

1. Peripheral: This is a situation in which the principles of the UNGC are implemented at a strategic level but not integrated into daily operations. Often, this is handled by a separate department or foundation. Examples of engaging employees through this model are as follows:
    a. Communication that makes employees aware of the organization's efforts, which in turn builds pride and loyalty (e.g., training programs, newsletters, conferences, meetings).
    b. Volunteering initiatives, which are conducted outside of one's own scope of work.
    c. Donating to philanthropy (note that strategic philanthropy makes more business sense, but from an employee perspective, it might or might not influence employee pride and values alignment).
2. Lone Ranger: Employees might be in roles or conduct tasks that contribute to the UNGC principles, but their overall organization is not deeply involved or, at best, pays lip service to the principles. Examples of such roles are:
    a. Officers such as those charged with ethics, sustainability, corporate responsibility, or running a corporate foundation.
    b. Tasks such as recycling, greening the office, waste reduction, water conservation.
    c. Functions that have elements that deal with labor issues, such as procurement managers.
3. Embedded: These employees not only work for organizations that contribute to the UNGC principles, but their individual jobs contribute as well. Examples can be combinations of the previous two (e.g., a corporate responsibility officer working in a responsible corporation), but some more innovative examples are as follows:
    a. Organization-wide integration into daily products and services, such as employees who work on ecomagination products at General Electric.
    b. Design teams that are more than green teams, in that employees meet to create new and innovative ways in which the organization can be socially and environmentally responsible. An example is what Nike did internally in having cross-sections of designers

come up with models to work toward the sustainability of all their products through closed loop supply chains, with the goals of zero waste, carbon neutrality, and toxic reduction.

c. My Sustainability Programs, as designed by the agency Saatchi & Saatchi S, through which employees proactively shape their own jobs to be more socially and environmentally responsible. An example is at Walmart, where employees came up with more than 35,000 group initiatives. (Note: This method is sometimes used for peripheral activities such as implementing sustainability in personal lives outside of work.)

In practice, the lines between the above three models are often blurred, and one can lead into another. For example, at Green Mountain Coffee Roasters, employees take time out of work to live for three months with coffee growers. When they return, their experience completely reshapes how they think about the supply chain. This goes beyond a commitment to Fair Trade; employees holistically think about the entire value chain and how shared value genuinely can be created.

The model with the greatest impact on employees is probably the "embedded" model. It is also perhaps the most difficult to implement and for many organizations will only be a state toward which they aspire. But for organizations willing to embark (or continue) on that journey, numerous resources exist, such as the work *Embedded Sustainability* by Laszlo and Zhexembayeva[41]; or a project at Case Western Reserve University called "World Inquiry," in which two thousand interviews were conducted to find examples of how corporations can both benefit society and the company as well.

WE STILL HAVE a lot to learn about the differences in how social and environmental responsibility should be implemented. There is definitely no "one size fits all" model. What motivates one employee might disengage another. Some might be motivated by messages of world peace, while others consider such attitudes "tree-hugging" and as having nothing to do with business. Others might be motivated by instrumental goals, while others consider arguments from enlightened self-interest as "greenwashing." Furthermore, strategies for engaging employees might differ by age group, gender, personality, and culture.

We are only at the tip of the iceberg in understanding how to engage employees.

But it is a journey on which it is worth embarking. If we are to truly take the principles of the UNGC from being an agenda of the CEOs to one that is implemented organization-wide, we need to understand how to engage our employees. In addition, the benefits to business and world could be immense. If employee performance can be increased even by a few percentage points, the impact on the bottom line can be enormous. In today's competitive marketplace, it might make all the difference. In today's struggling society and ecosystem, it also might make all the difference.

NOTES

1. J. H. Fleming, C. Coffman, and J. K. Harter, "Manage Your Human Sigma," *Harvard Business Review* 83, no. 7 (2005): 106–15.

2. A. M. Saks, "Antecedents and Consequences of Employee Engagement," *Journal of Managerial Psychology* 21, no. 7 (2006): 600–619.

3. C. Wallis, "The New Science of Happiness," *Time Magazine* (January 17, 2005), A3–A9.

4. T. W. H. Ng and D. C. Feldman, "Long Work Hours: A Social Identity Perspective on Meta-Analysis Data," *Journal of Organizational Behavior* 29 (2008): 853–80.

5. A. Wrzesniewski, J. E. Dutton, and G. Debebe, "Interpersonal Sensemaking and the Meaning of Work," *Research in Organizational Behavior* 25 (2003): 93–135.

6. See H. Aguinis, "Organizational Responsibility: Doing Good and Doing Well," in *APA Handbook of Industrial and Organizational Psychology: Maintaining, Expanding, and Contracting the Organization*, ed. S. Zedeck (Washington, DC: American Psychological Association, 2011), 855–79; and M. P. Lee, "A Review of the Theories of Corporate Social Responsibility: Its Evolutionary Path and the Road Ahead," *International Journal of Management Reviews* 10, no. 1 (2011): 53–73.

7. S. A. Waddock, "Parallel Universes: Companies, Academics, and the Progress of Corporate Citizenship," *Business and Society Review* 109 (2004): 5–42.

8. J. Margolis, H. A. Elfenbein, and J. Walsh, "Does It Pay to Be Good . . . and Does It Matter? A Meta-Analysis of the Relationship between Corporate Social and Financial Performance," unpublished manuscript (2009).

9. D. A. Jones, "Does Serving the Community Also Serve the Company? Using Organizational Identification and Social Exchange Theories to Understand Employee Responses to a Volunteerism Programme," *Journal of Occupational and Organizational Psychology* 83 (2010): 857–78.

10. A. Glavas and S. K. Piderit, "How Does Doing Good Matter? Effects of Corporate Citizenship on Employees," *Journal of Corporate Citizenship* 36 (2009): 51–70.

11. Jones, "Does Serving the Community Also Serve the Company?"

12. Glavas and Piderit, "How Does Doing Good Matter?"

13. I. Maignan, O. C. Ferrell, and G. T. M. Hult, "Corporate Citizenship: Cultural Antecedents and Business Benefits," *Journal of the Academy of Marketing Science* 27 (1999): 455–69.

14. See D. B. Turban and D. W. Greening, "Corporate Social Performance and Organizational Attractiveness to Prospective Employees," *Academy of Management Journal* 40 (1997): 658–72; and Greening and Turban, "Corporate Social Performance as a Competitive Advantage in Attracting a Quality Workforce," *Business & Society* 39 (2000): 254–80.

15. A. Carmeli, G. Gilat, and D. A. Waldman, "The Role of Perceived Organizational Performance in Organizational Identification, Adjustment and Job Performance," *Journal of Management Studies* 44 (2007): 972–92.

16. See M. S. de Luque, N. T. Washburn, D. A. Waldman, and R. J. House, "Unrequited Profit: How Stakeholder and Economic Values Relate to Subordinates' Perceptions of Leadership and Firm Performance," *Administrative Science Quarterly* 53 (2008): 626–54; Jones, "Does Serving the Community Also Serve the Company?"; and C. Lin, N. Lyau, Y. Tsai, W. Chen, and C. Chiu, "Modeling Corporate Citizenship and Its Relationship with Organizational Citizenship Behaviors," *Journal of Business Ethics* 95 (2010): 357–72.

17. See B. R. Agle, R. K. Mitchell, and J. A. Sonnenfeld, "Who Matters to CEOs? An Investigation of Stakeholder Attributes and Salience, Corporate Performance, and CEO Values," *Academy of Management Journal* 42 (1999): 507–25; and Glavas and Piderit, "How Does Doing Good Matter?"

18. S. E. Humphrey, J. D. Nahrgang, and F. P. Morgeson, "Integrating Motivational, Social, and Contextual Work Design Features: A Meta-Analytic Summary and Theoretical Extension of the Work Design Literature," *Journal of Applied Psychology* 92 (2007): 1332–56.

19. F. P. Morgeson, E. C. Dierdorff, and J. L. Hmurovic, "Work Design in situ: Understanding the Role of Occupational and Organizational Context," *Journal of Organizational Behavior* 31 (2010): 351–60, especially 351.

20. E. Diener and R. Biswas-Diener, "Will Money Increase Subjective Well-Being? A Literature Review Guide to Needed Research," *Social Indicators Research* 57 (2002): 119–69.

21. S. Kerr, "On the Folly of Rewarding A, While Hoping for B," *The Academy of Management Executive* 9, no. 1 (1995): 7–14.

22. A. G. Sanfey, J. K. Rilling, J. A. Aronson, L. E. Nystrom, and J. D. Cohen, "The Neural Basis of Economic Decision-Making in the Ultimatum Game," *Science* 300 (2003): 1755–58.

23. A. L. Kristof, "Person-Organization Fit: An Integrative Review of Its Conceptualizations, Measurement, and Implications," *Personnel Psychology* 49 (1996): 1–49.

24. S. A. Graves and S. A. Waddock, "Beyond Built to Last . . . Stakeholder Relations in 'Built-to-Last' Companies," *Business and Society Review* 106 (2000): 393–418.

25. W. A. Kahn, "Psychological Conditions of Personal Engagement and Disengagement at Work," *Academy of Management Journal* 33 (1990): 692–724.

26. J. E. Dutton, *Energize Your Workplace: How to Create and Sustain High-Quality Connections at Work* (San Francisco: Jossey-Bass, 2003).

27. Relevant sources include: P. Tierney, S. M. Farmer, and G. B. Graen, "An Examination of Leadership and Employee Creativity: The Relevance of Traits and Relationships," *Personnel Psychology* 52 (1999): 591–620; R. M. Ryan and E. L. Deci, "Self-Determination Theory and the Facilitation of Intrinsic Motivation, Social Development, and Well-Being," *American Psychologist* 55 (2000): 68–78; T. M. Amabile, *The Social Psychology of Creativity* (New York: Springer-Verlag, 1983); Amabile, "How to Kill Creativity," *Harvard Business Review* 76 (1998): 76–87; and C. E. Shalley, "Effects of Productivity Goals, Creativity Goals, and Personal Discretion on Individual Creativity," *Journal of Applied Psychology* 76 (1991): 179–85.

28. See S. L. Hart and C. M. Christensen, "The Great Leap: Driving Innovation from the Base of the Pyramid," *MIT Sloan Management Review* 44 (2002): 51–56; R. M. Kanter, *Men and Women of the Corporation*, 2nd ed. (New York: Basic Books, 1993); and C. K. Prahalad and A. Hammond, "Serving the World's Poor, Profitably," *Harvard Business Review* 80 (2002): 48–57.

29. See R. N. Bellah, R. Madsen, W. M. Sullivan, A. Swidler, and S. M. Tipton, *Habits of the Heart* (New York: Harper & Row, 1985); and A. Wrzesniewski, "Finding Positive Meaning in Work," in *Positive Organizational Scholarship: Foundations of a New Discipline*, ed. K. S. Cameron, J. E. Dutton, and R. E. Quinn (San Francisco: Berrett-Koehler, 2003).

30. Bellah et al., *Habits of the Heart.*

31. Wrzesniewski, "Finding Positive Meaning in Work," 301.

32. M. G. Pratt and B. E. Ashforth, "Fostering Meaningfulness in Working and Meaningfulness at Work: An Identity Perspective," in *Positive Organizational Scholarship*, ed. Cameron et al.

33. See Turban and Greening, "Corporate Social Performance and Organizational Attractiveness to Prospective Employees"; and K. Basu and G. Palazzo, "Corporate Social Responsibility: A Process Model of Sensemaking," *Academy of Management Review* 33, no. 1 (2008): 122–36.

34. Pratt and Ashforth, "Fostering Meaningfulness in Working and Meaningfulness at Work."

35. Humphrey, Nahrgang, and Morgeson, "Integrating Motivational, Social, and Contextual Work Design Features."

36. Relevant sources include: V. M. Buehler and Y. K. Shetty, "Motivations for Corporate Social Action," *Academy of Management Journal* 17 (1974): 767–71; A. Muller and A. Kolk, "Extrinsic and Intrinsic Drivers of Corporate Social Performance: Evidence from Foreign and Domestic Firms in Mexico," *Journal of Management Studies* 47 (2010): 1–26; C. A. Ramus and U. Steger, "The Roles of Supervisory Support Behaviors and Environmental Policy in Employee 'Ecoinitiatives' at Leading-Edge European Companies," *Academy of Management Journal* 43 (2000): 605–26; G. R. Weaver, L. K. Treviño, and P. L. Cochran, "Integrated and Decoupled Corporate Social Performance: Management Commitments, External Pressures, and Corporate Ethics Practices," *Academy of Management Journal* 42 (1999): 539–52; and Weaver, Treviño, and Cochran, "Corporate Ethics Programs as Control Systems: Influences of Executive Commitment and Environmental Factors," *Academy of Management Journal* 42 (1999): 41–57.

37. See P. Bansal, "From Issues to Actions: The Importance of Individual Concerns and Organizational Values in Responding to Natural Environmental Issues," *Organization Science* 14 (2003): 510–27; and P. Mudrack, "Individual Personality Factors That Affect Normative Beliefs about the Rightness of Corporate Social Responsibility," *Business & Society* 46 (2007): 33–62.

38. See R. A. Johnson and D. W. Greening, "The Effects of Corporate Governance and Institutional Ownership Types on Corporate Social Performance," *Academy of Management Journal* 42 (1999): 564–76; J. M. Stevens, H. K. Steensma, D. A. Harrison, and P. L. Cochran, "Symbolic or Substantive Document? The Influence of Ethics Codes on Financial Executives' Decisions," *Strategic Management Journal* 26 (2005): 181–95; and Weaver, Treviño, and Cochran, "Integrated and Decoupled Corporate Social Performance."

39. J. R. Deckop, K. K. Merriman, and S. Gupta, "The Effects of CEO Pay Structure on Corporate Social Performance," *Journal of Management* 32 (2006): 329–42.

40. Mudrack, "Individual Personality Factors That Affect Normative Beliefs about the Rightness of Corporate Social Responsibility."

41. C. Laszlo and N. Zhexembayeva, *Embedded Sustainability: The Next Big Competitive Advantage* (Stanford, CA: Stanford Business Books, 2011).

17 | **A Nonprofit Sector Perspective of the United Nations Global Compact and Millennium Goals**

Thomas J. Harvey

The primary function of the economy involves the creation of wealth. For most people, this statement is a given. Most of the essays in this book either attempt to demonstrate or else assume that the economy can fulfill this important function while at the same time accomplishing other worthwhile objectives that benefit the human condition, by respecting the environment and the rights of labor, and by showing a planned commitment to such goals as good primary education, improved health care, and the elimination of hunger and poverty. This essay will take the position that the economy indeed needs these incentives to play a more positive role in raising the quality of life throughout the world. Nonetheless, these incentives will have a long-term impact only if it is understood that the economy is the most powerful force shaping the agenda of virtually every human social institution, from religion to government. An investigation of social arrangements since the Industrial Revolution will indicate the power of economic forces.

Such a far-reaching analysis of the social impact of the economy does not diminish the value and importance of developments such as the Millennium Goals and the United Nations Global Compact. In fact, these developments will especially benefit the human community throughout the world if they become a catalyst to intensify the analysis and political awareness of economic power and influence.

The Millennium Goals, along with the Global Compact, uniquely craft an agenda for the common good of humanity in the modern world. As such, they stand in sharp contrast to the piecemeal economic development of much of the last two centuries, which too often created many of the extremes targeted in these initiatives at both national and international levels. The UN Millennium Goals and Global Compact may not be equal to meeting the entire challenge, but they squarely put the focus on the needs and accountability of all the community's stakeholders, not just investors, and they do so at an international level.

Fortunately, the UN Millennium Goals and Global Compact do not stand alone in promoting benchmarks for a more sustainable economy. They share in common an attempt to develop a pool of ethical guidance for the global economy and the businesses that drive it. These include the Global Reporting Initiative Guidelines (1997); the Organization for Economic Cooperation and Development (OEDC) Principles for Corporate Governance (1999); the OECD for Multinational Enterprises (2000); the United Nations Principles for Responsible Investment (2006); the United Nations Principles for Responsible Management Education (2007); and the UN Framework for Business and Human Rights (2008).

To begin the analysis offered here, we should remember that the Industrial Revolution introduced an axial shift that reshaped virtually every aspect of the organizational arrangements of the human community, from the social structure of the family, to the role of religion, and even to the development of new governmental structures. Prior to the Industrial Revolution, the basis of wealth throughout the world involved the ownership and control of land.[1] In Western societies, monarchical governments were led by land-owning, extended families. To give one example, in the sixteenth century, Catherine d'Medici of the famous Medici family of Florence, Italy, married Henry II of France, and six of their children in turn became monarchs of France and other European nations.[2] With the Industrial Revolution came the growing awareness of nationhood and national economies, which would eventually lead to the emergence of new parliamentary and democratic republics throughout the world. In the current global economy, we can see a growing shift beyond nationalism toward internationalism, through such developments as the United Nations, international courts, and even a shared currency among most of the nations of Europe.

The shift from land to capital as the basis of wealth led to other revolutionary results. Perhaps the most fundamental one centered around the separation of work from the family. For example, it is estimated that 80 percent of the workforce in preindustrial England was landless, yet these workers all worked for landowners, primarily in agriculture or in related support trades. Their work and their family settings existed in close proximity. This close relationship would be forever severed with the development of industries that drew the present populations into the mines and mills of the emerging modern economy.

For a full treatment of this transition in England, France, and other soon-to-be developing countries of Europe in the eighteenth and nineteenth centuries, one may refer to *Regulating the Poor: The Functions of Public Welfare*, by Frances Fox Piven and Richard Cloward.[3] With the separation of work from the family, education for the vast majority of people moved from the apprentice model, whereby fathers taught their sons basic skills to be productive, and mothers taught their daughters, to free-standing schools, where new knowledge, skills, and specialization brought about a diversity of opportunities. This development would eventually blur traditional gender roles. With specialization came the deferral of mate selection, marriage, and childbearing. From a twenty-first-century perspective, it is clear that traditional religious teachings on birth control by major Christian religions had less influence on actual behavior than economic forces. The birth rates of most developed countries today, regardless of the dominant religion, are not even sufficient to maintain current levels of the population. Consider, for example, Italy and Spain, which have predominantly Catholic populations; they also have some of the lowest birth rates in the world.

One can also say that the Industrial Revolution led eventually, and more remotely, to greater longevity (first through water purification and the development of fertilizers, and later through medical breakthroughs) and to more leisure time (as in the creation of the weekend). This cursory summary indicates that most of today's challenges—whether positive or negative—are still unfolding because of the power of the economy—not primarily because of religion, government, or other social realities, which themselves have been essentially changed by the economy.

My basic assumption, in short, is that the power of the economy affects the human community and its social arrangements more dramatically than either the government or nongovernmental sectors. Lack of attention to this reality has permitted centuries of poor public policies in the West intended to support and provide an adequate safety net for those on the margins or dislocated from the economy. Consider some examples from history, both recent and more distant.

As reported in 2011, New York City had approximately 37,000 homeless people, of whom about 80 percent were women and children. Instead of looking at the actual causes of homelessness, donors and policymakers focus on the behavior of people who became homeless—as if their homelessness could have been avoided if these people had made better choices. In recent years, the city has spent as much as $880 million per year to provide shelter to the homeless. Despite this investment, there has been little progress in solving the problem over three decades. This failure results because governments have disregarded research that has identified several of the major causes of homelessness. The most basic cause identified in New York City is gentrification, which permits luxury developers to buy up old neighborhoods without dealing with the very predictable increase in homelessness that results. The developers not only are free to act in their own interests but are often given incentives in the form of tax abatements or low municipal bond rates.[4]

Social welfare policies in Western societies on the whole favor the needs and perspectives of the economically elite. Piven and Cloward's *Regulating the Poor: The Functions of Public Welfare* has this as its central theme.[5] In tracing the public policies of the United States and of the European nations that have highly influenced such policies in the United States, their study shows how such policies tend less to give genuine relief or opportunity than to act as a vehicle to provide stability and avoid political disruption.

Piven and Cloward demonstrate that this bias actually predated the Industrial Revolution. The needs of an industrial society, however, created a new power that eventually ended three hundred years of such regressive policies, which primarily had benefited landowners. The new industrial society's power structures became the only societal reality strong enough to undo policies that had protected landowners, the power elite of pre-industrialization.

As a result of their research on the oldest social policies in Western societies, Piven and Cloward argue that the Black Death of the fourteenth century was the catalyst for perhaps the first attempt at social welfare legislation. In 1349, the plague decimated the British populace alone by as much as 50 percent. As a result, peasant laborers in England had opportunities for better work if they migrated in search of more rewarding employment opportunities. The British Parliament passed the so-called Residency or Settlement Laws to curtail such mobility. In 1350, a companion piece of legislation forbade the travel of laborers to find better working conditions. It even included a prohibition against giving alms to itinerant laborers from other regions.. In succeeding centuries, these laws were kept intact or made more stringent. Finally, in 1795, the British Parliament repealed the Settlement Laws because of the growing appetite of urban industries for more and more laborers. As this change indicates, although the political process always favors the power of economic interests, that power became intensely invested in the new industrial reality.[6]

In the United States, the expansion and contraction of the economy determines the level of demand for workers. Yet the prevailing bias in public policy formulation and in the attitude of the general public is that employment or unemployment involves a behavioral attitude, not an economic systemic reality.

Three examples will shed light on the issue and bring home how firmly entrenched this prejudice has become in the United States, a prejudice that regards poverty as basically a behavioral issue. First, in 1935, when the poor were the majority of this nation, their problems were considered the nation's problems. As a result, one of the more enlightened pieces of American social legislation was enacted during that year of the Great Depression, namely, the Social Security Act. The name itself, Social Security Act, is an objective attempt to describe the fundamental purpose of the legislation. A part of the legislation that focused on the needs of the poorest families was called Aid to Families with Dependent Children. In 1996, when the poor numbered only 13 percent of the nation's population, it was apparently easier to return to the bias that the causes of poverty were primarily behavioral. The so-called welfare reform act of 1996 was called the Personal Responsibility and Work Opportunity Reconciliation Act, and it did not address systemic issues arising from the economy.

Second, consider the disconnect between the title of the 1996 social legislation and the economic reality that preceded it. In 1982, I became the president of Catholic Charities USA, the national network of social services affiliated with the Catholic Church. At that time, this national service network had 3.5 million clients, of whom only 23 percent needed food or shelter. By 1992, my last year of leadership, the Catholic Charities clientele had grown to 13.5 million clients, of whom 64 percent needed food or shelter. The Rust Belt was being created as the U.S. economy shifted from an industrial manufacturing base to a service economy. Talented laborers whose skills were not well aligned with the needs of the new economy were dislocated. Donors of the recent past were now clients of Catholic Charities. Obviously, the United States did not suffer a behavioral collapse in the desire and willingness for work. Capital and jobs fled to overseas investment opportunities, leaving in their wake a massive dislocation of talented workers.

Third, research demonstrates empirically the power of economic reality on human behavior during times of economic dislocation. One of the oldest examples is a thirty-five-year longitudinal study, over the years 1940 to 1975, of the relationship between the economic dislocation caused by plant closing and the rise of suicides among the dislocated workers and their families.[7] The findings of Dr. Harvey Brenner indicated that, regardless of religious beliefs, suicide rates among those personally affected by plant closings were thirty times higher than the rates for the rest of the population. In the United States, it is commonly assumed that nonprofit organizations are able to provide a safety net to help the unemployed deal with their new needs. Unfortunately, this sector also suffers during times of economic downturn, with fewer donors, less philanthropic support from foundations whose portfolios have contracted, minimal and often misdirected governmental-supported programs, and the common attitude of blame toward the unemployed themselves, which interferes with the search for effective and viable relief programs.

The UN Millennium Goals and Global Compact offer a revolutionary approach, if only at an elementary level, to viewing and measuring profits, where "profits" go beyond the narrow focus on rewards for financial stakeholders as opposed to the larger community. These initiatives are emerging within the basic norms of capitalism. They do not seek to overthrow economic reality, but rather they aim to give it balance by promoting growth of profits for all stakeholders. That this is happening is being documented; see, for example, the description in "Creating Shared Value" by Michael E. Porter and Mark R. Kramer of how major corporations are demonstrating that new and more inclusively beneficial forms of economic investment can be a win-win both for investors and for the common good.[8]

Nonetheless, these initiatives will remain elementary if the general population and the social institutions of religion, education, and social welfare do not come to recognize the power of the economy in rewarding many with untold levels of wealth, while tolerating, if not causing, untold levels of hunger and homelessness, of abuse and addiction, and other symptoms of poverty. The ultimate improvement of this system relies on the narrowing of the gap between rich and poor by expanding the genuine involvement of people throughout the world in rewarding economies.

One of the haunting realities of the modern world is the growing polarization between wealth and poverty. To me, the UN Millennium Project and UN Global Compact, if successful, will give the world a catalyst to bridge this extreme in ways that the nonprofit or government sectors are obviously not able to do. The measure of success will be a growing participation in the rewards of a sustainable, global economy.

NOTES

1. See Stuart Hall, ed., *Modernity: An Introduction to Modern Societies* (Oxford: Blackwell Publishers, 1996), 129–30.

2. Milton Waldman, *Catherine d'Medici and Her Children* (Boston: Houghton Mifflin, 1936), iii.

3. Frances Fox Piven and Richard Cloward, *Regulating the Poor: The Functions of Public Welfare* (New York: Vintage Books, 1993).

4. For details, see *The Chronicle of Philanthropy* (February 18, 2011), 27 and 30.

5. Piven and Cloward, *Regulating the Poor*, 36–37.

6. Ibid., 415. Piven and Cloward describe the welfare state as less connected to the welfare of vulnerable people than to economic stability: "The logic of industrialism, nevertheless, posits that the welfare state is ultimately shaped by systemic imperatives and the system is industrial society."

7. For a summary of Dr. Harvey Brenner's sociological studies at Johns Hopkins University on how the impact of a negative economy provokes increases in suicides, heart attacks, homicides, and increased admissions to mental hospitals, consult Peter Drier's March 10, 2009, article "This Economy Is a Real Killer," available at http://www.huffingtonpost.com/peter-dreier /this-economy-is-a-real-ki_b_173515.html. See also M. Harvey Brenner, *Mental Illness and the Economy* (New York: Universe Press, 1999).

8. Michael E. Porter and Mark R. Kramer, "Creating Shared Value," *Harvard Business Review* 89, no. 1 (January–February 2011): 62–77.

18 | Millennium Development Goals, Business Planning, and the UN Global Compact Management Model

Gerald F. Cavanagh, S.J., and Eric Hespenheide

Preserving a livable planet and reducing global poverty are essential not only for sustaining vigorous markets but also for the future stability of the world. Moreover, it is essential for a business firm to plan for future products and markets. Thus the United Nations has invited business firms to become partners in providing jobs and products for the world's poor, reducing harmful pollutants, and combating poverty. Such activities may seem more properly to be the role of governments, since they are pledged to work for the benefit of citizens. However, governments generally seek the benefit of only their own citizens.

It comes as a surprise to many people that countless business firms now demonstrate more responsibility for the future of people and the planet than do governments. The United Nations Global Compact (UNGC) provides a consistent, straightforward, and universally accepted framework for business to cooperate with citizens around the world to improve human rights, worker rights, and the natural environment and to battle corruption. The UNGC Management Model is designed as an instrument to help business firms establish and then work toward accomplishing their own goals, and also, following the UNGC, contribute to achieving the United Nations Millennium Development Goals (MDGs). In this chapter we will address the following topics: the background of the UN Global Compact; the development of the UNGC Management Model; the model itself; and preliminary experience with the model by firms that are beginning to incorporate it as an aid to their planning. First, let us broaden our scope to consider the tools that are available to help business firms develop just, consistent, and sustainable business practices worldwide.

TREATIES, CODES, AND SELF-RESTRAINT

As has been widely reported in the media, some businesses engage in activities that result in sweatshops and environmental degradation. While free markets provide quality and product usefulness, the market system also gives incentives to keep costs low, so markets thus often reward poor wages and working conditions and the dumping of toxic wastes in the air or water. More than two decades ago there were several attempts to develop a code of ethics for global corporations. One of these was the Principles for Global Corporate Responsibility produced by the Interfaith Center on Corporate Responsibility, and another was drawn up by the United Nations itself.[1] These codes were unsuccessful, largely because they lacked the support of the business community.

Multilateral agreements on wages and working conditions have been in place for even longer. But such agreements are not enforced and thus have limited ability to affect these issues. The Kyoto Protocol to reduce greenhouse gas emissions, with its minimal goals, has not been ratified by the United States and a few other major emitters. The United States, which is still the world's biggest market, has been a major obstacle to enacting global treaties on similar issues. It has also refused to ratify treaties such as the Law of the Sea Treaty and the World Health Organization Infant Formula Agreement. So there seems to be little chance that effective and enforceable international treaties will be enacted on these essential issues.[2]

Global corporations provide jobs for poor people, and many firms have voluntarily taken steps to improve wages and working conditions and to preserve the environment. However, such actions can increase their costs and thereby give a short-term, competitive advantage to a lower-cost firm that is less responsible. This unfairly tilts the "level playing field" that efficient markets require; the long-term operation of an effective market requires that level playing field. Executives of global firms are aware of this dilemma and propose some solutions in the form of global codes of business behavior.

The Caux Round Table (CRT) is a group of top executives from global firms. Founded in 1986, they developed their Principles for Business in 1994. These principles provide a set of seven "general principles" and then specific sets of "stakeholder principles" covering customers, employees, owners/investors, suppliers, competitors, and communities in which they operate.[3] The Caux Principles are proposed as a benchmark to which executives can compare their own firm's code.

Another early initiative is the CERES Principles, which seek to reduce environmental degradation. The principles provide guidance for firms on acceptable and unacceptable policies and practices. Other codes have been proposed and adopted by business firms, but these codes have had limited success in providing consistent, ethical, and transparent global business behavior.[4] Therefore, executives of international firms continue to seek guidance on these vital issues. The United Nations has worked with global corporations for decades, and its Global Compact with Business provides a guide and tools that have aided business people.

THE UNITED NATIONS AND GLOBAL BUSINESS

The United Nations was formed by governments, but it has sought to influence global corporations from its founding. Governments operate within limited political boundaries and seek the welfare of their own constituents, while large corporations often have global goals. In its early years, the UN sought to limit the excesses of international firms; its relationship with business was adversarial.[5] A new chapter began when world business and political leaders invited Kofi Annan, then

Secretary-General of the United Nations, to address the World Economic Forum in 1999. In his talk Annan underscored the gap between global markets and the inability of governments and people worldwide to deal with them:

> Globalization is a fact of life. But I believe we have underestimated its fragility. The spread of markets far outpaces the ability of societies and their political systems to adjust to them, let alone guide the course they take. History teaches us that such an imbalance between the economic, social and political realms can never be sustained for very long.[6]

Annan offered business people the support of the United Nations if businesses would reinforce the good effects of global markets and reduce their undesirable effects. Following that meeting, business leaders from around the world worked with the United Nations in 2000 to formulate nine principles of the United Nations Global Compact with Business. These principles address human rights, worker rights, and the natural environment. A few years later an anti-corruption principle was added, bringing the number of Global Compact Principles to ten.

The United Nations Global Compact brings business firms together with labor, civil society, and UN agencies under the moral authority of the United Nations. The Global Compact champions sustainable business and provides a practical set of aids for business firms that seek to be successful socially and environmentally, as well as economically. It does this by urging business people to integrate the Compact's ten principles into the strategic planning of their business firm, and it also encourages business firms to support the UN Millennium Development Goals. The aim is to embed the principles of the Global Compact in the firm's business strategy, culture, and day-to-day operations. The Compact encourages business firms to use their economic and social power to provide jobs, education, and a healthy environment for the world's citizens, especially those who are the poorest, and it supports them in that process. The Compact is a voluntary organization that gains its strength from partnerships, dialogue, learning, transparency, and cooperation.

If a firm elects to join and thus follow the ten principles of the Global Compact, it must submit a letter of intent from its CEO and agree to publish in its annual report, or in a parallel sustainability report, a description of the ways in which the firm is supporting the Compact. The Compact requires the firm to submit this information, also known as a "Communication on Progress" (COP), on the Compact website. As of 2013, over 13,000 COPs were filed with the Compact from over 8,700 active Global Compact businesses from 135 countries, and over 4,000 firms were expelled or "delisted" for failing to file COPs.[7] A partial list of active participating business firms includes Cisco Systems, Deloitte, DuPont, eBay, Ford Motor, Hewlett-Packard, Novartis, Royal Dutch Shell, Eli Lilly, Intel, Unilever, Volvo, Microsoft, and General Electric.[8] Firms have an incentive to join the United Nations Global Compact, since many find that it provides a boost in reputation. This has especially been true for European firms.[9] The principles themselves, the learning forums sponsored by Compact, and the transparency provided by the annual "Communication on Progress" all provide stimuli for a firm to be innovative, balanced, and consistent in pursuing its social and environmental goals and responsibilities.

In its COP, a firm is required to report on each of the four areas of the Compact (human rights, worker rights, sustainable environment, and anti-corruption). However, the principles of the Compact are general, do not provide specific guidance, and are also sometimes perceived as minimum standards for corporate activities and policies.[10] Given this, the Compact has established levels of progress in meeting the ten principles. Firms are classified as "active level" or "advanced level," and they support that designation by their COP report.

Some executives have signed the Compact, proclaimed its high ethical standards, and displayed the UN logo on their website, but have not reported on their firm's progress toward Compact goals. Both the UN and these firms have been criticized for "blue washing," referring to the display of the blue United Nations logo. Researchers found that a significant number of firms did not report on their activities, and "that smaller companies are generally least likely to comply with current reporting requirements." They also found that a larger portion of firms from the Northern Hemisphere were likely to report than those from elsewhere.[11] The nonreporting firms either did not do much to integrate the principles of human rights, worker rights, protecting the environment, and anti-corruption into their business plans or did not take the time to report on their progress.[12] The Compact warned firms that did not report and, as indicated above, took the step of removing more than 4,000 of them from its list of participants as of 2013. Even after reducing the number of its members, the Compact still has a goal of 20,000 corporate signers by the year 2020. However, the number 20,000 represents only about a quarter of the estimated 75,000 to 80,000 firms operating in the world.

The Compact and the cooperation, dialogue, and learning that it fosters have had a positive impact on the thousands of businesses that participate, so the Compact has brought "a new era of cooperation [of the UN] with the business community and [overcome] a recent past of mutual suspicion."[13] The Compact has brought much-needed cooperation, discovery, and positive role models for international business and also for global development. The Compact also cooperates with other nongovernmental (NGO) institutions that have complementary goals, and provides learning forums, tools, and training materials to aid the efforts of business executives.

As already indicated, firms must upload their annual COPs to the Compact website. This is a public forum, so it provides transparency —anyone can see what a firm has done or claims to have done. This approach freed the Compact office from the burdensome task of evaluating each annual submission, and it also enabled the office to easily convey on its website which firms did not communicate progress.[14] The Compact is still criticized by many NGOs because it does not monitor and measure the firms who sign the Compact. Much of this criticism is misplaced, however, due to a lack of understanding of the role and goals of the UN and the Compact. The Compact has neither the authority nor the resources to undertake extensive monitoring.[15] However, the COPs are a form of monitoring. With the COPs in place, the information is available to anyone who wishes to monitor a firm's accomplishments on the issues on which the firm chooses to report.

On the other hand, when business firms do take initiatives that follow the Compact principles and help address the UN global development goals, they deserve to be acknowledged and given credit by various stakeholders, including NGOs. Business executives and their firms can then more readily be drawn into discussions on how to provide solutions to "failing markets" and "failing states."[16] In summary, the Compact's actions show how they are able to experiment and change their strategy in order to improve human rights, labor rights, the natural environment, and anti-corruption. Initiatives similar to the Compact also have been developed in cooperation with the UN for the investment community and for business schools.

PRINCIPLES FOR RESPONSIBLE INVESTMENT AND PRINCIPLES FOR RESPONSIBLE MANAGEMENT EDUCATION

The Principles for Responsible Investment (PRI) were established in 2005 by financial executives in cooperation with the United Nations. Recent financial crises, along with social and environmental problems, provide a compelling rationale for financial institutions to adopt such principles.[17] As of 2013, the PRI have been adopted by more than one thousand investing institutions from forty-five countries, which together represent more than $30 trillion of investments—in excess of 10 percent of global capital markets.[18]

Business schools influence business people and business practices. So, business educators, again in cooperation with the United Nations, launched the Principles for Responsible Management Education (PRME) in July 2007. Business schools from around the world were invited to embrace these principles. More than 500 business schools have pledged themselves to the PRME (as of 2013). They, like those who have signed the other principles, agree to annually report on progress.[19] Given the number of business firms, financial institutions, and business schools that have pledged to follow these sets of principles (the UNGC, the PRI, and the PRME) and to report on their progress, one may judge that the efforts of the United Nations have had considerable impact and success.

The four areas addressed by the United Nations Global Compact—human rights, worker rights, natural environment, and anti-corruption—are essential to the future health of peoples, their ability to lead decent lives, the stability of nations, and the health of the planet as a whole. One area of major concern is global climate change, but there has been little progress in efforts to reduce greenhouse gas emissions. More than 250 climate scientists have called for recognition of the scientific data that demonstrates a warming of the earth, the use of that data for formulating policy, and an end to attacks on the integrity and abilities of the scientists and the Intergovernmental Panel on Climate Change (IPCC).[20] Nevertheless, there is little likelihood of greenhouse gas regulation and carbon trading in the near term, at least in the United States, in spite of the data and reports by scientists from around the world and the work of the IPCC.[21] Yet major insurers must deal with the global risks of climate change. Munich Re, the largest reinsurer in the world, "has the world's most comprehensive database on natural disasters . . . going back centuries. It shows that the frequency of serious floods worldwide has more than tripled since 1980, while hurricanes and other severe windstorms have doubled." Munich Re states, "global warming is real, and it affects our business."[22]

International accountability standards, for example, ISO 14001, have been developed over the last decade in an attempt to provide agreed-upon environmental guidelines for firms. This has occurred because there is no international body that provides a comprehensive instrument to monitor human rights, worker rights, or environmental and transparency standards. Global business and government leaders have succeeded in supporting global markets by means of international regulations to ensure the protection of property, but there has been no parallel effort to ensure adequate working conditions.[23] To achieve their goals, the Compact has partnered with the International Organization for Standardization, the Global Reporting Initiative, the World Business Council for Sustainable Development, CERES, the Caux Round Table, and other NGOs with similar purposes.

BUSINESSES EMBRACE COMPACT PRINCIPLES

There are countless examples of global firms that embrace the Compact principles. Many business firms now operate by pursuing profit, while simultaneously recognizing the needs of workers, customers, the community, other stakeholders, and also the local and global environment.[24] Many firms on their own initiative improve wages and working conditions and require a reduction in waste and greenhouse gas emissions in supply chain firms. Business executives recognize that today's citizens have little trust in business firms and the managers who run them, yet they also know that trust is essential for the efficient operation of a business firm and the business system. Their actions promise to increase that trust.

Let us examine some examples of firms that are trying to act more responsibly and sustainably. McDonald's will no longer use foam clamshell containers. Wal-Mart has set targets to eliminate waste, rely only on renewable energy, and sell only sustainable products. Among other firms making similar efforts are Cisco Systems, Duke Energy, Eaton, and FedEx.[25] Business firms have significant opportunities to profit from long-term planning. Firms like Clorox, Nike, Dow Chemical, and Hewlett-Packard have implemented major programs to reduce energy use and waste and to produce attractive, profitable "green" products.[26] Most of these firms are active members of the Compact.

The United Nations Global Compact has consistently provided communication tools, learning forums, and other mechanisms to aid business firms as they implement the Compact principles. As part of this ongoing effort, the United Nations Global Compact Management Model was designed in 2010 to aid in this implementation. The model is being rolled out worldwide primarily through the Compact's local networks.

THE GLOBAL COMPACT MANAGEMENT MODEL

Over its history as an organization, the Compact has brought forward, often through collaboration with other groups, an impressive array of tools, such as communications and learning forums. These tools are designed to assist business in establishing useful and actionable programs to implement the ten principles.

From the beginning, the Compact has recognized that organizations would need assistance with embedding the ten principles into their day-to-day operations. While there are a wide variety of actions by which firms address their commitment to the principles, since "one size does not fit all," there are certain standard requirements, such as the annual Communication on Progress, which became a requirement for continued recognition as a Compact member in 2005.

The COP addresses several important purposes. First, it highlights a firm's actions and progress on the ten principles through transparency and accountability. Second, it assists organizations to implement actions by providing best-practice examples of how others are addressing the serious business of dealing with the world's problems that underlie the principles. Third, it provides a driver for continuous improvement.

This drive for continuous improvement is one of the factors that led the Compact to improve the tools available to organizations striving to demonstrate progress on the ten principles. While there have been a number of tools and approaches available through the Compact over the years, it became increasingly evident that a new approach was needed to help firms, particularly those just starting their journey with the Compact.

A book published in 2004, *Raising the Bar: Creating Value with the United Nations Global Compact*, introduced the concept of a Performance Model.[27] The book provides detailed guidance and examples of actions and disclosures for each of the ten UNGC principles. Although this was a comprehensive guide, the Global Compact received feedback that some organizations found it difficult to use, particularly recent signers and smaller organizations. Based on this feedback, the Compact undertook a project in 2009 to assess the need for additional guidance on implementation. As a help in developing a new approach, over one hundred companies were surveyed and provided suggestions on what was needed.

One finding indicated a need for a simpler method of illustrating the Performance Model and demonstrating the continuous improvement that underlies the objectives of the Compact. The Compact, in collaboration with Deloitte Touche Tohmatsu (Deloitte), therefore revisited the Performance Model and designed another approach to help organizations translate the ten principles into value-enhancing management practices.[28] The primary goal of the Global Compact Management Model is to support organizations' efforts to embrace corporate responsibility through integrating their mainstream business practices and their commitment to the Global Compact principles.

The Management Model is designed graphically as a circle to illustrate that progress is iterative and that there is neither a "right" entry point nor an end point to an organization's corporate responsibility or sustainability activities. Of course, there is an initial starting point on the circle, which is the organization's commitment to the Global

Compact principles as evidenced by the Letter of Commitment signed by the chief executive of the organization. The Management Model is designed to help organizations through a series of steps, starting with its formal commitment (and regular recommitment). The other five steps, moving clockwise around the circle from the step of commitment, are to assess, to define, to implement, to measure, and to communicate a strategy based on and supporting the Global Compact and its underlying ten principles.

The Management Model provides definitions and illustrations for each step of the process, which assists organizations with getting started. It also helps organizations maintain momentum over time, continuously improve their sustainability performance, and provide transparency regarding their operations and strategies for furthering the Compact principles. Specific reference to other Global Compact requirements and materials is provided throughout the Management Model document.

In addition to providing practical advice on how to achieve each process, the Management Model includes "Getting Started" and "Leadership Practices" sections that are intended to reinforce the idea of continuous improvement and demonstrate the model's relevance to all Global Compact signatories.

The six steps of the Management Model are described below:

1. COMMIT: *Leadership commitment to mainstream the Global Compact principles into strategies and operations and to take action in support of broader UN goals, in a transparent way.* During this step, company leadership publicly signals its commitment to stakeholders. Specifically, leadership commits to supporting the Global Compact and making the ten principles part of the strategy, culture, and day-to-day operations of the company, with oversight provided by transparent governance structures.

2. ASSESS: *Assess risks, opportunities, and impacts across Global Compact issue areas.* Euipped with a commitment to the Global Compact and in support of UN goals, the company assesses its risks and opportunities—in financial and extra-financial terms—as well as the impact of its operations and activities on the issue areas, on an ongoing basis in order to develop and refine its goals, strategies, and policies.

3. DEFINE: *Define goals, strategies, and policies.* Based on its assessment of risks, opportunities, and impacts, the company develops and refines goals and metrics specific to its operating context, and creates a roadmap to carry out its program.

4. IMPLEMENT: *Implement strategies and policies through the company and across the company's value chain.* The company establishes and ensures ongoing adjustments to core processes, engages and educates employees, builds capacity and resources, and works with supply chain partners to address and implement its strategy.

5. MEASURE: *Measure and monitor impacts and progress toward goals.* The organization adjusts its performance management systems to capture, analyze, and monitor the performance metrics established in the Assess and Define steps. Progress is monitored against goals and adjustments are made to improve performance.

6. COMMUNICATE: *Communicate progress and strategies and engage with stakeholders for continuous improvement.* During this step the company communicates its progress and forward-looking strategies for implementing its commitment by developing a Communication on Progress, and engages with stakeholders to identify ways to improve performance continuously.

Additional information on each of the six steps tailored to a firm's "Getting Started" and "Leadership Practices" are described in the appendix.

PRELIMINARY EXPERIENCE WITH THE MANAGEMENT MODEL

The Management Model was introduced at the UN Global Compact Leaders Summit in June 2010. Since then, there have been several learning events to promote the adoption of the model. These have been held in various locations including the United States, Mexico, Belgium, and Turkey, as well as countries in Africa and Asia. The Global Compact office made note of the inaugural training in a press release in February 2011.[29] The training events have been attended by over sixty companies, including PepsiCo, EMC, Citigroup, Campbell Soup Company, Merck, MolsenCoors, and Symantec. However, given the newness of the Management Model, actual experience with applying it has been limited. In an attempt to gauge its future adoption by organizations, and businesses in particular, we participated in the Compact learning events and interviewed several companies regarding the following attributes of the model. Interview questions included:

- What do you like about the model?
- What do you see as the benefits of the model?
- What are the challenges to implementation of the model?
- What components will be the easiest to implement, and what are your specific steps?
- What time frame are you considering for implementing the model?

Of the small sample of organizations from which we were able to obtain their views, none had yet formally adopted the full Management Model. Future research will be required to go beyond the anecdotal data presented here. But we were able to identify a few themes that emerged from the training and supplemental discussions.

Generally, the feedback has been very positive. Most respondents see the model as an effective means of communicating with executive management not only what it means to be a signatory of the Global Compact but, more importantly, what is involved in adhering to the commitments inherent in the ten principles.

Interviewees liked the model's simplicity, at least in concept. While there was support for the general description of the "Getting Started" and "Leadership Practices," most businesses attending the training sessions pressed for concrete and practical examples of each step in the process. Perceived benefits of the model included being able to use the framework as an overall communications tool within the organization, both at the executive level and also with the entire workforce.

The participants put most of the challenges into two broad categories. First, how does this fit into what we are already doing? Many saw a challenge in understanding how the model relates to and complements the other material provided by the Global Compact, such as the Global Compact Self-Assessment Tool and the Blueprint for Corporate Responsibility Leadership, and how to link it to other corporate responsibility and sustainability initiatives. Second, how does a firm practically implement some of the specifics included in the model, such as defining goals and measuring impact? There were strong concerns expressed regarding the establishment of specific goals, given the possible accountability and risk of litigation if the goals are not met.

There are currently several ways to measure and report sustainability actions. And there is a lack of useful and definitive guidance on what and how to measure certain sustainability attributes, particularly in the social dimension. Organizations expressed strong interest in obtaining additional guidance in this area.

A third area expressed by some related to establishing the "business case" for adopting a "formal" process such as the Management Model.

Not surprisingly, given the organizations participating, the easiest step was the Commit process. All of these organizations were at that stage, since they had already signed the Compact. Additionally, many of the organizations are already publishing some form of report on their activities, although most stated that improvements could be made in linking to the Compact's ten principles. This is one area where examples of best practices are especially important.

As to time frames for implementing the Management Model, the general consensus was that elements of the model either were already in place or were in the process of being implemented and that the model provides useful input and enhancement for these activities. Formal adoption of the model in its entirety was not specifically expressed, although the possibility was not ruled out.

THE UNITED NATIONS Global Compact continues to exert an important influence on numerous businesses that are committed to the long-term sustainability of their organizations and the people of the planet. The ten principles were formulated in cooperation with business executives, and they spell out in general actions that are needed to address some of the most serious problems facing the world.

The United Nations Global Compact Management Model is an aid for firms who sign the Compact and then strive for continuous improvement. While most firms have not yet adopted it in its entirety, many have found it useful in their attempt to embed the Compact principles in their own business strategic plans. They found the Model especially useful in communicating actions and progress both to their internal and external stakeholders.

APPENDIX

Step 1. Commit

Getting Started:
- CEO and Board (if applicable) sign the UN Global Compact Letter of Commitment.
- Leadership commits to adhering to the ten principles, submitting a Communication on Progress (COP) annually and taking action in broader UN goals.
- Leadership plans to put resources aside to carry out commitment over time.

Leadership Practices:
- Leadership team, including CEO, C-suite officers, the Board, and heads of business units and company subsidiaries, commits to adopting and promoting sustainability with its industry and communities.
- Company promotes its commitment by communicating it to shareholders and other stakeholders.

Step 2. Assess

Getting Started:
- Company makes sure it understands the ten principles and reviews appropriate issue area information and tools.
- Considers owned operations at a high level to see if it is in alignment with the principles
- Prioritizes risks and opportunities to address

Leadership Practices:
- Prioritizes risks, proactively identifies opportunities, and calculates impacts at both the interprise and product level on a regular basis across issue areas
- Forecasts future operating context scenarios, based on review of data and deep understanding of trends, so that it can address risks and capture opportunities

- Engages stakeholders in assessments and shares best practices with peers, suppliers, and other business partners

Step 3. Define

Getting Started:
- Starts by prioritizing high-level and achievable goals to address top risks, impacts, and opportunities identified in the Assess step
- Sets high-level strategy and action plan to achieve goals

Leadership Practices:
- Sustainability is an essential component of the company's mission statement and business strategy; sustainability strategy planning process is integrated into overall corporate strategy planning process.
- Develops strategy in consultation with internal and external stakeholders
- Develops roadmap of actions and investments to improve sustainability performance, with clear ownership and accountability
- Encourages or requires suppliers and business partners to operate in ways consistent with Global Compact principles

Step 4. Implement

Getting Started:
- Adjusts relevant processes and educates employees on the actions and behaviors that will help the company achieve its goals

Leadership Practices:
- Adjusts core processes to align with Global Compact principles and drive value for shareholders, stakeholders, and society
- Equips and empowers subsidiaries, business units, employees, business partners, and suppliers to carry out its sustainability strategies on a daily basis
- "Sustainability mindset" is adopted throughout the organization.

Step 5. Measure

Getting Started:
- Starts to measure and monitor corporate sustainability metrics set up in the Assess and Define steps

- Collects all available data, noting source of data and data it does not yet have; data will be refined and expanded over time to extract insights that will enable the company to continuously improve.

Leadership Practices:

- Implements system to measure and report performance toward achieving goals
- Makes performance broadly visible, regularly uses performance data to guide decisions and investments, and seeks to translate corporate sustainability impact into financial impact
- Works within industry and government to develop industry standards for impact metrics

Step 6. Communicate

Getting Started:

- Documents progress toward completing action plan by describing activities undertaken to align with the UN Global Compact principles in its COP
- Reconfirms commitment to the Global Compact

Leadership Practices:

- Documents sustainability goals, strategies, and performance in a credible manner, highlighting successes and shortcomings, and integrates relevant information into annual financial report ad supporting documentation
- Receives Board approval and third-party verification of COP
- Engages stakeholders to capture feedback to improve sustainability performance and promote alignment with current and emerging regulations and trends

NOTES

1. Duane Windsor, "Toward a Transnational Code of Business Conduct," in *Emerging Global Business Ethics*, ed. Michael Hoffman et al. (Westport, CT: Quorum Books, 1994), 165–76; "Principles for Global Corporate Responsibility," *The Corporate Examiner* 24 (September 1, 1995): 1–25.

2. Gerald F. Cavanagh, "Global Business Ethics: Regulation, Code or Self-Restraint," *Business Ethics Quarterly* 14 (December 2004): 625–42.

3. Kenneth Goodpaster, "The Caux Round Table Principles: Corporate Moral Reflection in a Global Business Environment," in *Global Codes of Conduct: An Idea Whose Time Has Come*, ed. Oliver F. Williams, C.S.C. (Notre Dame, IN: University of Notre Dame Press, 2000), 183–95. For the principles and background, see http://www.cauxroundtable.org/.

4. For a more complete list of principles and codes and additional insights, see Sandra Waddock, "Building a New Institutional Infrastructure for Corporate Responsibility," *Academy of Management Perspectives* (August 2008): 87–108.

5. Tagi Sagafi-nejad and John H. Dunning, *UN and Transnational Corporations: From Code of Conduct to Global Compact* (Bloomington: Indiana University Press, 2008).

6. Kofi Annan, "Business and the UN: A Global Compact of Shared Values and Principles," *Vital Speeches* (February 15, 1999), 260–61. See also Oliver F. Williams, C.S.C., ed., *Peace through Commerce: Responsible Corporate Citizenship and the Ideals of the United Nations Global Compact* (Notre Dame, IN: University of Notre Dame Press, 2008); S. Prakash Sethi, *Setting Global Standards: Guidelines for Creating Codes of Conduct in Multinational Corporations* (Hoboken, NJ: John Wiley, 2003); and Williams, ed., *Global Codes of Conduct*.

7. For expulsions, see "Expelled Participants" under http://www.unglobalcompact.org/COP/analyzing_progress/.

8. For a current list of participating firms, organized by country, see http://www.unglobalcompact.org/participants/search.

9. Jay Janney, Greg Dess, and Victor Forlani, "Glass Houses? Market Reactions to Firms Joining the UN Global Compact," *Journal of Business Ethics* 90 (December 2009): 409–23.

10. Hens Runhaar and Helene Lafferty, "Governing Corporate Social Responsibility: An Assessment of the Contribution of the UN Global Compact to CSR Strategies in the Telecommunications Industry," *Journal of Business Ethics* 84 (February 2009): 479–95.

11. Ralf Barkemeyer and Giulio Napolitono, "The UN Global Compact: Moving Towards a Critical Mass or a Critical State?" *Academy of Management Annual Meeting Proceedings* (2009): 1–6.

12. Michael Behnam and Tammy L. MacLean, "Where Is the Accountability in International Accountability Standards? A Decoupling Perspective," *Business Ethics Quarterly* 21 (January 2011): 64; and Robert W. Nason, "Structuring the Global Marketplace: The Impact of the United Nations Global Compact," *Journal of Macromarketing* 28 (December 2008): 418–25.

13. Georg Kell, "The Global Compact: Selected Experiences and Reflections," *Journal of Business Ethics* 59 (2005): 70.

14. Kell, "The Global Compact: Selected Experiences and Reflections," 72.

15. For an excellent summary of criticisms of the Compact and how they are misplaced, see Andreas Rasche, "A Necessary Supplement: What the United Nations Global Compact Is and Is Not," *Business and Society* 48 (December 2009): 511–37.

16. See Klaus M. Leisinger, "Capitalism with a Human Face," *Journal of Corporate Citizenship* 28 (Winter 2007): 113–32.

17. Georg Kell, "Responsible Investment: Why Should Private Equity Care?," *International Trade Forum* 4 (2009): 7–8.

18. See http://www.unpri.org.

19. See http://www.unprme.org.

20. See the letter "Climate Change and the Integrity of Science," *Science* 328, no. 5979 (May 7, 2010): 689–90.

21. The position of many people in the United States on these multilateral agreements is probably explained by the predominant values of individualism, self-interest, and survival of the fittest; see Gerald F. Cavanagh, *American Business Values*, 6th ed. (Upper Saddle River, NJ: Prentice Hall, 2010).

22. Carol Matlack, "The Growing Peril of a Connected World," *Bloomberg Businessweek* (November 29–December 5, 2010), 63–64.

23. See Dirk Ulrich Gilbert, Andreas Rasche, and Sandra Waddock, "Accountability in a Global Economy: The Emergence of International Accountability Standards," *Business Ethics Quarterly* 21, no. 1 (January 2011): 23–44.

24. Michael E. Porter and Mark R. Kramer, "Creating Shared Value," *Harvard Business Review* 89, no. 1 (January–February 2011): 62–77.

25. Helen M. Haugh and Alka Talwar, "How Do Corporations Embed Sustainability Across the Organization," *Academy of Management Learning and Education* 9 (September 2010): 384–93.

26. Eric Hespenheide, John DeRose, Jessica Bramhall, and Mark Tumiski, "A Profitable Shade of Green: Compounding the Benefits of Carbon Management and Sustainability Measures," *Deloitte Review* 7 (2010): 60–73.

27. Claude Fussler, Aron Cramer, and Sebastian van der Vegt, eds., *Raising the Bar: Creating Value with the United Nations Global Compact* (Sheffield, UK: Greenleaf Publishing, 2004).

28. Georg Kell, *UN Global Compact: Framework for Implementation*, 2010.

29. Available at http://www.unglobalcompact.org/NewsAnd Events; see February 3, 2011.

19 | Do The Principles of Responsible Management Education Matter?
One School's Perspective

Arvid C. Johnson

Dominican University is a private, Catholic university located in River Forest, Illinois, ten miles west of the Chicago Loop. With an enrollment of nearly 3,800 students—about half of whom are graduate students—it offers bachelor's degrees in more than fifty areas of study and master's degrees from our schools of library and information science, business, education, and social work. The *U.S. News & World Report* consistently ranks Dominican in the top tier of Midwest master's-level universities.

Founded in 1977, the School of Business at Dominican University was named in honor of Edward A. Brennan and his wife, Lois L. Brennan, in 2006. The Brennan School of Business is a leading small school provider of management education in the Chicago metropolitan area—with over five hundred students pursuing undergraduate and graduate degrees in the fields of accounting, business, economics, and international business. The student body, with representatives from around the world, is diverse in terms of both business experience and cultural backgrounds.

Since its inception, the Brennan School of Business has offered a curriculum that addresses issues of business ethics. The establishment of the Christopher Chair in Business Ethics in 2003 and the founding of the School's Center for Global Peace through Commerce in 2008 reflect its continuing commitment to educating the next generation of leaders to have impact with integrity in their communities and around the world.

BRENNAN AND THE PRINCIPLES OF RESPONSIBLE MANAGEMENT EDUCATION

Getting Started

As noted earlier, the Brennan School of Business has a deep and long-standing commitment to ethics-centered management education; and the six Principles of Responsible Management Education (PRME) of *purpose, values, method, research, partnership,* and *dialogue* resonated with our desire to prepare leaders to have impact with integrity. For the Brennan School of Business, the fact that the PRME are focused on both "impact" and "integrity" was critically important. We recognize that some business people have impact without integrity—we read about them in the press and follow their trials. At the same time, we know that many people of integrity lack the skills or understanding of how to have an impact. Our programs—and our mission—are about ensuring that those we serve are ready to have impact *with* integrity.

When the director of the Center for Global Peace through Commerce and one of the most respected faculty members—Al Rosenbloom, who has done a lot of work with CEEMAN[1] (the international management development association) and PRME on poverty as a challenge to management education—approached the Brennan School faculty with the request that the school "sign on" to the PRME, the idea was met with unanimous approval. The Brennan School of Business became a signatory to the PRME on April 13, 2009.

Our First Year

At that point, there was a decision to make about how—and whether—to reinforce intentionally the PRME during the coming 2009–10 academic year. Should there be regular discussions about activities at faculty meetings? Should we publish quarterly updates or check on status? Or, since the PRME were well-aligned with the Brennan School's fundamental values and mission, why not just let the faculty, staff, and students go about the "business" of the School?

The second approach obviously held the appeal of involving less up-front work—never a negligible factor in any academic's decision-making process. More important, it also avoided the potential pitfalls of the "new, new thing" or "flavor of the month" mentalities and the danger of the PRME becoming a matter of "checking the boxes." In consultation with the driving faculty behind the Brennan School of Business's engagement with the PRME, including the director of the Center for Global Peace through Commerce, the school opted for the "normal operations" approach.

When it came time to capture the actions and results for the first Sharing of Information on Progress (SIP) Report, this faith was affirmed. As you can read in the first SIP—published on October 6, 2010, and available at the PRME site—the faculty, staff, and students had great examples to share in each of the areas. Whether it was the tremendous fundraising success of the Kiva lending team in supporting entrepreneurs in developing economies, or the "social business" models studied by the students, or the faculty members' research on the impact of microfinance and on poverty and management education, or the "Power of Commerce for Social Good" symposium, the Brennan School lived its mission and embodied the PRME in word and deed.

However, the best result of this approach was evident when the faculty met to review and approve that first SIP for publication. In the discussion of the SIP at that meeting, faculty members realized two important things: (1) the PRME are precisely about *how* the Brennan School "does business"—which is more important than *what* the school does—and (2) there were opportunities for collaboration and reinforcement among colleagues that would form the next logical, mission-consistent evolution of practices. The dynamic interaction and level of energy present in that faculty meeting—yes, even in a faculty meeting—were remarkable.

It may be helpful to state here the full text of the six principles of the PRME:

As institutions of higher education involved in the development of current and future managers we declare our willingness to progress in the implementation, within our institution, of the following Principles, starting with those that are more relevant to our capacities and mission. We will report on progress to all our stakeholders and exchange effective practices related to these principles with other academic institutions:

1.   **Purpose**: We will develop the capabilities of students to be future generators of sustainable value for business and society at large and to work for an inclusive and sustainable global economy.
2.   **Values**: We will incorporate into our academic activities and curricula the values of global social responsibility as portrayed in international initiatives such as the United Nations Global Compact.
3.   **Method**: We will create educational frameworks, materials, processes and environments that enable effective learning experiences for responsible leadership.
4.   **Research**: We will engage in conceptual and empirical research that advances our understanding about the role, dynamics, and impact of corporations in the creation of sustainable social, environmental and economic value.
5.   **Partnership**: We will interact with managers of business corporations to extend our knowledge of their challenges in meeting social and environmental responsibilities and to explore jointly effective approaches to meeting these challenges.
6.   **Dialogue**: We will facilitate and support dialog and debate among educators, students, business, government, consumers, media, civil society organisations and other interested groups and stakeholders on critical issues related to global social responsibility and sustainability.

We understand that our own organisational practices should serve as example of the values and attitudes we convey to our students.[2]

As a result of Brennan's new commitment to PRME, there has been intensified and exciting progress. It might be helpful if I highlight one or two examples from the second, 2011 SIP of how the Brennan

School's actions align with each of the PRME. There is more information about these actions—and many others—in the Brennan School of Business's subsequent SIPs on the PRME website.

1. **Purpose**: Our 2010 Power of Commerce for Social Good Symposium brought together students, alumni, business people, and other leaders to explore trends in corporate social responsibility (CSR) and sustainability communications; creating, maintaining, and sustaining CSR commitment; the challenges to CSR and global commerce in the current economic climate; and enterprise for a sustainable world. Key speakers included Stuart Hart (Cornell's S. C. Johnson Chair of Sustainable Global Enterprise and author of *Capitalism at the Crossroads*) and Jane Madden (who leads Edelman's Chicago CSR & Sustainability practice).

2. **Values**: In the spring of 2011, the Brennan School of Business offered a "Special Topics" course on "Social Business and Sustainability" to our graduate students. In the summer, students participated in a newly developed "International Residency" program that provided an immersion experience working with small businesses and social entrepreneurs in the black township of Alexandria, South Africa.

3. **Method**: In addition to the many on-campus programs and activities coordinated by the Center for Global Peace through Commerce (including "Growth Can Be Good: Sustainability and Commerce in the 21st Century" and "The Road Ahead for Egypt: Social Justice and Social Responsibility"), the Center is in the process of developing a series of on-line modules on sustainability that are available to other institutions.

4. **Research**: Brennan faculty published journal articles and made presentations on subjects that included anti-corruption initiatives (specifically, the growing menace of money laundering); the recent financial crisis and how the "lessons learned" can be incorporated into accounting, economics, finance, and strategy classes; and likely relative effectiveness of carbon taxes versus cap-and-trade mechanisms for controlling global carbon emissions.

5. **Partnership**: The 2010 Ethics & Leadership Lecture saw Sam DiPiazza (the retired Global CEO of PricewaterhouseCoopers International) speak on responsible leadership in a multi-stakeholder world.

In addition, Brennan School of Business students regularly have opportunities to interact with social entrepreneurs such as Manish Shah, the Founder & CEO of Fos Biofuels.

6. **Dialogue**: Our panel on "Is Dreaming Illegal? Seeking Sustainable Solutions" brought together members of academia, nongovernmental organizations, the Catholic Church, and the business community to explore the issue of undocumented immigrants.

SO, DO THE PRME MATTER?

I think that you would be shocked if someone asked to write about the PRME answered with anything other than a resounding "Yes!"—and I won't disappoint you in that regard. However, I believe that you deserve a more complete answer than that.

Even before signing on to participate in the PRME, the Brennan School of Business was already a mission-driven, ethics-centered business school within a larger institution whose mission is to prepare students to pursue truth, to give compassionate service, and to participate in the creation of a more just and humane world. If anything, there was some chance that the PRME would have absolutely no impact on our School of Business.

That has not been the case, however. In fact, and in a very real way, the PRME have been *transformative* for the Brennan School of Business. The school is now part of a larger network of institutions that are committed not only to continuous improvement but also to sharing "what works" through their annual reports on progress. While the quality and utility of these reports can vary, they are an incredibly valuable resource—even if some of them can be a bit intimidating for a "little" school like Dominican.

More importantly, the PRME have provided the academic community with a framework for discussion, interaction, and collaboration *within* the Brennan School of Business. In that regard, Dominican can take great pride in the way that each and every member of the School— faculty, staff, or student—is helping us to put the PRME into practice.

So, do the PRME matter? I hope that my brief remarks above have shown you that the answer is "Absolutely!" If I have failed to convince you, then please chat with *any* Brennan School of Business faculty member—the ones really doing the work—and they will set the record straight.

NOTES

1. See http://www.ceeman.org.
2. See http://www.unprem.org/the-6-principles.

Part III

WHERE DO WE GO FROM HERE?

20 | The Future of the United Nations Global Compact

Kirk O. Hanson

Since the founding of the United Nations Global Compact in 2000, many have admired its perseverance and effectiveness in engaging corporations and their leaders in the pursuit of global economic and social development. The ten principles of the Global Compact summarize much of our collective hope for the contribution that corporations and other private businesses can make toward a world of peace and economic security. The credit for the accomplishments of the Global Compact over its first ten years is due to Secretaries-General Kofi Annan and Ban Ki-moon, but also to the leadership of business executives such as Sir Mark Moody Stuart, former chairman of Royal Dutch Shell and now chairman of the Global Compact Foundation, and the staff assembled and managed by Executive Director Georg Kell.

After celebrating the Global Compact's tenth anniversary in 2011, and moving into the next decade, it is appropriate to ask several questions about the future of the organization. How these questions are answered will determine the future direction and success of the Global Compact in its second decade.

WHAT WILL THE GLOBAL COMPACT'S
TEN PRINCIPLES MEAN IN 2021?

The first question is how the ten principles, which have formed the core commitments of the organization, will be elaborated upon and redefined over the coming years. In its first decade the Global Compact had a deliberate strategy of promoting the ten principles without full definition and elaboration, letting corporate practices brought forth by members define what it means not to be "complicit in human rights abuses," to eliminate "discrimination in respect of employment and occupation," or to "undertake initiatives to promote greater environmental responsibility," for example. Companies joining the Global Compact were asked simply to support the principles and report annually on efforts to implement them. At first, the simple statements of the ten principles raised as many questions as they answered. Slowly, since the principles were first formally adopted in 2004, a series of Global Compact meetings and conferences, as well as guidelines and best practices collected and published by the Global Compact, have amplified the meaning of these commitments.

In its second decade, the Global Compact will face important debates over the meaning of the ten principles in a truly global world. While the 1948 UN Declaration on Human Rights provides the foundation for much of the ethical discussion, many see a need for further reflection. For example, the business world of 2001 was dominated by American and Western European multinational firms. Therefore, the philosophical and religious ethical traditions that informed how one understood the ten principles were primarily Western. Categories of utilitarian thinking, concepts of rights and duties, notions of social justice, the common good, and the ancient verities of virtues were at the heart of one's understanding of the imperatives of business ethics and the meaning of the ten principles. The global economic world of the second decade is increasingly populated by globalizing firms from China, India, Central and Eastern Europe, South America, and Africa. These companies and their leaders bring the philosophical and ethical insights of Hinduism, Buddhism, Daoism, and other religions to global commerce. It is unclear what impact this will have on our understanding of the ten principles, but the dialogue with these traditions is an important agenda for the second decade.

This dialogue may lead to what has been called a "global ethic." There are several initiatives underway to understand the valuable insights that each religious and philosophical tradition brings to global commerce, and to ask whether one can formulate a truly global ethic. What is clear is that ten years from now we will understand the Global Compact principles differently because of the richness of these diverse traditions.

Closely related to the question of what insights will be drawn from different ethical and spiritual traditions is a cultural question. Do peoples in different cultures define the purpose of life and therefore the goals of the ten principles differently? Does human aspiration, happiness, and thriving mean different things in different cultures? Is "ethical" behavior to be defined differently in a country where people are more rather than less oriented toward spiritual fulfillment? Are the goals of the ten principles to be understood differently in a Buddhist society than in a secular society? Is good corporate citizenship to be defined very differently in one society versus another? What implications would this have for the global implementation of the commitments in the principles?

Another dimension of how the ten principles will be defined over the next years is the impact of the different national economic systems. Is corporate citizenship very different in a predominantly market economy from one primarily directed by the state? What difference does it make to desired corporate environmental performance that a company is based or operates in a market that is state-controlled versus another operating in free market economies? Is the meaning of each of the ten principles different in one economy versus another? How will the Global Compact cope with identified differences?

WHAT MECHANISMS AND INFLUENCES WILL THE GLOBAL COMPACT RELY ON?

The second question driving Global Compact strategy for its second decade is a long-standing one but central to its direction and success. What mechanisms, whether regulatory, otherwise coercive, or just encouraging, will lead companies to adopt and pursue the ten principles more aggressively? The Global Compact, emanating from the United

Nations, gives a few observers the hope that a regime of *global governance*, at least over our largest global businesses, may be in the early stages. Others discount this possibility, saying that the trend, even in more state-controlled economies, is toward less business regulation. Will a system, or partial system, of global economic governance be the mechanism by which companies in 2021 are held to the ten principles? There have been notable developments toward global governance in selected areas, including the Law of the Seas, which came into effect in 1994. Some see future governance developments in the need for global financial and environmental regulation and for setting common standards for telecommunications.

A second possible response to the question of what will be the primary mechanism by which the ten principles will be enforced is *state-based regulation* and controls created by individual governments, sometimes with extraterritorial extensions. Certainly, there are signs that some concerns of the ten principles are being enacted broadly by member states. In the field of corruption, for example, the 1978 United States Foreign Corrupt Practices Act has now been followed by the UK Anti-Bribery Act and other national laws designed to control corruption both within the nation's borders and beyond. This pattern may be repeated in the other areas of the ten principles, knitting together a web of national regulations and laws, each with some degree of extraterritoriality. This process may be aided by a more active adoption of United Nations "Conventions," legal commitments meant to be implemented by all member states.

A third possibility is a more active promotion of *best practices or voluntary global standards*, which would define more explicitly acceptable behavior for a global company. Already in some societies, including China, there is a concept of dividing companies into two groups, those that operate by local standards and those that operate by "international standards." Further development of this concept might incorporate many of the expectations of the ten principles, resulting in a common understanding of companies that meet international standards of corporate citizenship as well as financial reporting and otther activities.

There are innumerable voluntary international standards regimes and organizations created over the past two decades, covering workplace standards, operations in South Africa and Northern Ireland, environmental behavior, and other fields. In a few areas of Global Compact concern, these international standards efforts have achieved broad acceptance. Most notable among these are the human rights principles developed by John Ruggie and adopted in 2011 as the UN Guiding Principles for Business and Human Rights. Earlier, with the leadership of veteran diplomat Richard Holbrooke, the Business Coalition on AIDS was turned into the Business Coalition on HIV/AIDS, Tuberculosis and Malaria in 2002, and more recently into GBCHealth. The best practices and standards promulgated by these two organizations have a moral force beyond the norm of other voluntary international standards. They may even prove to have a legal force, since legal authorities in various countries use these standards to define what "normal care" or "prudent action" demands.

A fourth mechanism is *market demand*, as influenced by the attributes of product or a corporate reputation for citizenship. Will consumers demand that the global businesses they patronize adhere to the ten principles or produce products consistent with the principles? How much are consumers willing to pay for "green products" or "responsible behavior" by companies? There are clearly examples in each country of businesses that have developed devoted consumer followings by producing responsible products or demonstrating responsible behavior. However, there are also indications that consumers will make a "responsible choice" only if the prices for such products are at least comparable to the prices of competitors, and that they will flee quickly from high-priced responsible products or companies.

A fifth mechanism is through the succession of a *generation of responsible corporate executives* to the leadership of global firms. The Global Compact and other organizations have advocated for acceptance of the Principles for Responsible Management Education (PRME) as a way of changing the mind-set and values of the next generation of business leaders. These principles, which specify the kind of management education that should be offered in the world's MBA classrooms, are built on the hope that a more enlightened leadership will follow the ten principles as a matter of philosophy and commitment. It is difficult to evaluate this hope. The subject of business ethics and corporate responsibility was introduced into United States business education in the late 1970s, but there is little evidence that this has led in the last thirty-five years to more enlightened U.S. business leadership.

Finally, a new interest has grown over the last ten years in the possibility that *investor pressure* might become the most effective force promoting responsible business. Similar to educational standards for MBA programs, investor advocacy for responsible business behavior has a long history, beginning in 1970 with a campaign by a small group of reformist investors in General Motors. This led in the United States to an investor responsibility movement that focused on getting businesses out of apartheid South Africa, on environmental performance, and later, on human rights violations across the globe. In the last decade, however, there are signs that a new, more significant investor movement may lead to greater effects.

In the early 2000s, CERES, a coalition of environmental organizations promoting standards of global corporate environmental behavior, relaunched itself more deliberately as a coalition of environmentalists and *investors* committed to seeking solutions to the sustainability challenges of global climate change and water shortages. Most significantly, CERES started a campaign to educate large institutional investors on the financial impact of these environmental challenges. The results have been significant. Many of the world's largest institutional investors have joined the Investor Network on Climate Risk, created to encourage the disclosure of companies' climate-related risk. CERES has been successful convincing large investors that their long-term financial interests are inextricably tied to corporate environmental policies. This may represent a new model of investor activism that can be replicated in other areas of the concerns expressed in the ten principles. The Global Compact is now a partner in CERES' long-standing system of voluntary corporate environmental reporting, known as the Global Reporting Initiative.

HOW AGGRESSIVE WILL THE GLOBAL COMPACT BE IN PURSUING ITS OBJECTIVES?

The final question before the United Nations Global Compact is what it will expect of its own members. In its earliest days, the Global Compact welcomed all companies, expecting little beyond a one-page letter from the CEO by which the company endorsed the ten principles (originally, nine) and agreed to report once a year on some aspect of company efforts to implement the principles. After it became clear that many companies made the initial pledge but did little to implement the principles, the Global Compact took a second step to enforce the requirement that annual reports be filed. Over the last few years, the Compact has suspended the membership of more than 4,000 former members. As of 2013, even the initial commitment made by companies joining the Global Compact has been enhanced. Companies now pledge to make the ten principles "an integral part of business strategy, day-to-day operations and organizational culture," to integrate the Global Compact and its principles "in the decision-making processes of the highest-level governance body," and to "integrate in its annual report . . . a description of the ways in which it implements the principles and supports broader development objectives." The Global Compact also required that the commitment to join the Global Compact be "supported by the highest-level Governance body of the organization (e.g., the Board)" and that companies consider contributing financially to the support of the Global Compact. Suggested fees run from USD 500 to USD 10,000, depending on the firm's sales or revenue.

In a 2010 development, the Global Compact has established a new and enhanced level of Global Compact leadership, called the "Global Compact LEAD" program, for fifty companies that have a history of the most active engagement with the Global Compact, either locally or globally. While selection and participation in the LEAD program does not represent a "seal of approval" or "endorsement" by the United Nations, companies selected will undoubtedly reap some degree of reputational advantage. The Global Compact candidly states that the existence of the LEAD program "is designed to challenge highly engaged companies in the UN Global Compact to reach further, to experiment, to innovate, and to share learnings." This group of companies will set a higher standard, an "aspirational" standard, which can then be used to raise expectations of all Global Compact members.

Recent structural changes in the Global Compact have encouraged more active engagement with the principles. Over the first decade of the Global Compact, members gathered in committees to work on individual issues and principles. However, over the past few years, these issue groups have been increasingly formalized and have taken the lead both in networking with other global organizations that address the same issues and in publishing a growing body of best practices. Similarly, the Compact has enhanced the structure and responsibilities of its local and national networks, making the formation of national networks a greater priority. It is hoped that having an active Global Compact presence close to member companies will lead to greater engagement and greater implementation of the ten principles.

Some critics still question whether the Global Compact has asked enough of its members, but earlier, organized protests against the weaknesses of the Global Compact appear to have faded. Nonetheless, the Global Compact will continue to be faced with questions about how aggressive it should be in encouraging its members' progress in implementing the ten principles.

THE ACCOMPLISHMENTS OF the United Nations Global Compact in its first decade are significant. While some may hold that the organization did not press companies hard enough, it has continually enhanced the expectations of its members and upgraded its own capacity to influence and assist their efforts to implement the ten principles. One hopes that the Global Compact's leadership will continue to be as dedicated and effective as that of its first decade.

One also hopes that in 2021, on its twentieth anniversary, the meaning of the ten principles will be more fully elaborated and that every global company of that time will feel compelled to be an active member of the Global Compact process. But there is considerable work—and at least the three questions outlined in this essay—to be addressed over the second decade.

21 | **Beyond Corporate Responsibility to the Common Good**
The Millennium Development Goals, UN Global Compact, and Business Enterprise

Sandra Waddock

The breadth and depth of the issues that abound in the world suggest that they are systemic, and must be dealt with by seeking root causes and fundamental issues. Corporate responsibility measures—which generally accept the system as given—will not get us to the systemic changes that are needed for sustainability, social justice, and democracy to thrive. For that, we need more fundamental change—in the purpose of the corporation, in the dominance of financial interests over the "real" economy, in the distribution of profits, and in the conversation about what it means to be in society collectively. Certainly, the United Nations Global Compact (UNGC) and the Millennium Development Goals (MDGs) represent positive steps toward greater corporate citizenship from businesses and greater awareness of the steps that countries (and others) need to take in achieving a more equitable and just world. Capitalism, at least as it has evolved in the past few decades, needs reform, not only to deal with the obvious flaws exposed during the 2008 meltdown and ensuing Great Recession, but also to deal with the very real issues of climate change and all of its implications.

Business as usual will not get us there. We need a societal, if not a planetary, perspective on the role of business—and the other important institutions that constitute human civilization—to help us get there. Real wealth would find its basis in a just society and in a collective understanding that we are all on this planet together, that its resources are limited, and that we need to be stewards of those resources. It would be a wealth that is based on human connection and community, on sufficiency and equity, engagement with things that are really important in life—love, laughter, joy, connection with others, art and music—and not in the continual quest for more "stuff," with which our current form of capitalism seems to be obsessed.

A decade or more into the life of the Millennium Development Goals (MDGs) and the United Nations Global Compact (UNGC), the world arguably has significantly changed, but, perhaps more significantly, has not changed nearly enough. During the first ten years of the twenty-first century, we experienced the Enron, WorldCom, and related scandals, the advent of human-induced climate change,[1] a global financial crisis built upon a now collapsing and highly suspect mortgage industry, and a financial services industry that has created a global gambling casino focused mainly on speculation and the accumulation of wealth for those who are already well off, with little consideration for the health or well-being of others in society (or the natural environment), rather than on any genuinely productive activity. Global inequity has continued to increase, as the rich grow richer and the poor, with some exceptions, do not change their lot very much. Ecologists note that virtually every ecological system is in decline, many large mammals are on the verge of extinction, and species loss is occurring at devastating rates.

This list of the world's ills could go on. Consider the following:

- The continuing gaps between rich and poor (more than three billion of the world's nearly seven billion people live on less than $2.50 a day and 1.2 billion on less than $1 a day; 1.1 billion people have no access to clean water; 2.4 billion lack adequate sanitation facilities), North and South, haves and have-nots, and economically developed and undeveloped nations.
- The ecological devastation that is consistently wrought in the name of "progress," "economic development," and "competitive advantage"

by companies, who (among other practices) continue to produce numerous products using strategies of planned obsolescence, namely, products that will shortly become outdated, broken, unfashionable, or otherwise made useless within a relatively short period of time, ending up in overflowing landfills or incinerators.

- The seemingly unceasing wave of scandals that have hit company after company, not to mention financial institution after financial institution, which have created enormous government bailouts and the rhetoric of companies or institutions that are "too big to fail." Within these institutions, think of the many individuals within those companies who have been involved in "unethical" practices that have resulted in great harm for their stakeholders. And consider the many who have benefited from questionable practices by getting rich.

- Think beyond business. Consider the scandals that have hit institution after institution—from the Catholic Church to the Red Cross and United Way. Consider the insidious institutional corruption that seems rampant in governments today,[2] including notably the U.S. government after the already infamous 2010 U.S. Supreme Court *Citizens United* decision, which now allows corporations to make unlimited (and nontransparent) campaign contributions, thereby increasing the already powerful ties between industry and politics at some risk to democratic processes.

- Further, witness the enormous gaps between the pay of the average worker and the pay of CEOs, even when the companies they lead are not doing well even for shareholders.

This litany of social and ecological problems, institutional corruption, and increasing divides among peoples is discouraging at best. Yet the first years of this century also witnessed the emergence of corporate responsibility initiatives in many large (and many small and medium-sized) companies, along with numerous global institutions aimed at enhancing sustainability and the common good, raising awareness of these issues,[3] and building a new sense of responsibility among businesses and other institutions. Among these institutions is the UN Global Compact, which ten years after its launch, had more than 8,700 signatories, including more than 7,700 businesses operating in 130 countries.[4]

Also among major global initiatives are the Millennium Development Goals, which are aimed at reducing inequity and poverty in the world; the Principles for Responsible Investment, which were launched in 2005 and by 2013 had some one thousand signatories controlling more than $30 trillion (US);[5] and the Global Reporting Initiative, which has become the global standard for ESG (environmental, social, and governance) reporting. These represent only a small sampling of the many new initiatives that have sprung up that implicitly or explicitly try to articulate the relationship of business to society and make it a productive and healthy one.[6]

The breadth and depth of the problems that abound in the world suggest that they are systemic, meaning that they cannot be resolved by surface level or piecemeal approaches but must be dealt with by seeking root causes and fundamental issues. The macro-system that humanity (or, mainly, the world's richest industrialized nations) has created since World War II to organize the world has fostered this inequity. It has also fostered the squandering of planetary resources and possibly a significant misalignment between the interests of corporations and the goals on the basis of which many democratic societies were founded.[7] In other words, the current system tends to favor economic over societal or community interests, growth over stability, and use of resources rather than conservation of them. It has generated a situation in which issues of what might be termed the common good are frequently overlooked or shunted aside if they do not add to the bottom line. Yet entrenched interests, including the elite and powerful wealthy nations, corporations, and individuals who have benefited from this system, are unlikely to move willingly toward change.

It is clear to many observers that a "business as usual" orientation will not get us the necessary changes;[8] indeed, it is business as usual that has created and sustained the issues facing the planet. Yet we know that societies need enterprises and, in particular, businesses. Businesses play an essential social role in the provision of jobs, needed goods and services, and economic stability; they are foundational to the world we live in. Yet the problems identified above are systemic problems. They highlight a system that lacks integrity insofar as the *common* good of humanity and nature's other creatures is concerned: it lacks coherence, equity, sustainability, and fairness for all. It is a system that currently seems geared toward providing ever more for the already well off, while reaping advantage over the less fortunate. These issues, in my view, reflect a system that is badly broken and in need of significant repair and rethinking. They can only be changed if we begin thinking systemically about what needs to change and how it might change.

Currently, however, forces and dynamics in the system mitigate against ethical or responsible behavior aimed at the common good (beyond economics) for humanity over the long term and particularly for the planet as a whole. As we think about the implications of this system, we all need to begin to think more broadly, more systemically, and more pragmatically about the pressures and dynamics of the system as it currently exists, and how those pressures affect the planet and, importantly for us, its capacity to support human civilization.

When an entire system lacks integrity, it is, arguably, somewhat of a lost cause to expect all but the strongest individuals or companies to exhibit integrity (as a sense of the whole) because many of the pressures and dynamics of the system work against them. To achieve any fundamental change, we need to begin a new conversation or, as stakeholder theorist R. Edward Freeman would put it, a new narrative about the role of business in society, as well as about the common good and how all can contribute to it.

UNGC AND MDGS: CHANGE AND NO CHANGE

The UNGC and the MDGs are core elements of the emerging infrastructure that is pressuring companies for greater responsibility and seeking to raise the standards of corporate practice and corporate engagement with societal and ecological issues. Below, I present a brief overview of both initiatives and their status.

Progress on the UNGC

Ten years into its existence, or by 2011, the UNGC, which bills itself as the world's largest corporate citizenship initiative, has launched numerous other initiatives, including the Principles for Responsible Investment (PRI), the Principles for Responsible Management Education (PRME), the Women's Empowerment Principles, and the Principles for Social Investment (PSI). The UNGC has also produced numerous tools and resources to help companies implement its ten core principles (and the MDGs), including the 2010 launch of the Blueprint for Corporate Sustainability Leadership and the UN Global Compact Management Model, and other resources for dealing with human rights, labor principles, human trafficking, water policy, and anti-corruption. At its 2010 Leaders Summit in New York, the signatories signed the "New York Declaration," which calls for collective action to address the world's challenges related to global integration, sustainable development, and peace and security.[9]

During its first ten years, the UNGC has "done more than any initiative to globalise the idea that business can be both good for business, and important for the world," according to Jem Bendell.[10] But, as Bendell also notes and the data cited above suggest, the world has not notably changed the relationship between business and societies during these years of the Compact's existence. One could also note that even the approximately 7,700 members of the UNGC represent but a small fraction of the more than 70,000 multinational corporations and millions of small and medium-sized businesses in the world. Further, because the corporate responsibility agenda is now well established, the role of the UN and the UNGC in particular with respect to society needs to grow and evolve. Bendell also indicates that the UN needs to step up to the challenge of dealing with difficult issues related to companies, to widen its scope to deal with the economic governance issues facing the world, and to face the difficulties of coping with trade and investment policy agreements, as well as creating fair and sustainable economies.

There have been significant achievements for the UNGC. Yet critics also abound, frequently taking the UNGC to task for its lack of capacity to ensure that signatories actually live up to the ten principles. The fact that there are few requirements for signatories, other than submitting a letter of support for the UNGC from the chief executive officer, and an annual "Communication on Progress," means that virtually any interested company (or other type of enterprise or organization) can sign on to the Compact. One common criticism is that companies sign the Compact as part of a "bluewashing" strategy, wrapping themselves in the UN's blue flag to gain whatever reputational advantage might be associated with this action because of the legitimacy cast by the United Nations in most parts of the world.[11]

Progress on the MDGs

The Millennium Development Goals Report 2010[12] highlights some of the significant achievements of the MDGs during their first ten years:

- Generally, we are on track to reduce poverty by half (from 1990s number) by 2015, meaning that some 920 million people will live under the international poverty line.
- There have been significant advances in getting children into school in many poor nations, significantly, in sub-Saharan Africa.
- Malaria, HIV, and measles interventions (including bed nets and more effective treatments) have reduced childhood deaths from these diseases from 12.5 million in 1990 to 8.8 million in 2008.
- Tree planting and natural forest expansion have reduced the rate of deforestation (though it remains high).
- The gap in water availability between rural and urban areas has narrowed, though water safety is still a major issue.

Despite the progress in some areas, significant challenges to achieving the MDGs remain, including the impact of climate change on vulnerable populations, armed conflict, displacement of people from conflict or persecution, and undernourishment, and some 1.4 billion people still live in extreme poverty. Other aims that are proving intractable include equality and the empowerment of women, reducing the gap between rich and poor, ensuring that girls are educated on a par with boys, adequate maternal health care for the poor, and ending undernourishment, extreme poverty, and lack of access to sanitation, not to mention solving many ecological issues.

BUSINESS ENGAGEMENT WITH THE MDGS AND THE UNGC

One of the two main objectives of the UNGC (in addition to mainstreaming the ten UNGC principles into business practice) is to "catalyze actions in support of broader UN goals, including the Millennium Development Goals."[13] Just how businesses can engage on these goals, however, is the subject of some debate, particularly as the MDGs are aimed largely at governments. Still, according to a 2008 report by Jane Nelson and David Prescott, businesses can contribute to the achievement of the MDGs in multiple ways. For example, Nelson and Prescott argue that within the domain of business operations, businesses need to produce safe and affordable products and services and to generate income and investment as well as jobs that help to develop human resources in developing nations. They can help to foster entrepreneurial activities and local business infrastructure, while simultaneously spreading responsible practices and standards, supporting technology transfer, and otherwise building local infrastructure.[14]

Because expectations of businesses today include charitable contributions, Nelson and Prescott argue that they can also contribute to the achievement of the MDGs using their philanthropy. For example, companies could support training and educational programs (particularly around health and environmental issues), building local capacity for community leaders and social entrepreneurs, and enhancing capability for local governance and a civil society "voice,'" among other possibilities.[15]

A third role that Nelson and Prescott see for business has to do with public policy and involves creating frameworks for advocacy, policy dialogue, and institution building locally. Using numerous examples, these authors highlight the ways in which businesses can support each of the MDGS, which are aimed at eradicating extreme poverty and hunger, achieving universal primary education, promoting gender equity and empowering women, reducing child mortality, improving material health, combating HIV/AIDS, malaria, and other diseases, ensuring environmental sustainability, and developing a global partnership for development.[16]

NOT CHANGED ENOUGH

Even if businesses did all of the things that Nelson and Prescott call for, however, the necessary systemic changes are unlikely, partly because the UNGC, progressive as it is, pretty much accepts the system as it is currently structured—business as usual. Though much has changed in the first ten years of the UNGC and MDGs, the evidence indicates that, at the same time, in many respects little has changed. Business as usual means an increasing materialism and consumption, waste, and lack of progress on alleviating the worst of environmental problems (or even the easiest). These issues are among the significant problems the world now faces, not to mention a continued emphasis on growth—when it is exactly growth in many ways that has created our current global ecological problems.

We know from the market flaws and collapse of 2008 that the economic system has significant and fundamental problems. But at the same time, the assumption almost inevitably is that more growth is the solution for economic health—and even for achievement of the MDGs.[17] Indeed, in the 2010 report by the UN Development Program (UNDP) on the MDGs, the first of six roles articulated for business was that of economic growth, because growth (and, wrongly, productivity, which actually reduces the number of available jobs) is seen as the main driver of job creation, higher income, and new opportunities for producing income. Notably, this report also argues that the "trickle down" from corporate growth to jobs is insufficient and that companies need to assume five other roles, including what the UNDP calls "inclusive business models" that "consciously include poor people into [companies'] value chains."[18] These relationships are as producers, partners, employees, and consumers. Other roles for businesses in achieving the MDGs include the contribution of knowledge and capabilities, innovation, replication of successes, and advocacy.[19]

Note that in all of these examples the fundamental assumption remains one of continued growth, despite growing recognition that it is exactly the growth assumption that has created many of today's problems. Thus, there is a significant tension between the environmental imperative to deal much more effectively with climate change and all of the other ecological issues facing the planet, to which population growth and the needs and demands that come from a surging populace are surely contributors, and the "need" for economic growth.

SOCIETY OR ECONOMY?

Robert Reich, when he was labor secretary of the United States, starkly posed the fundamental issue being addressed here when he asked, "Do you want to live in an economy or a society?" It is the distinction between society and economy that underlies the issue of business's role in society, and whether business *is* the same as society and therefore dominated by wealth maximization and economic thinking, or whether we want and need, as humans, to think beyond economic values to what makes a world worth living in.

In many respects, the conversation about the business case for joining initiatives like the UNGC or working with the MDGs must recognize that there are really two conversations that are important. The first is based on economics, which is about money conceived as wealth as the central value. Let's call this conversation the economics perspective. Despite the fact that economics is often touted as being value free, it is actually far from "value free"—it is just that the set of values considered relevant and important is limited to financial wealth and material goods and the relevant stakeholder set is equally restricted to investors. Pretty much everything, other than the assumptions of rationality, self-interest, and market efficiency, represent externalities from the economics perspective. Further, measurement of wealth is based on indicators such as GDP (gross domestic product) or GNP (gross national product), in which "caring" work is not counted and the depletion of the natural environment (among other negatives) is considered an addition to wealth. Since their inception, these have been known to be limited measures.[20]

"Doing good" is narrowly bounded in the economics perspective to mean "doing well" (financially) for shareholders, even through a profitable firm may actually be doing harm, for instance, to the natural environment or to other stakeholders. As examples, think of the clear-cutting of forests, blowing off the tops of mountains to obtain coal or minerals beneath, or miles of monoculture crops that invite ever-increasing applications of man-made fertilizers and pesticides, which then run off into the local waters. Or consider what is sold as necessary through sophisticated marketing techniques that manufacture new needs among consumers. We could also mention toxic and addictive products such as tobacco, and many other consumer products that are essentially useless or filled with untested toxic materials. We could note many of the high-fat, high fructose corn syrup "food products" now sold on supermarket shelves as nutrition. The list goes on, all in the purported interest of maximizing shareholder wealth, which often means in practice maximizing executives' wealth.

The second conversation, which applies to the rationale behind the UNGC and MDGs, is really about a different set of values, beyond monetary ones, that involve ethics, responsibility, and the creation of what used to be talked about as a good society.[21] Let us call this second perspective the societal perspective. From the societal perspective, observers can claim that business has an important set of *roles* in creating a good society, but that business is not the only important element in constructing a healthy, viable, and connected society. In this context, many people try to make the so-called business case for corporate responsibility, claiming that somehow companies can "do well by doing good." Surely it is helpful when such a relationship works, but the role of business in society is not fundamentally about "doing well by doing good" as much as it is about the inherent responsibilities that companies bear simply because of their power, clout, and impact on society, nature, and stakeholders. The very existence of corporations originates in early corporate charters, according to which these companies exist to *serve* society's needs and interests, not to dominate them.

Unlike the economics perspective, which narrowly focuses on wealth maximization for a select set of stakeholders (the shareholders), the societal perspective focuses on issues of human values beyond the material and on a wide range of stakeholders. Such values might encompass, for example, community and connectedness, artistic, aesthetic, and spiritual values, social justice, equity, and other moral considerations, and ecological sustainability with all of its associated complexity. The societal perspective recognizes value (and values) in multiple spheres, including the natural environment with all of its manifold creatures and ecosystems, and spheres of human civilization encompassing political, civil society, *and* business activities.

In the societal perspective, wealth is not necessarily restricted to financial and material wealth. It is more closely related to some definition of well-being (which indicators like the Genuine Progress Indicator, a proposed alternative to GDP/GNP, attempt to capture).[22] Of course, as economists would probably be the first to argue, the measurement of noneconomic value(s) is much more complex, difficult, contested, and ambiguous than economic or financial measurement, and the societal perspective does not readily lend itself to any clearly defined set of assumptions. But it may present a more robust understanding of how human civilization actually works and what is valued.

Individuals embracing the societal perspective simply do not "buy" many of the fundamental assumptions of the economics perspective. Even without its limiting assumptions and distortions, the economics perspective also forgets the historical roots of the corporation. A corporation is intrinsically *embedded* in society and is granted a charter by a government (called papers of incorporation), at least in theory, to serve society's interests. At least, that was the original intent of the early legislation surrounding corporations, in part because of the fear that without such legal limits, there would be a narrowing of corporate logic and the power held by a corporation to serving a small set of powerful interests. Corporations, or any businesses for that matter, cannot thrive unless humanity is thriving.

THE PURPOSE OF THE FIRM

Milton Friedman and more recently Aneel Karnani have argued that the sole purpose of the firm is to maximize shareholder wealth.[23] The British/Irish thinker Charles Handy some years ago issued a robust refutation of this position, arguing in "What's a Business For?" that simply by playing by the existing rules, capitalists could potentially bring down capitalism. Handy's analysis was prescient, in light of the 2008 economic meltdown caused by what Alan Greenspan once called "irrational exuberance" in the purportedly "free" (but actually, notably distorted) financial markets. Handy suggested that what he called the "American disease" had distorted the nation's business culture, "a culture underpinned by a doctrine that proclaimed the market king, always gave priority to the shareholder, and believed that business was the key engine of progress and thus should take precedence in policy decisions."[24]

That, of course, is exactly what has taken place as the "purpose" of the firm was redirected to a shareholder-dominant perspective following the Reagan-Thatcher revolution of the early 1980s. Yet we know that the corporation is a creature *of* society, created in and by members of society, to serve society's interests—and those interests are broader than, although they certainly include, purely economic interests. Originally, corporate charters were granted only so long as the company continued to serve society's interests. Perhaps, as suggested by the instigators of the Corporation 2020 initiative, which is trying to redesign the corporation to meet twenty-first-century needs, and a more recent initiative called the Global Corporate Charter, corporations should be forced to return to those roots of serving society.[25] Minimally, according to the societal perspective, corporations should be expected to meet not only financial goals but also goals related to ESG—environment and ecology, society, and governance—as part of their charter.

The argument that the sole purpose of the firm is to maximize shareholder wealth presents business strategists with a conundrum, because one of the first questions that strategists always ask is, "What business are you in?" Exactly what is the "business" associated with maximizing shareholder wealth? Perhaps it is today's rampant speculation, but it is difficult to see how that activity has added much real value to the economy. Indeed, former Federal Reserve Chairman Paul Volker, an economist, has publicly stated that the only innovation of the financial services industry in the twenty-five years before the economic meltdown of 2008 that has improved society has been the ATM machine, "which at least is useful."[26]

Back to the point: how can any company or leader define a business without first taking into account what customers might need or want, what the company and its employees want to produce or deliver, what suppliers can provide to engage the production process, and what innovations are needed? Such are the questions that can begin to define a business and its purpose. As Freeman has noted, profits are like red blood cells—they are necessary for life, but creating red blood cells is certainly not the *purpose* of anyone's life.[27]

Customers actually *do* come first in business because, without them, the business does not exist, at least not for long. Nor can businesses exist without employees to do the necessary work, suppliers to supply needed raw materials or other resources, and, of course, investors to supply the capital (though these need not always be shareholders in the current sense). All of these stakeholders make important contributions to or investments in the business, just as investors do in providing funds. They also take risks with respect to the business, as do investors, though risks of a different sort. Purpose gives meaning and direction—and necessarily goes far beyond maximizing shareholder wealth if it is to achieve those ends.

NO MORE BUSINESS AS USUAL:
A "COMMON GOOD" CONCEPTION OF BUSINESS

Clive Crook, who argued against the concept of corporate social responsibility in a 2005 *Economist* article, correctly stated that CSR "is at best a gloss on capitalism, not the deep system reform that its champions deem desirable."[28] But he stated further that "capitalism does not need the fundamental reform that many CSR advocates wish for." Interestingly, the same journal published an article in 2008 entitled "Just Good Business," with the headline that CSR, "once a do-gooding sideshow, is now seen as mainstream" although "too few companies are doing it well."[29] Initiatives like the UNGC and the MDGs have helped to create this change in context for business.

But Crook, fundamentally, is wrong about capitalism not needing to be reformed. Capitalism, at least as it has evolved in the past few decades, *does* need fundamental reform, not only to deal with the obvious flaws exposed during the 2008 meltdown and ensuing Great Recession, but also to deal with the very real issues of climate change and all of its implications, on which there is global scientific agreement and limited capacity to respond within the current system.

There are many possibilities for regulatory change and reform, but I will mention only a few. As Corporation 2020 argues, there is a need for fundamental redefinition, redesign, and repurposing of the firm to incorporate responsible environmental, social, and governance (ESG) into the core purposes of the firm and meet twenty-first-century needs.[30] Given the externalities arising from doing business as usual—such things as air and water pollution—and in particular the growth-at-any-cost model embedded in today's capitalism, issues of climate change and sustainability imply a clear need for accounting and management practice reform that requires companies to internalize any externalities associated with their production and other processes, such as outsourcing, which have severely disruptive impacts on many local communities and their populace. The impact of rising levels of carbon dioxide on the environment also necessitates a move toward carbon neutrality by all types of enterprises.

Companies need to be encouraged, perhaps through legislation and regulatory reform and incentives, to take their stakeholder impacts into account in their decision-making processes; to use their considerable innovative capacities to produce new forms of carbon-neutral energy; to use and create many fewer toxic chemicals in their production of goods and services; to focus on producing durable and useful products rather than faddish products designed to be obsolete within six months of their release; and to use renewable (rather than nonrenewable) resources, while ensuring that the renewal actually takes place. The UNGC represents an important step in bringing these issues to the attention of corporate decision makers—albeit not in nearly sufficient depth or breadth as yet.

A business-as-usual perspective, with no changes to free market ideology, means continuing with an economic system premised on constant growth, planned obsolescence, increasing materialism and consumption patterns, and the shifting of financial wealth to the already wealthy elite. But is this linear and wasteful system really still feasible in the world that we now live in, if we are honest with ourselves?

A "common good" conception of business in society argues for something quite different. As Mallen Baker has argued,[31] we are creating a situation in which we are choosing to "test the carrying capacity of the planet," by living on the edge of potential planetary overload. As Baker notes, such a test has potentially catastrophic consequences if we fail it. Is it feasible to continue to push a growth agenda in any sense—whether population, economic, or other types of growth—on a planet in which humanity is already in "ecological overshoot," each year drawing more resources from the earth than can be replenished within that year?[32]

As I have tried to illustrate above, the economics perspective alone will not get us to what Malcolm McIntosh and I have called a "SEE change."[33] A SEE change is change to a sustainable enterprise economy, something that is desperately needed and in which businesses, big and small, play important, indeed crucial, roles. Yet it is exactly such a transition that we believe we need to effect on this planet if living conditions for our grandchildren are to support anything like today's lifestyles in developed nations. Business as usual will not get us there. Economics alone will not get us there, particularly with its current limiting set of assumptions. We need a societal, if not a planetary, perspective on the role of business—and the other important institutions that constitute human civilization—to help us get there. Antonio Argandoña has argued that a possible theoretical foundation for stakeholder theory is the common good.[34] SEE change—change to a sustainable enterprise economy—involves greater creativity, a human scale, businesses that inherently recognize their social purposes, multiple stakeholders, and an emphasis on preserving resources for the future. Growth cannot be at the heart of SEE change, since growth conflicts with the need for sustaining at least the current level of resources for future generations, and the need to think not just of the individual (or company) good but of the good of all of the planet's creatures, on which we are symbiotically dependent.

Stakeholders are the ones affected by the decisions, actions, practices, and behaviors of both individuals and organizations—and on a planetary level, all living creatures and systems are stakeholders.[35] So when leaders in companies make decisions to maximize wealth for shareholders that have serious detrimental consequences for other stakeholders, they are making decisions with significant ethical implications and consequences (for example, the community devastation that comes from large-scale layoffs, the negative ecological consequences of certain "efficient" industrial practices such as strip mining, or unsustainable industrial agricultural practices fostered by the profits-come-first mentality).

To the extent that such practices are established norms, based on the primacy of shareholders (who are not real owners in any sense of that word, as Charles Handy eloquently points out),[36] they highlight problems in the way that the economic system itself is structured. Just because we have put shareholders first for the past fifty years and more does not mean that they *are* necessarily more important than other stakeholders or than the natural environment, on whose conditions we depend for our very existence. Humans created the system and humans have the capacity to change it—but first they must recognize that changes are needed.

With common sense and a new sensibility toward what we really need to make our lives happy and fulfilling, we can arguably create a more equitable world, where businesses and other institutions serve everyone's interests rather than those of a few, and where all individuals have access to education, jobs, and opportunities for self-development and service to others. But I don't think achieving the necessary shift of mind away from materialism to a new understanding of wealth will be easy. The question is, where do we begin?

NOTES

1. Bill McKibben, *Eaarth: Making a Life on a Tough New Planet* (New York: Times Books, 2010); and Intergovernmental Panel on Climate Change, *Climate Change 2007: Synthesis Report: Summary for Policymakers* (2007), available at http://www.ipcc.ch/pdf/assessment-report/ar4/syr/ar4_syr_spm.pdf.

2. See, for example, Lawrence Lessig, "Institutional Integrity: *Citizens United* and the Path to a Better Democracy," *Huffington Post*, January 22, 2010, available at http://www.huffingtonpost.com/lawrence-lessig/institutional -integrity-c_b_433394.html.

3. See Sandra Waddock, "Building a New Institutional Infrastructure for Corporate Responsibility," *Academy of Management Perspectives* 22, no. 3 (August 2008): 87–108.

4. UN Global Compact, http://www.unglobalcompact.org, and Overview, http://unglobalcompact.org/HowToParticipate/Business_Participation /index.html.

5. Principles for Responsible Investment, press release of September 14, 2010, available at http://d2m27378y09r06.cloudfront.net/viewer/?file=wp -content/uploads/2010_Report-on-progress-press-release1.pdf.

6. For example, see Waddock, "Building a New Institutional Infrastructure."

7. See John Cavanagh et al., *Alternatives to Economic Globalization: A Better World Is Possible* (San Francisco: Berrett-Koehler, 2002).

8. See Juliet Schor, *Plentitude: The New Economics of Real Wealth* (New York: Penguin, 2010).

9. UN Global Compact, *UN Global Compact Leaders Summit 2010: Building a New Era of Sustainability, Summary Report 24–25 June, New York*, available at http://www.unglobalcompact.org/docs/summit2010/2010 _Leaders_Summit_Report.pdf.

10. Jem Bendell, "What If We Are Failing? Towards a Post-Crisis Compact for Systemic Change," *Journal of Corporate Citizenship* 38 (Summer 2010): 27–31; and Bendell, "From Global Compact to Global Impact," *Lifeworth* (August 1, 2010), available at either http://www.lifeworth .com/consult/2010/08/from-global-compact-to-global-impact/ or http://www .lifeworth.com/consult/wp-content/uploads/2010/08/globalimpact.pdf.

11. Many of these critiques can be found linked at the website Global Compact Critics, http://globalcompactcritics.blogspot.com/. Also see Elaine Cohen, "The UN Global Compact Celebrates 10 Years of What?" *CSR Wire*

(2010), available at http://www.csrwire.com/csrlive/commentary_detail/3325 -The-UN-Global-Compact-celebrates-10-years-of-what-.

12. United Nations, *Millennium Development Goals Report 2010* (New York: United Nations Department of Economic and Social Affairs, 2010); also available at http://www.un.org/millenniumgoals/pdf/MDG%20Report%2020 10%20En%20r15%20-low%20res%2020100615%20-.pdf.

13. UN Global Compact, "Overview of the UN Global Compact," available at http://unglobalcompact.org/AboutTheGC/index.html.

14. Jane Nelson and David Prescott, *Business and the Millennium Development Goals: A Framework for Action*, 2nd ed. (London: International Business Leaders Forum, 2008), 8.

15. Ibid.

16. For information on the Millennium Development Goals, see http://www.un.org/millenniumgoals/.

17. See Christina Gradl, Subathirai Sivakumaran, and Sahba Sobhani, *The MDGs: Everyone's Business—How Inclusive Business Models Contribute to Development and Who Supports Them* (New York: United Nations Development Program, 2010); also available at http://www.growinginclusivemarkets.org/media/mdgreport/mdgreport_full.pdf.

18. Ibid., 4.

19. Ibid.

20. Robert Costanza, Maureen Hart, Stephen Posner, and John Talbert, "Beyond GDP: The Need for New Measures of Progress," *The Pardee Papers* 4 (January 2009): 7; and Bart Wesselink, Jan Bakkes, Aaron Best, Friedrich Hinterberger, and Patrick ten Brink, "Measurement Beyond GDP," prepared for "Beyond GDP: Measuring Progress, True Wealth, and the Well-Being of Nations," International Conference, November 19–29, 2007, Brussels, Belgium.

21. For example, see Robert Bellah, Richard Madsen, William M. Sullivan, Ann Swidler, and Steven M. Tipton, *The Good Society* (New York: Knopf, 1991).

22. See the initiative "Beyond GDP" at http://www.beyond-gdp.eu/; and "NextStep," Minnesota Sustainable Communities Network, at http://www.nextstep.state.mn.us/res_detail.cfm?id=358, for background on alternatives to GDP.

23. See Milton Friedman, "The Social Responsibility of Business Is to Increase Its Profits," *The New York Times Sunday Magazine* (September 13, 1970); and Aneel Karnani, "The Case Against Corporate Social Responsibility," *Wall Street Journal* (August 23, 2010), available at http://online.wsj.com/article/SB1 0001424052748703338004575230112664504890.html; and Karnani, "Doing Well by Doing Good: The Grand Illusion," *California Management Review* 53, no. 2 (Winter 2011): 69–86.

24. Charles Handy, "What's a Business For?" *Harvard Business Review* (December 2002): 50.

25. Corporation 2020 (at www.corporation2020.org) and Global Corporate Charter (at http://www.gtinitiative.org/documents/IssuePerspectives/GTI-Perspectives-Global_Corporate_Charters.pdf) are initiatives of the Tellus Institute in Boston.

26. "Paul Volcker: Think More Boldly," *Wall Street Journal* (December 14, 2009), available at http://online.wsj.com/article/SB100014240527487048255504574586330960597134.html.

27. See R. Edward Freeman, *Strategic Management: A Stakeholder Approach* (Boston: Pitman, 1984); and Freeman, Jeffrey S. Harrison, and Andrew C. Wicks, *Managing for Stakeholders: Survival, Reputation, and Success* (New Haven: Yale University Press, 2007).

28. Clive Crook, "The Good Company," *The Economist* (January 20, 2005): 9.

29. "Just Good Business: Special Report on Corporate Social Responsibility," *The Economist* (January 17, 2008).

30. See www.corporation2020.org.

31. Mallen Baker, "Global Risks in 2011: The Scale of the Challenge," *Ethical Corporation* (January 18, 2011); available at http://www.ethicalcorp.com/governance-regulation/global-risks-2011-scale-challenge.

32. The Global Footprint Network calculates an approximate date in any given year at which the resource consumption for that year exceeds the planet's ability to replenish those resources within a year. See http://www.footprintnetwork.org/en/index.php/GFN/page/earth_overshoot_day/.

33. Sandra Waddock and Malcolm McIntosh, *SEE Change: Making the Transition to a Sustainable Enterprise Economy* (Sheffield, UK: Greenleaf Publishing, 2011).

34. Antonio Argandoña, "The Stakeholder Theory and the Common Good," *Journal of Business Ethics* 17 (1998): 1093–1102.

35. Sandra Waddock, "A Gaia-Centric Perspective on Stakeholder Theory," presented at the 3rd Stakeholder Conference in Solitude, Utah, December 4–5, 2010.

36. Handy, "What's a Business For?"

22 | **Advancing Human Rights in Developing Countries**

A Voluntary Opportunity or a Moral Obligation for Business?

Oliver F. Williams, C.S.C.

Each of the companies profiled in this volume discusses how they are advancing human rights in accordance with the UN Millennium Development Goals. The question often arises as to whether a company should take on some of the problems of the wider society out of a sense of moral obligation or if these efforts are just examples of corporate philanthropy. What is the role of business when it comes to human rights, and what constructs are helpful in guiding business in making decisions on this issue? This final chapter argues that under certain conditions, a company has the moral responsibility to take on some of the problems in the wider society.

With the advent of the globalization of the economy, multinational firms with operations in developing countries increasingly have been criticized for their human rights records. A subsidiary body of the UN Commission on Human Rights presented in 2003 a draft of a study called the Norms on Transnational Corporations and Other Business Enterprises.[1] The key finding of this study was that businesses and states have the *same* human rights responsibilities: "to promote, secure the fulfillment of, respect, ensure respect of, and protect human rights." Needless to say, this controversial position was received with many misgivings in the business community. To equate the roles of states and business in regard to promoting human rights was a principle most in business could not accept. As a result of the controversy, the UN appointed a Special Representative of the Secretary-General (SRSG) on human rights who was charged to develop a coherent position. This assignment was given to Professor John Ruggie, a lawyer and advisor to the UN and now a professor at the Kennedy School of Harvard University.

After more than five years of research and extensive consultation, in March 2011, Ruggie presented what he called the "Protect, Respect and Remedy" Framework along with "Guiding Principles" that provide helpful recommendations for applying the Framework.[2] The Framework essentially gives business the responsibility to do no harm, to avoid infringing on human rights, and to correct any infringement of rights that is connected to its activity. This responsibility of business to respect human rights entails acting with due diligence, taking measures to be proactive, and avoiding human rights violations. The state in the Framework has the primary duty, and it includes developing "policies, regulation, and adjudication" to protect against human rights violations by business and others and to promote rights. Finally, the Framework calls for effective remedies for those who believe they have been victims of human rights abuses.

The Ruggie Framework puts limits on the obligations of a business in regard to human rights, namely, the responsibility is to do no harm. The Framework makes it clear that the state, and not business, has the positive duty to advance human rights. This position gives considerable comfort to business, which has been the object of increasing demands by NGOs and other civil society actors to accept new social responsibilities to balance their newly acquired power in the global community. For example, one article on the HIV/AIDS pandemic in sub-Saharan Africa, where over twenty-five million people have the disease, cited a critic who "unleashed a verbal broadside against the pharmaceutical companies, and their refusal to provide drugs at cost or, even better, no cost at all." In a similar vein, another article noted that pharmaceutical companies are being "threatened by the National Association of

People Living With AIDS if the firms continued to refuse to provide antiretroviral drugs free of charge."[3] The critics based their arguments on the premise that access to life-saving medicines is a human right and that business, in particular, pharmaceutical companies, ought to meet this right.

Georges Enderle, in chapter 8, presents an excellent reflection on Ruggie's "Protect, Respect and Remedy" Framework. Much of that chapter, which presents the ethical implications of this UN Framework, is assumed in this discussion. Enderle celebrates the fact that the Framework applies to all human rights: civil, political, economic, social, and cultural, as well as the right to development. This is a significant point since some discussions limit the responsibility for business to just some of these rights. He notes that transnational corporations should be conceived of as moral actors, collective entities that act with intention, and therefore can be held accountable by the public. He concludes with a very insightful reflection on whether a business case, enlightened self-interest, is always a sufficient motivation for business to respect human rights. He argues that human rights are "public goods" and therefore "the relevant motivation of the corporation cannot be only self-interest, but has to include, in one form or another, the public interest of securing human rights."

In this final chapter I focus on an issue that Enderle does not discuss: whether corporate responsibility sometimes partially includes the general *promotion* of human rights. What follows are some preliminary reflections on this matter.

WHERE THERE IS POWER, IS THERE ALSO RESPONSIBILITY?

In 2000, the Economic and Social Council of the United Nations stated that "health is a fundamental human right indispensable for the exercise of other human rights."[4] This right is based on the human dignity of the person, and while there is a fairly wide consensus on this right in the global community, views on how to fairly apportion the responsibilities of meeting the right diverge widely. The Ruggie Framework comes down squarely on the side of the state as the entity charged to protect and advance this and all crucial human rights. While some scholars argue that where there is power, there is also responsibility, Ruggie dismissed the possibility of anchoring the responsibility of a company in its power and resources.

A number of stakeholders have asked whether companies have core human rights responsibilities beyond respecting rights. Some have even advocated that businesses' ability to fulfill rights should translate into a responsibility to do so, particularly where government capacity is limited.

Companies may undertake additional human rights commitments for philanthropic reasons, to protect and promote their brand, or to develop new business opportunities. Operational conditions may dictate additional responsibilities in specific circumstances, while contracts with public authorities for particular projects may require them. In other instances, such as natural disasters or public health emergencies, there may be compelling reasons for any social actor with capacity to contribute temporarily. Such contingent and time-bound actions by some companies in certain situations may be both reasonable and desirable.

However, the proposition that corporate human rights responsibilities as a general rule should be determined by companies' capacity, whether absolute or relative to states, is troubling. On that premise, a large and profitable company operating in a small and poor country could soon find itself called upon to perform ever-expanding social and even governance functions—lacking democratic legitimacy, diminishing the state's incentive to build sustainable capacity, and undermining the company's own economic role and possibly its commercial viability. Indeed, the proposition invites undesirable strategic gaming in any kind of country context.

In contrast, the corporate responsibility to respect human rights exists independently of states' duties or capacity. It constitutes a universally applicable human rights responsibility for all companies, in all situations.[5]

The logic of Ruggie's position is that while it is true that a company with power and resources is able to discharge its social responsibility, power and resources alone are not the source of the responsibility; "can does not imply ought." As will become evident in this chapter, I am not arguing that "can implies ought" but rather that serious human rights violations imply "ought." The "can" or capability of an actor is one of the criteria for distributing responsibilities among members of the community for remedying the human rights deficit. In my view, under certain conditions, this responsibility to remedy is a moral obligation and not an optional philanthropic endeavor.

THE KEW GARDENS PRINCIPLE

In the Framework, Ruggie never explicitly discusses whether businesses should take on the advancement of crucial human rights when a state is unable or unwilling to do so. For example, did Microsoft have a moral obligation to do something about the education of some of the poor students in developing countries? Did Merck have a moral obligation to do something for *some* of the 25 million people in sub-Saharan Africa with HIV? We know these companies did do something, but were these projects a result of simply voluntary philanthropy or a moral obligation? While Ruggie acknowledges that there are situations "such as natural disasters or public health emergencies" where "any social actor with capacity" might find compelling reasons to assist, this contribution would only be temporary. We never hear from the SRSG that business has a moral obligation to assist in the problems of society, although I will argue that a case might be made using the Framework that under certain conditions such a duty is present.

In a study on ethical investing by Simon, Powers, and Gunnemann,[6] the authors propose that business may, under certain circumstances, have a moral duty to try to advance and protect human rights, even when the business did not in any way cause the problem. To make the case, the authors recount the original news story of the 1964 stabbing and death of Kitty Genovese in Kew Gardens, New York City. Reportedly, thirty-eight people heard what was happening but took no action, not even the simple action of calling the police. There was a huge public outcry in the press because people who could have taken some action to try to save her life did nothing. From this incident, the authors formulate what they call the "Kew Gardens Principle." There is a moral obligation to provide assistance when four features are present: (1) critical need; (2) the proximity of potential actors; (3) the capability of those knowing of the problem to assist; and (4) last resort, that is, the absence of others who might assist.

Need is clear when human life is at stake, but in our global economy, need can take on a variety of forms in poor and developing countries.

Proximity can be spatial, but at the root it is the awareness—the knowledge—of the problem. There is a "network of social expectations" that flow from our various roles, for example, as a citizen, as a father, and so on, and our responsibility to act flows from these expectations.

Capability follows from Immanuel Kant's dictum that "ought" assumes "can." There is no moral responsibility, even in the face of need and proximity, unless there is some action that I am capable of doing to ameliorate the situation.

Last Resort is difficult to determine, but often large companies with ample resources know that very few others are able to respond to unique challenges that only they can resolve.

"The Kew Gardens Principle" is an explicit moral or ethical argument that a business has a moral obligation to assist in promoting human rights under certain conditions. Although some see implicit moral arguments in Ruggie's presentation, he never employs an explicit *moral* argument to justify respecting human rights but relies only on making a business case. Respecting human rights will protect a company's reputation, preserve its social license to operate, and perhaps enhance its brand. While making the business case for the corporate responsibility to respect human rights is surely important to persuade some leaders, the lack of any explicit moral foundation is puzzling. Human rights surely have an instrumental value, but they also have an intrinsic moral value. Advancing human rights can advance business interests but, more importantly, will advance human interests. Ruggie is very clear that business has a responsibility to respect human rights, especially in cases where governments are unwilling or unable to enforce international and national human rights law, but the justification for this responsibility is "business self-interest" (instrumental) rather than a moral argument (intrinsic). Many of us teaching ethics to future business leaders would like to see an explicit focus on doing the right thing because it is the right thing, and not simply because it will serve the self-interest of business. However, according to the Framework:

> In addition to compliance with national laws, the baseline responsibility of companies is to respect human rights. Failure to meet this responsibility can subject companies to the courts of public opinion—comprising employees, communities, consumers, civil society, as well as investors—and occasionally to charges in actual courts. Whereas governments define the scope of legal compliance, the broader scope of the responsibility to respect is defined by social expectations—as part of what is sometimes called a company's social license to operate.[7]

Thus, business should respect human rights in order to meet society's expectations and therefore avoid sanctions or penalties. A moral argument would focus instead on respecting the rights of a person because of the inherent dignity of that person, and not simply because not respecting rights would have adverse consequences for the business.

A MORAL ARGUMENT FOR ADVANCING RIGHTS IN BUSINESS

In an earlier article of mine, I discussed the question of whether research pharmaceutical companies, which have medicines that can contain HIV/AIDS, have a moral obligation to provide those antiretroviral drugs for at least some of those infected.[8] As indicated above, many NGOs are pressuring multinational pharmaceutical corporations to accept a widening of their role in society based on their immense power and resources, both financial and human. This would clearly be giving business part of a state's role—the role to protect and advance human rights. The Ruggie Framework would preclude giving business such a *moral duty*, although business would certainly be free to accept such a duty should it decide it is in its interest. In my view, the pharmaceutical/HIV/AIDS case is an early warning signal that there is a paradigm shift underway in formulating the role of business in society; and hence, it is an insightful case to consider.

It may be helpful to consider the logic of the Ruggie Framework in limiting the role of business to respecting human rights, rather than protecting and advancing human rights. Ruggie assumes that, while multinational corporations do sometimes assume extraordinary social responsibilities and corporate citizenship duties in developing countries, there is a limit to business's role in society. Individuals (especially wealthy individuals) and nations can and should help provide medicines to all who need them, limited only by their capability. For-profit corporations should see their primary duty as providing good products at a fair price in the context of listening to their many stakeholders. If a pharmaceutical company, for example, depleted its revenue in the process of providing antiretroviral medicines and developing medical clinics for the poor of sub-Saharan Africa, it could not generate the money necessary for research for a cure for HIV/AIDS. Consumers would ultimately pay, either by much higher prices for drugs or by the absence of new, innovative products or cures (assuming the company survived). To assign the pharmaceutical business the *moral obligation* of aiding those deprived of antiretroviral medicines and care would undermine the genius of the free enterprise system.

In spite of the compelling logic of the above position, there are a growing number of scholars who argue that with the huge aggregates of money and power under the control of multinational businesses, these organizations *do have moral obligations* as corporate citizens in the global community to assume some responsibility for providing medicines. The very title of the UN program, namely, the Global Compact, points us to the basis of these obligations. All organizations producing goods and services have an implied contract with society. Similar to the argument for the moral and political foundations of the state advanced by Locke, Rousseau, and Hobbes, this approach argues that companies have a duty to be socially responsible, and this duty involves honoring human rights. That being said, the theory does not spell out just what responsibilities are appropriate for multinational firms.

Michael A. Santoro, in discussing the duties of multinational firms in the face of human rights violations in China, offers a conceptual framework to assist in the analysis and clarification of the situation. Calling it a "fair share" theory of human rights, Santoro points us to four factors: "the diversity of actors; the diversity of duties; an allocation of duties among various actors; and principles for a fair allocation."[9] In any human rights problem, there are a number of possible actors, for example, international institutions, nation-states, multinational firms,

NGOs, and individuals, and each should be allocated a fair share of the duties. The principles proposed for a fair allocation of duties are similar to the Kew Gardens Principle: relationship to those whose rights are violated; the likely effectiveness of the agent in remedying the problem; and the capacity of the agent. Santoro's point is that while companies must do something, they should not be asked to do "more" than they are capable of doing effectively.

Many of our best companies have formulated a philosophy of corporate citizenship and have taken steps to institutionalize this philosophy in their corporate culture. U.S. companies involved with producing antiretroviral medications include Abbott, Bristol-Myers Squibb, and Merck. Each of these has initiated programs to deliver better health care and treatment, in some limited way, to those suffering HIV/AIDS. I believe these companies correctly perceive that they must do these activities as a matter of moral obligation as corporate citizens and not merely as a matter of philanthropy or as a public relations gesture. From my discussions with some of the companies, I believe they are employing allocation principles similar to Santoro's, largely principles of effectiveness and capacity, and thus are trying to meet what is morally required.[10]

The kind of moral leadership exemplified in Merck's Botswana Comprehensive HIV/AIDS Partnership, discussed in chapter 2 in this volume, may set a standard of how corporate citizenship can contribute to solving the pandemic. This case may also exemplify how a business can determine its moral obligation to advance human rights.

THE FRAMEWORK AND THE KEW GARDENS PRINCIPLE

The Kew Gardens Principle and the "fair share" theory discussed above both assume that respecting and promoting human rights are important for their own sake, as well as for their instrumental value. Most people assume that respect for the law is a basic moral obligation, and thus, it is not debatable that a company follow the law, even if being lawful might lower profits somewhat. Similarly, making the case that respecting human rights is a *moral* obligation for business, that is, that it is done because of the inherent dignity of the person, provides the substantive argument that could help develop consensus in the global community that business ought to advance rights, even if some profit is sacrificed. In the context of a moral argument, the difference between *respecting* human rights and *protecting* and *advancing* those rights pales.

Does Ruggie believe there is a place for the intrinsic moral significance of human rights in the thinking of business? The Ruggie Framework implicitly moves toward an ethical or moral basis when it discusses due diligence. Due diligence involves identifying all possible risks to the success of the business, including political, environmental, financial, and even ethical risks. In speaking of due diligence, the Framework states:

> Companies routinely conduct due diligence to ensure that a contemplated transaction has no hidden risks. Starting in the 1990s, companies added internal controls for the ongoing management of risks to both the company and stakeholders who could be harmed by its conduct; for example, to prevent employment discrimination, environmental damage or criminal misconduct. Drawing on well-established practices and combining them with what is unique to human rights, the "protect, respect and remedy" framework lays out the basic parameters of human rights due diligence. Because the process is a means for companies to address their responsibility to respect human rights, it must go beyond simply identifying and managing material risks to the company itself to include the risks a company's activities and associated relationships may pose to the rights of affected individuals and communities.[11]

It is important to note that the concern is for risks to the company itself as well as to the rights of *affected individuals and community*. The report also suggests that companies engage stakeholders and listen to their concerns about their rights. Here, rights are being discussed not because it will save the company money (although it might), but simply because people have a right to have their human rights respected. This may be an opening to developing a moral basis for not only respecting but also protecting and advancing human rights on the part of business. More research and discussion on this and related issues will be helpful.

THEORY AND PRACTICE IN THE AREA OF HUMAN RIGHTS: THE UN GLOBAL COMPACT

This chapter has argued that, at present, there is no generally accepted theory that mandates that business take on some of the problems of the wider society as a matter of moral obligation. John Ruggie, in the Guiding Principles on Business and Human Rights for implementing the UN "Protect, Respect and Remedy" Framework, postulates that business has a limited obligation. Business must avoid "causing or contributing to adverse human rights impacts through their own activities" and "seek to prevent or mitigate impacts that are directly linked to their operations, products or services by their business relationships." The basic justification of this injunction against "doing harm" is a business case, that is, that doing harm will have adverse economic impacts on the firm.

Rosabeth Moss Kanter, a highly regarded business scholar, opens her reflections on the new role of business in society as follows: "It's time that beliefs and theories about business catch up with the way great companies operate and how they see their role in the world today."[12] She argues, similarly to this chapter, for more than a merely financial logic—for "a social or institutional logic." As she puts it, "Institutional logic holds that companies are more than instruments for generating money; they are also vehicles for accomplishing societal purposes and for providing meaningful livelihoods for those who work in them."[13]

My conclusions as a board member of the United Nations Global Compact Foundation are similar to those of Kanter: many businesses already voluntarily commit to projects that support and advance human rights. Some examples of such projects are discussed in the first seven chapters of this volume. The UN document *Blueprint for Corporate Sustainability Leadership* reminds signatory companies to the Global Compact that "corporate sustainability is defined as a company's delivery of long-term value in financial, social, environmental and ethical terms."[14] Thus, in this context, "to do no harm" means, in ethical terms, to respect human rights *because* they are the rights of a human, even if it might cost some money. From an ethical perspective, the difference between respecting and promoting human rights when it comes to advancing the Millennium Development Goals may not be as great as the

Ruggie Framework suggests. Does business have a moral responsibility to advance the MDGs when it can? I think so.

NOTES

1. United Nations, *Norms on the Responsibilities of Transnational Corporations and Other Business Enterprises with Regard to Human Rights* (Commission on Human Rights, Sub-Commission on the Promotion and Protection of Human Rights, Fifty-fifth Session, E/CN.4/Sub.2/2003/12/Rev.2: 2003).

2. United Nations, *Guiding Principles on Business and Human Rights: Implementing the United Nations "Protect, Respect and Remedy" Framework,* Report of the Special Representative of the Secretary-General on the issue of human rights and transnational corporations and other business enterprises, John Ruggie (Human Rights Council, Seventeenth Session, A/HRC/17/31: 2011).

3. Stephen Lewis, "Silence=Death: AIDS, Africa and Pharmaceuticals," *Toronto Globe and Mail* (January 26, 2001), 12; and "Threatened," *Johannesburg Sunday Times* (April 2, 2003), 2.

4. "General Comment No. 14 on Substantive Issues Arising from the Implementation of the International Covenant of Economic, Social and Cultural Rights (ICESCR)," United Nations Economic and Social Council, 2000.

5. United Nations, *Business and Human Rights: Further Steps Toward the Operationalization of the "Protect, Respect and Remedy" Framework*, Report of the Special Representative of the Secretary-General on the issue of human rights and transnational corporations and other business enterpieses, John Ruggie (Human Rights Council, A/HRC/14/27: 2010), para. 62–65.

6. J. G. Simon, C. W. Powers, and J. P. Gunneman, *The Ethical Investor: Universities and Corporate Responsibility* (New Haven: Yale University Press, 1972), 22–25.

7. United Nations, *Protect, Respect and Remedy: A Framework for Business and Human Rights*, Report of the Special Representative of the Secretary-General on the issue of human rights and transnational corporations and other business enterprises, John Ruggie (Human Rights Council, A/HRC/8/5: 2008), para. 54. For discussion of this point, see Wesley Cragg, "Ethics, Enlightened Self-Interest, the Corporate Responsibility to Respect Human Rights: A Critical Look at the Justificatory Foundations of the UN Framework," *Business Ethics Quarterly* 22, no. 1 (2012): 9–36.

8. The next four paragraphs follow closely an earlier article of mine: see Oliver F. Williams, "The UN Global Compact: The Challenge and the Promise," *Business Ethics Quarterly* 14, no. 4 (2004): 755–74.

9. Michael A. Santoro, "Engagement with Integrity: What We Should Expect Multinational Firms to Do about Human Rights in China," *Business and the Contemporary World* 10, no. 1 (1998): 30.

10. The next four paragraphs follow closely an earlier article of mine: see Oliver F. Williams, "The UN Global Compact: The Challenge and the Promise," *Business Ethics Quarterly* 14, no. 4 (2004): 755–74.

11. United Nations, *Business and Human Rights: Further Steps . . .*, John Ruggie (Human Rights Council, A/HRC/14/27: 2010), para. 81.

12. Rosabeth Moss Kanter, "How Great Companies Think Differently," *Harvard Business Review* (November 2011): 68.

13. Ibid.

14. United Nations Global Compact, *Blueprint For Corporate Sustainability Leadership*, 2010. In a July 2011 document, *The UN Guiding Principles on Business and Human Rights: Relationship to UN Global Compact Commitments*, the Global Compact acknowledges that signatories to the Compact should not only respect human rights but also advance human rights. "In addition to respect for human rights, participants in the Global Compact have committed to support the promotion of human rights, that is, to make a positive contribution to the realization of human rights especially in ways that are relevant for their business" (see http://unglobalcompact.org). For further discussion of these issues, see Oliver F. Williams, *Corporate Social Responsibility: The Role of Business in Sustainable Development* (London: Routledge, 2013).

CONTRIBUTORS

JOHN BEE is currently Public Affairs Communications Manager with Nestlé SA, based in Vevey, Switzerland. John's career in communications began in the UK. Having headed the Communications team at UK outsourcing specialist Capita Group, John joined the Consumer Health division of Swiss Pharmaceutical multinational Novartis in 2000 as Worldwide Internal Communications manager. A move to Zurich-based global human resource solutions leader Adecco as Internet and Knowledge Management Director followed, before his appointment to his current position in February 2004. While at Nestlé, he has helped develop the company's Creating Shared Value strategy. He is responsible for producing Nestlé's Creating Shared Value reports, together with its annual Global Creating Shared Value Forum, and for accompanying global communications strategies that comprise physical events and corresponding online programs. He is a graduate in German from the University of London and is fluent in French and German. He is also a member of the Chartered Institute of Public Relations.

DANIEL BROSS is Senior Director of Corporate Citizenship at Microsoft. With a background in public policy, government and public affairs, and corporate reputation management, Dan has led government affairs and policy teams at both the federal and state levels for two Fortune 100 companies. His corporate experience includes strategic planning; policy development and advocacy; grassroots program development and management; strategic relationship identification and engagement; and investor relations. In addition to his corporate experience, he has significant management and program development experience in the nonprofit sector.

DOUGLASS CASSEL is a scholar, attorney, and journalist specializing in international human rights and international criminal and humanitarian law. Current or former president of two international organizations assisting justice reform in the Americas, he has been human rights consultant to numerous nongovernmental organizations as well as the United

Nations, the Organization of American States, the U.S. Department of State and U.S. Department of Justice, and the Ford Foundation. He lectures worldwide, and his articles are published internationally in English and Spanish. He is currently professor of law, and was formerly director of the Center for Civil and Human Rights, at the University of Notre Dame Law School.

GERALD F. CAVANAGH, S.J., holds the Charles T. Fisher III Chair of Business Ethics and is professor of management at the University of Detroit Mercy. He is the author of more than forty research articles and five books, the latest being *American Business Values: A Global Perspective*, 6th ed. (Prentice Hall, 2010). Cavanagh was academic vice president and provost at the University of Detroit Mercy and held the Gasson Chair at Boston College and the Dirksen Chair of Business Ethics at Santa Clara University. He has received honorary doctorates from Loyola of Baltimore and Siena Heights University. He chaired the Social Issues Division of the Academy of Management and the All-Academy of Management Task Force on Ethics. He referees papers for several journals and for national professional conferences. Cavanagh has served on the board of trustees of Fordham, Santa Clara, Xavier, Holy Cross, Loyola University of New Orleans, John Carroll University, and the University of Detroit Mercy. He holds a B.S. in engineering, graduate degrees in philosophy, theology, and education, and a doctorate in management.

INNOCENT CHINGOMBE is a Senior Programme Officer for Research and Documentation for the African Comprehensive HIV/AIDS Partnerships. Prior to joining ACHAP, he was working in Zimbabwe with Zimbabwe Parents of Handicapped Children Association as head of the Research Monitoring and Evaluation Unit. He has also worked for the Training and Research Support Centre as a programme coordinator in Public Health Training. He has been with Zimbabwe Aids Policy and Advocacy (ZAPA) Project–Futures Group International as a Senior Programme Monitoring and Evaluation Officer and with the Government of Zimbabwe Census as a statistician. He holds an M.S. degree in Population Studies (University of Zimbabwe), a Post-Graduate Diploma in Monitoring and Evaluation Methods (University of Stellenbosch), and a Bachelor of Science Honours in Psychology from the University of Zimbabwe.

HAL CULBERTSON is Executive Director of the Kroc Institute for International Peace Studies at the University of Notre Dame. He joined the Kroc Institute in 1997 and was appointed associate director in 2001 and executive director in 2007. He oversees daily operations of the Institute, including finances, staffing, and programs. He holds an M.A. in philosophy (1990), a J.D. (1991) from the University of Illinois at Urbana-Champaign, and an M.A. in peace studies from the University of Notre Dame (1996). From 1992 to 1995, Mr. Culbertson completed a term of service with Mennonite Central Committee–Bangladesh, where he served as a program administrator for a large rural development program. In addition to his administrative role at the Kroc Institute, he also teaches a course on International NGO Management and contributes to research and outreach projects focusing on the management of peace initiatives.

KEVIN DOWLING, C.Ss.R., is the Bishop of Rustenburg, South Africa, a poor mining area with a very high rate of HIV/AIDS infection. In 2005, Bishop Dowling was awarded *Time Magazine*'s European Hero Award in recognition of his efforts to build the largest and most comprehensive HIV/AIDS program in the North West Province (State) in South Africa, encompassing home-based nursing care by 120 community care workers, an in-patient unit for the dying, thirteen anti-retroviral clinics, and an orphan and vulnerable children's program caring for two thousand children. He has been involved in justice and human rights issues throughout his life. He played a leadership role in the Southern African Bishops' Conference Justice and Peace Commission for seventeen years, and started the Conference's Aids Commission, the Conference's Parliamentary Liaison Office for advocacy with the government, the Denis Hurley Peace Institute for solidarity with African countries experiencing war and violence, and the Conference's Professional Conduct Commission for Church workers. He served for many years as the co-chair of the Sudan Ecumenical Forum and is in his second term as co-president of Pax Christi International, together with Marie Dennis of the Maryknoll Office for Global Concerns.

GEORGES ENDERLE is the John T. Ryan Jr. Professor of International Business Ethics at the Mendoza College of Business, University of Notre Dame, and former president of the International Society of Business, Economics, and Ethics (2001–2004). Educated in philosophy (Munich), theology (Lyon), economics (Fribourg), and business ethics (St. Gallen), he has extensive research and teaching experiences in Europe (1983–1992), the United States (since 1992), and China (since 1994). He serves on the board of advisors of several academic journals and Centers for Business Ethics in various countries and has authored and edited eighteen books and over 130 articles, including "Three Major Challenges for Business and Economic Ethics in the Next Ten Years: Wealth Creation, Human Rights, and Active Involvement of the World's Religions" (2011); *Developing Business Ethics in China* (2006); *International Business Ethics: Challenges and Approaches* (1999); *Lexikon der Wirtschaftsethik* [Encyclopedia of Business Ethics] (1993, in Portuguese 1997 and in Chinese 2001).

DEBORAH RIGLING GALLAGHER is Associate Professor of the Practice of Environmental Policy at the Nicholas School of Environment and Executive Director of the Duke Environmental Leadership program. She has also served as Associate Faculty Director of Duke's Corporate Sustainability Initiative. Dr. Gallagher's research focuses on public policies related to the interaction of business and the environment. Her work has been published in a variety of business and public policy journals and edited volumes on sustainability. She received her Ph.D. in Public Policy from the University of North Carolina at Chapel Hill, a master's degree in Public Policy from Harvard University, and a B.S. in Chemical Engineering from Northwestern University. Prior to her academic career, Dr. Gallagher held leadership positions in the public and private sector. She has consulted firms on the design and implementation of business strategies to promote sustainability. She is editor of the two-volume *Environmental Leadership: A Reference Handbook* (2012).

ANTE GLAVAS is Assistant Professor of Management at the University of Notre Dame. He received his Ph.D. in Organizational Behavior from Case Western Reserve University, where he was also Executive Director of BAWB, the Center for Business as an Agent of World Benefit, now known as the Fowler Center for Sustainable Value. Prior to academia, he worked as an organizational consultant with over one hundred companies and has lived in five countries. He was a senior manager in Diageo, a Fortune 500 company; started an organic foods company; founded Horizon, a leadership institute in Croatia; and led a team that built CBA, the first private graduate business school in Croatia, becoming its first CEO. He has received numerous awards for his work contributing to society, including the medal of honor from the President of Croatia.

KIRK O. HANSON is the Executive Director of the Markkula Center for Applied Ethics and the John Courtney Murray, S.J., University Professor of Social Ethics, Santa Clara University. At Stanford University from

1978 through 2001, Hanson was Senior Lecturer in Business Administration and a pioneer in the study of business ethics and business responsibility. He was also Faculty Director of the Stanford Sloan Program, Stanford's master's program for mid-career executives. He taught in Stanford's MBA and Executive Programs throughout his Stanford career. Hanson writes on managing the ethical and public behavior of corporations. He is co-editor of the four-volume *The Accountable Corporation* (2006). His current research interests include the design of corporate ethics programs and the responsibilities of boards for the ethical culture of the organization. He was the founding president of The Business Enterprise Trust, a national organization created by leaders in business, labor, media, and academia to promote exemplary behavior in business organizations; the first chairman of the Santa Clara County Political Ethics Commission; and has written a weekly column on workplace ethics for the *San Jose Mercury News*. He has served on the boards of the Social Venture Network and Students for Responsible Business, national organizations; and on the board of American Leadership Forum Silicon Valley. He served on the advisory board of the Markkula Center for Applied Ethics from 1995 until his appointment to head the center. He has twice chaired Stanford's Committee on Investment Responsibility, which advises the Stanford Board of Trustees on social investment issues. Hanson currently serves on the board of directors of the Skoll Community Fund and the advisory board of the Entrepreneurs' Foundation of Silicon Valley. In October 2005 he was appointed the Honorary Chair of the Center for International Business Ethics in Beijing, China's first center for the study of business ethics. Mr. Hanson is a graduate of Stanford University and the Stanford Graduate School of Business. He has held graduate fellowships and research appointments at the Yale Divinity School and the Harvard Business School.

THOMAS J. HARVEY is Director of Nonprofit Professional Development at the Mendoza College of Business, University of Notre Dame. He joined the staff of the Mendoza College in 2005. Over the course of his forty-year career, he has led local and national organizations committed to confronting the challenges of poverty, discrimination, and access to health care and human services. In October 2003, the Council on Social Work Education chose Harvey as one of the fifty pioneers within the field of social work during the past fifty years, as highlighted in its published work, *Celebrating Social Work: Faces and Voices of the Formative Years*. From 1998 until 2005, Mr. Harvey served as the Senior Vice President of the Alliance for Children & Families, an international association of 350 private, nonprofit child- and family-serving agencies that strengthen the lives of over 5 million disadvantaged families annually. Earlier in his career, he served as the president and CEO of Catholic Charities USA, one of the nation's largest networks of religiously affiliated social service organizations. He is coauthor of *Nonprofit Governance* (2009).

HOLLY HERMES is a 2012 graduate of the M.B.A. program of the University of Notre Dame's Mendoza College of Business, where she focused on business leadership, ethics, and corporate social responsibility. She was a Brogan Fellow and teacher's assistant for two marketing courses and served on the leadership team for the MBA Net Impact Chapter. Prior to graduate school, Holly worked for Young Life, recruiting, training, and supervising volunteer leaders. She was instrumental in fundraising for her local area and completed a Certificate in Youth Ministry from Fuller Theological Seminary. Holly holds a degree in Business Marketing with an International Emphasis from the College of William and Mary in Virginia.

ERIC HESPENHEIDE serves as the Global Leader of the Deloitte Touche Tohmatsu (DTT) member firms' Climate Change and Sustainability group within Audit and Enterprise Risk Services. He represents DTT in various forums, such as the Liaison Delegate to the World Business Council for Sustainable Development, and is the Organizational Stakeholder for the Global Reporting Intitative (GRI). He is a frequent speaker on the topic of sustainability, particularly relating to reporting and insurance matters. Eric is a CPA and has served numerous global companies during his career.

ARVID C. JOHNSON is currently President of St. Francis University in Illinois and is former dean and professor of management at Dominican University's Brennan School of Business. He has served on the board of trustees (including its executive committee) of the Illinois Council on Economic Education, as a member (and president) of the Lincoln-Way Community High School District Board of Education, and as an officer (including president) of the Midwest Decision Sciences Institute. Johnson also founded and served as the chair of Information Resources, Inc.'s Analytics Advisory Board from 2003 to 2008. He led that company's efforts to establish a global Research & Development function that included over 120 personnel in nine countries. Prior to joining Dominican University in 2001, he had over fifteen years of engineering, manufacturing, and management experience in a variety of business environments, primarily in the defense/aerospace industry at Northrop Grumman Corporation, at Varian Associates, and at Microwave Development Laboratories. Johnson has published and spoken extensively in the areas of quantitative analysis, strategic management, and advanced manufacturing practices. In addition to a B.S. in physics (Lewis University, Romeoville, IL) and a master's degree in electrical engineering (Northeastern University, Boston), Arvid holds an M.B.A. from the Kenan-Flagler Business School at the University of North Carolina and a Ph.D. in management science from the Stuart School of Business at the Illinois Institute of Technology.

MARK R. KENNEDY is Director and Professor of Political Management at the Graduate School of Political Management at George Washington University. He was CEO of Chartwell Strategic Advisors. He teaches, speaks, and advises across the globe on success as a "Business in a Political Age." Kennedy shows how businesses can effectively engage with political, regulatory, media, and activist-group forces to simultaneously advance their market strategies and benefit society. Previously, Kennedy led as Senior Vice President and Treasurer of a Fortune 100 company (Macy's); served three terms in the U.S. Congress (2001–2007); and was a presidentially appointed trade advisor under both President Bush and President Obama. Kennedy is an Executive in Residence at Johns Hopkins University's Carey Business School. He has lectured or led research projects at Wharton, London Business School, HEC-Paris, Mannheim Business School, National University of Singapore Business School, Fundação Getulio Vargas (São Paulo), and the University of Maryland. He is Chairman of the Economic Club of Minnesota.

YORK LUNAU is Corporate Responsibility Advisor at the Novartis Foundation for Sustainable Development (Switzerland), a corporate responsibility think tank and development cooperation center with special focus on health care in contexts of poverty. Apart from developing and managing projects to drive innovation and improve stakeholder cooperation in international health, York is particularly active in the debate on business and human rights. Before joining the Novartis Foundation in 2006, he was a freelance consultant based at the Institute for Business Ethics at the University of St. Gallen (Switzerland), where he completed his doctoral thesis on "Business Ethics Consulting" in 2000.

DANIEL MALAN is a Senior Lecturer in Ethics and Governance at the University of Stellenbosch Business School (USB) in South Africa and

Director of the Centre for Corporate Governance in Africa at the USB. His focus areas are corporate governance, business ethics, and corporate responsibility. He is a member of the following initiatives: the World Economic Forum's Global Agenda Council on Values in Decision Making, the International Corporate Governance Network's Integrated Business Reporting Committee, and the Anti-Corruption Working Group of the United Nations Principles for Responsible Management Education (PRME). His educational qualifications include a master's degree in philosophy as well as a master's degree in Business Administration (MBA), both from the University of Stellenbosch in South Africa. He is the residential head of Wilgenhof in Stellenbosch, the oldest university men's residence in Africa.

SCOTT MITCHELL is Vice President at the corporate branch of Sumitomo Chemical America. He supports the work of several departments within Sumitomo Chemical, including the Vector Health Department, as well as other company initiatives, including the promotion of corporate social responsibility activities with particular focus on the Olyset® Nets long-lasting, insecticide-treated nets business. Mr. Mitchell compiled the information in this volume with the assistance and support of the CSR and Vector Control Departments in Tokyo. He is a graduate of Purdue University (B.S., M.S.).

THEMBA L. MOETI is the Managing Director of the African Comprehensive HIV/AIDS Partnerships (ACHAP), a public/private development partnership between the Government of Botswana, Merck/The Merck Company Foundation, and the Bill & Melinda Gates Foundation, which provides support to Botswana's national HIV and TB responses. Prior to joining ACHAP in 2006, Dr. Moeti served as Deputy Permanent Secretary, Support Services, at the Ministry of Health with responsibility for the departments of Policy, Planning, Monitoring and Evaluation, and Health Sector Relations and Partnership. From 2001 to 2004 he served as Deputy Director Health Services. In these and other roles he has provided public health strategy and policy guidance at the national level to HIV/AIDS, TB, and communicable disease control and prevention efforts since the late 1990s, with a special interest in the linkages between health and development. He has coauthored several papers on the topics of TB and HIV and has served on national and regional task forces addressing HIV/AIDS, TB, and communicable disease prevention. He holds degrees in medicine and a postgraduate degree in public health from the University of London.

GODFREY MUSUKA is Director of Monitoring, Research, and Evaluation at the African Comprehensive HIV/AIDS Partnerships (ACHAP). Previously, he was the head of the Research Monitoring and Evaluation Unit at the Southern African HIV and AIDS Information Dissemination Service (SAfAIDS). He holds a Bachelor of Veterinary Science degree from the University of Zimbabwe, an M.Phil. in Applied Epidemiology from the University of Hertfordshire (UK), and a Master of Science in Medicine, MSc (Med) degree in the area of Epidemiology and Biostatistics from the School of Public Health of the University of the Witwatersrand, Johannesburg.

JAMES S. O'ROURKE, IV, is Teaching Professor of Management and the Arthur F. and Mary J. O'Neill Director of the Fanning Center for Business Communication, Mendoza College of Business, University of Notre Dame. O'Rourke, whose Ph.D. is from the Newhouse School at Syracuse University, teaches management and corporate communication and is an expert on business writing and speaking. He is the author of numerous books, including *Management Communication: A Case-Analysis Approach*, now in its fifth edition from Prentice Hall (2013), as well as *The Truth about Confident Presenting* and *Effective Communication*. He is principal author or directing editor of more than two hundred management and corporate communication case studies. O'Rourke is a trustee of both the Arthur W. Page Society and the Institute for Public Relations. He is a member of the Reputation Institute and the Management Communication Association, and a regular consultant to Fortune 500 and mid-size businesses throughout North America.

PHILIP PARHAM is Ambassador and the Deputy Permanent Representative to the United Nations from the United Kingdom. Before working in government service, he served ten years as an investment banker with Morgan Grenfell and then Barclays de Zoete Wedd, spending six of those years in Japan. Ambassador Parham's first foreign service assignment was as Head of the Pakistan/Afghanistan Section from 1992 to 1994. He also served in the British Embassy in Washington, DC, as First Secretary covering the UN, Africa, and Asia; then in Riyadh as Director, Trade & Investment for Saudi Arabia; then as Head of the Iraq Operations Unit; and as Head of the Counter-Terrorism Policy Department. Before coming to the UN, Parham was the British High Commissioner to Tanzania (2006–2009).

SANDRA WADDOCK is Galligan Chair of Strategy and Professor of Management at Boston College's Carroll School of Management. She received the 2004 Sumner Marcus Award for Distinguished Service from the Social Issues in Management (SIM) Division of the Academy of Management, the 2005 Faculty Pioneer Award for External Impact by the Aspen Institute, and the 2011 David L. Bradford Outstanding Educator Award from the Organizational Behavior Teaching Society. She has been a visiting scholar at the Harvard Kennedy School of Government (2006–2007) and the University of Virginia Darden Graduate School of Business (2000). The author of over one hundred papers on corporate responsibility/citizenship, system change, management education, and related topics, her recent books include *Building Responsible Enterprise* (2012), with Andreas Rasche; SEE *Change: Making the Transition to a Sustainable Enterprise Economy* (2011), with Malcolm McIntosh; and *The Difference Makers* (2008, winner of the SIM Best Book Award in 2011).

OLIVER F. WILLIAMS, C.S.C., is Associate Professor of Management in the Mendoza School of Business and Director of the Center for Ethics and Religious Values in Business at the University of Notre Dame. He is an ordained Catholic priest in the Congregation of Holy Cross. Williams is the editor or author of seventeen books, including *Economic Imperatives and Ethical Values in Global Business: The South African Experience and International Codes Today* (2000), coauthored with S. Prakash Sethi; as well as numerous articles on business ethics in journals such as *Harvard Business Review, California Management Review, Business Ethics Quarterly,* the *Journal of Business Ethics, Business Horizons,* and *Theology Today*. He served as associate provost of the University of Notre Dame from 1987 to 1994 and is a past chair of the Social Issues Division of the Academy of Management. In 2006 he was appointed a member of the three-person board of directors at the United Nations Global Compact Foundation. Williams serves as a visiting professor in the Graduate School of Business of the University of Cape Town and in the Global Collaborative Summer Program in Global Governance & East Asian Civilization at Kyung Hee University in Seoul, South Korea. While at Notre Dame he has also served as the Christopher Chair in Business Ethics for the Brennan School of Business at Dominican University in Chicago (2011–2012). For the 2012–2013 academic year he served as an "International Scholar" at Kyung Hee University in Seoul.

INDEX